The Persistence of Race

THE PERSISTENCE OF RACE

Continuity and Change in Germany
from the Wilhelmine Empire to National Socialism

Edited by
Lara Day and Oliver Haag

berghahn
NEW YORK · OXFORD
www.berghahnbooks.com

First published in 2017 by
Berghahn Books
www.berghahnbooks.com

© 2017, 2024 Lara Day and Oliver Haag
First paperback edition published in 2024

All rights reserved. Except for the quotation of short passages
for the purposes of criticism and review, no part of this book
may be reproduced in any form or by any means, electronic or
mechanical, including photocopying, recording, or any information
storage and retrieval system now known or to be invented,
without written permission of the publisher.

Library of Congress Cataloging-in-Publication Data

Names: Day, Lara, author | Haag, Oliver, author.
Title: The persistence of race : change and continuity in Germany from the
    Wilhelmine Empire to national socialism / edited by Lara Day and Oliver
    Haag.
Description: New York : Berghahn Books, [2017] | Includes bibliographical
    references and index.
Identifiers: LCCN 2017014895 (print) | LCCN 2017034836 (ebook) | ISBN
    9781785335952 (e-book) | ISBN 9781785335945 (hardback : alk. paper)
Subjects: LCSH: Racism—Germany—History. | Race awareness—Germany. |
    Imperialism—Social aspects—Germany—History. | National socialism. |
    Germany—Intellectual life.
Classification: LCC DD74 (ebook) | LCC DD74 D37 2017 (print) | DDC
    305.800943/09041—dc23
LC record available at https://lccn.loc.gov/2017014895

British Library Cataloguing in Publication Data

A catalogue record for this book is available from the British Library

ISBN 978-1-78533-594-5 hardback
ISBN 978-1-80539-334-4 paperback
ISBN 978-1-80539-443-3 epub
ISBN 978-1-78533-595-2 web pdf

https://doi.org/10.3167/9781785335945

Contents

Acknowledgments — viii

Introduction — 1
Oliver Haag & Lara Day

I. Categories: Continuous, Heterogeneous Narratives

1. The "Origin of the Germans": Narratives, Academic Research, and Bad Cognitive Practice — 27
   Ulrich Charpa

2. Fantasies of Mixture, Politics of Purity: Narratives of Miscegenation in Colonial Literature, Literary Primitivism, and Theories of Race (1900–1933) — 44
   Eva Blome

3. *Blüte und Zerfall*: "Schematic Narrative Templates" of Decline and Fall in *Völkisch* and National Socialist Racial Ideology — 65
   Helen Roche

II. Germany and Internal Otherness

4. Ernst Lissauer: Advocating *Deutschtum* Against Cultural Narratives of Race — 89
   Arne Offermanns

5. The Jewish CEO and the Lutheran Bishop: The Impact of German Colonial Studies on Young Jewish and Christian Academics' Cultural Narratives of Race — 108
   Lukas Bormann

III. GERMANY AND TRANSNATIONAL OTHERNESS

6. Race and Ethnicity in German Criminology: On Crime Rates and the Polish Population in the *Kaiserreich* (1871–1914) 129
   Volker Zimmermann

7. Narratives of Race, Constructions of Community, and the Demand for Female Participation in German-Nationalist Movements in Austria and the German *Reich* 154
   Johanna Gehmacher

8. In the Crosshairs of Degeneracy and Race: The Wilhelmine Origins of the Construction of a National Aesthetic and Parameters of Normalcy in Weimar Germany 174
   Lara Day

IV. GERMANY AND COLONIAL OTHERNESS

9. "The White Goddess of the Masses": Stardom, Whiteness, and Racial Masquerade in Weimar Popular Culture 209
   Pablo Dominguez Andersen

10. Idealized Australian Aboriginality in German Narratives of Race 230
    Oliver Haag

Index 258

List of Figures

Figure 1.1. A closed process.	38
Figure 1.2. An open-ended process.	39
Figure 1.3. The point of closure.	40
Figure 5.1. Friedrich Samuel Blach, ca. 1929	112
Figure 5.2. Hans Meiser around 1928.	115
Figure 5.3. Cover and table of contents of Friedrich Blach's *The Jews in Germany* (*Die Juden in Deutschland*), Berlin, 1911.	116
Figure 5.4. Headline of *Der Stürmer: Nuremberg weekly to struggle for the truth*, July 1925: "500 Jews as dictators of the Protestant church."	119
Figure 6.1. Total number of crimes and misdemeanors against Imperial Laws in 1882 (broken down by administrative districts). Convicted offenders per 100,000 inhabitants of the age of criminal responsibility.	137
Figure 9.1. Film star Henny Porten photographed in blackface makeup as part of a popular weekly quiz.	210
Figure 9.2. Collection of Henry Porten star postcards.	215
Figure 9.3. *Meine Tante, Deine Tante*, 1927.	225
Figure 10.1. Value judgments of Aboriginal Australians in German publications, 1870–1945.	243
Figure 10.2. Australian throws his boomerang.	249
Figure 10.3. Bee-hunting scene.	250
Figure 10.4. Australians hunting kangaroos.	252

Acknowledgments

The impetus for this volume arose in 2012, when the editors first discussed the transnational implications of cultural constructions of race in German history. The project was influenced by our considerations of different cultural narratives impacting on the formation of racial categories. Constructs of race in German history and beyond, we had the impression, often appear fluid and contradictory, and not homogeneous and linear. We wanted to explore the complexities of cultural narratives' impact on the conception of race in German history. We determined to include a broad disciplinary scope and present the formation of different racial narratives in tandem – from anthropology, over popular culture to political propaganda. This book brings together an international group of scholars to share work on "cultural narratives of race in the German empire, 1871–1945." The project was made possible by an Innovation Initiative Grant from the University of Edinburgh, as well as grants from the Centre for the Study of Modern Conflict, the German History Society, and the Visual Arts Research Institute Edinburgh. Donald Bloxham and Pertti Ahonen supported this effort wholeheartedly, generously taking the time to advise, question, and confirm our thoughts. We are very grateful to Stephan Malinowski, Fabian Hilfrich, and Anne Brockington of the University of Edinburgh's School of History, Classics and Archeology, and to Iain Boyd Whyte and Christian Weikop of the Edinburgh College of Art.

Introduction

Oliver Haag and Lara Day

This volume, as its title implies, initially developed out of the editors' interest in dis/continuities within Imperial Germany's cultural narratives of race and their correspondence and perhaps correlation to events in political history—particularly to the oft-cited national caesuras of 1871, 1918, 1933, and 1945. This interest subsequently broadened to a theoretical reconsideration of race as an intricate component of cultural narratives. If caesuras in political history, such as the formation of national unity and independence or the loss of colonies, indeed affect racial narratives, what does this tell us about the seeming fixity of a scientific category? What does it say about the relationship between the cultural and the biological as well as the national and the transnational in narratives of race?

Race is obviously not a German brainchild, yet the German iterations have been widely considered the product of a largely national evolution, inherently and fundamentally different from racial narratives originating from other national contexts. While this is true for actual events, such as particular policies and atrocities, it is far less clear for ideas and narratives. Is a colonial trope of black beauty in German discourse, for example, quintessentially German, and if so, what are the implications of such a national attribution in the theoretical conception of race? Is the German idealization of Aboriginal Australians specifically German or is it comparable to international constructions of Australian Aboriginality? If race supersedes national border, how then can it be analyzed in a spatial frame? At which other level—global, transnational, or regional seem to be the obvious alternatives—can the concept be examined? This volume points out the global nature of racial narratives and does not juxtapose the national with the transnational. It shows the ways in which racial narratives were quintessentially cultural and thus able to be nationalized without losing their regional or transnational character. This book suggests that the approach to these questions is not one of either-or, but that the national, local, transnational, cultural, and biological were intermingled and resulted in conceptions of race that were simultaneously rigid and adaptable. Race could align with the national, strengthen it, all while being transnational in origin.

Race has never been confined to the realm of intellectual ideas but exerted veritable influence on social and political action. With the development and establishment of the natural sciences begun in the Enlightenment, biological ideas of human races became the basis for national politics, a process that Ivan Hannaford has called the "racialization of the West" (1996: 185). Race informed a wide spectrum of processes of social ordering from democratic participation to the point of lethal destruction without losing momentum. As Richard Delgado and Jean Stefancic argue, racial stereotypes have been historically malleable and pandered to changing political and economic demands (2001: 8). Race was thus imbued with a range of connotations in differing political, historical, and national settings. The presumed changes in narratives and conceptions of race imply a strong level of persistence and tenaciousness of the concept of race as such.

This volume illustrates that the concept has been not only a central but a persistent sociopolitical category, easily adaptable to changing political and cultural settings without curtailing its exclusionary and often hierarchical nature in sociopolitical ordering. Indeed its dynamic character can be considered one of the central reasons for the endurance of racial thought. Racial thought, we argue, evinced continuity between the Wilhelmine and National Socialist era in the sense that processes of racialization remained central parameters of cultural narratives. Race, in other words, mattered greatly in these periods. Yet while these narratives transcended political caesura, they were also informed by political changes and thus reimagined and repositioned. As the chapters in this book illustrate, racial narratives about colonized peoples continued to be hierarchical and essentialist while being reinterpreted with the value judgments inherent to changing political demands, as in the singular example of the establishment and loss of the German colonies. The end of World War I resulted in increasingly idealized narratives of colonized peoples. These persisted through the National Socialist era and were remodeled in accordance to its polity—Papuan peoples, for example, were first recast as Germany's allied friends after 1918 and then conveniently aligned with National Socialism after 1933 (Haag 2014: 149).

This book eschews defining race as a necessarily biological and physical entity and seeks, in Robert Miles's sense, to deconstruct it to expose the different processes of racialization (1993: 49). It analyzes the different modes in which race came into being; it iterated, changed, and was conceived of in different times and spaces. Uli Linke argues that in

German discourses, racial attributes were based less on physical difference than imaginings of blood typology (1997: 560). Although ideas of blood-based difference did not preclude the attribution of physical signifiers, race assumed a greater variety of forms than construed physical difference. Thus the editors understand race as a sociohistorical construct established in intersecting modes by reference to cultural perceptions of, *inter alia,* gender, sexuality, national affiliations, class, and dis/ability (Hill Collins and Andersen 2004; Campt 2004: 6–7, 22; Theweleit 1980; Mosse 1985: 36, 42; Jarman 2012: 90–91). As Volker Zimmermann's chapter shows, what race was understood to be (or not to be) was a product of complex cultural narratives, and not necessarily preconditioned.

We understand cultural narratives as ideas thought to be commonly shared (Hoggart 1972; Hall 1996: 2)—hence a "culture of race" that manifested differently by different agents in academia, popular culture, literature, legal and political domains, and religious circles, among others. The dynamic interplay between these agents in re-creating ideas of race constituted what we suggest to be read as narratives, that is, tales of social entities that were explicated—for all their fixity—as historically grown. Ulrich Charpa's contribution analyzes the origin stories of (Aryan) races that were legitimated with recourse to ancestral tales of ancient birth and common provenance. Cultural narratives were immersed in power relations—hence discursive in a Foucauldian sense—but also specifically historical and at the same time provisional, or, in Mark Currie's sense, less retrospective than prospective tales that re-created spaces in the present (2007). These narratives seem to have naturalized race as a stable category juxtaposing in-groups with out-groups. Yet, while racial narratives could take such oppositional direction, especially when asymmetrical power relations attributed racial signifiers, they were often multidimensional and contradictory (JanMohamed 1985: 63). To elucidate this multidimensional and contradictory character, this collection presents a wide spectrum of instances of racial formation—from popular culture and history to scientific and legal domains.

Scholarship on German history of race is highly complex, both regionally and thematically. The construction and often the persecution of European races, especially in iterations of anti-Semitism, have and continue to engage scholars. German attitudes toward non-European races, especially through the lens of retracing the reciprocal images of alterity and a German national self, have also been scrutinized, increasingly in studies on the former German colonies and German affiliation for particular areas like North America (e.g., Schmokel 1964; Zantop

1997; Berman 1998; Friedrichsmeyer, Lennox, and Zantop 1998; El-Tayeb 2001; Wildenthal 2001; Lutz 2002; Kundrus 2003; Campt 2004; Ames, Klotz, and Wildenthal 2005; Penny 2007; Steinmetz 2007; Graichen and Gründer 2007; Langbehn 2010; Perraudin and Zimmerer 2011; Rash 2011; Langbehn and Salama 2011; Rash 2012). These studies use the German nation as a central theoretical framework for explaining the development of race, and the German history of race as exceptional. As George Williamson argues in his work on the longing for myth in Germany, German mythology drew on a fusion of Protestant, classic, and ancient Germanic traditions in its development of a specifically German connotation of race (2004: 3–4, 18). Sara Eigen and Mark Larrimore's edited volume *The German Invention of Race* (2006) also returns to the nation as a central parameter in its conception of the formation of race in Germany as decidedly different from other national contexts. Michael Hau's monograph on hygienic culture detects a specifically German trait of racial ideas as expressed in the *Lebensreformbewegung* (2003). Moreover, these three studies state that, particularly for German authors of the nineteenth century, human difference was not necessarily racialized and point out that some authors rejected the very concept of race. This implies a contrast between earlier concepts of culture and later paradigms of biology (race).

An assessment of the development of nationalism and race in Germany in the late nineteenth and twentieth centuries is inextricable from the movement of conservatism. German nationalism was promoted in response to the Napoleonic invasions, drawing on the revolutionary idea of replacing individual states and their ruling dynasties with a unified Germany.

Scholarship of German history is often defined by its focus on National Socialism and the so-called Third Reich. Beginning with the canonical studies of Fritz Stern (1961) and Georg Mosse (1981), a common point of departure has been the sense of a "politics of cultural despair" coupled with a particularly German reactionary romanticism, which presaged and perhaps enabled the development of National Socialism. In combination with the generally acknowledged lag in unification and industrialization (albeit the latter only up to the late nineteenth century), this consensus describes the *Sonderweg* hypothesis, which Geoff Eley has dismissed as the "backwardness syndrome" (2003: 129). Eley describes this hypothesis as a determinist teleologist approach of causality, which seeks to situate the origins of National Socialism somewhere in the nineteenth century, when Germany supposedly strayed from the "normal" western European liberal democratic evolution (1991: 209). His definition of fascism as "a qualitative departure from previous conservative practice, which is negatively defined against liberalism, social democracy and communism or any creed that seems to elevate difference, division and conflict over the essential unity of the race-people as the organizing principle of political life" (2003: 132) illustrates the centrality of race to sociocultural political process and polity development.

This volume rejects as inherently flawed the concepts of the *Sonderweg* and of "reactionary modernism" proposed in such scholarship as Jeffery Herf's benchmark *Reactionary Modernism: Technology, Culture, and Politics in Weimar and the Third Reich* (1986). Herf casts Romanticism and technology in opposition to one another, ultimately suggesting that technology was usually rejected by those of reactionary political persuasion and wholeheartedly accepted by liberals, democrats, and socialists. Enmeshed with Herf's "reactionary modernism" is the debate over whether the proponents of *völkisch* nationalism and National Socialism were essentially antimodern, anti-Enlightenment, and antitechnology, seeking only to turn back the clock, even while embracing some facets of modernity, or whether they were active modernizers themselves. The debate on the disparity between a linear, chronological historical development and the thematization of rupture in cultural criticism and history leaves these questions unanswered. In 1935, Ernst Bloch identified the potential tension within fascism, between the "affirmation of capitalism through its intensive rationalization of industrialization on the one hand, and its rural, *völkisch*, and romantic anti-capitalism on the other" (in Rabinbach 1977: 13), prefiguring the debate over the relationship of the *völkisch* Nationalists and National Socialists to modernity.

Bloch's explanation of the appeal of the radical right presupposes the acceptance of the thesis that its visions were more than "mere ideology," and that they were searching for a "*Glaubensraum*," a space for belief in a better future (Rohkrämer 2007: 18). It is this space that the conservative members of the *Lebensreform* movements sought to fill with their ideology of a new social system grounded on aesthetics. Conservatism in Germany has usually been understood as backward looking, instead of an iteration of bourgeois modernism, which exists beyond the dialectic of left and right, modernism and antimodernism, and suggests an entirely alternative future. As Anson Rabinbach points out, Bloch argues that the "explosive tradition of mystical and romantic anti-capitalism was not merely composed of 'irrational' and archaic myths, but of dynamic components of the present" (1977: 6). Rabinbach explains Bloch's hopeful position: "For Bloch the past is a beacon within the present, it illuminates the horizon of that possibility which has not yet come fully into view, which has yet to be constructed.

Tradition is not the handed-down relic of past generations, but an image of the future, which, though geographically located in a familiar landscape, points beyond the given" (ibid.: 7). In this position Bloch is not alone, but in the company of many conservative, so-called reactionary modernists in Germany. Rolf Peter Sieferle proposed a "descriptive notion of modernity" that considered everything that occurred after a certain point "modern," regardless of its outcome. Extending his argument to the limit, he even identifies mass extermination—i.e., Himmler's camps—as a modern process, which did not exist in premodern society by definition (Sieferle 1984).

Lest we be misunderstood, we do not wish to negate that racial ideas, having spread through the Western world, were differently received in varying locations (Glick 1988). Racial ideas certainly adapted to German contexts and developed national and regional peculiarities. However, we suggest a conceptually different approach to race—that is, to conceive of it not as a biogenetic category but more broadly as a set of narratives resulting from racialization. Racialization acts as a normative process that re-creates social entities, culture, and identities (Murji and Solomos 2005: 4; Breitenfellner and Kohn-Ley 1998; Martinot 2010). We consider the nation as *co*-formative with processes of racialization and as intrinsically enmeshed with constructions of race.

The appropriation of scientific ideas within cultural discourse was crucial to the development of new systems of racialization. The monistic philosopher and scientist Ernst Haeckel (1834–1919) popularized Charles Darwin's written work and his concept of evolution in Germany (Humble 2003: 109). Haeckel also espoused the morphology of Goethe in *Generelle Morphologie* (1866)—in which he coined the tem "ecology"—*Natürliche Schöpfungsgeschichte* (1868), *Welträthsel* (1899), and *Die Lebenswunder* (1904), which were aimed at and well received by a large lay audience. Paul Gilroy proposes that these texts helped "conceptualize the state as an organism and to specify necessary connections between the nation and its dwelling area" (2000: 39), thus beginning or at least preparing the *Lebensraum* debate, which was easily linked by way of social Darwinism to eugenics. As Lara Day's chapter examines, the discussion around the body, evolution, eugenics, and racial theory was very widely represented in Wilhelmine popular discourse on the fine arts, literature, and philosophy. In this cross-disciplinary move, many ambiguities and doubts inherent in the concept's scientific origin were lost, or indeed resolved by the authorities in the individual disciplinary area, be it theology, philosophy, or the sciences. Kevin Repp suggests that "eugenics offered the possibility of reconciliation between science and humanism" (2000: 687) as a product of ongoing debates over heredity, Darwinism, and improvement for all. To dismiss Wilhelmine racial discourse as pseudo-scientific and thus irrelevant, or to "segregate the participants of this debate into modern and anti-modern camps on the basis of their subsequent development rather than contemporary perceptions" (ibid.: 687), is to ignore their wider contemporary contexts.

This book does not endorse a national framework, which tries to explicate the development of race in Germany primarily through a national lens, or even a German *Sonderweg*, which assumes a teleological progression of German exceptionality to National Socialism. Instead, it posits that the nation did not create race and race did not create the nation, but that racialization produced images of race and nation that appeared as fundamentally German and hence established expressions of sociocultural reality. This reality is widely seen as a "negative" history, as the outcome of lethal destruction and epitome of the humane failings of modernity. Yet it is also occasionally read as having shown a liberal development at the popularization of Social Darwinian thought in the nineteenth century (Weindling 1991; Weikart 1993; Hawkins 1997: 132–133). As Russell Berman's reference to German imperialism suggests, racial thought was more "humane" in the "liberal" era of the nineteenth century in Germany than in other European countries (1998: 15). Historians of German social anthropology have argued in a similar vein that racial ideas changed from a more liberal (i.e., culturally based) to a more exclusive (i.e., biologically based) understanding of race at the close of the nineteenth century. However, while scholarship has acknowledged the complexity and nonteleological character of racial thought in German history, the processes of racialization in culturally driven liberalism remain undertheorized. As Woodruf Smith asserts, German social anthropologists were initially influenced by ideas of liberalism and, partly in opposition to physical anthropology, increasingly focused on the study of human cultures. Human sameness, the underlying anthropological concept of cultural sciences, is cast in opposition to (physical) racialism. Although Smith acknowledges the racial hierarchies construed in cultural sciences, his study suggests that cultural racism seems to have borne less negative weight than biological racism:

> Indeed, Ratzel (in theory, at any rate) was less of a racist than Virchow. Although allowing that racial features had some bearing on the adaptability of a migrating people to a new physical environment, Ratzel (like Boas) emphasized the adaptability of human physical features to the environment through natural selection. A *Volk* was a cultural, not a racial entity. Ratzel shared his era's prejudices against some *existing* races (Africans, for instance). On the other hand, he had enormous respect for

the peoples of East Asia. And in the long run, he argued, racial factors did not matter very much. It was culture that counted. (1991: 147)

The conceptual problems with this interpretation are manifold. First, the passage suggests that embracing cultural concepts rendered social anthropologists less racist than the more physically oriented anthropologists, because they, the argument runs, allowed the possibility of change. This understanding confuses racism with theories of race, ignoring the manifold effect of racism as a complex set of hierarchies. This interpretation posits that racial assimilation (which presupposed alteration) was implicitly less racist than biogenetic racism. The second major problem is the differentiation between culture and race, as if cultural views were not fundamentally entangled in racial views and vice versa. Pascal Grosse has argued that culture was conceived of in (German) colonial discourse as a fundamentally racialized category intended to secure white supremacy (2005: 121). Differentiations between biological and "cultural/social" conceptions of race overlook first the construction of nonmalleable hierarchies in both concepts and second the biologizing nature of race that predates the nineteenth century (Stoler 1995: 68). Imperial perceptions of culture were racialized and informed by biological and bodily scripting. Given the apparent understanding of culture as deracialized, Smith's interpretation implies the view of a more lenient—that is, less racist—German discourse on colonized peoples. The third and perhaps gravest problem is the way the author balances Ratzel's varied attitudes toward human groups: applying the undefined concept of "prejudice" (instead of racism), Smith reduces Ratzel's racism to an attitude toward "Africans," while he excludes his so-called respectful views. Alongside the dubious nondefinition of "respectfulness" (and "East Asians"), the salient point here is the oppositional value judgment drawn between negative views (= "prejudices/racism") and "good" or "free-of-racism" views (= "respectfulness"). Such oppositional views remain theoretically underdeveloped and oversimplify the complexity of racism, since "positive" views *are* racist views, just as the differentiation between cultural and biological racism represents a grave misjudgment of the basic principles of the ideology of racism. The theorization about the intricacies of racial representation should increase awareness of racism's accommodation of idealizing views, but not produce the unraveling of the racist nature of metropolitan constructions of race.

The aforementioned is exemplary. Several historians of German anthropology have argued that by the end of the nineteenth century the discipline lost much of its liberal stance in conceiving race (Penny 2003:

2–3, 23, 32; Massin 1996: 79–154; Evans 2008: 87–108; Penny and Bunzl 2003: 1–30; Evans 2010: 8). Benoit Massin explains the liberal character of nineteenth-century German anthropology in three references: first, that Arthur de Gobineau's racial theories were initially badly received in German anthropological circles; second, concepts of monogenism (i.e., the idea of a single human ancestry) prevailed at the beginning of the twentieth century; third, many liberal anthropologists tried to rebut the popular image of Indigenous peoples' primitivity (1996: 81, 88). This reading results from a narrow understanding of racism as an expression of somatic difference. But conceptual differences in theory did not mean differences in racial hierarchies that, in construing racial hierarchy as a normative principle, fueled anthropological discourses worldwide (Anderson and Perrin 2008: 962–964; Freeman 2005: 42–69; Smedley 1993: 244–246; Marks 2008: 242–243.). The theorems of polygenism and monogenism rested on a hierarchical order informed by implicit (white) racial hierarchy and a racialization of culture. The "lenient" description of liberal anthropologists does not mean that the superior act of "knowing" the racialized subject would not disclose their racially superior positioning. Glenn Penny goes further still and juxtaposes the anti-Darwinian and cosmopolitan German anthropology of the nineteenth century with the "more" racist anthropology of the twentieth century. He argues that the former was characterized by humanist and liberal scholars who, he contends, were partly critical of German colonialism, while the latter was prone to colonialism: "Then, in the early twentieth century, central European ethnologists and anthropologists abandoned their cosmopolitan heritage. A narrowly nationalistic and increasingly racist orientation became dominant during the interwar years" (2008: 79–80). The author does not define racism and antiracism, though "well-intentioned" worldly attitudes appear to constitute the latter. Judging whether racial representations constituted racism simplifies the complexity of racism that rests on a web of generalization, hierarchy, and paternalism, which John Dixon and Mark Levine posit can accommodate "a blend of positive and negative feelings" (2012: 11). Penny's statement unduly equates theory with social narrative, resulting in a narrow understanding of racism as biological hierarchy. The author's theory also fails to explain the replication of racial scaling in nineteenth-century German anthropology. As Oliver Haag's chapter shows, nineteenth-century German discourses, including anthropology, mirrored the low scaling of the most stigmatized Indigenous group in Darwinian and evolutionist discourse, Aboriginal Australians (Anderson and Perrin 2007). If nineteenth-century anthropologists were free of hierarchical scaling, how might their taxonomy be explained? A theoretically more nuanced approach is necessary to understand the discourse of "positive" racial views in German history.

This ostensible paradigm shift in value attitudes of the German history of race—expanding with the scholarship of the history of German anthropology and German representations of Indigenous peoples—has major implications for this study, which considers a broad spectrum of annihilating and idealizing racial narratives. We argue that, conceptually, culture and race should be studied in tandem, and that "positivity" and "negativity" derive from the common concept of racialization, however different their practical results. Bringing together annihilating racism with idealizing or liberal racism increases understanding of the mechanism of racial thought, which served not as a politics of hatred alone, but also as idealization and self-identification, as Arne Offermanns's analysis of Jewish-German nationalism shows. Especially the German adoption of specific non-European racial identities, as paradigmatically shown in what Hartmut Lutz terms *Indianthusiasm*, begs theorization of racial admiration (Lutz 2002; Sieg 2009; Usbeck 2012; Usbeck 2015).

Theories of philosemitism offer analytical keys to decipher the racist current of idealizing imaginings (Edelstein 1982; Lassner and Trubowitz 2008: 7–9; Karp and Sutcliffe 2011a; Rubinstein and Rubinstein 1999; Kushner and Valman 2004). Coined in Germany in the 1880s, the term "philosemitism" initially indicated an opposition toward the hatred of Jewish people and was used to defame the opponents of anti-Semitism (Karp and Sutcliffe 2011b: 1; Levenson 2004: xii). Philosemitism is now largely understood as a set of actions and value-attitudes that do not form a calcified opposite to anti-Semitism, but instead draw upon similar mechanisms of processes of racialization. Zygmunt Bauman considers philosemitism and anti-Semitism different value directions of a repository of ambivalent images dubbed "allosemitism" (Bauman 1998: 143). This allosemitic repository is explicated as resting on constructions of Jewish essence and difference, thus constructions of a potentially racializing nature. Jonathan Judaken exposes that philosemitism, in its construction of "positive views of Jewishness," produces a one-sided power relationship in defining Jewishness (2008: 27, 29). The power to ascribe the primordial essence of Jewishness rests with philosemitic discourse and manifests, we argue, much like metropolitan definitions of colonized subjects. These definitions, as David Theo Goldberg delineates, rest on the principle of tolerance that constituted a common practice of civilization in nineteenth-century colonial discourses (2004: 37). The act of tolerance equipped the colonizing power to redefine the nature and limits of the tolerated subject. With the consolidation of European colonialism in late nineteenth century, views of colonial tolerance emerged. Gustav Jahoda has demonstrated that primitivism shifted increasingly from tropes of ferocious animalism to tolerated childlikeness, which cast the colonized subject as a semiotic object of colonial enterprise and parental guidance (1999: 85–87, 125, 145). The child-parent relation, reified in possessive form, was conferred upon the colonizer-colonized relation and replaced the previous constructs of outright animalism, no longer conducive to the economic exploitation of colonial work. Anthropophagy as a part of animalist imagery, the author argues, persisted but became less moralized than ridiculed and partly excused, thus tolerated. Additionally, German figures of anthropophagy, as Eva Bischoff argues, served the purpose of education and began to exhibit signs of partial tolerance (2011). Jan Nederveen Pieterse elaborates on the same shift from animalist to childlike savageness in European constructs of Africanism. Consolidated colonialism, the author argues, necessitated different images of tolerated servants to legitimize its rule (1990: 89). To govern colonized subjects, they first had to be tolerated, with the extent of toleration set by the colonizer.

Philosemitism as a practice of tolerance, we contend, suggests reading seemingly positive images of racialized Otherness not as a deracialized sign of worldly liberalism but rather an eminent practice of racialization and hegemony. As the instance of Indianthusiasm, as well as the partial idealization of African populations—such as the so-called Hamitic races—show, German and other colonial narratives of race tended to not only tolerate but also to idealize certain races in certain circumstances (Pugach 2012: 102–114; Hesse 1995: 115–118; Wilke 2006: 297; Gruesser 1992: 6–7; Waller 1976: 547–548; Coombes 1995: 66–67). As Sander Gilman asserts, philosemitism does not only rest on the superiority of tolerance but also on more inclusive constructions of idealization (2008: 83). Psychoanalytic theory conceives of idealization as a mechanism to develop one-dimensional positive views that accommodate complexity in the evaluation of an attitude object (Lerner and Van-Der Keshet 1995: 88–89). Idealization is understood as a narcissistic process that values objects by reference to traits perceived as "positive." This construction preconditions cultural familiarity of that trait which, in Serge Moscovici's sense, anchors the foreign object in socially familiar meaning (1984: 7–10, 29). Thus, the idealization of a culture is either the process of projecting familiar values onto a foreign culture or the identification of a lack or loss of such values in the familiar culture. The processes set the familiar culture as the parameter value and thus familiarize the foreign culture and insist that the familiar culture acts as the marker of normativity.

One trope of racial idealization, which Pablo Dominguez Andersen's chapter discusses, was the partial adoption of colonized and Indigenous identities. Masquerading and performing Indigenous identities in juvenile and adventure literature, for example by Karl May, were established elements of idealized German narratives of race (Carlson 2002). Scholarship on German–Indigenous American relations suggests a specifically national trait in conceiving Indigenous (North) Americans. Glenn Penny argues that German authors of the nineteenth century incorporated their affinity for North Americans into a broader concept of German anti-Americanism and a critique of modernity (2007: 145–146, 154). Barbara McCloskey suggests that figures of "traditionalist" North Americans fused with German nationalist ideals of antimaterialism and antimodernism (2007: 302, 312). The assumed naturalness of Indigenous North Americans, the argument runs, invited idealization. Susanne Zantop explains German interest in North Americans as exceptional in Europe. She suggests an assumed political bonding–produced idealization: the Germans, as victims of French imperialism, understood the defeat and political disunity as an elevation of Indigenous North Americans to a similar victim status (2002: 4–5). Christian Feest contends that identification with Indigenous North Americans constituted a European phenomenon (2002: 29, 31; 1999: 612), and rejects the existence of a specifically German exception.

Identification, we argue, needs to be conceived of in a theoretically broader context than national history. As Haag's chapter shows, national specificities, such as the loss of the German colonies, influenced the representation of racial narratives, yet without necessarily changing the nature of whitened racial dominance. The national fused with what Aileen Moreton-Robinson, Maryrose Casey, and Fiona Nicoll describe as transnational whiteness that evinced flexibility to maintain the unmarked norms of whitened hegemony (2008: ix). Racial idealization and the adoption of racialized identities in nineteenth- and early twentieth-century German discourses must be contextualized within a wider framework of colonialism that related not only to the German colonies but to the quest for imperial dominance, as Haag's chapter outlines. As Gayatri Chakravorty Spivak proposes, the conversion of the (racial) Other into a self is an imperialist endeavor to strengthen the imperialist self by domesticating the Other (1985: 253). The identification with the racialized Other posed a one-sided project that inscribed whitened supremacy in the "adored" subject and thus neutralized its sovereignty, since the racialized Other was not supposed to adopt German identity. In fact the full adoption of European culture was met with harsh satire (black people with top hats cast as objects of derision; the hateful trope of the *Hosenneger*). We theorize idealization in the context of colonial history and the German ambition of having a share in the imperial world order. This focus enables the understanding of idealization as a complex set of national demands in the transnational web of colonial domination. Gilles Deleuze and Félix Guattari have argued that "home" is not a given social space but a negotiation of "limited space" (1987: 311). The notion of a German share in the imperial world order is a product of such negotiation, in which idealization, however partial, was a means of gaining (imperial) space. Analyzing settler appropriations of Indigenous identity (called "indigenization"), Terrie Goldie argues that it bestowed settlers with a native identity in locations in which they were fundamentally nonindigenous (1988: 63). The process of indigenization connected the imperialist self with the immersive presence of a racially unwritten space into which nationalism could be inscribed. Through indigenization, the imperialist self could acquire imperial space, while neutralizing the presence of the racialized Other by refracting and absorbing its pieces into its national self. Idealization, we theorize, inscribed racial difference and white superiority into a system of indigenizing nationalism. The system of indigenizing nationalism thus rested on a deindigenization of other races.

This book shows that the idealization of racial out-groups was a complex process in which racial narratives were under constant transformation and reinvention. Racial narratives were not monolithic and not always of an annihilating nature. They could and did fuse with different factors, such as Indigeneity, colonial politics, and national identities, as this book's chapters discuss. These narratives were often determined by changing political necessities and shifting identities in which conceptions of cultural space informed the formation of race. Cultural practice, this book shows, was not opposed to racialization. Race and culture formed a field of mutual influence that remained flexible toward political necessities, without ensuing dissolution of racial hegemonies. Instead, this volume argues that cultural narratives rendered the fixity of race more dynamic and adaptable to changing political conditions. Cultural narratives of race were of an "ambivalent consistency" and anticipated the future of race.

• • •

This book falls into four subsections organized along the aforementioned theoretical framework of the seeming persistency and transnational dynamics of racial narratives. The first section theorizes the structure and functioning of racial categories. Cultural narratives of race evoke notions of immutability and permanence. One of the most visible examples of such notions of persistence is the narrative of origin, which marries cultural with biological conceptions of a people's provenience.

Applying the concept of mental mechanism, Ulrich Charpa's chapter presents a theoretical elaboration of origin metaphors. It discusses the link forged between racialist diachronics and synchronics to reexamine those historical phenomena commonly discussed in terms of "ideologies," "discourses," and "patterns of prejudice." Utilizing such diverse popular narratives as that of an Aryan race of Germanic peoples, the writings of Karl Penka, and the *Ahnenerbe*'s interpretation of Bronze Age lurs, Charpa draws attention to the highly complex mental mechanisms determining the "origin mechanism." A mechanism, Charpa argues, consists of entities and processes organized to be productive in the racist's demarcation. The chapter explains the origin mechanism as two-dimensional: one dimension consists of ordinary racist synchronics, demarcating the "superior" Germans from "inferior" nations, while the other dimension are diachronics aimed at beliefs related to the origin of Germans. Charpa's delineation suggests that scholarly research on origins never leads to ultimate justified beliefs but to more complex and still open views on the ways in which an entity came into being.

Eva Blome's essay investigates the reciprocal influences of racial narratives in (popular) culture and the realms of biopolitics and science. She examines the alleged threat of "racial intermixture" (*Rassenmischung*) in early twentieth-century German colonial discourse, which supposedly endangered the German culture and nation. She explores the premise that this *Rassenmischung* endangered German culture, and by extension the nation, by discussing points of intersection between this discourse, colonial novels, and canonical texts. Blome's focus is the relationship between political and aesthetic concepts of miscegenation and the discussion of "interracial sexuality," which she identifies simultaneously as a threat to and precondition of the collective that lies at the crux of colonial strategies or power and narration. The chapter investigates intersections of these discourses visible in texts published between 1900 and 1930, which seem contrary only superficially. Arguing that literary concepts of purity and mixture cannot superficially be associated with racist eugenicist programs, Blome analyzes the echo of a figuration used in the biopolitical discourse within the context of poetological visions—and vice versa. The chapter shows that imperialist imagination of miscegenation in the colonial discourse of the German *Kaiserreich* between 1900 and 1915 operated as literary laboratories of racial intermixture. Blome's chapter concludes that the relationship between the biopolitical and the cultural sphere functioned as a crucial element in the colonial and early postcolonial representation of races.

The second section of this book highlights the construction of Germany's internal Other. Cultural narratives of race did not construe simplistic opposites between in-groups and out-groups, but evinced highly complex and at times conflicting formations of identity categories.

Arne Offermanns's chapter presents an analysis of the strongly assimilated German Jew, poet, and literary critic Ernst Lissauer (1882–1937) as an example of such intricate mechanisms of racialized identity formation. Before World War I, Lissauer occupied a public stance for total assimilation and participated in literary attempts to revitalize *Deutschtum*. Later, he reframed his goal as a synthesis of Germanness and Jewishness. Offermanns shows that Lissauer neither developed nor rediscovered his Jewish identity, but continued to defend himself against attempts to exclude him from Germanness in the face of increasing anti-Semitism. Simultaneously, he rejected Zionist criticism of his affiliation with German culture and the demands of anti-Semites and Zionists to accept what they called his Jewish nature. Over time, Lissauer emphasized that he "felt exclusively German." Offermanns's thorough and careful investigation brings to light the ways in which Lissauer's notion of Germanness was rooted in culture and language. In both, there was room for the inclusion of ethnic minorities, and so, for Lissauer and others, this functioned as an alternative to a notion of Germanness based exclusively on race and blood.

Lukas Bormann's contribution examines the racial cultural narratives of the Jewish student Friedrich Samuel Blach's book, *Die Juden in Deutschland,* for traces of the impact of his colonial studies (*Kolonialwissenschaften*). The author compares Blach's consideration of Jewish "germanization" by participation in sports, social activities, and intermarriage—which the latter hoped might combine the best characteristics of Jewishness and Germanness—with the ideas of the Lutheran clergyman Hans Meiser. This chapter reveals the impact that racial theories enmeshed with German colonial studies had on the generation of young Christian and Jewish academics born around 1880, the year of the *Berliner Antisemitismusstreit.* Colonial studies students developed new cultural narratives based on theories of race and added their voices to the cultural debate of Jewish and Christian communities between 1910 and 1930, before the radical racial activism of the NSDAP dominated the cultural debate and the social lives of Germany, silencing both Blach and Meiser.

The third section engages with German constructions of the European Other, which were not only manifold but also equally complex, ranging from degradation to idealization.

Helen Roche's chapter maps the ways in which schematic narrative templates of race came to dominate intellectual and historical thought during the 1930s and 1940s. At the turn of the twentieth century, Roche explains, the idea that the destinies of races, nations, and empires were universal and biologically determined was held by a minority of racial theorists. However, within a few decades, such ideas came to dominate National Socialist thought and were propagated in ideological and educational material throughout the Third Reich. Drawing on a variety of examples drawn from these racial interpretations of history, concerning both the ancient and the modern world, Roche argues that this inculcation of a particular racial historical framework follows very closely the model of "schematic narrative templates" devised by the sociologist James Wertsch. His work shows that a crucial element to collective identity formation is provided by forcing historical occurrences to fit into a consistent, immutable narrative framework, which can then be used both to justify and legitimize the actions of the nation or ruling power. The chapter outlines that historical events, in relation to the rise and fall of the Roman Empire and the Greek city-states, the workings of the British Empire, and the supposed mission of the Third Reich itself, were presented in a way that assumed the dominance of the Nazis' desired racial schematic narrative template, and which ultimately attempted to discredit all deviant, non–racially motivated interpretations of world history.

Volker Zimmermann's chapter elaborates on quantitative questions connected to a "racial" interpretation of crime in nineteenth-century Germany. It asks what crimes were presented by statistics as typical for the eastern provinces in comparison to other German regions, which circumstances might be responsible, and how influential the stereotype of a typically "Slavic" crime was in scientific and political discourses. The chapter begins by pointing out that in 1882 (in the first publication of official crime statistics of the German Empire) more people were convicted in the eastern parts of the Empire than elsewhere. The statistical bureau in Berlin assumed that the Polish population in these areas was responsible, while the German residents were understood to have less affinity for criminal activity. In the following years, a number of criminologists analyzed the possible connection between crime rate and the Polish population of Prussia. Zimmermann highlights the influence of Cesare Lombroso and his concept of "born criminals," on some authors, but points out that some scientists linked higher crime rates primarily to social and economic problems and not to questions of "race" or "nationality."

Johanna Gehmacher's gender-based analysis of the German-nationalist women's movements in Austria provides insights into the dynamics of racialized narratives in transnational settings. Beyond Germany, racial narratives were adapted to serve local and national ends. Gehmacher argues that while women's rights activists enthusiastically embraced newly implemented women's suffrage in 1918, the latter was rejected as indicative of the collapse of state and society. Political parties in Germany and Austria realized the political potential of the women's vote in the electorate. With the single exception of the social democrats, however, political parties hesitated to integrate them into higher party offices. Female activists of the pre-war women's movements who searched for political contexts to exercise their newly won rights did not meet a warm welcome. Gehmacher's research exposes the ways in which German-nationalist women employed the racist ideology of *Volksgemeinschaft* (Community of the People) in two seemingly contradictory arguments: they used it to promote women's equality and to pacify virulent gender conflicts. The author argues that this ambiguity is inherent to the concept, which arises from the mutually reinforcing cultural narratives and narratives of race. Gehmacher points out that the ostensible openness of the concept not only allowed for liberals and even former feminist activists to embrace the racist politics of nationalist parties, but provided an important background for the integration of former liberal German nationalists into National Socialist politics. This chapter demonstrates that the concept of *Volksgemeinschaft* gained its power from its inextricable combination of race and culture.

Lara Day's chapter considers ongoing narratives of race, degeneracy, and deviance present in the German architect and critic Paul Schultze-Naumburg's writings of the Wilhelmine and Weimar period. Its examination of his *Die Kultur des weiblichen Körpers als Grundlage der Frauenkleidung* of 1901 and *Kunst und Rasse* of 1926 questions the presumed homogeneity of the *entartete Kunst* discourse. It posits that the continuity visible in Schultze-Naumburg's writing is indicative of a wider continuity of broader cultural parameters, tested and optimized in the so-called *Trutzgau* Weimar, before they became official National Socialist cultural politics and policy. His published work—37 books, over 230 articles, and countless lectures—ranging from art and architectural pedagogy, practice, and criticism to cultural and racial theory, made him one of the most widely read German authors of the first half of the twentieth century. Renowned during his lifetime, his racial and eugenic writing prompted his relegation in postwar German historiography, which ignored his impact and central position in the cultural and architectural landscape of German modernism. This chapter examines his role as a specific cultural catalyst of radical nationalist and racist art and architectural history and theory, and traces his trajectory through Wilhelmine, Weimar, and National Socialist Germany. His idealistic vision of the German *Volkskörper* was constructed in opposition to and at the expense of "the other," the non-Germans, who could not possibly measure up. This chapter traces the ways in which the development and introduction of these ideas shaped cultural criticism before and after 1933, to construct an aesthetic counterworld, which addressed dreams, desires, anxieties, and cultural and political criticism and was cast as a possible future waiting to be realized. In it, *Lebenskunst* and the fine arts were figured as palingenetic defenses against decadence and degeneration.

The fourth section makes inquiry into German constructions of the non-European Other that were neither simplistic nor opposite, but could evince radical dynamic and malleability.

Pablo Dominguez Andersen's essay analyzes the public persona of Henny Porten, Germany's first film star. To her contemporaries, Porten was *the* embodiment of an unambiguously white, German, and motherly femininity. In her films, the star represented a femininity characterized by its ability to suffer and endure the most tragic fate. By contextualizing Porten's white stardom within contemporary racial discourses, the author seeks to uncover her persona's understudied racial dimensions. Despite (or rather, because of) Germany's sudden decolonization in 1918, Weimar popular culture was obsessed with racial difference. Against the widespread feeling of national crisis and racial decline, scientists like Carl Heinrich Stratz conceptualized white female beauty as an important biopolitical resource. In scientific as well as popular discourses, white film stars like Porten came to stand for Germany's supposedly unabated racial superiority. Dominguez Andersen reads Porten's staging as a white woman against the background of a perceived crisis of white hegemony during the 1920s. The chapter shows that in Porten's films, Weimar blackface was simultaneously driven by desire for and aversion to the Black other. Weimar blackface was expressive of a widespread desire to incorporate valued characteristics associated with racial otherness into hegemonic white identity. Simultaneously, blackface performances like Porten's ridiculed and denigrated Blackness. While Porten's blackface act spoke of a widespread desire for racial difference, the article demonstrates that it ultimately served to perpetuate and reformulate existing racist stereotypes and hierarchies.

Oliver Haag's analysis focuses on German representations of Aboriginal Australians from the nineteenth century to the demise of National Socialism. Based on more than 150 publications stretching from the 1870s to 1945, his research investigates the changes in German narratives of Aboriginal people, particularly in widely read journals such as *Die Woche, Kolonie & Heimat,* and *Globus.* Haag compares Australian with German discourses of Aboriginal Australians, investigating, from transnational perspective, the influences of Australian narratives on German discourse and German specificities in imaging Aboriginal cultures. Based on international theories of evolutionism, Aboriginal Australians were placed at the bottom of the ladder of human development. The view of the "most primitive stone age people on earth" was a tenacious racist stereotype in the imagining of Aboriginal Australians around the world. This dehumanizing stereotype permeated German cultural narratives of Aboriginal Australians of the latter half of the nineteenth century. Not a single German publication revealed a trace of idealizing representation. This persisting representation changed suddenly in the mid-1920s, when one of the first articles idealized Aboriginal people as a beautiful, intelligent, and proud race. This idealization continued through the late 1920s and only intensified in the National Socialist era when Aboriginal Australians were celebrated as strong, intelligent, and racially pure. The "most primitive" race on earth was suddenly seen as a direct link to Germanic tribes, occasionally rendering Aboriginal Australians the allegorical "brother" race of the Germanic Aryans, the so-called Australian Aryans (*Australarier*). Haag's chapter elaborates on the reasons for this perceptible shift in racial perceptions, investigating both the influence that Australian debates exerted on German authors and the nature of (German) nationalism that resulted in cultural narratives of Aboriginal people, which were at times specifically German. Haag's research finds that the post–World War I narratives of regaining the former German colonies and rebutting reproaches of German colonial guilt primarily pandered to an increase of the idealization of Aboriginal Australians.

Lara Day is an art and cultural historian who studied at the University of Edinburgh's Edinburgh College of Art, and the School of History, Classics and Archaeology. She has written on twentieth-century German art, architecture, and culture, on such topics as the artist Anselm Kiefer and collective guilt, and the Wilhelmine *Heimatschutz* movement. She is currently preparing an intellectual biography of Paul Schultze-Naumburg for publication. She works for Artsy.net in Berlin.

Oliver Haag teaches at the University of Barcelona and is visiting professorial fellow at Queen Mary's College, Chennai. Oliver has coedited a book on ego-histoire and Indigenous studies, *Ngapartji Ngapartji: Reciprocal Engagement* (Australian National University Press), and authored a special issue of *National Identities* (Routledge). His scholarship has appeared, among others, in *Continuum, Aboriginal History, Journal of New Zealand Studies,* and *Neohelicon*. He is coeditor of the bilingual *Australian Studies Journal* (*Zeitschrift für Australienstudien*).

References

Ames, E., M. Klotz, and L. Wildenthal, eds. 2005. *Germany's Colonial Pasts*. Lincoln, NE.

Anderson, K., and C. Perrin. 2007. "'The Miserablest People in the World': Race, Humanism and the Australian Aborigines." *The Australian Journal of Anthropology* 18, no. 1: 18–39.

———. 2008. "How Race Became Everything: Australia and Polygenism." *Ethnic and Racial Studies* 31, no. 5: 962–990.

Bauman, Z. 1998. "Allosemitism: Premodern, Modern, Postmodern." In *Modernity, Culture and "the Jew"*, eds. B. Cheyette and L. Marcus. Cambridge.

Berman, R. 1998. *Enlightenment or Empire: Colonial Discourse in German Culture*. Lincoln, NE, and London.

Bischoff, E. 2011. *Kannibale-Werden. Eine postkoloniale Geschichte deutscher Männlichkeit um 1900*. Bielefeld.

Breitenfellner, K., and C. Kohn-Ley, eds. 1998. *Wie ein Monster entsteht. Zur Konstruktion des anderen in RAssismus und Antisemitismus*. Bodenheim.

Campt, T. 2004. *Other Germans: Black Germans and the Politics of Race, Gender, and Memory in the Third Reich*. Ann Arbor, MI.

Carlson, M. 2002. "Germans Playing Indian." In *Germans & Indians: Fantasies, Encounters, Projections*, eds. C. Calloway, G. Gemünden, and S. Zantop. Lincoln, NE.

Coombes, A. 1995. "Making the Nation: Primitivism and Modernity at the Franco-British Exhibition of 1908." In *Kolonialausstellungen—Begegnungen mit Afrika?* eds. R. Debusmann and J. Riesz. Frankfurt am Main.

Currie, M. 2007. *About Time: Fiction and the Philosophy of Time*. Edinburgh.

Deleuze, G., and F. Guattari. 1987. *A Thousand Plateaus: Capitalism and Schizophrenia*. Minneapolis, MN.

Delgado, R., and J. Stefancic. 2001. *Critical Race Theory: An Introduction*. New York and London.

Dixon J., and M. Levine. 2012. "Introduction." In *Beyond Prejudice: Extending the Social Psychology of Conflict, Inequality and Social Change*, eds. J. Dixon and M. Levine. Cambridge.

Edelstein, A. 1982. *An Unacknowledged Harmony: Philo-Semitism and the Survival of European Jewry*. Westport, CT.

Eigen S., and M. Larrimore, eds. 2006. *The German Invention of Race*. New York.

El-Tayeb, F. 2001. *Schwarze Deutsche. Der Diskurs um "Rasse" und nationale Identität 1890–1933*. Frankfurt and New York.
Eley, G. 1991. *Wilhelminismus, Nationalismus, Faschismus*. Münster.
———. 2003. "Fascism as the Product of Crisis." In *The Fascism Reader*, ed. A. Kallis. London.
Evans, A. 2008. "Race Made Visible: The Transformation of Museum Exhibits in Early-Twentieth-Century German Anthropology." *German Studies Review* 31, no. 1: 87–108.
———. 2010. *Anthropology at War: World War I and the Science of Race in Germany*. Chicago, IL, and London.
Feest, C. 1999. "Indians and Europe? Editor's Postscript." In *Indians & Europe: An Interdisciplinary Collection of Essays*, ed. C. Feest. Lincoln, NE.
———. 2002. "Germany's Indians in a European Perspective." In *Germans & Indians: Fantasies, Encounters, Projections*, eds. C. Calloway, G. Gemünden, and S. Zantop. Lincoln, NE.
Freeman, V. 2005. "Attitudes Toward 'Miscegenation' in Canada, the United States, New Zealand, and Australia, 1860–1914." *Native Studies Review* 16, no. 1: 42–69.
Friedrichsmeyer, S., S. Lennox, and S. Zantop, eds. 1998. *The Imperialist Imagination: German Colonialism and Its Legacy*. Ann Arbor, MI.
Gilman, S. 2008. "Points of Conflict: Cultural Values in 'Green' and 'Racial' Antisemitism." In *Antisemitism and Philosemitism in the Twentieth and Twenty-first Centuries: Representing Jews, Jewishness, and Modern Culture*, eds. P. Lassner and L. Trubowitz. Newark, NJ.
Gilroy, P. 2000. *Between Camps: Nations, Cultures and the Allure of Races*. London.
Glick, T., ed. 1988. *The Comparative Reception of Darwinism*. Chicago, IL, and London.
Goldberg, D. T. 2004. "The Power of Tolerance." In *Philosemitism, Antisemitism and "The Jews": Perspectives from the Middle Ages to the Twentieth Century*, eds. T. Kushner and N. Valman. Aldershot.
Goldie, T. 1988. "Signifier Resignified: Aborigines in Australian Literature." In *Aboriginal Culture Today*, ed. A. Rutherford. Sydney.
Graichen, G., and H. Gründer. 2007. *Deutsche Kolonien. Traum und Trauma*. Berlin.
Grosse, P. 2005. "What Does German Colonialism Have to Do with National Socialism? A Conceptual Framework." In *Germany's Colonial Pasts*, eds. E. Ames, M. Klotz, and L. Wildenthal. Lincoln, NE, and London.
Gruesser, J. C. 1992. *White on Black: Contemporary Literature about Africa*. Chicago, IL.
Hall, S. 1996. "Who Needs Identity?" In *Questions of Cultural Identity*, eds. S. Hall and P. du Gay. London.
Hannaford, I. 1996. *Race: The History of an Idea in the West*. Baltimore, MD.
Hau, M. 2003. *The Cult of Health and Beauty in Germany: A Social History, 1890–1930*. Chicago, IL.
Hawkins, M. 1997. *Social Darwinism in European and American Thought, 1860–1945: Nature as Model and Nature as Threat*. Cambridge.
Herf, J. 1986. *Reactionary Modernism: Technology, Culture and Politics in Weimar and the Third Reich*. Cambridge.

Hesse, A. 1996. *Malerei des Nationalsozialismus: Der Maler Werner Peiner, 1897–1984*. Hildesheim.
Hill Collins, P., and M. Andersen. 2004. *Race, Class, and Gender: An Anthology*. Wadsworth.
Hoggart, R. 1972. *On Culture and Communication*. New York and Oxford.
Humble, M. 2003. "Das Reich der Erfüllung: A Theme in Wihelmine Counter Culture." In *Counter-Cultures in Germany and Central Europe: From Sturm und Drang to Baader-Meinhof*, eds. S. Giles and M. Oergel. Bern et al.
Jahoda, G. 1999. *Images of Savages: Ancient Roots of Modern Prejudice in Western Culture*. London.
JanMohamed, A. 1985. "The Economy of Manichean Allegory: The Function of Racial Difference in Colonialist Literature." *Critical Inquiry* 12, no. 1: 59–87.
Jarman, M. 2012. "Dismembering the Lynch Mob: Intersecting Narratives of Disability, Race, and Sexual Menace." In *Sex and Disability*, ed. R. McRuer and A. Mollow. Durham, NC, 89–107.
Judaken, J. 2008. "Between Philosemitism and Antisemitism: The Frankfurt School's Anti-Antisemitism." In *Antisemitism and Philosemitism in the Twentieth and Twenty-first Centuries: Representing Jews, Jewishness, and Modern Culture*, eds. P. Lassner and L. Trubowitz. Newark, NJ.
Karp, J., and A. Sutcliffe, eds. 2011a. *Philosemitism in History*. Cambridge.
———. 2011b. "Introduction: A Brief History of Philosemitism." In *Philosemitism in History*, eds. J. Karp and A. Sutcliffe. Cambridge.
Kundrus, B. 2003. *Moderne Imperialisten. Das Kaiserreich im Spiegel seiner Kolonien*. Cologne.
Kushner, T., and N. Valman. 2004. *Philosemitism, Antisemitism and "The Jews": Perspectives from the Middle Ages to the Twentieth Century*. Aldershot.
Langbehn, V. 2010. *German Colonialism, Visual Culture, and Modern Memory*. New York and London.
Langbehn, V., and M. Salama, eds. 2011. *German Colonialism: Race, the Holocaust, and Postwar Germany*. New York.
Lassner, P., and L. Trubowitz. 2008. "Introduction." In *Antisemitism and Philosemitism in the Twentieth and Twenty-first Centuries: Representing Jews, Jewishness, and Modern Culture*, eds. P. Lassner and L. Trubowitz. Newark, NJ.
Lerner, P., and Y. Van-Der Keshet. 1995. "A Note on the Assessment of Idealization." *Journal of Personality Assessment* 65, no. 1: 77–90.
Levenson, A. 2004. *Between Philosemitism and Antisemitism: Defenses of Jews and Judaism in Germany, 1871–1932*. Lincoln, NE, and London.
Linke, U. 1997. "Gendered Difference, Violent Imagination: Blood, Race, Nation." *American Anthropologist* 99, no. 3: 559–573.
Lutz, H. 2002. "German Indianthusiasm: A Socially Constructed German National(ist) Myth." In *'Germans & Indians: Fantasies, Encounters, Projections*, eds. C. Calloway, G. Gemünden, and S. Zantop. Lincoln, NE.
McCloskey, B. 2007. "Von der 'Frontier' zum Wilden Westen. Deutsche Künstler, nordamerikanische Indianer und die Inszenierung von Rasse und Nation im 19. und frühen 20. Jahrhundert." In *I like America. Fiktionen des Wilden Westens*, eds. P. Kort and M. Hollein. Munich.
Marks, J. 2008. "Race across the Physical-Cultural Divide in American Anthropology." In *A New History of Anthropology*, ed. H. Kuklick. Malden, MA.

Martinot, S. 2010. *The Machinery of Whiteness: Studies in the Structure of Racialization*. Philadelphia, PA.
Massin, B. 1996. "From Virchow to Fischer: Physical Anthropology and 'Modern Race Theories' in Wilhelmine Germany." In *Volksgeist as Method and Ethic: Essays on Boasian Ethnography and the German Anthropological Tradition*, ed. G. Stocking. Madison, WI.
Miles, R. 1993. *Racism after "Race Relations."* New York and London.
Moreton-Robinson, A., M. Casey, and F. Nicoll. 2008. *Transnational Whiteness Matters*. Lanham, MD.
Moscovici, S. 1984. "The Phenomenon of Social Representations." In *Social Representations: Explorations in Social Psychology*, eds. R. Farr and S. Moscovici. Cambridge.
Mosse, G. 1981. *The Crisis of German Ideology: Intellectual Origins of the Third Reich*. New York.
———. 1985. *Nationalism and Sexuality: Middle-Class Morality and Sexual Norms in Modern Europe*. Madison, WI.
Murji, K., and J. Solomos. 2005. "Introduction: Racialization in Theory and Practice." In *Racialization: Studies in Theory and Practice*, eds. Karim Murji and John Solomos. Oxford.
Nederveen Pieterse, J. 1990. *Wit over zwart. Beelden van Afrika en zwarten in the westerse populaire cultuur*. Amsterdam.
Penny, G. H. 2003. *Objects of Culture: Ethnography and Ethnographic Museums in Imperial Germany*. Chapel Hill, NC.
———. "Illustriertes Amerika. Der Wilde Westen in deutschen Zeitschriften 1825–1890.'" In *I like America. Fiktionen des Wilden Westens*, eds. P. Kort and M. Hollein. Munich.
———. 2008. "Traditions in the German Language." In *A New History of Anthropology*, ed. H. Kuklick. Malden, MA.
Penny G., and M. Bunzl. 2003. "Introduction: Rethinking German Anthropology, Colonialism, and Race." In *Worldly Provincialism: German Anthropology in the Age of Empire*, eds. G. H. Penny and M. Bunzl. Ann Arbor, MI.
Perraudin, M., and J. Zimmerer, eds. 2011. *German Colonialism and National Identity*. New York and London.
Pugach, S. 2012. *Africa in Transition: A History of Colonial Linguistics in Germany and Beyond, 1814–1945*. Ann Arbor, MI.
Rabinbach, A. 1977. "Unclaimed Heritage: Ernst Bloch's Heritage of Our Times and the Theory of Fascism." *New German Critique*, no 11: 5–21.
Rash, Felicity. 2011. "Images of the Self and the Other in Paul Rohrbach's 'German Idea.'" *Patterns of Prejudice* 45, no. 5: 381–397.
———. 2012. *German Images of the Self and the Other: Nationalist, Colonialist and Anti-Semitic Discourse, 1871–1918*. Basingstoke.
Repp, K. 2000. "'More Corporeal, More Concrete': Liberal Humanism, Eugenics, and German Progressives at the Last Fin de Siècle." *The Journal of Modern History* 72, no. 3: 683–730.
Rohkrämer, T. 2007. *A Single Communal Faith? The German Right from Conservatism to National Socialism*. New York.
Rubinstein, W., and H. Rubinstein. 1999. *Philosemitism: Admiration and Support in the English-Speaking World for Jews, 1840–1939*. Basingstoke.

Schmokel, W. 1964. *Dream of Empire: German Colonialism, 1919–1945*. New Haven, CT.
Sieferle, R.-P. 1984. *Fortschrittsfeinde? Opposition gegen Technik und Industrie von der Romantik bis zur Gegenwart*. Munich.
Sieg, K. 2009. *Ethnic Drag: Performing Race, Nation, Sexuality in West Germany*. Ann Arbor, MI.
Smedley, A. 1993. *Race in North America: Origin and Evolution of a Worldview*. Boulder, CO.
Smith, W. 1991. *Politics and the Sciences of Culture in Germany 1840–1920*. New York.
Spivak, G. C. 1985. "Three Women's Texts and a Critique of Imperialism." *Critical Inquiry* 12, no. 1: 243–261.
Steinmetz, G. 2007. *The Devil's Handwriting: Precoloniality and the German Colonial State in Qingdao, Samoa, and Southwest Africa*. Chicago, IL, and London.
Stern, F. 1961. *The Politics of Cultural Despair: A Study in the Rise of the Germanic Ideology*. Berkeley, CA.
Stoler, A. L. 1995. *Race and the Education of Desire: Foucault's History of Sexuality and the Colonial Order of Things*. Durham, NC, and London.
Theweleit, K. 1980. *Männerphantasien*. 2 vols. Reinbek bei Hamburg.
Usbeck, F. 2012. "'We are Indigenous!' National Socialist Constructions of German Indigeneity and the American Indian Image during the Third Reich." In *Erinnerungskulturen in transnationaler Perspektive. Memory Cultures in Transnational Perspective*, eds. U. Engel, M. Middell, and S. Troebst. Leipzig.
———. 2015. *Fellow Tribesmen: The Image of Native Americans, National Identity, and Nazi Ideology in Germany*. New York.
Waller, R. 1976. "The Maasai and the British 1895–1905: The Origin of an Alliance." *Journal of African History* 17, no. 4: 539–553.
Weikart, R. 1993. "The Origins of Social Darwinism in Germany, 1859–1895." *Journal of the History of Ideas* 54: 469–488.
Weindling, P. J. 1991. *Darwinism and Social Darwinism in Imperial Germany: The Contribution of the Cell Biologist Oscar Hertwig, 1849–1922*. Stuttgart.
Wildenthal, L. 2001. *German Women for Empire, 1884–1945*. Durham, NC.
Wilke, S. 2006. "Images of Africa: Paradigms of German Colonial Paintings." *German Studies Review* 29, no. 2: 285–298.
Williamson, G. 2004. *The Longing for Myth in Germany: Religion and Aesthetic Culture from Romanticism to Nietzsche*. Chicago, IL.
Zantop, S. 1997. *Colonial Fantasies: Conquest, Family, and Nation in Pre-Colonial Germany, 1770–1870*. Durham, NC.
———. "Close Encounters: Deutsche and Indianer." In *Germans & Indians: Fantasies, Encounters, Projections*, eds. C. Calloway, G. Gemünden, and S. Zantop. Lincoln, NE.

PART I

CATEGORIES: CONTINUOUS, HETEROGENEOUS NARRATIVES

 1

THE "ORIGIN OF THE GERMANS"
Narratives, Academic Research, and Bad Cognitive Practice
Ulrich Charpa

Stuart Hall has identified five components of a nationalist ideology, or—as he would describe it—"discursive strategies" for a narration about that which is called a "nation" within such a "discourse":

1. The narration itself as it can be identified in history books, literature, symbols etc.
2. An emphasis on origin, continuity, tradition etc. providing an essentialist image of an "eternal" national character.
3. The invention of new practices declared as a reawakening of what has already been practiced since the "old days."
4. Myths of origin related to the earliest beginnings of the nation.
5. Establishing a link between the origin myth and certain characteristics of the nation and its eligibility to exercise power over others. (1995: 594; see also Rush 2013: 7–8)

This is a helpful survey in accordance with the way in which most scholars from Ernest Renan on would have characterized nationalist ideology (Lemberg 1964: 52, 65). The reason I prefer to speak about true or false opinions and of bad or good practice but not of discourses has to do with the epistemological relativism and the ethical neutrality at the basis of postmodern talk. Along with historical relativism in general, discourse analysis describes the meaning of past opinions and practices to those who considered them adequate. Group A believes in *a*, group B believes in *b*, and there is no option for a group C on the outside who knows better or acts superior. In everyday life, there are many situations in which a C knows better or has a better practice. Modern social epistemology has given such ordinary experiences a precise philosophical form (one may think of the writings of Alvin Goldman and others). In view of this I consider much of what nationalist ideologies, including their racist ingredients, put forward as false and the corresponding practices as something that can be shown as being unsound.

In this regard I will focus on components 4 and 5 from Hall's list, and touch upon the other items to the extent to which they are intertwined with notions of origin and the idea of a historically justifiable national superiority. Taking the omnipresence of historical relativism into consideration, it may not be superfluous to say some general words about scrutinizing nationalist and racist ideas in compliance with ordinary philosophical epistemology as well as with the common sense attitude toward truth and sound practice.

Criticizing in Place of Relativizing False Opinions and Bad Cognitive Practices

At first sight, the matter seems settled: most historians are relativists in a moral as well as in epistemological sense. To say that, for example, the crusaders naively believed in the fraudulent relics of biblical figures may be correct, but it is not the *façon de parler* that professional historians appreciate. Leopold von Ranke's often-cited dictum, "each epoch is immediate to God," puts this historical relativism in a nutshell. Indeed, it does not present itself as a promising strategy to start by anachronistically questioning the crusaders' "truth" with the help of later insights. Such procedure appears unproductive to historians (though not to devout Catholics or historians of ideas who compare Catholic ideas of the time to those of their skeptical contemporaries like Maimonides). The ordinary historian's preference in cases of this type seems to be relativist in the sense presented above. Historians see their task in analyzing the significance of such "biblical" relics to those who experienced them as such within their own context.

After World War II many historians—among them some who were personally affected by radical nationalism and racism—were far from considering such ideologies as epistemologically undetermined, as mere antiquarian stuff. To them these were matters of right or wrong, or as—Eric Hobsbawm put it—something that presupposes "much belief in what is patently not so" (1992). It needs not be discussed here whether Stephen Toulmin (1990) has a point with his assumption that peaceful decades (as western Europeans experienced them after 1945) promote relativism, but it is apparent that nowadays Hobsbawm's attitude is no longer an integral component of discussing nationalism and racism. There is an increasing tendency to focus on *how* certain "imagined communities" are created by concepts (Anderson 1983), discursive events, text genres, and other constituents (Wodak 2006). Such an approach includes reconstructing nationalism, racism, and the like "from inside" and not from an (actually or alleged) epistemologically superior position. The question of whether a community is merely imagined or not, is an illusion or a real entity, no longer seems relevant. Such a retreat from Hobsbawn's "veritism" has not become a controversial issue, as one could perhaps think. In a way, veritism simply seems to fade away and relativism disseminates as something like a natural attitude for modern academics. Moreover, this modern tendency matches to the venerable tradition already mentioned. Seen from a general epistemological point of view, the orientation of modern discourse analysis is similar to Ranke's habit of conceiving historical phenomena in their own terms as "immediate to God."

But is this preference based on more than a heuristic routine? Is it in fact unavoidably linked to *accepting* the idea that the truth of an opinion is always a daughter of times and spaces? Historians do not lose their sanity and reason because they do their work in a certain way. I doubt that they consider a medieval belief, e.g., in the authenticity of the bones preserved in the Cologne Shrine of the Three Kings, as *epistemically* justified because of the fact that in the Middle Ages people held it and we remain interested in their belief system. Historians accept relativism *methodologically*, in other words, simply because discussing the naïveté of a crusader's opinions does not promise deeper historical insight. Instead of inquiring into the reality of the kings' bones, they would emphasize their religious, political, and economic functionality, e.g., their motivational force for warriors. One may take for granted that as ordinary people in an ordinary life-world most modern academics would not seriously consider the crusaders' "truth" as a candidate for being true at all. But this is a more or less tacit *presupposition* of their work and not a constituent.

Irrespective of that, in another regard "nation" or "race" should not be treated as modern variants of the kings' relics. Notions like nation or race, which are part of our own current political and social talk, cannot seriously avoid questions of cognitive value and of pragmatics. They are related to *our* questions to an extent the bones of the Cologne shrine are not. It is of relevance to what extent a racist *Weltanschauung* is right or wrong. The ordinary academic usage of "racism" is not that of a disinterested observer. In most cases this usage is pejorative and linked to a moral rejection based on negative epistemic and ethic appraisals. Accepting this fact is not the same as assuming that all sorts of talk about nation and race can be socially destructed to zero (Sesardic 2010). For example, the existence of geographically, morphologically, or otherwise differentiated human populations is an unquestionable fact in the sense that it is in correspondence with some fundamental ways of experiencing the world. Most people we encounter walking through the streets of Mumbai differ in many respects from most of those we might see on the Isle of Wight. It is not racism to concede that most people in Mumbai behave differently, look different, etc. Racism does not originate from the empirical world as it is. It results from linking the obvious to the dubious, e.g., by declaring the phenotype of people in Mumbai or their behavioral traditions as emerging from an inferior genotype. The popular social deconstruction of racist ideologies is unnecessarily founded on the denial of the empirical, e.g., the fact that something like skin color exists. Seen from the viewpoint of philosophical epistemology, the deconstructionist's relativism mirrors the confusion of the old self-defeating skeptic who denies the reality of horses and afterward mounts one of them. There is not a single professional representative of modern epistemology who would agree that our vision of a black spot on a wall is merely a matter of social rules. What do exist are borderline cases. Here, observers would prefer to speak of a gray spot, without calling into question that this spot is brighter than another "really" black one. Writers such as Scott Atran have even shown that the highly sophisticated classification of animals and plants in, e.g., Maya terminology on the one hand and in Linné's system on the other, widely coincide (1990). At the empirical level, people of different cultural contexts are not living in different worlds. The opposite view is based on bad science (e.g., of the Sapir/Whorf type). Criticizing an ideology is not bound to questioning actuality, not even "awkward" facts such as that more than two-thirds of the top twenty-five individuals (according to Forbes' List) whose success arose from real estate are Jewish. The point at issue is how an ideology *links* such facts to explanatory grounds, predictive statements, and ideas on appropriate political and social action. This indicates certain mental mechanisms and not interchangeableness of facts at will (Charpa 2013). My first point of inquiry is the way in which the "mechanics" of an ideological conception works. The second is to what extent this functioning can be deceptive, misled, and provide a basis for inadequate actions. I abstain from a discussion of moral relativism because it is not a problem at issue among twentieth- and twenty-first-century historians. While, e.g., medieval jurisdiction is seldom condemned, ordinary academic historians would not let themselves be carried away into dealing with the Nazi attitude as something legitimate "in its time." What if anything could perhaps be seen as a tendency in this regard rests on confounding deliberate ethics with mere moral or moral-like attitudes (as "Nazi-morality"). Nevertheless, the philosophical position of moral relativism is much better than that of relativism in epistemology (Gowan 2013).

The "Origin-Story" in Narratives and Visual Representations

That which lies at the core of a nationalist ideology with regard to components 4 and 5 in Hall's list may be called the "origin-story." It is a mechanism of thought connecting diachronic and systematic opinions. This origin-story manifests itself in pictures, narratives, songs, and many other ways. Characterized in a somewhat sarcastic manner, the origin-story presents fictitious "Germans" who look and act like the Vikings of Hal Foster's comics. These figures become related to a nineteenth- and twentieth-century world where, in fact, women wear two-piece dresses, men colored ties, and both take Aspirin pills to fight headaches. Of course, the origin-story does not present itself as such an absurdity. It weakens the absurd by concealing the differences between modern and ancient life and stressing real or alleged similarities.

Let us start with a very simple case: a typical pictorial example is Nazi artist Anton M. Kolnberger's poster announcing the exhibition "Vom Ringwall zum Bunker" at the Army Museum, Munich, in 1943. It shows two young men of similar physiognomy, with same-sized heads and the same "determined" facial expression. Both men are wearing helmets, one the modern type of the *Wehrmacht,* the other the alleged type of helmet for "Nordic" warriors with its festooned horns (which in fact no ancient hero ever wore, if we consider the archaeological evidence). The message is obvious: the modern *Wehrmacht* soldier is an heir of the old warriors. He stands at the end of chain that began in the age of swords and battleaxes. A much more colorful example of a visualized version of the origin-story was presented some years before the army exhibition in the same town, the parade *Zweitausend Jahre deutsche Kultur,* with more than three thousand participants (mostly members of the *Wehrmacht* and the *SS*) wearing old-fashioned costumes and aiming at a kind of documentation of German culture from the "Germanic Age" to the NS era (Hermann 2000: 203–207). Among the groups that caused the most sensation was an ensemble of lure blowers. The story behind the story in this case was that some Nazi experts considered the Bronze Age natural trumpets (Focke Museum 2013) as proof that the early Germans invented polyphonic music and used D major as a specifically "Nordic" musical key (Potter 1998).

As to written versions of the origin-story, it is worth noting that, statistically, two-thirds of the German schoolbooks, published between 1850 and 1918, identified the Germans in the sense of "Germanen" with the Germans as "Deutsche" (Wolfrum 2002: 17). Regarding literary fiction, what immediately crosses a literary historian's mind are books like Felix Dahn's *Ein Kampf um Rom,* celebrating the noble mind of the "hochgewachsenen, blonden Goten" (the tall blond Goths). It was published in 1876, ran through countless editions, and was among the bestselling books of the "long nineteenth century." From beginning to end it varies the story. The novel starts with a meeting of Gothic warriors and a solemn speech by of one of these heroes that includes sentences such as: "It is this alone which can save us now as then; if once the Goths feel that they fight for their nationality, and to protect the secret jewel that lies in the customs and speech of a people, like a miraculous well-spring, then they may laugh at the hate of the Greeks and the wiles of the Italians" (1878: I, 1).

Roughly speaking, the novel, the *Festzug*, and countless other versions of the origin-story include the following components:

- In the beginning there existed a Germanic race that was in many respects superior to others;
- it emerged in Scandinavia and northern Germany;
- it had physical characteristics like blond hair and blue eyes;
- it showed noble character traits;
- it had as its language Germanic idioms going back to a common "*Ursprache*";
- it had the modern Germans as its principal heirs.

In other words, due to its (presumed) origin the modern German nation is construed as superior to other nations. Its nineteenth-century political claims are deeply rooted in the history of this nation and are justified by its "origin" as starting point.

The Academic Correspondence to the "Origin-Story"

Today, the idea of national superiority tends to whip up most enthusiasm among groups with reasons to doubt their own achievements. In recent years the most serious conflicts motivated by nationalistic ideologies have flared up in regions where a lack of life perspectives and high rates of unemployment are relevant social factors. The situation in nineteenth-century Germany was totally different. Due to dramatic transformations in several domains, Germany had advanced to being the dominant industrial, scientific, and cultural force worldwide. Recently, under the title *The German Genius*, the English journalist Peter Watson published a lengthy compilation of essays describing this process, which became one of the bestselling books of recent years in the

Anglo-Saxon world (2010). In fact, the Germany of the "long nineteenth century" may even have proved superior in some scientific and technical contexts. However, this superiority did not play an important role in academic discourses. Richard Wagner was no academic, and a racist and chauvinist like Eugen Dühring lost his *venia legendi* under the auspices of Hermann von Helmholtz, the mandarin of mandarins within the German university system. All German academics were probably nationalists to a remarkable extent, and not a few of them were racists, but influential figures like Helmholtz were nationalists of a different type than Dühring or Wagner. They shared their work with British and other foreign colleagues, promoted their Jewish disciples equitably, and showed no interest in Gothic chieftains, Siegfrieds, and helmets with horns (Charpa 2004).

The academic background of the origin-story cannot be found in the realms of those academics in fact contributing impressively to the worldwide reputation of German universities before 1933. Its academic home is a rather specific field of historical investigation where professional and amateur work converged. It has been said that the survival of myths is dependent on their historicization (Pollmann 2013). What this means is that in the long run they need to be supported by information on time, space, material evidences, and so on. In this regard literary fiction seems to be a genre close to historiography, which connects raw imagination to historical assumptions. The nonfictional publications and the fictional novels of Felix Dahn are illuminating in this regard. Dahn, a professor of history at the University of Königsberg and its *Rector Magnificus* for a time, was—one of his many nationalistic practices—notorious for discriminating against Polish students. His academic work includes *Urgeschichte der germanischen und romanischen Völker,* a voluminous study in four parts. As its first part, it presents the *Geschichte der deutschen Urzeit* (published in 1883); one does not necessarily need to study these volumes intensively to grasp the point at issue here. In a way, it is already announced by the titles and the words "Urgeschichte" and "Urzeit." For translations into English one might think of "primordial time" and "prehistory," but such English expressions do not adequately mirror the German concepts, which are in a way untranslatable. The term "prehistory" simply refers to events that occurred before a certain time span. The prehistory of the Roman Empire embraces the Etruscan state building, the prehistory of shipbuilding has to do with the construction of primitive canoes, etc. "Primordial" is a more theoretical term coined by late-medieval scholars to describe the beginning states of things. The most common modern usage is to be found in developmental biology and refers to the first recognizable state of the development of a cell. Of importance with regard to the semantic features of the terminology used here is that what is seen as primordial has to do with our capabilities as observers. What was primordial in microscopic biology around 1850 is not the same as in our times. It changes. This points to an interesting difference if we compare "primordial" to German expressions with the prefix *ur-*. *Urzeit, Ursprache, Urgeschichte,* etc., are much more common in German than expressions with "primordial" are in English. And what is more important, *ur-* is not relative to different stages of a process and does not depend on the changing cognitive status of the observers. *Urzeit* and *Urgeschichte* are *absolute* and not simply something that was before a certain historical epoch. It resembles the *bershit* of Genesis 1,1—it is *first*. This is a very important point because it marks the crossroads of methodologically deliberated nineteenth-century historical research and quasi-theological approaches of ideologists. We will return to this point.

Variants of the "origin-story" have been presented by historically minded linguists such as Karl Penka (1847–1912), a grammar school teacher from Vienna. In his publications, the line of thought does not primarily emerge from the vague a priori idea of a "first" epoch but from an extension of some definitive and more or less neutral findings. Penka's first relevant book, *Die Nominalflexion der indogermanischen Sprachen* (1878), deals with historical and systematic questions of the declension in Indo-European languages. It does not require much effort to see that it is a scholarly publication and that the author is not only a trained classical philologist but also acquainted at a professional level with at least a dozen modern and ancient languages. The fundamental issue of the book is within a disciplinary horizon that had been determined by August Schleicher in his famous *Compendium* (1861–1862). Penka's genuine question was: how did the system of cases, outlined in classical grammar, and as carried out with nouns, pronouns, and adjectives of different languages, evolve?

Compared to Schleicher's approach, Penka's explanatory patterns are derived to an even greater extent from mere linguistic rules, and have to do with similarities of case endings in distant languages—for example, with sophisticated shifts of accentuation, etc. In contrast to Schleicher, Penka seems less attracted by the romantic idea of an Indo-Germanic *Urvolk*. Especially Schleicher's famous "fable" (1868: 206–208), a text written in the hypothetical protolanguage of the Indo-European *Urvolk*, did a lot to integrate the idea of origin as a definite status into the academic discourse. Compared to this, in his first book Penka presents himself as a modest philologist *in rebus grammaticae*. What he announces as his next publication is an investigation of the inflection of verbs, obviously an attempt to complement his work on nouns. This book was not published and in its place we come across *Origines Ariacae* (Penka 1883), a speculative book on the anthropology of a speculative historical group, enriched by a lot of linguistic details but no longer attempting to contribute to linguistics. Nevertheless, the subtitle "linguistisch-ethnologische Untersuchungen" of the book indicates the philological background. Furthermore, what Penka published was free of the thematic commitments of his beginnings:

Die Herkunft der Arier. Neue Beiträge zur historischen Anthropologie der europäischen Völker (1886)

Die Entstehung der arischen Rasse (1891)

Neue Hypothesen über die Urheimat der Arier (1906)

The chronological succession of Penka's books makes clear how the academic version of the origin-story in his case evolved. First, Penka began by comparing languages under a certain and purely linguistic aspect. He did what philologists have done since the ancient Alexandrian Grammarians. He then interpreted some systematic linguistic features historically, toward the "origins." This was Schleicher's program, which itself was deeply influenced by the pioneers of the historical-critical method as it was first employed by Robert Estienne (1581) and others. He then connects the "original" linguistic features to a speculatively "original" ethnicity. This matches the Romantic perspective of Johann Gottfried Herder, Johann Georg Hamann, and other authors on language and folk. The final step was to link this speculative ethnicity (that—inspired by the evolutionist natural history of the time—meanwhile turned itself into a race) to existing geographical regions named with the help of the politico-geographical terminology of modern times. The "Indo-Germans" became "Germans" and afterward "Deutsche." Irritating facts such as that Slavic languages belong to the family of Indo-European idioms as well are explained by the auxiliary hypothesis about a secondary usage—due to the adoption of the superior language by so-called inferior ethnicities.

What motivated Penka's shift from linguistics to anthropology cannot definitely be determined. One possible reason may be found in the reaction of the academic experts to Penka's *Nominalflexion* (Meyer 1878). Another is the changing "market situation" because the popular origin narrative had meanwhile become widespread in the German-speaking countries. A quasi-academic support for the "origin-story" appeared more than welcome to many contemporaries such as the readers of "völkische" literature and the admirers of Richard Wagner and his racist writings, not to mention the nationalistic handling of sagas in his operas.

The "Origin of the Germans" and the Historical Method

There is no necessity with regard to logics, methodology, or to content that forces one to end with the Germans as a noble race when one starts with the declension of Greek nouns. To note this is not an anachronistic appraisal as some relativists might assume. Penka does *not* make explicit what the average scholars in the same domain might have presented on the same topic. Admittedly, philologists like Schleicher and many other high-ranking specialists in the same field may also have promoted racist tendencies and romantic ideas about Germans as an original nation at that time, but they were much more cautious as far as the "origin-story" was concerned. This has to do with serious obstacles rooted in the traditions of classical philology that deeply influenced the orientation of nineteenth-century historical research. The era of Schleicher was at the same time the heyday of historical methodology. The writings of Johann Gustav Droysen, Ernst Bernheim, and others on method were compulsory reading for all students of history and historically minded academics in general. The way in which, for example, Bernheim comments on research investigating "primitive folks" (*Völker*) is telling. He emphasizes that, due to the poor reliability of the data, gaining any knowledge *at all* in this regard is very difficult. And in the same context he complains that the most simple principles of source criticism seem not to exist in the field of "ethnological" research whereas—in his opinion—they would be more relevant here than anywhere else in historical studies (1908 [1889]: 610–611).

What can be reliably stated about those issues that the origin-story acquires? As to the Indo-Germans or "Aryans," there is an overwhelming body of linguistic evidence concerning the close relationships between certain languages. This evidence is not tied to an ethnographical conception (Untermann 1985). Methodologically, referring to an Indo-European (as most philologists today would prefer to say) *Urvolk* as explanatory ground for related linguistic phenomena of the Indo-European languages is *self-referential* if these linguistic phenomena provide the only evidence for the existence of an ethnicity as explanatory ground. It would need an independent archaeological record documenting the existence of the "Indo-Germans." Indeed, there are plenty of materials from nonlinguistic sources found in middle and northern Europe, relics of settlements, pottery, funerals, etc.

However, not a single one of such relics is definitely related to a certain language. There is not a single clay jug left with the inscription in *Ursprache,* not to mention one that might provide evidence of a certain folk. The runes that for a while and by some ideologists have naively been considered as "original" scriptures are relatively young (some centuries younger than Latin script), and they are in fact derived from Italic alphabets (which themselves have an Oriental prehistory). So much for evidence supporting the idea of the Indo-European *Urvolk*. I shall now consider the "Germans," who, according to the origin-story, have their forefathers among the Indo-Europeans and who themselves are seen as the origin of the modern "Deutsche."

One may start with the most relevant document from antiquity that can be related to the early history of people named "Germans" in the sense of "Germanen" (even if the term "Germanii" causes a lot of interpretive problems [Krebs 2012]). It is the famous *Germania*, written at the end of the first century CE by the Roman author Cornelius Tacitus. The *Germania* is a minor work celebrating the Germans as "pure" people with a lot of praiseworthy characteristics in contrast to the "decadent" Romans of the time. Irrespective of this tendency, Tacitus's approach to history has often been characterized as "objective" or neutral. He himself speaks of his orientation as "sine ira et studio" (*Annales* I,1), a description that later became a colloquialism. There are many hypotheses concerning the possible aim of Tacitus's allegedly neutral writing, but none has shown itself as decisive. We simply do not know whether Tacitus had in mind to provide ethnographic information, to criticize contemporary Roman society, or indirectly to warn his fellow politicians in Rome of war against the Germanic tribes. Whatever Tacitus's ambitions may have been, the text itself became a major point of reference whenever the history of the ancient "Germans" was at issue. Due to the fact that no alternative to the *Germania* as a rich and colorful source existed, it is no surprise that it shaped the historical imagination over many generations. However, it is precisely this unrivaled position that weakens its reliability as a source. With a side glance at Tacitus's *Germania*, Bernheim ascribes it to the weakness of our minds that we tend to take for granted what we cannot countercheck, simply in order to have any information at all (1908 [1889]: 545). He advises great caution in such cases and bases his hopes for a change on recent philological progress (ibid.: 546).

The "Origin-Story": A Cognitive Mechanism

If one builds a clock following a construction manual, the mechanism may not work, for a variety of reasons. We may distinguish two cases

- At least one of the pieces of the mechanism is damaged.
- At least one of the pieces does not work with the others (perhaps it has been interchanged with another piece).

What has been described above is an example of the first case. The conception of modern Germans as heirs to the Indo-European *Urvolk* and later to Tacitus's *Germanii* is flawed. It cannot be taken as an essential part of a reliable cognitive process. This negative appraisal does not result from anachronistic arrogance. It becomes obvious if we—as we did—check it against the standards of nineteenth-century historical methodology. In the second case, we enter the realms of a somewhat formal examination of the origin-story. A clockwork does not run if a gear-wheel needs to transport a movement to a simple slice. In case of the origin-story there are two main aspects with regard to functionality of the mechanism:

- The investigation of an origin is fundamentally different from merely tracing the arc of a story.
- Fixing an origin does not provide a functional part of a reliable origin-research because it is not compatible with the guiding idea of such research.

In combination, this shows that the origin-story is an unsound cognitive mechanism. Accepting it destroys the reliability of processes aiming at an understanding of relevant prehistorical, ethnological, and political issues.

The first aspect needs little explanation. A story is a story because it tells us about a process of change. New events occur. The situation is no longer the same. Characters and things change—for example, a heroic figure falls from his position in an orderly world into chaos. If we characterize our intuition about a story with the help of a primitive pictorial representation of the diachronics, a story is a process with A as the beginning and B as the end (figure 1.1).

Let us now have a closer look at the second topic, the concept of origin. It belongs to the realm of our handling of the past. The meaning of "origin" results from sharpening ordinary questions of the type, "What happened before?" If we are not content with such answers as, "before the event (process, action, structure,

Figure 1.1. A closed process.

etc.) *A* there was a *B*," we go on and look for more and more remote units. As stated, origin in this context is *first.* Among other narratives, creation myths tell us what the first event, thing, force, etc., was. However, with widening the span of origin thinking from the end of the eighteenth century on, the concept of origin as a last achievable aim came under skeptical attack and lost its function as referring to a definite entity (Charpa 2012). The eighteenth-century German physicist and philosopher Georg Christoph Lichtenberg puts it like this: "If a higher being were ever to tell us about the origin of the world, I wonder whether we should be capable of understanding him" (Stern 1959: 312). No longer a fixable unit, origin became a methodological device directing vaguely to a vanishing point in the succession of before-questions. Now the concept of origin became what William Whewell and Matthias Schleiden, two of the outstanding methodologists of the time, called a "leading idea," which in depth is a *maxim* to act on in the course of further research. Oriented in this way, Charles Darwin in *Origin of Species* demarcates his own studies from last fundamental investigations. He explicitly informs the reader that it is not his issue "how life itself first originated" (1859: 187).

Compared to an ordinary story, the methodologically sound processes investigating origins present themselves as essentially different. In a simple illustration the diachronics would present itself as shown in figure 1.2. What is lacking is the definite end. In other words, seen from the perspective of nineteenth-century methodology, the origin-story is a contradiction in terms. Looking for the origin of something does not amount to telling a fixed story that could support any systematic view. The popular version and authors like Penka avoid the contradiction by using a specific "trick" of linking diachronics to synchronics. This mechanism makes something fit again that fitted in an outdated theological context of historical thinking. The methodological idea of origin as a vanishing point that diachronic research can at best approximate becomes substituted by the conception of *closing* research at a certain point with the help of a speculative entity. In the beginning there was the Indo-German *Urvolk*, a step analogous to the Bible that positions the creator at the origin of everything that constitutes our world.

Figure 1.2. An open-ended process.

Having turned scholarly origin-questions into quasi-theological ones with definite answers, it became possible to establish an argumentative link from a now closed diachronics to the synchronic ambitions shared by nationalists and racists through the ages (see figure 1.3). As a mere mechanism, the origin-story does not really justify the systematic claims of racial and national superiority, but it works *in place* of a sound justification. The "origin-discourse" on nation, origin, and superiority is a piece of unsound thinking, and within the context of historical research we have to do with bad practice.

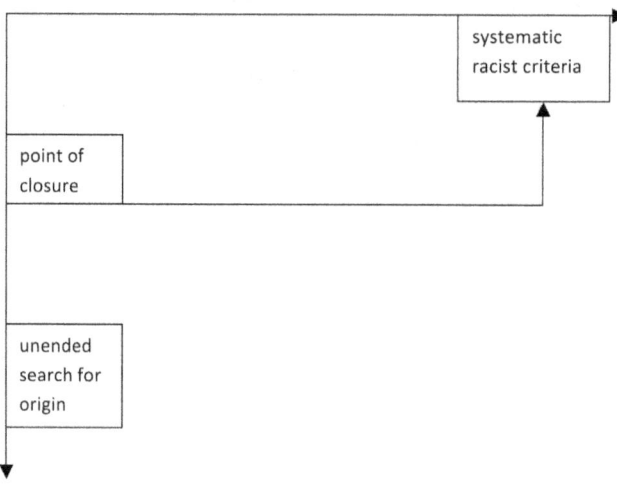

Figure 1.3. The point of closure.

The Mechanism and its Function: Power and Motivational Strength

To build on the work of the relativist author cited above, it can be easily seen in which regard the relativist and the antirelativist approaches could meet one another. Both allow room to determine the *functionality* of practices and patterns of thinking. Hall links it to the effect on the chance to "exercise power over others." The fact that "power" is the pivotal concept in Hall's and other Foucauldian authors' approaches should not detract from noticing that "exercising power" can also be understood as a meaningful description in an antirelativist context. Power is the capacity of directing the actions of others, of oneself, or the course of events. In the realm of human interactions: *A* forces *B* to act in the way *C* acts—irrespective of what *B*'s intentions are. Power presents itself as the disposition to generate such a structure of interaction as a *fact* of which we are informed by the agents' utterances, gestures, obviously unrequested and requested effects, etc. "Power" stands for certain mental states that play an explanatory role in our understanding of human behavior. In other terms, one could speak of motivational force, its intensity and constancy (Mele 2009). It needs no deeper investigation to realize that motivational force and its robustness are very favorable conditions for a power-exercising person and are the opposite for his potential victim. The same applies to groups. In other words, when the historical element of nationalist thought is fastened to a definite "origin" and the systematic elements can be handled optionally, mere nationalist attitudes are turned into a robust mental mechanism that works functionally as far as ignoring other peoples' historical legitimacy and fading out all kinds of systematically irritating facts are concerned.

Ulrich Charpa is professor of philosophy and a member of the Research School at Ruhr University, Bochum. He has taught courses in philosophy, history of science, and Jewish thought side by side at various institutions and for many years worked as research professor at Leo Baeck Institute London. He has published several books and over one hundred articles in academic journals and collections, mostly in the fields of history and philosophy of science, as well in the humanities.

References

Anderson, B. 1983. *Imagined Communities: Reflections on the Origins and Spread of Nationalism.* London.
Atran, S. 1990. *Cognitive Foundations of Natural History: Towards an Anthropology of Science.* Cambridge.
Bernheim, E. 1908 (1889). *Lehrbuch der historischen Methode und der Geschichtsphilosophie.* 6th edition. Leipzig.
Charpa, U. 2004. "Judentum und wissenschaftliche Forschung. Einstellungscluster im späten 19. Jahrhundert und ihr Fortwirken." *Simon Dubnow Institute Yearbook* 3: 175–198.
———. 2012. "'Origin,' 'Creation,' and 'Origin of Life': Some Conceptual Considerations." *History and Philosophy of the Life Sciences* 34: 439–460.

———. 2013. "Anti-Semitism as Mental Mechanism: A Model Suggested by some Similarities between Nineteenth-Century Anti-Semitisms in Music and Science." In *English and German Nationalist and Anti-Semitic Discourse 1871–1945*, eds. G. Horan et al. Oxford, 21–48.
Dahn, F. 1878. *A Struggle for Rome*, translated by L. Wolffsohn. London.
———. 1881–1889. *Urgeschichte der germanischen und romanischen Völker.* Leipzig.
Darwin, C. 1859. *On the Origin of Species by Means of Natural Selection.* London.
Estienne, R. 1581. *Recueil de l'origine de la langue et poesie françoise, ryme et romans. Plus les noms et sommaire des oeuvres de CXXVII poetes françois, vivans avant l'an MCCC.* Paris.
Focke Museum. 2013. *Graben für Germanien: Archäologie unterm Hakenkreuz.* Stuttgart.
Gowan, C. 2012. "Moral Relativism." In *The Stanford Encyclopedia of Philosophy* (Spring Edition), ed. E. N. Zalta. http://plato.stanford.edu/archives/spr2012/entries/moral-relativism/.
Hall, S. 1995. "The Question of Cultural Identity." In *Modernity: An Introduction to English and German Nationalist and Anti-Semitic Discourse 1871–1945*, eds. S. Hall et al., *Modern Societies*. Oxford, 594–634.
Hermann, M. 2000. "Kompetenzrivalität und Selbstinszenierung. Theater in der 'Hauptstadt der deutschen Kunst.'" In *Münchner Theatergeschichtliches Symposium 2000*, eds. H. M. Koerner and J. Schlaeder. Munich, 189–210.
Hobsbawn, E. 1992. *Nations and Nationalities since 1780.* Cambridge.
Krebs, C. B. 2012. *A Most Dangerous Book: Tacitus's Germania from the Roman Empire to the Third Reich.* New York.
Lemberg, E. 1964. *Nationalismus.* Vol. 2. Reinbek.
Mele, A. 2008. *Motivation and Agency.* Oxford.
Meyer, G. 1878. Review. *Jenaer Literaturzeitung* 15, no. 15: 226–227.
Penka, K. 1878. *Die Nominalflexion der indogermanischen Sprachen.* Vienna.
———. 1883. *Origines Ariacae. Linguistisch-ethnologische Untersuchungen zur ältesten Geschichte der arischen Völker und Sprachen.* Vienna.
———. 1886. *Die Herkunft der Arier. Neue Beiträge zur historischen Anthropologie der europäischen Völker.* Vienna.
———. 1891. *Die Entstehung der arischen Rasse.* Vienna.
———. 1906. *Neue Hypothesen über die Urheimat der Arier.* Leipzig.
Pollmann, J. 2013. "Of Living Legends and Authentic Tales: How to Get Remembered in Early Modern Europe." *Transactions of the RHS* 23: 103–125.
Potter, P. 1998. *Most German of the Arts: Musicology and Society from the Weimar Republic to the End of Hitler's Reich.* New Haven, CT.
Rush, F. 2013. "Contextualizing Nationalism and Anti-Semitism 1871–1945." In *English and German Nationalist and Anti-Semitic Discourse 1871–1945*, eds. G. Horan et al. Oxford, 5–19.
Schleicher, A. 1868. "Fabel in indogermanischer Ursprache." In *Beiträge zur vergleichenden Sprachforschung auf dem Gebiete der arischen, celtischen und slawischen Sprachen.* Berlin, 206–208.
———. *Compendium der vergleichenden Grammatik der indogermanischen Sprachen. Kurzer Abriss der indogermanischen Ursprache, des Altindischen, Altiranischen, Altgriechischen, Altitalischen, Altkeltischen, Altslawischen, Litauischen und Altdeutschen.* 2 vols. Weimar.

Sesardic, N. 2010. "Race: A Social Destruction of a Biological Concept." *Biology and Philosophy* 25: 143–162.
Stern, J. P. 1059. *Lichtenberg: A Doctrine of Scattered Occasions.* Bloomington, IN.
Toulmin, S. 1990. *Cosmopolis: The Hidden Agenda of Modernity.* Chicago, IL.
Untermann, J. 1985. "Ursprache und historische Realität. Der Beitrag der Indogermanistik zu Fragen der Ethnogenese." In *Studien zur Ethnogenese,* ed. Rheinisch-Westfälische Akademie der Wissenschaften. Opladen, 133–163.
Watson, P. 2010. *The German Genius.* London.
Wodak, R. 2006. "Discourse-analytic and Socio-linguistic Approaches to the Study of Nationalism(s)". In *The Sage Handbook of Nations and Nationalism,* eds. G. Delanty and K. Kumar. London, 104–117.
Wolfrum, E. 2002. *Geschichte als Waffe. Vom Kaiserreich zur Wiedervereinigung.* 2nd edition. Göttingen.

 2

Fantasies of Mixture, Politics of Purity
Narratives of Miscegenation in Colonial Literature,
Literary Primitivism, and Theories of Race (1900–1933)

Eva Blome

New conceptualizations of race emerged in the late nineteenth-century German Kaiserreich. The process of nation building (see Anderson 1991) and the beginning of German colonialism led to a stronger focus on a collective identity centered on German culture, the German nation, and the German *Volk*. The concept of race here functioned as a marker of national collectiveness, with German identity conflated with racially defined "whiteness." In this manner, with racial hierarchies within and especially outside of Europe now receiving definition, "race" became a "boundary marker" (McClintock 1995) of Germanness. Consequently, we should not understand the racist theory articulated in this period as the result of "constructions of race," but rather as a driving force for social and cultural processes that involve proclaiming the existence of something called "race." That claim thus served as the catalyst for a politics of social exclusion and racism.

The breach with earlier racial concepts that developed in the late nineteenth century was manifest in the individual and social bodies being grasped as intertwined, by way of a concept of propagation. Michel Foucault has, famously, described the scenario at work here as "biopolitics" (2004). Fatima El-Tayeb and Pascal Grosse have thus been able to show that under the impression of Social Darwinism and the emergence of nationalist and colonial population policies, sexual contact between members of various "races" was viewed within the perspective of reproduction and the endangerment of the national collective (El-Tayeb 2001; Grosse 2000). El-Tayeb concluded that on this process *Volk* and "race" became nearly identical concepts (2001: 132; see also Sarasin 2003: 65). For this reason, early twentieth-century German colonial discourse obsessively focused on a threat of miscegenation (*Rassenmischung*; lit. "racial intermixing"). In the sphere of social anthropology, which was at the time a nearly new academic discipline, in medical debates and political conflicts concerning how to behave in the colonies, and finally in popular literature and culture, questions such as the following were being asked: were sexual contacts to be allowed between different "races"? What did such contacts lead to? And what role did the children stemming from the contacts play for and in the German nation and German culture? In view of this question, it is clear, to speak with Ronald Hyam, that "sex is at the very heart of racism" (1990: 203).

For its fantastic and dialectic character, the race concept needed shoring up and confirming in the form of cultural evidence. In the fin-de-siècle context, Christina Hanke has observed that a permanent "dissolving" of the category of race demanded its permanent fixation. According to Hanke, the circle that thus formed between these two poles itself points to the emptiness of "race" as an ontological quantity (2007). In addition, we find a biopolitical paradigm that starting in the late nineteenth century increasingly placed "purity" at the center of its racial-ideological demands and premises—and this not without the idea's counterpart, "mixing." Hence in his study *Colonial Desire: Hybridity in Theory, Culture and Race,* Robert Young argues that "the idea of race … shows itself to be profoundly dialectical: it only works when defined against potential intermixture, which also threatens to undo its calculations altogether. This antagonistic structure acts out the tensions of a conflictual culture which defines itself through racial ideologies" (2003: 19; see also Zack 1993). Werner Sollors argues in a similar fashion: "The hackneyed notion of 'pure blood' always rests on the possibility and the reality of 'mixed blood'—though violent 'cleansing' may be deemed necessary to constitute 'purity'" (1999: 4).

As Kien Nghi Ha has shown in detail in the context of the German-speaking world, "racial purity" and "racial mixing" were bound together in a contradictory way (2010; see also Blome 2011: 45–51). Precisely in light of the imaginary and contradictory character of racial conceptions, the question of a specific *poetics* of "racial purity" and "racial mixing," applied in a wide range of literary-cultural paradigms, appears to call all the more strongly for consideration. In this regard, the project of colonial racism requires figures of hybridity. For while, to be sure, the so-called racial bastard or mixed-race person on the one hand repeatedly call into question the opposition between self and other in imaginary colonial topography; on the other hand, due to their liminal status, they refer time and again to the difference of "races."[1]

At the same time, we need to examine aesthetic and narrative factors revealing the diverse political and theoretical paradigms of sexuality and "race." The present chapter is meant to fulfill this double purpose, thus contributing to the literary-historical study of a thematic field of great significance for the self-understanding of both the Kaiserreich and the Weimar Republic, but that has until now been examined mainly in a framework of historical research.²

Politics and Aesthetics

In the following discussion, I will thus consider diverse forms of narrative staging of the theme of "racial mixing," as unfolding in a variety of cultural contexts. Broadly speaking, two major lines of argument were at work in such staging: In the political sphere, the emergence of colonial biopolitics resulted in a wide range of negative scenarios of "racial intermixing" centered around interconnections between gender, race, and (colonial) space. As a consequence, so-called mixed-marriage prohibitions were decreed for "German Southwest Africa" as early as 1905 (see El-Tayeb 2001: 92–109) and for "German East Africa" in 1906; in 1907, marriages in the German colonies in Africa prior to 1905 were declared invalid, and those who had entered into such marriages lost their civil as well as voting rights.³

At the same time, in the first two decades of the twentieth century, contemporary literary avantgardes enthusiastically embraced utopias of miscegenation, with literary primitivism being the most prominent example of such visions. Writers such as Robert Müller, Klabund, and Carl Sternheim were fascinated by the far-reaching consequences of miscegenation. In addition, literary constructions of "racial purity and intermixing" connected the phenomenon with poetic and artistic production itself. But in making this connection, the authors involved applied stereotypes of race and gender manifested in colonial and early fascist discourse. Indeed, primitivist visions of "interraciality" as either a prototype of humanity's future or as a product of poetics of commixture themselves depended on a logic of purity and on the concept of breeding a "new race." Finally, the primitivist texts conveying these visions could not escape the double movement of mixture and separation. In this manner, progressive poetic fantasies of "race mixing" demonstrably reflected and sometimes generated metaphors and narratives of race that would move toward hegemony in the Weimar Republic and attain it in the Nazi "racial state."

This discussion considers intersections between relevant German colonial and avantgarde discourse on the basis of political and cultural-theoretical texts, colonial novels, and other literary work appearing between 1900 and 1933—a body of writing that, I argue, is only internally contradictory on first view. In my analysis, I will focus on the relationship between political and aesthetic concepts of miscegenation and consider the discussion of "interracial sexuality"—constructed as a threat to the social collective but also functioning as a precondition for it—that unfolded in this period. This discussion represented a central moment in a colonial strategy for maintaining power with the aid of narration.

It is clear, in any case, that on the surface literary concepts of purity and mixture are not tied to racist eugenicist programs. This essay is an analysis of the echoes of a figuration used in biopolitical discourse within a corpus of poetological visions, and vice versa. To that end the essay will be divided into three parts. First, I will argue that imperialist imagination of miscegenation in German colonial discourse of the early twentieth century evolved in a literary laboratory of "racial intermixture." The main question here will be how that imagination was represented in and through literary texts conveying that colonial discourse, and how the programmatic novels in question made a significant contribution to colonial politics of race. Next, I will consider literary primitivism. Here, I wish to show how both biological and poetic paradigms of mixture became influential in the primitivist movements of classical modernity, and how the biological meaning of "racial intermixture" changed in the course of this transformation. Finally, I will focus on theories of race promulgated after World War I. In examining the influence of aesthetic concepts of purity on prefascist theories of "racial purity," I will consider interconnections between earlier, primitivist literary concepts of "racial intermixing" and the aesthetic component of Weimar Republic race theories circulating between 1920 and 1933. In this way, I hope to show that the relationship between biopolitical and cultural spheres was an important element in Germany's (colonial) representation of race in the Kaiserreich and the Weimar Republic.

Importantly, this argumentation should not be understood to suggest a demonstrable, consequential development from (colonial-)literary dystopias of "racial mixing" in the Kaiserreich, to utopias of mixing in avantgarde writing of literary expressionists and primitivists, and onward to proto-Nazi racial theories circulating in the Weimar Republic. Rather, the concern here is with displacements and transformations of both concepts and contents evident in the representation and assessment of "interracial" sexuality in this period.

Literary Imaginations of Colonial Sexuality

The popularity of cultural and literary figurations of miscegenation at the end of the nineteenth century was a product of European imperialism. The broad political debate regarding the political and social consequences, including gradual "hybridization" of sexual contact with people not belonging to one's own collective, can be viewed as an outcome on the basis of a new biopolitical paradigm (see Foucault 1998). With regard to this development, Ann Laura Stoler has noted that in "linking domestic arrangements to the public order, family to the state, sex to subversion, and psychological essence to racial type, *métissage* might be read as a metonym for the biopolitics of empire at large" (2002: 80). Within colonial discourse, figures of sexual and reproductive miscegenation appear to have come to the fore in the context of such a linkage, the figures conveyed in terms of a dialectical relationship between pureness and mixing. As I will argue below, literary texts produced in the period around 1900 mediated such a paradoxical racial ideology in a special way, with a wide range of authors—the list includes Frieda von Bülow, Hanna Christaller, Gustav Frenssen, Lene Haase, Hans Grimm, Richard Küas, and Willy Seidel—repeatedly representing sexual relationships between colonizers and the colonized in identical form (see Blome 2011: 85–141).

A problem with the biopolitical regime operating in the German colonial context was that the possibility of legally controlling male sexuality was restricted to a prohibition on "mixed marriages." Extramarital sexual activity by men in the colonies remained widely beyond the state's reach, since male sexuality itself was considered essentially autonomous, as Pascal Grosse (2000: 148, 156) has indicated. Thus finding other forms of regulation became necessary. Imaginative literature was called on to fulfill this role since what we might term "fictional thought experiments" offered the possibility of representing perceived far-reaching consequences of "mixed" sexual relationships. Within the texts in question, the story of an individual protagonist was represented as part of the history of the German *Volk* or "race" and the act of "race mixing" as a contamination of the individual and collective body (see Planert 2000: 571). Most of these programmatic texts were written in autobiographical form; considering colonial literature as a whole, the percentage of highly personalized genres, such as the epistolary novel and coming-of-age narratives, was strikingly high (see Schneider 2003: 30). At the same time, in forewords, postscripts, or fictive editor's statements, the texts addressed the larger framework of German colonial racial policy in which they were meant to be read, thus relocating individual, intimate narratives in an exemplary realm of German collective identity.[4] Affiliation with the *Volk* was emphasized here by drawing a connection between heroic actions or transgressions on the one hand, thriving or incurred damage on the other hand. The "imperial pairings" depicted in colonial literature always stood for the relationship between Germany and its colonies, with a focus on presenting the figure of a "white" German nation to which the sexual behavior of each German was wed.

This double strategy of individualizing the narrative plot, favoring readers' participation, while contextualizing the narrated action as relevant for the national community, characterizes the narrative approach to sexual contact within the colonial and racial-political program. The dramatic results of crossing the sexual gap between white and black persons was presented through themes of biological reproduction and a group of questions tied to the death of the protagonists: Did children issue from these relationships? What happened to the children? Who was allowed to survive the illegitimate union and who had to die? For whom was reintegration into the German national collective permissible after the "racial intermixing"?[5] The answers offered in these works of fiction depended both on the particular constellation of the relationship in question and on the historical moment in which the text was written. This becomes clear in a comparison of early twentieth-century German colonial novels. All of them finally define the relationship between German colonists and those who are colonized as illegitimate and indeed dangerous both at an individual level and at the level of the collective race or nation. But the narratives diverge strikingly depending on the gender of the work's German protagonist, the race of the corresponding non-European figure, and the location of the plot. In the following observations I will focus on the gender/race-constellation.

As we can see in a number of colonial novels, for the white woman, the narrative paradigm for sexual contact with non-European men is seduction or rape and, for the most part, total and irreversible contamination; by contrast, the paradigm for such contacts between white males and non-European women is referred to in the colonial discourse as *Verkafferung* (literally "becoming a Kaffir")—that is, sociocultural degeneration through sexual intercourse with African women. The *German Colonial Dictionary* (*Deutsches Koloniallexikon*) from 1920 explains the key word "Verkafferung" in the following terms:

> V. refers in German Southwest Africa to the degeneration of a European to the cultural level of the native, a phenomenon for which in other protectorates the terms *Vernegern* or *Verkanakern* are used. Lonely life in the field, in constant contact with colored persons, but mixed marriage with them in particular, foster this regrettable degeneration of white settlers. The kaffirred European is, despite previous personal intelligence, always a lost member of the white population, because even in the best case he

completely loses one of the most essential requirements of his domestic culture, namely energetic drive and adherence to a definite plan. ... Only through legislative (prohibition of mixed marriage) and social measures can this scourge be steered [sic] in the long run. The most reliable means to combat this danger, which is not to be underestimated, is to facilitate marriage with white women. (Schnee 1920: 606)[6]

The phenomenon of "Verkafferung" ("kaffirring") is construed here in a way that establishes a clear connection between the behavior of an individual and the resulting consequences for the entire "white population." It is striking, however, that men exclusively are thought to be affected by "kaffirring," and marriage with "white women" is regarded as a type of antidote.

Typical literary examples of this paradigm are offered in Hanna Christaller's novel *Alfreds Frauen* (1903) and the widely read colonial novel *Wie Grete aufhörte ein Kind zu sein* (1913) by Hans Grimm, who later became a prominent "blood and soil" novelist.[7] Both these texts incorporate a systematic element in programmatic German colonial scenarios of miscegenation: the integration of another white woman into the plot as a figure of pureness. Through this figure, the perceived "racial gap" between the male colonizer and his indigenous mistress is brought to the fore. In Christaller's novel, whose title already indicates the symptomatic triangulation, this is the settler's bride, arrived from Germany. In Grimm's novel, the role is occupied by the colonizer's daughter—let us dwell for a moment on this colonial narrative: Grimm's male protagonist, Troyna, a widower who lives alone on a farm in "German Southwest Africa," shoots another European, who has two children with a native woman, in a confrontation with smugglers. These now-orphaned young siblings, Ellen and Alfred, then take up with Troyna, which might appear strange at first glance, since he is responsible for the death of their father. Ellen's explanation for this decision is: "What should I do? These are not my people [*Volk*] here!" (Grimm 1975: 87).[8] Yet not only Ellen and her brother Alfred feel like they do not belong to the "people," but also Troyna's belonging to his own culture is at issue: he enters into a sexual relationship with Ellen, which calls into question his superior role as a European in the African colony, as in his relation to her the colonial hierarchies between "white" and "black" begin to reverse: "She [Ellen] was the queen of the night, and here power had long since become so great that the man, as with many men who believe to pull the strings when it comes to women, had for some time now become subject to her rule and sank, sank, sank all the more that she loved him passionately and he loved her in return" (ibid.: 106).[9]

Racial and sexual hierarchies consort with one another in the process of "kaffirring" represented here (see Axster 2007). Ellen is thereby characterized by a cunning, wildcat-like dangerousness that is also connected to her hybrid descent but that does not only present a danger to the individual settler, since it increases her sexual proximity and attractiveness, but also poses a problem of population politics and power. A lieutenant had explained to Troyna that Ellen and Alfred are so-called Hundasi, "the only pretty bastards of the colony" (Grimm 1975: 88). Ellen and Alfred already embody the topic of the narrative, "racial mixing," which is thus evoked as a danger for colonial politics in order to maintain colonial hierarchies and the predominance of Europeans in the African colonies. Grete, Troya's daughter who returns from Europe, has the function of symbolizing colonial purity—yet in her case, too, it remains contradictorily tied to the "danger of intermixing." Therein lies the narrative challenge for a programmatic author such as Grimm and the paradox to be overcome by narrative of a colonial border that first comes into being in its transgression. It is resolved—merely—in Grete's dream in which a sexual relationship is insinuated between her and Alfred (see Grimm 1913: 124f.). However, the imagery of the dream suggests that the relationship is meant to be reinterpreted. Erotic desire becomes thirsting for water, potential amour turns into a caring and nourishing relationship of a mother to her child. Grete explicitly says as much in her dream: "Oh you, ah you, I thought you were a foreigner and I loved you, and now, now I know that I am mother to you, and you, you are my child" (Grimm 1975: 125). The motif of caring is mounted here against the danger of a sexual encounter. When Homi Bhabha emphasizes that the Black "is the embodiment of rampant sexuality and yet innocent as a child" (Bhahba 1994: 82), we find in Grimm's story the narrative attempt to limit the black figure to the figure of a nondangerous child, hence the attempt to conceive the colonial relation as a paternalistic one that here appears in a maternalistic variation, since Grete's father cannot assume this position as a "kaffirred colonizer" (see Blome 2013: 99f.). In the end, Grete shoots the siblings Ellen and Alfred and thus restores the colonial racial order. Within a triangular structure, the white woman Grete acts as a boundary marker (McClintock 1995: 24)[10] between the white man and the black woman. In the process, the white woman not only embodies the imperative of racial purity but functions as a figure burdened with the task of compensating for the transgressions and inadequacies of the white man in the colonies. In this manner the "German woman," as a differentiating and demarcating figure, emerges as a fixed topos in German colonial literature. Richard Küas's novel *Vom Baum der Erkenntnis* (1911) includes a song of praise of a young female settler's biopolitical mission sung at her deathbed:

> For us who are here ... you are not just any random little white woman [*Weibchen*] who succumbs to her herd instinct and drives and can wander, like some black woman, from the arms of one man into those of another. For us you are *the* white woman [*Weib*]! The woman who must fulfill a mission, sent to us by a will controlling all our fates, out here among us white heathens in order to make us believe in the inner beauty and purity of the white woman and the holiness and inviolability of marriage! In order to tear us away from pleasure in the arms of these black women and sustain strong men for your and our race, and your children, you must sustain our faith in you! That is your mission out here, your highest and most noble mission, alongside many others you have to fulfill here! (Küas 1911: 259f.)[11]

In this way, for the German settler the white female sustains the hierarchical opposition threatened by "racial mixing," between the colonial masters and their subjects. The African woman is usually presented as a seducer and threat to such racial integrity.

Such fictional, narrative establishing of a distinct colonial-racial order shows the mechanisms involved in the equivalent real-life process. The texts reveal the imaginary origins of the racial concept at work in biopolitical modernism. In turn the imaginary construction of racial borders took explicit poetic-aesthetic form in early twentieth-century German avantgarde primitivist literature.[12] German colonial literature's laboratories of "racial intermixture" and hierarchies of race and gender generated a poetics of miscegenation of some importance to authors working within that particular framework of German modernism.

Miscegenation as a Poetic Concept

It is unsurprising that a weighty but complicated relationship is manifest between an increasingly aggressive colonial response to purported "bastardization" of the German population abroad and increasing popularity of the theme of miscegenation within early twentieth-century German antibourgeois artistic avantgardes. While, as suggested, in the colonial novels appearing around 1900 miscegenation was understood to signify the downfall of both individual identity and the national racial collective, in the second decade of the twentieth century, more artistically ambitious literary texts proposed, not a threat to German culture by miscegenation or "foreign blood," but instead a high degree of interdependency between "mixed" procreation and literary-cultural production, the two phenomena now serving to articulate a poetological perspective.

The idea that art and artistic production were closely and even necessarily connected with "race mixing" was rooted in tradition. An early version of the idea of art as a product of miscegenation with considerable influence on relevant German discourse is Joseph-Arthur Gobineau's *Essai sur l'inégalité des races humaines*, written between 1853 and 1855 and first published in German in 1898 (1940: 239). Gobineau constructed the racial characteristics through the conceptual figure of an opposition between rationality and sensuality; he defined the former as a decisive characteristic of "white peoples," the latter of "black peoples" (ibid.: 240f.). The art produced by "black peoples," he indicated, neglected the spiritual realm, being rather focused on the body and the factual; in addition, it had more sexual energy at its disposal (ibid.: 243). But in a manner tied to eighteenth-century aesthetic traditions, Gobineau assumed that consummated art consisted of a blend of reason and sensuality—meaning that for him in the end a mixture of "races" was a prerequisite for cultural development and artistic innovation.[13] With initial consideration, such a view on the part of an author whose ideas formed the basis for modern racial theory (see Lemonon 1982), including Nazi biological racism, might seem astonishing. It is the case that Gobineau maintained that for a "real victory of the arts" "white blood" had to dominate the mixture (Gobineau 1940: 249). Nevertheless, his basic idea corresponds to a direction emerging in a range of philosophical and literary texts published at the turn of the nineteenth century, in such texts as the observations of Nietzsche[14] and in Heinrich Mann's novel *Zwischen den Rassen* (1906), which argues that artists and others of interracial descent are something like "soulmates" (see Blome 2011: 57–61).

In a body of German expressionist and primitivist literature, the idea of racial intermixture was actualized and modified, its avantgarde authors developing both poetological concepts and social utopias based on the idea. It is realized, for example, in Robert Müller's expressionist novel *Tropen* (1915). According to the first-person narrator, a central "mixed race" figure in this book, Jack Slim, represents the "prototype of future humanity" (Müller 1990: 28).[15] Overall, in this novel and other (literary) texts, Müller presented a program of racial intermixture that was aimed at nothing short of a new aesthetics resulting from such a new "bastardized" type of humanity (see also Blome 2010). At one point, he writes: "If races come together it will be an artistic or erotic occasion for the individual. Conquest is always love; synthesis of peoples is always poetry" (1917: 79).[16] For Müller and many other writers of that period, art was closely connected to a general process of overcoming formal boundaries and the phenomenon of "racial mixing" was considered an optimal form of this process. In the eyes of various German authors, miscegenation was not only capable of overcoming differences between races, nations, and cultures, but between the artist and his production, art and life, and even between form and content. For Müller, this applied to all the arts, and in particular music. When the narrator in *Tropen* notices the unusual appearance of jungle-dwelling musicians, his alter-ego, Slim, comments with lapidary coolness: "Mixed race, like all musicians" (1990: 82).[17] In *Tropen* and various other novels of the period emerging from an avantgarde and primitivist milieu, (non-European) music is understood as the most intuitive of the arts, because in music there is no difference between the artwork and its meaning. Congruence between form and content was the ideal of expressionist aesthetics in general—an ideal primitivist writers (and such painters as Paul Gauguin and Ernst Ludwig Kirchner[18]) saw realized in the art of "primitive" societies, and in particular in the work of artists of interracial descent. Other prominent authors to incorporate this theme included Carl Sternheim and Klabund, both of whom used the motif of interracial pairing to articulate a desired overcoming of the boundaries between European and "primitive" art and aesthetics.[19]

But if miscegenation here led to creativity and artistic production, then the writing of literature had no less capacity to produce a new, mixed human being, the poet thus defined as humanity's potential savior. In *Tropen* this not exactly modest definition of the artist is expressed by the narrator: "O, Brazil is enormous and a country of the future; but who knows anything about Brazil and who knows its soul than I, the poet? I was created to become its emperor; I will found not only an empire but a new race, for which I will invent a modern soul of its own reflecting the latest style; I will create a Brazilian and human archetype in which the talents of all organisms are united" (Müller 1990: 83f.).[20] In any event, all such expressionist and primitivist identifications with intermixing inevitably run up against their own limits—the intermixture being evoked can only constitute a reference to the very components making up its mixed nature. In other words, the concept of purity is inherent in any such aesthetic of indifferentiation. Ultimately, the novels in question cannot escape a double movement of intermixture and separation, which is precisely what made them attractive to theorists of race after World War I. A certain literary-historical paradox was at work here: on the one hand, expressionist-primitivist art was spurned by these theorists, while on the other, their racial and eugenic theories were based on the very concepts to which they were opposed.

Bio-Aesthetics: Theories of Race in the Weimar Republic

After World War I, the conception of "race" shifted from a more or less strictly biological concept to one defined mainly in terms of culture. Hence in 1933, in his book *Rasse und Staat,* Eric Voegelin described the difference between "racial theories" around 1900 and the "racial idea" of the postwar period as demonstrating both the intellectual-historical and "mythic [*mythischen*]" content of "race" (1933: 15). Voegelin here confirmed a decisive shift in that concept in the first third of the twentieth century: whereas an older understanding of "race" focused on an essence of human beings meant to be defined in natural-scientific terms, "race" was now declared an "idea," its necessity asserted, but at the same time its "mythic" character not denied. Correspondingly, the *Volkskörper*—the *"Volk* body"—was no longer conceived in biological but rather in spiritual terms.[21] Voegelin is here describing a displacement already to be found in Oswald Spengler's *The Decline of the West* (written between 1918 and 1922). In his book Spengler declared that race was composed not only of "blood and soil" but also of a "feeling for the beauty of the race" ("Gefühl für Rassenschönheit," Spengler 1922: 150). In his view, the beauty of a piece of art and racial beauty (of the artist) stemmed from the same sources, from "something entirely primordial and rising from the soul's deepest grounding" (ibid.: 233).[22] Just as artworks are assessed on their expressive strength, Spengler assumes a hierarchy for "races," based on the standard of how well a "race" succeeds in leading its "underlying form" to a goal (ibid.: 233). For Spengler, the "struggle between the races" unfolded through racial concepts. We read, for example, that "the energy of form is so strong that it seizes and reshapes neighboring peoples" (ibid.: 204).[23] While in earlier, colonial discourse fear of biological fusion through sexual contact and propagation was the dominant focus, Spengler offers a new, aesthetic interpretation: the danger of degeneration no longer lay in biological mixing or the power of assimilation of other races, but in the "energy of form." It would appear, then, that in Spengler's theory, racist and imperialist potential was bound up with the implementation of aesthetic concepts.

With the term "form," Spengler made use of a concept central to writings on aesthetics since Plato and Aristotle. In the Weimar Republic, the embrace of bioaesthetics—the alliance between aesthetics and racist conceptualizations—became even more pronounced in the writings of theorists of race that lay the basis for Nazi racial policy and theory. Three such theorists were Hans F. K. Günther (1891–1968), Paul Schultze-Naumburg (1869–1949), and Alfred Rosenberg (1893–1946); in the 1920s all consciously carried forward the analogy between biological reproduction and the production of art. In his 1926 book on *Rasse und Stil,* Günther argued that Gothic art was marked by an absence of any separation between form and content.[24] That separation, he indicated, only emerged during the Italian Renaissance, around 1500 (1926: 7). In Günther's view, whether the German *Volk* would be able to realize "sufficient northern essence [*Wesen*]" depended on its capacity to overcome the form-content separation and create a new totality (ibid.: 14). He saw "racial mixing" as a central danger, in this manner bringing the concept of "racial purity" together with a unity of form and content in art and its consideration. Conversely, the sundering of form from content was understood as catalyzed by "racial mixing" in a very essential way (ibid.: 14).

In his book *Kunst und Rasse,* first published in 1928, Paul Schultze-Naumburg likewise expounded on the concept of "artistic purity" in the sense of an absence of "racially alien" influences. He viewed the diversity of artistic expression and style on the one hand and aesthetic judgments on the other hand as grounded in the differing "corporeality" of the artists or art-recipients involved (Schultze-Naumburg 1928: 1). This assumption allowed him to in turn infer an artist's specific corporeality from the artwork. But for Schultze-Naumburg, the "corporeal principle" ("*leibliches Prinzip*"; ibid.: 22) was identical with a "'racial' principle" ("'*rassisches*' *Prinzip*"; ibid.: 23). With corresponding inevitability, "purely physical propagation" here emerged as the model for developing the idea that "spiritual creation" depended on its creator's racial affiliation (ibid.: 18). As a starting point, for his connection between race and art, Schultze-Naumburg takes up a definition of artistic production that had been generally virulent in aesthetic theory for centuries: a definition operating in the framework of mainly literary semantics of propagation (see Wellbery 2002: 13), which he then—and this is new—connected to racial concepts. But he also tied outer appearance, physiognomy—in his understanding, the artist's race—with the specific aesthetic of a given artwork, which received its own racial affiliation through the racially defined artist's act of creation. In this way the artist as it were bequeathed his "corporeality" or "race" to his or her work, the realization of a fundamental biologization of art and aesthetics.

In his *Myth of the Twentieth Century* (with the telling subtitle *An Evaluation of the Spiritual-Intellectual* [seelisch-geistigen] *Confrontations of Our Age*), first published in 1930, Alfred Rosenberg carried forward and radicalized the same basic approach. In a fanatic *völkish*, "blood and soil" mode that would prompt the Nazis to draw on the book to justify a ban on marriage between Jews and Aryans, Rosenberg offered a plea for a "religion of blood" that would replace Christianity; the "Nordic *Volk*," he argued, were a single culture and race, whose survival was to be expected according to developmental laws and whose purest expression was the "German *Volk*," a "race of Aryans." Importantly, a theory of art was inherent in this racial theory as well, in that Rosenberg saw Europe's art as a genuine "medium for overcoming the world" and "a religion in itself" (1938: 443).[25] For Rosenberg, artistic creation was all the more valuable in proportion to the formative will it displayed; the Aryan race here displayed the most strength. In this way aesthetic expression and perception served for Rosenberg, as it had for Schultze-Naumburg, to establish an essential differentiation and hierarchization of races, the concept of race no longer conceived of in merely biological terms but aestheticized in an essentialistic way (Hebekus 2009: 65–74; Lacoue-Labarthe and Nancy 1997).

Rosenberg viewed race as a kind of artwork that developed by a process of selection and elimination of material elements. Crucially, he viewed the selection process as a decidedly male activity that formed a contrast to the "lyrical passion" characterizing the female: A passion rendering her responsible for a task with much in common with the expressionist project of creating a "new race," namely "to live a myth and create a t y p e" (1938: 481).[26] Thus for Rosenberg, women were meant to guarantee "purity of the race" (ibid.: 511).[27] In the framework of such an aesthetical-biological labor division between men and women, biological reproduction and artificial production were bound together through a presumption of natural heterosexual desire, at this point, the concept of creation and the notion of "creating a new breed" had been given an entirely racist turn.

Conclusion

In the laboratory of modernity, a literary program with biopolitical content prepared the ground for a commonly held understanding of miscegenation and its implications. Within this process, various scenarios and their consequences, both for the individual and the German *Volk*, were played through in ways akin to fictitious experiments. Expressionist and primitivist authors adopted these scenarios, redefining them from a poetic perspective. On the basis of perceived similarities between art and "racial intermixing," they developed utopias of creative production and propagation, and, through miscegenation, of new kinds of human beings. Even if unintentional, this development served as a kind of conceptual blueprint for the approach taken by later racial theorists, who used the combination of aesthetics and conceptualizations of race to propose a fascist and anti-Semitic utopia, achieved through a purification and refinement of the Aryan race. Where, however, in texts stamped by literary primitivism purity, collectivizing power, and an indifference of form and content in the primitive artwork are foregrounded, in the last-discussed racial and cultural theorists of the Weimar Republic, these conceptual figures are used in relation to *creating* a *Volkskörper* defined as a "race."

With this as our starting point, we can more precisely define the significance of the phenomenon of "racial mixing" for Nazi ideology. The subject of "racial mixing" was already spelled out in colonialism's cultural and literary imagination as a dystopia; as a kind of counter-movement, it was not only utopized but also aestheticized in the primitivism of the artistic avantgarde. In the context of the Weimar racial theories treated here, this subject is presented in colonial and primitivist literature as a particular type of juncture between dystopian and aesthetic-utopian manifestations: as Pierre-André Taguieff has shown, Nazi doctrine constructed its myth of race and blood upon the assertion of racial mixing as the greatest of all dangers (2000: 290), hence as a dystopia, one we already encounter in the colonial discourse around 1900. But at the same time, a conception of "race" projects itself into the Weimar Republic's various racial theories that explicitly approaches "race" as an idea, a project located under an aesthetic sign (see also Hebekus 2009: 395). Importantly, however, while "mixing" served primitivism as an aesthetic ideal, in Nazi anti-Semitism it was defined as an essential characteristic of the Jew, hence as impure and thus per se without shape or form. Consequently, on a substantive level we find no connection between the literary primitivism in circulation around 1910 and the racial theory of the interwar period. Rather, the connection lies in the idea, held in common despite all contrary political and racial-ideological positions, that the concept of "race" is a specific accomplishment of the faculty of the imagination, and thus in the end of a bioaesthetic mythology.

Eva Blome is assistant professor of gender studies at the Ernst-Moritz-Arndt-University of Greifswald. Her research interests include: literature from the eighteenth to the twenty-first century, "Bildung" and social inequality around 1800, body and gender politics, postcolonial theory, and intersectionality. In 2011 she published the monograph *Reinheit und Vermischung. Literarisch-kulturelle Entwürfe von "Rasse" und*

Sexualität (1900–1930). More recently, she coedited the special issue *Bildung, verweigert. Zum Verhältnis von Bildung, Institution und Romanform von "Anton Reiser" bis zu "Der Hals der Giraffe"* (IASL Bd. 41 (2016), Heft 2).

Notes

1. In particular the transfer of Gregor Mendel's doctrine of heredity, recorded in his *Treatise on Plant Hybrids* (Versuch über Pflanzenhybride) (1866), from botany to anthropology and the study of races in the early twentieth century introduced the concepts of the "hybrid" and the "bastard" into the debates over racial mixing. Eugenic theories and biopolitical ambitions invoked Mendel's laws, in order to propagate the practice of guaranteeing "racial purity" in the sense of a qualitative improvement of "genetic material," for instance Eugen Fischer in his study from 1909, *The Rehoboth Bastards and the Problem of Human Bastardization* (1913). With this work, which made him into an internationally recognized expert on "racial mixing," Fischer pushed for the study of "racial cross-breeding" as the basis for a eugenic praxis (see El-Tayeb 2001: 83–92).
2. Alongside the already mentioned studies by El-Tayeb (2001) and Grosse (2000), the work of Anette Dietrich (2007), Christian Geulen (2004), Christine Hanke (2007), Birthe Kundrus (2003), Ann Laura Stoler (2002), Katharina Walgenbach (2005), and Lora Wildenthal (2001) should be noted in this context, together with an anthology edited by Frank Becker (2004) and an earlier, foundational essay by Franz-Josef Schulte-Althoff (1985). It is striking that a large portion of work on the present theme appearing in the context of German studies has emerged from the United States and Great Britain. A basis was established by Susanne Zantop with her relatively early examination of literary and cultural colonial fantasies in the precolonial period (1997). Since then some work within literary studies has considered the significance of sexuality in German colonial discourse, for example the anthology *The Imperialist Imagination: German Colonialism and its Legacy* (Friedrichsmeyer, Lennox, and Zantop 1998) and books by Russell A. Berman (1998), Christl Grießhaber-Weninger (2000), Rosa B. Schneider (2003), and Herbert Uerlings (2006). In any event, the main emphasis of this work on colonial and postcolonial German-language literature has consistently been the categories of race and gender and not literary paradigms of race and sexuality. To my knowledge, there has been remarkably scant reception in Germany of a study by the American scholar Werner Sollors treating the theme of miscegenation from a comparative perspective, with a discussion of some relevant German-language authors such as Theodor Storm and Hans Grimm (Sollors 1999).
3. In Samoa, in contrast, "mixed marriages" were not prohibited until 1912.
4. Later texts still do the same, as in, for instance, the preface to Franz Schmidt-Olden's novel *Black Country—White Woman (Schwarzes Land—weiße Frau)* from 1937.

5. For the special significance of murder and suicide in German colonial literature and its configuration of the theme of "racial mixing," see Warmbold (1982: 248).
6. "Unter V. versteht man in Deutsch-Südwestafrika das Herabsinken eines Europäers auf die Kulturstufe des Eingeborenen, eine Erscheinung, für die man in anderen Schutzgebieten Vernegern oder Verkanakern gebraucht. Einsames Leben im Felde, in stetem Verkehr mit Farbigen, ganz besonders aber die Mischehe mit jenen begünstigen diese bedauerliche Entartung weißer Ansiedler. Der verkafferte Europäer ist trotz bisweilen vorhandener persönlicher Intelligenz stets ein verlorenes Glied der weißen Bevölkerung, da ihm selbst in diesem besten Falle eine der wesentlichsten Förderungen der heimischen Kultur, das energische Wollen und das Festhalten an einem bestimmten Plane, völlig abgehen. ... Nur durch gesetzgeberische (Verbot der Mischehe) und gesellschaftliche Maßnahmen läßt sich diesem Übel auf die Dauer steuern [sic] Das sicherste Mittel gegen diese keineswegs zu unterschätzende Gefahr besteht in der Erleichterung der Eheschließung mit weißen Frauen."
7. See Hans Grimm's book *Volk ohne Raum* from 1928.
8. "Was soll ich tun? Dies ist nicht mein Volk hier herum!"
9. "Des Nachts aber war sie [Ellen] Königin, und ihre Macht war längst so groß, daß der Mann, wie viele Mäner, die meinen, den Frauen gegenüber die Fäden in der Hand zu halten, längst von ihr beherrscht wurde und sank, sank, sank, um so heißer sie ihn liebte und er sie wieder liebte."
10. In a similar context, Nira Yuval-Davis (1997: 23) refers to women as the "border guards" of a national or colonial collective.
11. "Für uns, die wir hier sind ... bist du nicht irgendein beliebiges, zufälliges, weißes Weibchen, das ihrem Herdeninstinkte und Triebe nachgebe und aus dem Arm des einen in den Arm des anderen wandern darf wie irgendeine Schwarze auch. Für uns bist Du das weiße Weib! Das Weib, das hier eine Mission zu erfüllen hat, das ein Wille, der über unser aller Schicksal schwebt, zwischen uns weiße Heiden hier draußen gesandt hat, um uns an die innere Schönheit und an die Reinheit des weißen Weibes und an die Heiligkeit und Unverletzlichkeit der Ehe glauben zu machen! Um uns der Lust in den Armen dieser schwarzen Weiber zu entreißen, um deiner und unserer Rasse die starken Männer zu erhalten, und ihre Kinder, darum mußt du uns in dem Glauben erhalten, den wir an dich haben! Das ist deine Mission hier draußen, deine höchste und vornehmste Mission, neben vielen anderen, die du hier zu erfüllen hast!"
12. For the concept of literary primitivism, see Blome (2011: 161–163), Gess (2013: 19–22), Schultz (1995), Schüttpelz (2013), and Werkmeister (2010).
13. On Gobineau's racial theory, see Geulen (2004: 217).
14. For Nietzsche (1971: 216), "mixing" is the preliminary step before rich cultural "purity". Hence because of their character of being a "mixed people", the ancient Greeks are a prototype of a pure, consequently strong and beautiful, people.
15. "Prototyp des zukünftigen Menschen."
16. "Wenn Rassen zusammenkommen sollen, wird es eine künstlerische oder

erotische Angelegenheit für den einzelnen. Eroberung ist immer Liebe, die Völkersynthese ist immer Dichtung."
17. "Mischrasse, wie alle Musiker."
18. For a more detailed discussion of the influence between primitivistic painters, writers, and also theorists like Wilhelm Worringer, see Blome (2011: 143–163).
19. See, for example, Carl Sternheim's short story *Ulrike* (1916) and Klabund's long poem *Der Neger* (1917).
20. "O, Brasilien ist ungeheuer und ein Land der Zukunft, wer aber weiß etwas von Brasilien und wer kennt seine Seele als ich, der Dichter? Ich bin dazu geschaffen, sein Kaiser zu werden, ich gründe nicht bloß ein Reich, ich gründe eine neue Rasse, ich erfinde ihr eine eigene moderne Seele nach dem neuesten Schnitte, ich kreiere einen brasilianischen und menschlichen Erztypus, in dem die Talente aller Organismen vereinigt sind."
21. For a critical analysis of Eric Voegelin's *Rasse und Staat*, see Kerner (2009: 84–96).
22. "Etwas ganz Ursprüngliches und aus den tiefsten Gründen des Seelentums Aufsteigendes."
23. "Die Energie der Form ist so stark, dass sie Nachbarvölker ergreift und umprägt."
24. For detailed information about the life and work of Hans F. K. Günther, see Lutzhöft (1971: 28–46). For the relation between Schultze-Naumburg and Günther, see Borrmann (1989: 216).
25. For the meaning of art in Rosenberg's race theory, see the chapter "Art as Racial Product" in Nova (1986: 79–102), and Mathieu (1997: 164–243).
26. "Einen Mythos zu erleben und einen Typus zu schaffen."
27. "Reinerhaltung der Rasse."

References

Anderson, B. 1991. *Imagined Communities: Reflections on the Origin and Spread of Nationalism*. London and New York.
Axster, F. 2007. "Vom *Sinken*. Figurationen von Handlungsmacht im kolonialen Diskurs." In *Unmengen. Wie teilt sich Handlungsmacht?* eds. I. Becker, M. Cuntz, and A. Kusser. Cologne, 321–335.
Becker, F., ed. 2004. *Rassenmischehen—Mischlinge—Rassentrennung. Zur Politik der Rasse im deutschen Kolonialreich*. Stuttgart.
Berman, R. A. 1998. *Enlightenment or Empire: Colonial Discourse in German Culture*. Lincoln, NE, and London.
Bhabha, H. 1994. *The Location of Culture*. London and New York.
Blome, E. 2010. "'Schwarze Schmach' und 'Prototyp des zukünftigen Menschen'. Zur Figur des Rassenbastards in der Weimarer Republik." In *Bastard. Figurationen des Hybriden zwischen Ausgrenzung und Entgrenzung*, eds. A. Bartl and S. Catani. Würzburg, 125–144.
———. 2011. *Reinheit und Vermischung. Literarisch-kulturelle Entwürfe von "Rasse" und Sexualität*. Cologne, Weimar, and Vienna.

———. 2013. "Koloniale Reinigungsarbeit." In *Zeitschrift für Kulturwissenschaften* 1/2013, eds. N. Ghanbari and M. Hahn. Bielefeld, 95–107.

Borrmann, N. 1989. *Paul Schultze Naumburg 1869–1949. Maler—Publizist—Architekt. Vom Kulturreformer der Jahrhundertwende zum Kulturpolitiker im Dritten Reich.* Essen.

Brehl, M. 2011. "'Grenzläufer' und 'Mischlinge'. Abgrenzung und Entgrenzung kollektiver Identitäten in der deutschen Kolonialliteratur." In *Maskeraden des (Post)Kolonialismus. Verschattete Repräsentationen "der Anderen" in der deutschsprachigen Literatur und im Film,* eds. O. Gutjahr and S. Hermes. Würzburg, 77–94.

Christaller, H. 1904 (1903). *Alfreds Frauen. Novelle aus den deutschen Kolonien.* 2nd ed. Stuttgart.

Dietrich, A. 2007. *Weiße Weiblichkeiten. Konstruktionen von "Rasse" und Geschlecht im deutschen Kolonialismus.* Bielefeld.

El-Tayeb, F. 2001. *Schwarze Deutsche. "Rasse" und nationale Identität 1890–1933.* Frankfurt am Main.

Fischer, E. 1913. *Die Rehobother Bastards und das Bastardisierungsproblem beim Menschen. Anthropologische und ethnographische Studien am Rehobother Bastardvolk in Deutsch-Südwestafrika.* Jena.

Foucault, M. 1998. *Der Wille zum Wissen. Sexualität und Wahrheit I.* Frankfurt am Main.

———. 2004. *Geschichte der Gouvermentalität I. Die Geburt der Biopolitik. Vorlesung am Collège de France 1978–1979.* Frankfurt am Main.

Friedrichsmeyer, S., S. Lennox, and S. Zantop, eds. 1998. *The Imperialist Imagination: German Colonialism and Its Legacy.* Ann Arbor, MI.

Gess, N. 2013. *Primitives Denken. Wilde, Kinder und Wahnsinnige in der literarischen Moderne (Müller, Musil, Benn, Benjamin).* Munich.

Geulen, C. 2004. *Wahlverwandte. Rassendiskurs und Nationalismus im späten 19. Jahrhundert.* Hamburg.

Gobineau, J.-A. 1940 (1853–1855). *Versuch über die Ungleichheit der Menschenrassen.* 5th ed. Stuttgart.

Grießhaber-Weninger, C. 2000. *Rasse und Geschlecht. Hybride Frauenfiguren in der Literatur um 1900.* Cologne, Weimar, and Vienna.

Grimm, H. 1931 (1928). *Volk ohne Raum.* Munich.

———. 1975 (1913). "Wie Grete aufhörte ein Kind zu sein." In *Südafrikanische Novellen,* ed. H. Grimm. Lippoldsberg, 79–134.

Grosse, P. 2000. *Kolonialismus, Eugenik und bürgerliche Gesellschaft in Deutschland 1850–1918.* Frankfurt am Main and New York.

Günther, H. F. K. 1926. *Rasse und Stil. Gedanken über die Beziehungen von Rasse und Stil im Leben und in der Geistesgeschichte der europäischen Völker, insbesondere des deutschen Volkes.* 2nd ed. Munich.

Ha, K. N. 2010. *Unrein und vermischt. Postkoloniale Grenzgänge durch die Kulturgeschichte der Hybridität und der kolonialen "Rassenbastarde."* Bielefeld.

Hanke, C. 2007. *Zwischen Auflösung und Fixierung. Zur Konstitution von "Rasse" und "Geschlecht" in der physiologischen Anthropologie um 1900.* Bielefeld.

Hebekus, U. 2009. *Ästhetische Ermächtigung. Zum politischen Ort der Literatur im Zeitraum der Klassischen Moderne.* Munich.

Hyam, R. 1990. *Empire and Sexuality: The British Experience.* Manchester.
Kerner, I. 2009. *Differenzen und Macht. Zur Anatomie von Rassismus und Sexismus.* Frankfurt am Main and New York.
Klabund, 2000 (1817). "Der Neger." In *Werke — Band 4. Gedichte. Teil I,* ed. R. G. Bogner. Heidelberg, 461–484.
Küas, R. 1911. *Vom Baum der Erkenntnis. Deutscher Kolonialroman.* Leipzig.
Kundrus, B. 2003. *Moderne Imperialisten. Das Kaiserreich im Spiegel seiner Kolonien.* Cologne, Weimar, and Vienna.
Lacoue-Labarthe, P., and J.-L. Nancy. 1997. "Der Nazi-Mythos." In *Das Vergessen(e). Anamnesen des Undarstellbaren,* eds. E. Weber and G. C. Tholen. Vienna, 158–190.
Lemonon, M. 1982. "Gobineau, père du racisme? La diffusion en Allemagne des idées de Gobineau sur les races." *Recherches Germaniques* 12: 78–108.
Lutzhöft, H.-J. 1971. *Der Nordische Gedanke in Deutschland 1920–1940.* Stuttgart.
Mann, H. 1976 (1906). "Zwischen den Rassen." In *Werksauswahl in 10 Bänden.* Bd. 8. Düsseldorf, 207–630.
Mathieu, T. 1997. *Kunstauffassungen und Kulturpolitik im Nationalsozialismus. Studien zu Adolf Hitler — Joseph Goebbels — Alfred Rosenberg — Baldur von Schirach — Heinrich Himmler — Alber Speer — Wilhelm Frick.* Saarbrücken.
McClintock, A. 1995. *Imperial Leather: Race, Gender and Sexuality in the Colonial Contest.* New York and London.
Müller, R. 1917. *Europäische Wege. Im Kampf um den Typus.* Berlin.
———. 1990 (1915). *Tropen. Der Mythos der Reise. Urkunden eines deutschen Ingenieurs. Herausgegeben von Robert Müller Anno 1915.* Paderborn.
Nietzsche, F. 1971. *Werke. Kritische Gesamtausgabe. Fünfte Abteilung. Erster Band,* eds. G. Colli and M. Montinari. Berlin and New York.
Nova, F. 1986. *Alfred Rosenberg: Nazi Theorist of the Holocaust.* New York.
Planert, U. 2000. "Der dreifache Körper des Volkes. Sexualität, Biopolitik und die Wissenschaft vom Leben." *Geschichte und Gesellschaft* 26, no. 4: 539.
Rosenberg, A. 1938 (1930). *Der Mythus des 20. Jahrhunderts. Eine Wertung der seelisch-geistigen Gestaltenkämpfe unserer Zeit.* Munich.
Sarasin, P. 2003. "Zweierlei Rassismus. Die Selektion des Fremden als Problem in Michel Foucaults Verbindung von Biopolitik und Rassismus." In *Biopolitik und Rassismus,* ed. M. Stingelin. Frankfurt am Main, 55–79.
Schmidt-Olden, F. G. 1937. *Schwarzes Land — weiße Frau.* Oldenburg.
Schnee, H., ed. 1920. *Deutsches Kolonial-Lexikon.* 3. Bd. Leipzig.
Schneider, R. B. 2003. *Um Scholle und Leben. Zur Konstruktion von "Rasse" und Geschlecht in der kolonialen Afrikaliteratur um 1900.* Frankfurt am Main.
Schulte-Althoff, F.-J. 1985. "Rassenmischung im kolonialen System. Zur deutschen Kolonialpolitik im letzten Jahrzehnt vor dem Ersten Weltkrieg." *Historisches Jahrbuch* 105: 52.
Schultz, J. 1995. *Wild, irre und rein. Wörterbuch zum Primitivismus der literarischen Avantgarden in Deutschland und Frankreich zwischen 1900 und 1940.* Gießen.
Schultze-Naumburg, P. 1928. *Kunst und Rasse.* Munich.
Schüttpelz, E. 2013. "Zur Definition des literarischen Primitivismus." In *Literarischer Primitivismus,* ed. N. Gess. Berlin and Boston, MA, 13–27.

Seidel, W. 1947 (1914). *Yali und sein Weib. Drei Erzählungen.* Munich.
Sollors, W. 1999. *Neither black nor white yet both: Thematic Explorations of Interracial Literature.* Cambridge, MA, and London.
Spengler, O. 1922. *Der Untergang des Abendlandes. Umrisse einer Morphologie der Weltgeschichte. Zweiter Band. Welthistorische Perspektiven.* Munich.
Sternheim, C. 1918 (1917). *Ulrike. Eine Erzählung.* Leipzig.
Stoler, A. L. 2002. *Carnal Knowledge and Imperial Power: Race and the Intimate in Colonial Rule.* Berkeley, CA, and London.
Taguieff, P.-A. 2000. *Die Macht des Vorurteils. Der Rassismus und sein Double.* Hamburg.
Uerlings, H. 2006. *"Ich bin von niedriger Rasse". (Post-)Kolonialismus und Geschlechterdifferenz in der deutschen Literatur.* Cologne, Weimar, and Vienna.
Voegelin, E. 1993. *Rasse und Staat.* Tübingen.
Walgenbach, K. 2005. *"Die weiße Frau als Trägerin weißer Kultur". Koloniale Diskurse über Geschlecht, "Rasse" und Klasse im Kaiserreich.* Frankfurt am Main and New York.
Warmbold, J. 1982 *"Ein Stückchen neudeutsche Erd". Deutsche Kolonial-Literatur. Aspekte ihrer Geschichte, Eigenart und Wirkung, dargestellt am Beispiel Afrikas.* Frankfurt am Main.
Wellbery, D. E. 2002. "Kunst—Zeugung—Geburt. Überlegungen zu einer anthropologischen Grundfigur." In *Kunst—Zeugung—Geburt. Theorien und Metaphern ästhetischer Produktion in der Neuzeit,* eds. C. Begemann and D. E. Wellbery. Freiburg im Breisgau, 9–36.
Werkmeister, S. 2010. *Kulturen jenseits der Schrift. Zur Figur des Primitiven in Ethnologie, Kulturtheorie und Literatur um 1900.* Munich.
Wildenthal, L. 2001. *German Women for Empire, 1884–1945.* Durham, NC, and London.
Young, R. 2003. *Colonial Desire, Hybridity in Theory, Culture and Race.* London and New York.
Yuval-Davis, N. 1997. *Gender & Nation.* London.
Zack, N. 1993. *Race and Mixed Race.* Philadelphia, PA.
Zantop, S. M. 1997. *Colonial Fantasies: Conquest, Family and Nation in Precolonial Germany, 1770–1870.* Durham, NC, and London.

BLÜTE UND ZERFALL
"Schematic Narrative Templates" of Decline and Fall in *Völkisch* and National Socialist Racial Ideology

Helen Roche

It has long been a commonplace that the National Socialist interpretation of history was dominated by an ethnic and biological teleology — as opposed to Marxist views, which were grounded in socioeconomic theory (e.g., Blackburn 1985: 51). Although the notion that the destinies of all races, nations, and empires were governed by universal, biologically determined "laws of nature" had first begun to gain ground during the latter half of the nineteenth century and the beginning of the twentieth, when popularized by authors such as Houston Stewart Chamberlain, such ideas truly came into their own during the Third Reich. Whether in relation to the rise and fall of the Roman Empire and the Greek city-states, or the workings of the British Empire and the supposed mission of the Third Reich itself, historical events began to be presented in a way that ultimately attempted to discredit all deviant, non–racially motivated interpretations of world history. In particular, it had to be "proved" that declines and falls were always the product of "racial degeneration," the intermarriage of "superior" races with "inferior" races, and that Nazi Germany would fulfill the promise of the "Thousand-Year Reich" precisely because its inhabitants would not commit the mistakes of their supposedly Aryan or Nordic forebears (such as the Persians, the Spartans, and the ancient Romans).

Indeed, such conceptions are arguably crucial to what we might call "the metaphysics of [National Socialist] history" (ibid.: 20). These ideas were often seen as a refinement of, and great improvement upon, theories of cultural decline put forward by commentators such as Oswald Spengler (Günther 1927: 192ff.),[1] and were eagerly taken up by leading Nazi ideologues such as Hans Günther and Alfred Rosenberg, as well as by Hitler himself. This new *"Geschichtsdogmatik"* or historical dogma (Apel and Bittner 1994: 243) could be combined unproblematically with other key aspects of Nazi historico-racial thought, such as the emphasis on the Darwinian struggle for existence, superior races' need for *Lebensraum*, and the drive for national and racial self-preservation in face of the supposed "threat" posed by what was called the Jewish race (Blackburn 1985: 22).

This chapter will give a brief overview of the development of these overarching historical narratives of racial degeneration, beginning with their genesis in Joseph Arthur Comte de Gobineau's *Essai sur l'inégalité des races humaines* (1853–1855), and then tracing their subsequent reception by Houston Stewart Chamberlain and the National Socialist ideologues mentioned above. However, I do not aim solely to consider such racial interpretations of historical "declines and falls" on their own terms. Rather, I shall be seeking to demonstrate that, from initially being the preserve of a minority of racial theorists and pseudo-scholars at the turn of the twentieth century, these ideas ultimately came to influence actual policy making in the Third Reich, especially (though not exclusively) in the sphere of education. Examination of a range of Reich Education Ministry–approved textbooks that were used in secondary schools during this period reveals how widespread these narratives of racial decline had become, and the importance that was accorded them in pedagogical terms—in full conformity with Hitler's own *Weltanschauung*.

I would argue that this inculcation of a particular racial historical framework follows very closely the model of "schematic narrative templates" devised by the sociologist James V. Wertsch. Wertsch's work has shown that a crucial element in the formation of collective identity is provided by forcing historical occurrences to fit into a consistent, immutable narrative framework, which can be used both to justify and to legitimize the actions of the nation or ruling power in question.

Although I will be modifying Wertsch's theory in certain respects, his ideas seem to form a valuable springboard for considering the form and impact of these Nazified and racialized versions of history. Therefore, before moving on to analyze some specific aspects of the phenomenon, I will present a brief exposition of the main points of Wertsch's theory, as initially set out in his monograph *Voices of Collective Remembering* (2002), and later clarified in his article "Collective Memory" (2009).

Wertsch's main area of expertise is Russian history, particularly with reference to its portrayal in Soviet and post-Soviet educational material. His classic example of a "schematic narrative template" at work therefore derives from this context, and is much influenced by Vladimir Propp's work on the schematization of Russian folk tales, as well as Frederick Bartlett's seminal work on "Remembering" (Wertsch 2009:

129). The schematic narrative template in question imposes a basic plot structure on a wide range of specific characters, events, and circumstances, and always comprises the following elements:

1. An "initial situation" in which Russia is peaceful and not interfering with others.
2. The initiation of trouble in which a foreign enemy viciously and wantonly attacks Russia without provocation.
3. Russia almost loses everything in total defeat as it suffers from the enemy's attempts to destroy it as a civilization.
4. Through heroism and exceptionalism, and against all odds, Russia, acting alone, triumphs and succeeds in expelling the foreign enemy. (Ibid.: 130–131)

Wertsch terms this the "expulsion of foreign enemies" narrative template, and argues that it frames Russian understanding of many crucial historical episodes, including the Napoleonic invasion and the Second World War from Operation Barbarossa onward (the so-called Great Patriotic War).

Wertsch also argues that, although such a framework may not at first glance seem intrinsically "Russian"—inasmuch as one could replace "Russia" with "America" in any given instance, and produce a narrative that could be used to explain an event such as Pearl Harbor to a tee—it is particularly prevalent in the Russian narrative tradition and in Russian collective remembering (ibid.). The template is also, he suggests, strikingly different both from those favored in narratives featured in US collective memory—which focus upon the "reluctant hegemon," "mystique of Manifest Destiny," or "quest for freedom" narrative templates—or even from an alternative trope used most often by outsiders considering Russian history; that of "expansive imperialism" (2002: 177). He concludes by remarking: "The expulsion-of-foreign-enemies template clearly plays a central role in Russian collective memory, even in instances when it would not seem relevant, at least to those who are not 'native speakers' of this tradition" (2009: 131).

In his monograph, Wertsch then goes on to analyze a corpus of Soviet and post-Communist textbooks on Russian history—all of which can clearly be seen to conform to this schematic narrative template in one form or another. At the core of his argument, there lies the assumption that state-sponsored histories are intended to provide the foundation for a strong collective identity (2002: 28), and some of his observations in this regard seem particularly relevant to the case in hand:

> Modern states differ from many other collectives in the importance they attach to assumptions about national characteristics, or essences, that bind their members together. Such assumptions are often widely shared and strongly defended by the members of a nation-state. A common language, history, religion, genetic make-up, or some other characteristic has been variously proposed as the essence that binds people together into a natural national community. Claims about these matters are often accompanied by assertions about the purity of the essence, and hence the group, and about how ancient this essence and group are. The temptation for states to inculcate such views [through the state educational system] is very strong, and such practices can be found the world over. (Ibid.: 68–69; cf., e.g., Anderson 1991)

Building upon this foundation, therefore, I would suggest that what we find in analogous racial theories and textbooks in the Third Reich—which persistently portray history in terms of victorious conquering Nordic races taking over weaker ones, then suffering denordification through defilement of their blood—are part of a state-sponsored attempt to *create* a schematic narrative template of this type from scratch, and to impose it upon the population at large. It would be interesting to speculate—though impossible to prove—whether this invented (narrative) tradition might have led eventually to the embedding of a racial schematic narrative template in German collective memory, if this educational experiment had continued over several generations. Certainly, recent psychological research by Henry Roediger, Franklin Zaromb, and Andrew Butler has stressed the importance of school textbooks in shaping collective national identities (2009).

The Development of a Schematic Narrative Template of Decline and Fall: From Gobineau to Hitler

Joseph Arthur Comte de Gobineau (1816–1882) has long been hailed as "a seminal figure in the history of European racism"—or even as the "father of racist ideology" (Biddiss 1970: 3). Although the ideas contained in his four-volume *Essai sur l'inégalité des races humaines* (Essay on the inequality of human races), published between 1853 and 1855, received little attention when the work first appeared, they were to prove extremely influential from the end of the nineteenth century onward—particularly in Germany (cf. Biddiss 1970: 256–258; Snyder 1939: 105, 140ff.).[2] The *Essai* was read and admired by figures such as Nietzsche, Schopenhauer, and particularly Wagner—with whom Gobineau had a close friendship (Grimes and Horwitz 1959: 340). Wagner printed some of Gobineau's pieces in a specially prepared translation in the *Bayreuther Blätter* during the 1880s, as well as publishing various essays on his thought; this relationship later led to Gobineau's work having a profound influence on the dedicated Wagnerite Houston Stewart Chamberlain, and thence—via figures such as Spengler, Günther, and Rosenberg—to Hitler himself (Biddiss 1970: 256–258; Young 1968: 301, 315, 327).

I will examine this chain of personal and intellectual connections in more detail below; however, it is the first few chapters of the first book of Gobineau's *Essai* that are of most immediate concern, since they constitute one of the earliest and most influential attempts systematically to ascribe the decline and fall of civilizations and nations to racial causes.[3] This assumption, moreover, is the basis on which the entirety of the rest of the *Essai* rests; unless this fundamental piece of racial "logic" is accepted unquestioningly, Gobineau's theory becomes simply unintelligible.

In his introductory dedication to George V of Hanover, Gobineau explicitly states that he wants to clarify the causes of the rise and decay of nations in new (racial) terms, not merely "in the light of the purely abstract and hypothetical arguments supplied by a sceptical philosophy" (1915: xiii). He goes on to explain: "I was gradually penetrated by the conviction that the racial question overshadows all other problems of history, that it holds the key to them all, and that the inequality of the races from whose fusion a people is formed is enough to explain the whole course of its destiny" (ibid.: xiv). In the first chapter, entitled "The mortal disease of civilizations and societies proceeds from general causes common to them all," Gobineau then sets out the aims of his investigation more clearly—he is determined to provide an explanation for the decline and fall of civilizations ("this seed, this principle of death")—which at first glance seem much more mysterious than any of their successes, since the latter can easily be attributed to human agency. Although, due to different clashes of events, every empire (such as Assyria or Egypt, Greece or Rome) seems to come to an end in a different way, their varied manners of death still presuppose a universal cause (ibid.: 1–2).

Gobineau subsequently attempts to prove that the fall of societies is not caused per se by fanaticism, luxury, corruption of morals, and irreligion (chapter 2) or by the merit—or otherwise—of their governments (chapter 3). Rather, these potential causes are no "mere unmeaning accidents," but "the consequences of a hidden plague more terrible still" (ibid.: 23). In a word, such societies have become "degenerate."

The *Essai* is therefore intended (at least in part) to prove that civilizations fall because, at the time of their death, they are no longer possessed of a sufficient quotient of their original blood (ibid.: 26). This degeneration occurs because all successful civilizations end up incorporating others within themselves. The greater the number of races that are assimilated, whether by conquest or by other means, the more the blood of the original race will change, until it is swamped by the plurality of other races, which are often more fertile and breed more quickly; additionally, the original race is often disproportionately affected by wars, proscriptions, and so forth, since it necessarily forms the highest social class (ibid.: 31–32). Therefore, the only way for a people to survive forever and to avoid degeneration is to ensure that "it remains eternally composed of the same national elements" (ibid.: 33).

The major difference between these ideas, and those of Gobineau's successors, is that Gobineau's racial worldview was wholly and fundamentally pessimistic (Biddiss 1997: 81–82). He did not believe that the racial decay of civilizations could ever be reversed; as Michael Biddiss has shown, he was strongly influenced by nineteenth-century discourses of decadence and "social pessimism"—in part because of his somewhat anomalous social position as an aristocrat in post-revolutionary France (1970). However, later racial theorists both wanted and needed to believe that *re*generation was also possible, and that the rigorous application of eugenic principles could lead to the resurrection of a purely Nordic race. It was ultimately due to this "dynamism" in subsequent racial theory that the use of such models to facilitate actual eugenic practices could gradually become a reality (cf. Field 1981: 205–206, 220–221).

This strand of thought can be seen very clearly in the work of the "renegade Englishman" Houston Stewart Chamberlain (1855–1927). In addition to his extremely close relationship with the Wagner family,[4] Chamberlain was a keen supporter of the German "Gobinists," led by Professor Ludwig Schemann of Freiburg, translator and proselytizer of Gobineau's works and founder of the "Gobineau-Vereinigung," which was established in 1894 (Biddiss 1970: 256–257; Mosse 1964: 91–92). Whilst fear of miscegenation is also a recurring theme in Chamberlain's two-volume racial treatise *Die Grundlagen des neunzehnten Jahrhunderts* (The Foundations of the Nineteenth Century), published in 1899, Biddiss has noted that Chamberlain was reluctant to acknowledge the extent of his debt to Gobineau, despite the similarity of the *Grundlagen* and the *Essai* in terms of both scope and method: "Where he differed principally from Gobineau was in his evocation of modern Teutonic-German potential, in his explicit polarization between its virtue and Jewish vice, and in the fact that he claimed to provide not merely a racial diagnosis of the ills of civilization but also an actively racist cure"

(Biddiss 1970: 257; Field 1981: 221).[5] In this context, Chamberlain went so far as to deride Gobineau for his "hopelessly pessimistic view of the future of the human race" (1912: 263).

Chamberlain's views on the decline and fall of civilizations come to the fore most clearly during his disquisition on the end of the Roman Empire, and the racial "chaos" that followed. He frequently intersperses his narrative with examples from animal breeding, arguing, for instance, that the human races are as different from one another in form and qualities as the greyhound, the bulldog, the poodle, and the Newfoundland. The only type of racial mixing that can ever be considered desirable, in order to create a "noble race," must take place within an extremely short time, between two "appropriate" races, and then never take place again (ibid.: 283–284). Otherwise, "a loss of the purity of the blood, revealed by the diminution of the characteristic qualities, is involved. We have an instance of this in Italy, where the proudly passionate and brilliant families of strong Teutons, who had kept their blood pure till the fourteenth century, later gradually mingled with absolutely mongrel Italians and Italiots and so entirely disappeared" (ibid.: 290).

Chamberlain's ideas met with instant adulation and acclaim, not only by racial theorists and the adherents of *völkisch* ideology, but even by Kaiser Wilhelm II; more than sixty thousand copies of the *Grundlagen* were sold just in the year of publication, and the work subsequently went through eight editions within the next ten years.[6] However, during the following two decades, his theories were most eagerly taken up by those with a National Socialist bent; in early October 1923, Hitler himself came to pay his respects to the aging Chamberlain, and, as the title indicates, Alfred Rosenberg's *Mythos des 20. Jahrhunderts* (1930) was explicitly conceived as an homage to Chamberlain's *Grundlagen*.[7]

Another key figure in Nazi racial theory, Hans F. K. Günther (1891–1968)—sometimes referred to as the *Rassepapst*, or "race pope," due to the extent of his supposed authority in the field—praised both Chamberlain and Gobineau for their contribution to racial "science." In his *Rassenkunde Europas* (1924), Günther devoted part of his final chapter to an encomium of his two intellectual forebears (including portrait photographs of them both), and hailed Gobineau as the first thinker to see the importance of the mixture of Nordic and other races and its contribution to the "decline of the West" (Günther 1927: 254–256).

In his quest for a general typology with which to prevent further "denordicization" of the German people in the present, Günther cleaves even more comprehensively to the idea of racial "*Blüte und Zerfall*" as the key to European history. Because Nordic peoples are so warlike, and thus so well-equipped to conquer lesser races, they are all too liable to end up fighting each other and destroying themselves, unless they awaken their racial consciousness and take explicit measures to strengthen their Nordic blood afresh—Günther's historical examples of this mutually destructive phenomenon include the Trojan War, the Medes versus the Persians, the Celts versus the Romans, and the Germans versus the Celts (ibid.: 130). He therefore draws the conclusion: "In the life of all peoples under Nordic leadership it has always been imperialism that has brought about decay and death by this same using up of the Nordic part of the people. Always the Nordic class (which at first even carries on the wars alone) spreads itself out over wide regions, thus ever growing thinner and thinner, and in the end dying out" (ibid.; 146–147).

He then proceeds to elaborate upon this theory with reference both to Greek and Roman history: "Always the decay of a culture founded by Nordic tribes has been brought about by theories of 'enlightenment' and 'individualism.' Decadent Athens shows this in her age of enlightenment. ... In Athens, as in Sparta, the decline is clearly marked by the exhaustion of the blood of the Nordic race" (ibid.: 167). As mentioned above, Günther was not the only staunchly National Socialist theorist who fully subscribed to such theories of racial decline. Alfred Rosenberg, Hitler's "chief ideologue," betrayed similar propensities in his turgid and rabidly anti-Christian ideological tract *The Myth of the Twentieth Century*, which was first published in 1930. After *Mein Kampf*, Rosenberg's *Mythos* was one of the Third Reich's biggest bestsellers, though a great many copies—including, rumor had it, the Führer's own—languished largely unread. According to one Anglophone reviewer, the work consisted of "a wild mumbo-jumbo of bad Nietzscheanism and stale ethnology out of Chamberlain, out of Gobineau, out of Spengler" (Snyder 1939: 185, citing Ernest Boyd).[8] Rosenberg's debt to Chamberlain did not only extend to his choice of title, however; he was also wholly committed to his conception of "racial chaos" and the ways in which this might be combatted, stressing it as a "foundational feature of Chamberlain's thought which is ... of decisive importance today" (1930: 42ff.; cf. Piper 2005: 207).

Even those readers who failed to get very far in their perusal of the *Mythos* could not have avoided encountering Rosenberg's theories on the racial decline and fall of civilizations, since these formed a substantial part of his opening chapter, entitled "Race and Race Soul" (*Rasse und Rassenseele*). Within the first three paragraphs, Rosenberg declares: "It is through ... desecration of the blood [i.e., mixing with alien blood] that personality, people, race and culture perish. None who have disregarded the religion of the blood have escaped this nemesis—neither the Indians nor the Persians, neither the Greeks nor the Romans. Nor will Nordic Europe escape if it does not call a halt, turning away from bloodless absolutes and spiritually empty delusions, and begin to hearken trustingly once again to the subtle welling up of the ancient sap of life and values" (1930: 13). He then proceeds, as did Günther, to demonstrate the ways in which this phenomenon could be discerned in Greek and Roman myth and history—concluding these historical observations by proclaiming: "If it does not triumph in the great struggle which is coming, the West and its blood will perish, just as India and Hellas were dissolved forever in chaos" (ibid.: 63).

It is at this point that we shall turn to the figure whom Louis L. Snyder has termed the "apostle of the apostles of Gobineau and Chamberlain"—Adolf Hitler (1889–1945).[9] It has become something of a scholarly commonplace to suggest that Hitler in some way "plagiarized" Gobineau's ideas (although, in all probability, he had never read the *Essai* himself); referring to certain passages from *Mein Kampf*, Michael Biddiss has remarked that "such words could almost be Gobineau's own," whilst E. J. Young complains of an "almost word-for-word repetition of Gobineau's racial theory"; Snyder also claims that *"Mein Kampf* expresses in a more elementary form precisely [Chamberlain's] thesis of Nordic superiority and Semitic decadence" (Biddiss 1970: 259; Young 1968: 301; Snyder 1939: 139).

In his autobiography, composed during his sojourn in Landsberg prison following the Beer Hall Putsch of 1923, and published in 1925–1926, Hitler unleashed his own views on racial degeneration, particularly in the chapters entitled *"Volk und Rasse"* (People and Race) and *"Der Staat"* (The State). Replete with references to breeding in the animal kingdom, Hitler's arguments aimed to substantiate his contention that "historical experience ... shows with terrifying clarity that in every mingling of Aryan blood with that of lower peoples the result was the end of the cultured people" (1969: 260). He believed that racial crossing always resulted in two phenomena—the lowering of the level of the higher race, and its physical and intellectual regression. Therefore, "all great cultures of the past perished only because the originally creative race died out from blood poisoning" (ibid.: 262). Using an argument somewhat similar to Günther's, Hitler claims that the Aryans frequently suffered from their role as culture-creating conquerors, since the moment that they relaxed the most ruthless attitude of mastery over their racially inferior subjects, they were liable to lose the purity of their blood and become "submerged in the racial mixture" (ibid.: 268–269). This would lead inevitably to a loss in mental, physical, and cultural capacity that would leave them no better off than their inferiors:

> For a time [the Aryan] could live on the existing cultural benefits, but then petrifaction set in and he fell a prey to oblivion. Thus cultures and empires collapsed to make place for new formations. Blood mixture and the resultant drop in the racial level is the sole cause of the dying out of old cultures; for men do not perish as a result of lost wars, but by the loss of that force of resistance which is contained only in pure blood. All who are not of good race in this world are chaff. And all occurrences in world history are only the expression of the races' instinct of self-preservation, in the good or bad sense. (Ibid.: 269)

Yet such warnings were by no means of purely academic or historical significance; they needed to be heeded immediately by the contemporary German people, which was no longer based on a unified racial nucleus—Hitler believed that "poisonings of the blood ... have led not only to a decomposition of our blood, but also of our soul" (ibid.: 360). It was therefore the duty of the Reich in the future to safeguard the truly German racial elements at all costs, and to put into place policies that would privilege the racially pure and ensure that only they could perpetuate themselves, without any danger of that miscegenation that would inevitably lead to racial decline. Human rights should be no guide to the state's action; the preservation of the racial foundations of the nation should be the only consideration (ibid.: 360–368). From a similar perspective, every single child in Germany should be branded with "racial sense and racial feeling," so that they would have no doubt whatsoever as to the "necessity and essence" of racial purity (ibid.: 389).

Here, perhaps, we can see the first inklings of those lethal policies that led to the "eradication of unworthy life," forced sterilizations, and the "Aktion T4" euthanasia program.[10] For the twin motors of Hitler's racial philosophy in *Mein Kampf* were fear (of degeneration) and hope (of regeneration); both, in his eyes, required systematic and speedy action in order to prevent the worst-case scenario and facilitate the best. It was therefore no coincidence that the National Socialist Party's 25-point plan, and, later, the Nuremberg Laws, made belief in these dangers part of policy, and "turned ... theory into law," nor that educational materials and school syllabuses became completely saturated in such narratives of racial degeneration (cf. Snyder 1939: 182–183).[11]

Schematic Narrative Templates of Race in Nazi Textbooks

In order to elucidate the ways in which such racial narratives were adapted and incorporated into the historical canon of National Socialist pedagogy as a form of "schematic narrative template," I analyzed two series of textbooks, the first entitled *Volk und Führer: Deutsche Geschichte für Schulen,* and the second *Geschichts[bücher] für die deutsche Jugend*; both were widely used in secondary schools throughout the Third Reich. Although the Nazi educational propagandist Dietrich Klagges was the overall editor of the first series, each book was devised by a different author or group of authors, so that the collection as a whole provides a sort of microcosm or laboratory where we can observe these schematic narrative templates being used in practice; the second series was entirely written by a group of three or four authors. As a control, I used Gilmer W. Blackburn's *Education in the Third Reich: A Study of Race and History in Nazi Textbooks* (1985), and Hans Jürgen Apel and Stefan Bittner's *Humanistische Schulbildung 1890–1945. Anspruch und Wirklichkeit der altertumskundlichen Unterrichtsfächer* (1994), both of which have engaged with a larger corpus of primary sources, to verify whether my hypotheses might be endorsed by more general analyses of the educational material in question.

Of course, there are other patterns that the accounts in these textbooks bring to the fore—such as the predominance of the "evil Jew," or the inevitability of nations or races needing to strike out for themselves to win more living space—yet, arguably, such elements can largely be incorporated into the broader "decline and fall" racial narrative.[12] Indeed, when it comes to explaining the destruction of civilizations, this appears to be the template very often closest to hand. This phenomenon is made particularly apparent by the organization and presentation of the textbooks—not merely in terms of the titles of chapters, or the numerous headings and subheadings within them, but even (at least in the case of Bernhard Kumsteller's series) in the boxes containing relevant buzzwords and slogans placed in the margins of the text. The same could also be said of the use of emphasis; very often, it is precisely those features of any given historical narrative that highlight aspects of the schematic narrative template of decline and fall that are italicized. It is certainly true that certain periods of history lend themselves more readily to this form of schematization—particularly the ancient world, which, with its ready-made set of empires and civilizations, must have seemed most eminently suited to synoptic analysis. Nevertheless, even though the model might seem harder to apply to more modern eras, the authors of the textbooks in question did not shrink even from this, as we shall see.

The second textbook in the *Volk und Führer* series, Paul Vogel's *Die Germanen,* contains a plethora of examples, from which I have selected the account that forms the denouement of the volume to serve as an extended example. The template for a classic "decline and fall" is very much apparent even in the title and subtitle of the section in question, respectively: "*Das Reich Karls zerbricht*" (Charles's Empire Disintegrates) and "*Völkischer Zerfall*" (Racial Ruin). The account that follows is also very strongly imbued with antireligious, and particularly anti-Catholic, sentiment:

> Since the Merovingian era, a disastrous development had already begun in the western Frankish regions of Gaul. Under Frankish, Gothic and Burgundian masters, there lived ... a numerous *Romano-Celtic* population. ... Their strength was soon increased by countless Germanic farmers, who had had to give up their liberty due to the burdens of war and the depression. After they had become slaves, they felt a closer bond with the racially alien [Romano-Celtic] subjects—in that the disenfranchisement and poverty which they shared was identical—than they did with their free, ruling compatriots. As slaves, they were no longer allowed to contract marriages with their kindred freemen, yet they were permitted to marry slaves of an alien blood and alien race. Soon there commenced a *full [sexual] blending between the destitute element of the Frankish people and the Romano-Celtic subjects.* Therefore the Franks, due to their small numbers, almost always abandoned their language. The leading Franks seemed to have been struck blind. [Those few who saw the danger] dared say nothing, since Latin was simultaneously the language of the Church. Soon, however, the decline had progressed so far that Kaiser Karl himself could no longer prevent it. ... Now the few remaining Frankish families confronted a new race, which was neither Roman nor Frankish. ... *Very often, a subject people absorbs a racially alien ruling caste into itself.* The Franks experienced this truth at first hand in the West of their Empire. The German conquerors had become too shortsighted and credulous, they had done too little for the preservation and strengthening of the Frankish people. (Vogel 1941: 138–139)[13]

In this and in the following sections, all those passages that particularly highlight the racial narrative and its adherence to the "schematic narrative template" in question are emphasized in the original text itself, leaving the moral of the story in no doubt. Meanwhile, the second part of the story, subtitled "*Staatlicher Zerfall*" (Political Ruin), is evidently considered both far less important and utterly contingent upon the racial decline that has previously been outlined (ibid.: 140ff.).

Moving on to the next textbook in the series, *Das Erste Deutsche Reich (900–1648)* by Paul Vogel and Waldemar Halfmann, a similar template is used to explain the demise of the Holy Roman Empire. The authors argue that, although Otto the Great managed to remain both an emperor and a "German King," this was impossible for the sovereigns who succeeded him. Concentrating far too much upon conquering and subduing Italy, rather than on consolidating their position in the East, they ended up wasting untold German lives in their quest for a hopeless victory in the South (1941: 61–62; cf. Blackburn 1985: 56): *"Fatal consequences!* The more brilliant and glorious the German emperors' Italian policy, the more alarming the consequences. Thousands and thousands of men of the best German blood were sacrificed, centuries wasted, in which the German emperors could have achieved something great and long-lasting on German soil" (1941: 62). This exhaustion of the power of Nordic blood thus led eventually to the loss of the entire Empire, and most particularly that unity that Otto I had fought so long and hard to defend. Germany was now merely a *"Länderstaat"* to which other nations could dictate at will. "Soon all that was left of the proud greatness of the 'Holy Roman Empire of the German Nation' was a name" (ibid.: 63).

In Book 4, similar considerations are used by Gerhard Staak and Walter Franke to explain Germany's extreme weakness in the wake of the Thirty Years' War: the blood of the Germanic peasantry has been weakened to such a degree that the ultimate success of France and Europe's other *"Randstaaten"* in dictating Germany's fate becomes a foregone conclusion. Even mass emigration (both to the East, and to the United States) is considered in terms of the grave dangers for Germany of the loss of Germanic blood (1943).

However, it is the sixth volume in the series, by Johannes Silomon and Walter Franke, that betrays the widest range of deployments of the relevant schematic narrative template. Beginning with a short section on the Persians (again, tellingly titled "The Persian Global Empire under Darius and its Collapse" [*Das Persische Weltreich unter Dareios und sein Verfall*]) (1941: 47),[14] we discover: "The Nordic trait of clemency towards conquered peoples and races and their suggestibility to alien influences was the Persians' downfall. ... Thus the language and culture of the oriental peoples gained ever stronger influence and led to the degeneration and bastardization of this Nordic race. ... Oriental pomp grew among the Great King's successors, who abetted the racial mixing of the Persians with the conquered peoples. Thus the old warrior spirit disappeared. Aliens continually took up the most important positions as officers in the army and officials at court" (ibid.: 49). The chapter ends with the resounding conclusion: "The history of the Aryans in the Eastern world confirms the truth of the saying: '*All great past cultures perish only because the original creative race died out through poisoning of the blood*'" (ibid.) — and this seems to be precisely what the rest of the work is designed to prove. For instance, just take this selection of chapter titles and subtitles from the section on the Classical world:

Creation and decline of the world of the Greek city-states.

Greece destroys itself in a fratricidal war (440–338) [the Peloponnesian War].

Blossoming and decay of Greek culture.

The political and cultural destruction of the Greek world.

Causes of the collapse [of the Roman Republic]: Corruption of the Nordic race; Degeneration of community spirit. ...

The Flavians (69–66) grasp at oriental despotism.

Ruin in all territories.

Final last-ditch rescue efforts and collapse. (Ibid.: IV–VI)

An example from this penultimate section (*Zerfall auf allen Gebieten*) demonstrates how very well the schematic narrative template functions with a completely different caste of characters, this time from the Later Roman Empire—yet the outcome, once again, seems strangely familiar:

> *Racial corruption*: Hand in hand [with migration from the country and depopulation], *the alienization of Italy* continued unstoppably. Hundreds of thousands of slaves from all countries of the world overwhelmed Italy and became Roman citizens through emancipation, while the Nordic population dwindled away due to wars and civil wars, proscriptions, mass executions and emigration. The last dam was destroyed by the son of an African and a Syrian woman, *Caracalla*, when in 212 AD he granted *Roman citizenship to all free inhabitants of the entire Empire*, even to Jews: in doing so, *racial death* became [the Romans'] implacable fate. (Ibid.: 146)

If we take the analogous textbook in the second series, Bernhard Kumsteller, Ulrich Haacke, and Benno Schneider's *Geschichtsbuch für die deutsche Jugend (Klasse 6)*, we find a very similar series of racial narratives, once again highlighted even on the contents page and elsewhere by a succession of telling titles and subtitles, including "*Zersetzung des alten Römertums*" (Decay of Ancient Romanhood), "*Verfall des Merwingerreichs*" (Decline of the Merovingian Kingdom), and "*Verfall der Rassenpflege*" (Decline of Racial Nurturing—this last in connection with the Carolingians). The authors are also keen to prove that Germanic peoples have always been very well aware of the dangers of racial mixing, and taken active steps to prevent it. This is the reason given for the creation of the Indian caste system, which was impressively upheld for centuries, until the pernicious effects of the native climate led to an ever-sinking birth rate, and the way was made open for women of a lower caste to marry into a higher caste, whilst their children kept their father's status: "It was inevitable that the alien blood of the dark-skinned native population should infiltrate the master caste ever more powerfully—the *denordification of the Indians* had begun" (Kumsteller, Haacke, and Schneider 1940b: 49). The remnants of Nordic blood, "exhausted with the struggle," turned instead toward escapist asceticism (i.e., Buddhism), and when Alexander the Great reached India in 327 BC, he did not even recognize the Indians as a people who had supposedly also once been of Nordic blood (ibid.: 50).

Similarly, the Spartans are praised for their *"Rassenpflege"* (preservation of racial integrity), and for the fact that they devoted all their care to the task of upholding the power of their race (ibid.: 67). Yet Sparta, too, eventually suffered her own downfall due to her inability to sustain her citizen numbers; her political decline was also rooted in a *"Rückgang der Volkskraft"* (decline in racial power).[15]

The fall of Athens is also explained according to the customary template—chapter 5, itself entitled *"Bruderkrieg und Zerfall"* (Fratricidal War and Decline), referring to the Peloponnesian War, contains subsections entitled *"Wirtschaftlicher, politischer, rassischer Verfall"* (Economic, Political, and Racial Decline) and *"Weitere Entartung der Demokratie"* (Further Degeneration of the Democracy; ibid.: 106–107). The explanation for this state of affairs runs as follows:

> The deepest cause for this transformation of outlook and custom was the fact that the people had become another race in terms of blood. The Nordic master-caste, which was responsible for the great deeds and creations of the Greek people, had become extinct. Countless ancient families were wiped out in the civil wars. The peasantry disappeared. Many of the metics and slaves, the majority of whom came from the Orient, rose into the bourgeoisie. ... People promised slaves freedom and citizenship rights if they fought in the army. It was the custom that skilled slaves ran their own business and bought their freedom from their masters. Close-knit groups of money-changers and speculators attained prosperity, and old indigenous families considered it an honour, when one married into them. "Money mixes the blood of the noble and the base," lamented one perspicacious observer. (Ibid.: 107)

Socrates and Plato are then characterized as *"Ungehörte Warner"* (unheard prophets of doom), who saw these dangers, but to whom no one listened. Plato, in particular, is praised for realizing that *"the recovery of the people is a racial question"* (ibid.: 107–109).

Meanwhile, chapter VI.6, entitled *"Der Untergang der antiken Welt"* (The Demise of the Ancient World), could almost have been lifted straight from Chamberlain's *Grundlagen*, with its appeals to the concept of *"Rassechaos"* and its castigation of mixed marriages with the Oriental and Asiatic slave populations during the Roman Empire. The fact that freedmen could marry citizens and quickly (within the space of a few generations) make their way up the political and social hierarchy is seen as the key to comprehensive racial mixing and consequent denordicization; moreover, the destruction of the peasantry, the republican civil wars, and imperial proscriptions are blamed for a dangerously incessant weakening of the Nordic proportion of the Roman population. Finally, immigration from the East and declining birth rates led to the triumph of Orientalism (ibid.: 180ff.). The section concludes:

> The history of the Roman people shows us in a unique fashion how a people can rise from the humblest beginnings to become a world power, and how it then sinks again to utter destruction. It shows us the strengths which enabled its rise; it shows us the powers which led to its decay. The Nordic peoples of Greece and Rome had, in the same manner as the Indians and the Persians, to fight the great fight for physical and cultural self-determination in the midst of a hostile environment. They were beaten in this battle, as were the Indians and the Persians. With insistent warning, their history speaks to us, when we trace the causes behind their inability to assert their nature. (Ibid.: 189)

This interpretation of the ancient history of the Indo-European peoples can also be found in the second book of the series. Following a depiction of the life of prehistoric tribes in Germany, from Cro-Magnon man to the "*Streitaxtleute*," the authors describe the migration of this Nordic people all over southern and eastern Europe and Asia, including their incredible artistic and cultural achievements (such as the Parthenon), the "light" that they brought with them from the Northlands (*ex septentrione lux*). The Indians, Persians, Greeks, Romans, Slavs, Celts, and Baltic peoples all come under this category. Yet, despite the vigorous rigor with which they strove to uphold their ancient Germanic laws and forbid intermarriage with the lesser peoples whom they had conquered, they were ultimately beaten; their culture and way of life gradually came to resemble that of the "*Südvölker*," and their racial power was broken—their temples crumbled and their states decayed: "They had been strong enough to conquer, but in the long run, in relation to the masses whom they ruled, they were far too weak" (Kumsteller, Haacke, and Schneider 1940a: 28–30).[16]

Other books in the series interpret German history itself in similar terms; thus, in Book 3, the crusades are criticized because "German blood was ever and again sacrificed for a cause which had nothing to do with the German people" (Kumsteller, Haacke, and Schneider 1942: 29), and, like the Peloponnesian War, the Thirty Years' War, and the wars with Austria-Hungary, are castigated as "three-hundred years of senseless fratricidal war," which has squandered the German people's plentiful powers and led to Germany becoming the only great power in the world which is still a *"Volk ohne Raum"* (ibid.: 109).[17] Book 8, however, is perhaps the most illuminating of all, since it extends the narrative template even to encompass modern Germany. The chapter in question, entitled *"Innerer Verfall und Erneuerungswille"* (Inner Decline and the Will for Renewal) begins with a section on "the liberal Zeitgeist," which warns of the myriad *"Verfallserscheinungen"* (phenomena of decline) that had become noticeable in Germany in the past half-century. Despite Germany's incredible ability to achieve in decades what other countries had only been able to achieve in centuries (national unity, colonial rights, and an industrial revolution), it cannot rest on its laurels, for it is threatened with racial death—in the form of rural migration to the cities, a dramatically sinking birth rate, and the proliferation of asylums that protect the racially unworthy (Kumsteller, Haacke and Schneider 1941: 90–97).[18]

Here, the antiurban, antimodernist *Blut-und-Boden* elements of National Socialist thought are fused with the racial decline model, to place the blame fairly and squarely on the "asphalt" of the metropolis:

> Now, millions suddenly lived a completely different life from that which had given their ancestors purchase and safety. The roots which they had laid in their homeland and in the community of clan and village ... were cut clean through. In the city, the most various impressions stormed in upon them. The men who found themselves here came from the most varied regions of Germany. The population which came into being was racially and intellectually a variegated mixture, without any distinctive character. That caused the individual to become inwardly insecure. He no longer trusted the voice of his instinctive emotions. ... Irreplaceable values and connections were lost, without which men cannot exist in the long run. (Ibid.: 92)

Germany was thus considered in danger of being taken over by a sort of rootless internationalism that wished to lump the West together as a single entity, after the model of the British and French democracies, with no regard for the specifics of German culture and nationhood (this development is ultimately blamed on the Jews) (ibid.: 96–97).

However, the German people have (apparently) been saved from this hellish fate—a disunity that is both *"unter-"* and *"über-"*national—by the truly nationalist and unifying *Weltanschauung* of National Socialism. In keeping with this message of hope, which characterizes pre-Nazi Germany as having been on the cusp of a process of racial destruction that was only prevented by the "national revolution," the second section of the chapter identifies *"Die Gegenkräfte,"* a series of nineteenth- and twentieth-century figures who are credited with prefiguring or fighting for the Nazi *Weltanschauung,* including Wagner, Lagarde, Treitschke, Nietzsche, and Houston Stewart Chamberlain. Although direct quotations from some of their works—particularly Nietzsche's—are also used to highlight the dangers of racial mixing (as well, of course, as the dangers of international Jewry), it is Chamberlain who is explicitly praised as being "the first man who raised the *racial question* in the battle against liberalism," and the quotations selected are those most specifically relevant to this subject (ibid.: 103–104). The fact that it is first and foremost this aspect of Chamberlain's thought that is singled out for summarization and adulation, rather than his more all-pervasive attitudes toward Christianity and Jewry, both brings us almost full circle, and shows how fundamental Chamberlain's theories of decline and fall (and those of his disciples) had become in National Socialist pedagogy.

In conclusion, then, we might concur with Gilmer Blackburn's observation: "The Nazis considered education an exercise for development of human will. Because all living things struggled to overcome a hostile environment, the school's function was to equip Germans to prevail in this struggle for existence. National Socialists, acutely anxious about the future of their race, decreed an education that would equip and unite youth to prevent the reversal of evolution. The urgent tone and the melancholy obsession with death and sacrifice found in National Socialist history grew out of this apprehension" (1985: 178). Ultimately, as the Third Reich collapsed around him, Hitler himself was consumed with the belief that this racial narrative had to reach its cataclysmic culmination in the extinction of the people whom he had led, first to victory, and then to disaster.

Helen Roche is an affiliated lecturer in history at the University of Cambridge, and a Fellow of Lucy Cavendish College. Her first monograph, *Sparta's German Children: The Ideal of Ancient Sparta in the Royal Prussian Cadet Corps, 1818–1920, and in National Socialist Elite Schools (the Napolas), 1933–1945*, was published in 2013, and her second book, *The Third Reich's Elite Schools: A History of the Napolas*, is forthcoming from Oxford University Press. She has also published extensively on German philhellenism, classical reception, and the history of education in modern Germany.

Notes

1. Indeed, one might suggest that these theories of racial decline were to a large extent parasitic on fears of cultural decline, as delineated by intellec-

tuals such as Paul de Lagarde, Julius Langbehn, and Moeller van den Bruck (cf. Stern 1965; also Mosse 1964).
2. This despite the fact that Gobineau himself would probably have disagreed with many elements of the subsequent German reinterpretations of his theory.
3. On Gobineau's anxiety to distance himself as far as possible from any intellectual forebears, see Beasley (2010: 50).
4. Chamberlain later married Wagner's stepdaughter, Eva von Bülow-Wagner, in 1908.
5. On Chamberlain's relationship with the development of "the Aryan myth," see Poliakov (1974).
6. On Chamberlain's relationship with Kaiser Wilhelm II, see Biddiss (1997: 85); on the popularity of the *Grundlagen*, see Snyder (1939: 140); Stackelberg (1981: 114). It is also worth noting the immense influence that, directly or indirectly, these theories had on *völkisch* and biological thought more generally during this period, both among scholars, amateur researchers, and mere dilettantes (the boundaries between these categories were often extremely fluid, in any case—cf. Wiedemann 2010: 113).
7. On the exchanges between Chamberlain and Hitler, see Biddiss (1997: 87); Mosse (1964: 93); on Rosenberg's relationship with Chamberlain's work, see Nova (1986: 11–17).
8. On the connections between Rosenberg's thought and Gobineau's, see Young (1968: 315).
9. Snyder (1939: 138)—the first set of apostles being Günther and Rosenberg.
10. For more on these developments and their connection with racial theory, see Weingart, Kroll, and Bayertz (1988); Weindling (1989); Weikart (2004); and Hutton (2005).
11. Cf. Piper (2005: 207): "Rosenberg and Hitler adopted this concept [of racial chaos], combined with the conviction that one both could and must fight it, that a teutonic regeneration was possible, and that anyone who stood in its way was a traitor to his people. From this spirit there later arose the *Bestimmungen zur Verhütung erbkranken Nachwuchses* as well as the Nuremberg Laws."
12. It is also worth noting, perhaps, that even in accounts where the question of *Blüte und Zerfall* is not explicitly raised, it often seems to be understood as an implicit—or even "transparent"—background (cf. Wertsch 2002). A good example of this comes from the penultimate textbook in the first series (Huth, Halfmann, and Malthan 1943: 159–160)—despite not being spelled out, the fact that Sweden was utterly unable to triumph in the early eighteenth century can be implicitly understood as due to the fact that the nation spread itself too thin, and then could not stem the endless losses suffered when fighting against the Poles, Danes, Russians, and Austrians.
13. Cf. Blackburn 1985: 79–80, for similar approaches in other textbooks. N.B. All emphasis in the following passages is original unless stated otherwise.
14. For more on such templates in teaching on the ancient world more generally, see Apel and Bittner (1994: 245ff).
15. Ibid.: 109: For an illuminating example of a textbook specific to the Adolf Hitler Schools (elite schools intended to train the future Nazi elite) that

fuses contemporary academic scholarship on Sparta with the decline and fall narrative template discussed here, see Vacano (1943), and the discussion in Roche (2012: particularly pp. 327–328). See also Meid (2012: 276–280).
16. For similar sentiments in yet another series of textbooks, see Schmidthenner and Fliedner (1941: 24).
17. See also Schmidthenner and Fliedner (1939: 139ff).
18. On the prevalence of such ideas more generally, see Hutton (2005: 10ff).

References

Anderson, B. 1991. *Imagined Communities: Reflections on the Origin and Spread of Nationalism.* London.
Apel, H. J., and S. Bittner. 1994. *Humanistische Schulbildung 1890–1945. Anspruch und Wirklichkeit der altertumskundlichen Unterrichtsfächer.* Cologne.
Beasley, E. 2010. *The Victorian Reinvention of Race: New Racisms and the Problem of Grouping in the Human Sciences.* London.
Biddiss, M. 1970. *Father of Racist Ideology: The Social and Political Thought of Count Gobineau.* London.
———. 1997. "History as Destiny: Gobineau, H. S. Chamberlain and Spengler." *Transactions of the Royal Historical Society* 7: 73–100.
Blackburn, G. W. 1985. *Education in the Third Reich: A Study of Race and History in Nazi Textbooks.* New York.
Chamberlain, H. S. 1912. *Foundations of the Nineteenth Century.* Trans. J. Lees. London.
Field, G. G. 1981. *Evangelist of Race: The Germanic Vision of Houston Stewart Chamberlain.* New York.
Franke, W. 1939. *Volk und Führer: Deutsche Geschichte für Schulen. Klasse 5: Nun wieder Volk.* Frankfurt am Main.
Gobineau, A. de. 1915. *The Inequality of Human Races.* Trans. A. Collins. New York.
Grimes, A. P., and R. H. Horwitz. 1959. *Modern Political Ideologies.* New York.
Günther, H. F. K. 1927. *The Racial Elements of European History.* Trans. G. C. Wheeler. London.
Hitler, A. 1969. *Mein Kampf.* Trans. R. Manheim. London.
Huth, E., W. Halfmann, and P. Malthan. 1943. *Volk und Führer: Deutsche Geschichte für Schulen. Ausgabe für Oberschulen und Gymnasien. Klasse 7: Deutsches Ringen um Lebensraum, Freiheit und Einheit.* 2nd ed. Frankfurt am Main.
Hutton, C. M. 2005. *Race and the Third Reich: Linguistics, Racial Anthropology and Genetics in the Dialetic of Volk.* Cambridge.
Kumsteller, B., U. Haacke, and B. Schneider. 1940a. *Geschichtsbuch für die deutsche Jugend. Klasse 2.* 3rd ed. Leipzig.
———. 1940b. *Geschichtsbuch für die deutsche Jugend. Klasse 6.* Leipzig.
———. 1941. *Geschichtsbuch für die deutsche Jugend. Klasse 8.* Leipzig.
———. 1942. *Geschichtsbuch für die deutsche Jugend. Klasse 3.* 3rd ed. Leipzig.
Malthan, P. 1941. *Volk und Führer: Deutsche Geschichte für Schulen. Ausgabe für Oberschulen und Gymnasien. Klasse 8: Der Weg zum Großdeutschen Reich.* Frankfurt am Main.

Massin, B. 1996. "From Virchow to Fischer: Physical Anthropology and 'Modern Race Theories' in Wilhelmine Germany." In *"Volksgeist" as Method and Ethic: Essays in Boasian Ethnography and the German Anthropological Tradition*, ed. G. W. Stocking. Madison, WI.

Meid, C. 2012. *Griechenland-Imaginationen. Reiseberichte im 20. Jahrhundert von Gerhart Hauptmann bis Wolfgang Koeppen*. Berlin.

Mosse, G. 1964. *The Crisis of German Ideology: Intellectual Origins of the Third Reich*. New York.

Nova, F. 1986. *Alfred Rosenberg: Nazi Theorist of the Holocaust*. New York.

Piper, E. 2005. *Alfred Rosenberg: Hitlers Chefideologe*. Munich.

Poliakov, L. 1974. *The Aryan Myth: A History of Racist and Nationalist Ideas in Europe*. Trans. E. Howard. London.

Roche, H. B. E. 2012. "*Spartanische Pimpfe:* The Importance of Sparta in the Educational Ideology of the Adolf Hitler Schools." In *Sparta in Modern Thought: Politics, History and Culture*, eds. S. Hodkinson and I. Macgregor Morris. Swansea.

Roediger, H. L., F. M. Zaromb, and A. C. Butler. 2009. "The Role of Repeated Retrieval in Shaping Collective Memory." In *Memory in Mind and Culture*, eds J. V. Wertsch and P. Boyer. Cambridge.

Rosenberg, A. 1930. *The Myth of the Twentieth Century*. https://archive.org/stream/DerMythusDes20Jahrhunderts/DerMythusDes20.Jahrhunderts#page/n1/mode/2up (retrieved 1 November 2013).

Schmidthenner, P., and F. Fliedner. 1939. *Führer und Völker: Geschichtsbuch für höhere Schulen. Geschichte des deutschen Volkes von der Gründung des Ersten Reiches bis 1648 — Klasse 3*. 2nd ed. Bielefeld.

———. 1941. *Führer und Völker: Geschichtsbuch für höhere Schulen. Geschichte des deutschen Volkes und seiner Vorfahren von den Anfängen bis Kaiser Karl — Klasse 2*. 4th ed. Bielefeld.

Silomon, J., and W. Franke. 1941. *Volk und Führer: Deutsche Geschichte für Schulen. Klasse 6: Von der Vorgeschichte bis zum Ende der Staufenzeit*. 3rd ed. Frankfurt am Main.

Snyder, L. L. 1939. *Race: A History of Modern Ethnic Theories*. New York.

Staak, G., and W. Franke. 1943. *Volk und Führer: Deutsche Geschichte für Schulen. Klasse 4: Preußen gestaltet das Reich*. 4th ed. Frankfurt am Main.

Stackelberg, R. 1981. *Idealism Debased: From Völkisch Ideology to National Socialism*. Kent, OH.

Stern, F. 1965. *The Politics of Cultural Despair: A Study in the Rise of Germanic Ideology*. New York.

Vacano, O. W. von. 1943. *Sparta: Der Lebenskampf einer nordischen Herrenschicht*. 2nd ed. Kempten.

Vogel, P. 1941. *Volk und Führer: Deutsche Geschichte für Schulen. Klasse 2: Die Germanen*. 2nd ed. Frankfurt am Main.

Vogel, P., and W. Halfmann. 1941. *Volk und Führer: Deutsche Geschichte für Schulen. Klasse 3: Das Erste Deutsche Reich (900–1648)*. 2nd ed. Frankfurt am Main.

Weikart, R. 2004. *From Darwin to Hitler: Revolutionary Ethics, Eugenics, and Racism in Germany*. Basingstoke.

Weindling, P. 1989. *Health, Race and German Politics between National Unification and Nazism, 1870–1945*. Cambridge.

Weingart, P., J. Kroll, and K. Bayertz. 1988. *Rasse, Blut und Gene. Geschichte der Eugenik und Rassenhygiene in Deutschland*. Frankfurt am Main.

Wertsch, J. V. 2002. *Voices of Collective Remembering*. Cambridge.

———. 2009. "Collective Memory." In *Memory in Mind and Culture*, eds. J. V. Wertsch and P. Boyer. Cambridge.

Wiedemann, F. 2010. "Von arischen Ursprüngen und rassischer Wiedergeburt: Themen und Figuren völkischer Geschichtskonstruktionen." In *Wege zur Geschichte: Konvergenzen—Divergenzen—Interdisziplinäre Dimensionen*, eds. H. Reza Yousefi et al. Nordhausen.

Young, E. J. 1968. *Gobineau und der Rassismus: Eine Kritik der anthropologischen Geschichtstheorie*. Meisenheim am Glan.

PART II

GERMANY AND INTERNAL OTHERNESS

 4

Ernst Lissauer
Advocating *Deutschtum* Against Cultural Narratives of Race
Arne Offermanns

In a volume addressing such a broad social topic as racial narratives, readers may ask what could be gained by an analysis focusing on a single individual. Yet, while the title of this volume emphasizes—and with good reason—the *persistence* of race from the Wilhelmine Empire to National Socialism, the narrative of "race" underwent different permutations during that period. Its influence on public debate, on politics, and on individual lives varied. The discourse about race itself was diverse and conflicting, and individuals were not only able, but often forced against their will to participate in it, especially, if they were seen as "internal others" by their contemporaries. They were called upon to defend their views and social standing, make decisions between the alternatives discussed, and champion those they wanted to prevail in the public arena. At different times individuals had to come up with a variety of (often tentative) answers to the situation at hand and were required to reflect upon or even change their attitudes and positions. Therefore, a close examination of the ramifications that the changing discourse about race had on an individual's self-perception and public stance may increase our awareness of the possibilities and limits of asserting personal identity and social position under these conditions. It may even help to better understand positions and decisions that, with hindsight and through the lens of later events, may appear inexplicable at first glance.

From this perspective, the case of poet and writer Ernst Lissauer is fascinating. Born to a Reform Jewish family from Berlin in 1882, he never practiced Judaism until his death in Vienna in 1937. Instead, he initially sympathized with Protestant reform movements of the time. Perceived as a "Jew" by most of his German contemporaries, he even participated in *völkisch* endeavors to revitalize *Deutschtum* ("Germanness") in the literary field, advocating a definition of this term that offered an alternative to definitions based on race. In this way, he may have unintentionally or even *against* his intentions contributed to the rise of precisely that body of thought that he later suffered from, when he became one of the early victims of the resurgence of anti-Semitic prejudice over the course of World War I, as will be shown. Later, after the Nazis' rise to power, he was effectively exiled in Vienna, to where he had moved in 1924. Lissauer's contradictory ideology and experiences highlight the complexity of social and political circumstances at the time.

This chapter analyzes Lissauer's conception of Germanness and the development of his position between Germanness and Jewishness over the course of his life. Previous studies have come up with widely differing assessments of Lissauer's beliefs and ethics. While some scholars went so far as to list him among the forerunners of National Socialism (see Haarmann, Huder, and Siebenhaar 1983: 117–127), others endeavored to rehabilitate him by stating that he underwent a "transformation from committed German to developing a Jewish identity" over the years (Albanis 2002: 262; see Brändle 2002). The coexistence of such divergent views calls for a reexamination of Lissauer's self-perception and convictions. In this context, I will also explore to what extent it might be true to say that Lissauer "develop[ed] a Jewish identity" and question whether such an observation should be used as a means to exonerate him from an infamous reputation or criticism for his ideological positions.

Lissauer's "Extreme Assimilationist" Stance in the *Kunstwart* Debate of 1912

Lissauer's first volume of poetry, *Der Acker* (1907), and his fast-growing body of critical writing gained renown, even from conservative circles, before his first prominent participation in a public discussion on issues of race. *Der Kunstwart,* one of the most influential cultural journals of Wilhelmine Germany, published in 1912 Moritz Goldstein's provocative essay *Deutsch-jüdischer Parnaß,* which triggered a heated debate about the role of Jews in German culture. In response to persistent anti-Semitism in Wilhelmine society, Goldstein (1912) promoted a cultural Zionist stance. He suggested that instead of contributing to German culture, the German Jews should separate themselves from it and begin developing an original Jewish culture and literature.

Lissauer was the first respondent to Goldstein's article and was heralded by the *Kunstwart* as "one of our best German-Jewish writers" (*Der Kunstwart* 1912: 6).[1] Lissauer advocated "an extreme assimilationist view" (Albanis 1998: 197). The most cited passage from his essay reads: "Only two things are possible: either to emigrate; or: to become German. But then: [you have] to dig yourself in, to root yourself with all your might, with all your veins, with all your muscles, [you must] educate yourself towards Germanness and make the cause of the Germans your own" (1912: 12). In retrospect, his next sentence proved to be almost prophetic: "And [you have] to persist in your duty: in spite of ridicule and mockery from anti-Semites and Zionists" (ibid.: 12).

Elisabeth Albanis, whose chapter on Lissauer in her book *German-Jewish Cultural Identity from 1900 to the Aftermath of the First World War* is probably the most balanced study about him to date, sums up Lissauer's *Kunstwart* essay as a call "for the total assimilation of all Jews preceded by the dissolution of any historical, cultural or religious links with Judaism" (2002: 94). Though this is an accurate observation, Lissauer's essay is more differentiated than Albanis's phrasing suggests. To start with, Lissauer did not *demand* the dissolution of the bonds that had held the German Jews together as a distinctive national group—a *Volk*—in the past. Instead, he argued that these bonds had already disintegrated. Therefore, in his opinion, the German Jews could not be regarded as a separate nation in its own right anymore: "I dispute the view that the Jews, who still were a nation in the ghetto, still are a nation today: all criteria are lacking. They lack the shared language, shared customs, a shared territory, the shared climate, and shared laws" (1912: 7).

According to Lissauer, the German Jews had been able to preserve a distinctive national culture as long as they had lived in the confined, almost exclusively Jewish area of the ghetto, and had maintained their national religion. After the liberation from the ghetto, the situation had changed dramatically. As a result of the process of emancipation and the dissolution of their religious bond over the course of the nineteenth century, in Lissauer's eyes, they were about to "evaporate their nationhood" (ibid.: 7). Even though they were still "recognizable" (ibid.: 7), their remaining specific features would disappear with temporal distance to the ghetto and its sociological effects: "I do not know what those indelible traits of the Jewish race might be; I only see that the ghetto has instilled characteristics in them, which, in freedom, are slowly (slowly!) disappearing" (ibid.: 9–10).

The concept of nation and nationhood that Lissauer advocated in his article was principally grounded in society, culture, language, and territory, with race being a subordinate factor at best. From this standpoint, Lissauer even criticized Goldstein for resorting to race-based thinking: "Goldstein's opinions are based upon the dogma of the unchangeable nature of the Semitic race; he operates as carelessly with this dogma as the anti-Semitic enemies do" (ibid.: 9).

In parts of his essay, Lissauer drew on the book *Die Nationalitätenfrage und die Sozialdemokratie* (The Question of Nationalities and Social Democracy), first published in 1907 and authored by Jewish Social Democrat Otto Bauer. In this study, Bauer, one of the leading theorists of Austro-Marxism at the time, defined "nation" as follows: "*The nation is the totality of human beings bound together by a community of fate into a community of character*" (2000: 117). Bauer regarded "nations and ethnic groups as historical and social constructs," "polemizing with equal vigor against nationalists and ethnicists who see nations and ethnic groups as essentializied and primordial" (Nimni 2000: XXXV). Lissauer borrowed the term "community of fate," and his assessments were obviously inspired by Bauer's arguments. This also holds true for Bauer's ideas on the development of European Jewry. As shown by the quotes given above, Lissauer shared Bauer's view that the Jews were "without a common territory, a common language or culture" (Wistrich 2012: 275; see Bauer 2000: 291–302) and, as a result, were "ceasing to be a nation" (Bauer 2000: 296). Lissauer's assertion "that the ghetto has instilled characteristics in them [the Jews], which, in freedom, are slowly (slowly!) disappearing" (1912: 9–10) reflects Bauer's ideas, too. Bauer stressed that, as long as they lived in the Ghetto, the Jews, "although they lived in the midst of European peoples, maintained such a loose interactive community with these peoples that they were able to preserve their own cultural community" (2000: 300). Therefore, he acknowledged that the Jews shared "certain habits of thinking and feeling derived from common experience in the past" (Wistrich 2012: 277). But Bauer was also convinced that the processes of modern capitalism "would inexorably consign … the historic Jewish nation to self-*dissolution*" (ibid.: 279) and were "already creating the conditions for the definitive assimilation of the Jews" (ibid.: 280). In his article, Lissauer offered arguments reminiscent of these ideas (1912: 7). The conclusions he drew were in line with Bauer's belief that "total assimilation was possible, desirable, and even a natural, *inevitable* process conditioned by the laws of economic development" (Wistrich 2012: 282).

Thus, Lissauer's historical and sociological assertions were by no means uninformed, but in accordance with established contemporary theory. Therefore, his assimilationist stance cannot be discarded as only a result of his personal bias, reactionary thinking, or Jewish "self-hatred," as has been done in the past (e.g., Wistrich 1982: 64). Interestingly, even Moritz Goldstein (1957: 246) did not raise accusations like that against Lissauer, but, instead, spoke of his "high reputation" and his "intelligent reply." Nevertheless, there is a certain disturbing ambivalence to Lissauer's arguments, especially in connection with his dismissive attitude toward Eastern Jewry and his passionate avowal of Germanness.

In his article, Lissauer distanced himself and all assimilated German Jews from the Eastern Jewry with vigor. He emphasized that the German Jews had "nothing in common with those [Eastern Jews] but the outward label of a denomination unknown to themselves for the most part" (1912: 7). He acknowledged that Eastern Jews continued to adhere to common traditions, shared a common language, lived in more or less separate communities and were still held together by a religious bond. Therefore, he allowed for a Jewish nationality in their case. The German Jews, however, "simply do not speak jargon, [and] have discarded the caftan and the payot" (ibid.: 7).

Such statements led Albanis (2002: 96) to the conclusion that Lissauer "equates Jewish characteristics with 'defects' requiring eradication." It would be too easy, however, to view his statements merely as an expression of Jewish "self-hatred." The link to Bauer's theory may help to make the picture more complete. Bauer feared "that the emergence of Jewish nationalism, by reinforcing traditional Jewish identity, would only exacerbate antisemitism [sic] and make the socialist class struggle more difficult" (Wistrich 2012: 283). For these reasons, he was very critical of Eastern Jewry and the Zionist movement. Similar reasons were applicable to Lissauer, if "the socialist class struggle" is replaced with the quest for social reform and unification of the German nation. Lissauer's stance was at least partly motivated by political considerations and can be understood as a comprehensible reaction to the contemporary social and political situation, especially in the light of "the common over-confidence of so many German Jews in the rootedness of their German identity" (Wistrich 1982: 64).

This leads to the second aspect of Lissauer's essay that may be slightly unpalatable: his passionate avowal of Germanness, which can be seen as a result of his proximity to *völkisch* ideas. Yet, such thinking was by no means uncommon even among Jews at the time, as George L. Mosse (1971) has shown. In the German society in the years before World War I, *völkisch* thinking was "part of a general climate of opinion which was crystallized by the Youth Movement" (ibid.: 80), for which Lissauer held great sympathies. According to Mosse, "the response of many young people to the crisis of modernity" was a "deepened feeling toward the Volk of which they felt themselves a part" (ibid.: 78). This affected German Jews as well. In the social and political climate of the time, even "some of those against whom it [*völkisch* thinking, AO] was potentially directed came to share many of its presuppositions" (ibid.:

114). In this context, the German Jews "were not merely objects of such a world view, but ... many also embraced it as their own, in different ways, whether it was in the form of a *völkisch* German or a *völkisch* Jewish nationalism" (Nicosia 2008: 7). It stands to reason that the majority of those German Jews who, like Lissauer, embraced the former adhered to a concept of nationhood based rather on culture and language than on race.

As a result, the concept of nation advocated by Lissauer in the *Kunstwart* was shaped to provide room for the inclusion of racial minorities, even though on condition of complete assimilation. Taking on a historical and sociological perspective, Lissauer defined nationality "as character stemming from territorial community and common economic and political conditions, *thus excluding any ethnic factors*" (Albanis 2002: 94–95; emphasis added). Even though the votes for anti-Semitic parties decreased in the years before 1912, Lissauer's assessment of German anti-Semitic attitudes may have been too optimistic to succeed in his goals (1912: 10; see Albanis 2002: 96). However, the political dimension of his intentions in writing the essay is obvious. At the core of Lissauer's essay lies a legitimate attempt to defend his interests in the political field against the threat of racial ostracism. To this end, Lissauer advocated an alternative to an idea of Germanness exclusively based on race and blood. At the time, it was possible for him to do so in a widely followed debate in one of the most influential German cultural journals, engaging with the broad German public.

The strategy Lissauer employed was ambivalent and not without its dangers, though. With his attempt to advocate an alternative concept of Germanness within the framework of *völkisch* thought, he ran the risk of unintentionally boosting exactly those ideas he argued against: "For even where Volkish thought was not overtly racial, it tended to separate Germans and Jews and thus worked for the exclusion of Jews from German life" (Mosse 1971: 114). Soon afterward his strategy backfired.

The *Haßgesang gegen England* and its Repercussions

At the time of Lissauer's contribution to the *Kunstwart* debate, he seemed to be fairly successful in realizing his own program. From around 1910 to the beginning of World War I, Lissauer was closely connected to the influential publisher Eugen Diederichs. As Diederich's "crucial literary advisor" (Heidler 1998: 501) he participated in the publisher's attempts to revitalize *Deutschtum* ("Germanness") and to promote Paul de Lagarde's (1913: 1924) ideas of reinforcing German *Volkstum* through the establishment of a national religion. Lissauer's work from 1910 to around 1915 might even be classified as German national religious poetry. In the April 1913 issue of Diederich's journal *Die Tat*, Lissauer was even advertised as a writer who had given a "living form" to Lagarde's thoughts and had thus enabled the German people to embrace them (see Wittner 1913).

Despite Lissauer's above-mentioned contiguity to *völkisch* thought, his ideological proximity to Lagarde, whose fervent anti-Semitism was widely known, may seem surprising at first. Yet, in spite of his anti-Semitic attitudes, Lagarde seems to have held a strong attraction for many German Jews, as his concept of nationhood was not primarily grounded in biology, but in culture and religion and thus at least seemed to allow for successful assimilation (see Valentin 1937: 42). Statements by Lagarde such as "the spirit can overcome even the race" (1924: 223) or "Germanness does not lie in the blood, but rests in the mind" (1913: 153) may explain the attraction his ideas held for many assimilation-oriented German Jews. Even as late as June 1933, Fritz Friedländer put an article in the *C.V.-Zeitung* under an epigraph by Lagarde, sympathized with the justifiable attraction Lagarde's "broadly defined essential determination of Germanness" had had for German Jews, and emphasized its contrast to the "well-defined borderline" drawn by the Nazis, under whose rule "race had become the pivot and criterion of nationhood" (1933: 249).

In the years before World War I, Lissauer was convinced that his affiliation to Germanness lay beyond doubt. After the positive reception of his volume *1813. Ein Zyklus* (1913), a poetic rendering of events connected to the German wars of liberation, he had good reason to feel himself widely accepted as "exclusively German" (1924: 4), with the exception of incorrigible *racial* anti-Semites. But this was not the only quarter that objected to him. The Zionist-minded author Kurt Hiller (1913: 106–107) also voiced scathing criticism and accused Lissauer of promoting anti-Semitic clichés. Later, Lissauer remembered the reactions to this work as follows: "When, quite impartially, I made events of German history the subject of my works, anti-Semitic quarters accused me of impairing Germanness, and Zionist quarters of betraying Jewishness" (1918: 270).

Then, at the beginning of World War I, Lissauer published his *Haßgesang gegen England* (Hymn of Hate against England). In strong rhetoric he drew a picture of a nation unified in hatred against a common enemy. In her detailed analysis of the ensuing debate, Elisabeth Albanis (1998; 2002) describes the work's public reception: "No other German war publication was as well known and as widely distributed as the

'Haßgesang.' ... The poem's impact, both in Germany and abroad, was immense. It was translated into other languages and regional dialects, its first verse was printed on postcards, and parts of it were used as headings of official leaflets. ... In addition, it was sent to all regiments, by order of the Bavarian Crown Prince" (2002: 216).

For a short time, the *Haßgesang*'s enormous public success seemed to ultimately prove Lissauer's affiliation with Germanness. But soon afterward it resulted in a serious backlash. Some extracts from the translation by Barbara Henderson, which was published on 15 October 1914 in the *New York Times*, help to better understand the heated discussions sparked by the poem:

> We love as one, we hate as one,
> We have one foe and one alone:
> He is known to you all, he is known to you all,
> He crouches behind the dark grey flood,
> Full of envy, of rage, of craft, of gall,
> Cut off by waves, that are thicker than blood.
> ...
> Take you the folk of the Earth in pay,
> With bars of gold your ramparts lay,
> Bedeck the ocean with bow on bow,
> Ye reckon well, but not-well enough now,
> ...
> You will we hate with a lasting hate,
> We will never forgo our hate,
> Hate by water and hate by land,
> Hate of the head and hate of the hand,
> Hate of the hammer and hate of the crown,
> Hate of seventy millions, choking down,
> They love as one, they hate as one,
> They have one foe, and one alone—
> England.[2]

These lines might easily prejudice today's reader against Lissauer, too, and their passionate nationalism is certainly difficult to swallow. Yet, Lissauer was by no means the only writer who supported the German war effort. Other works, such as Heinrich Vierordt's *Germany, hate!*, are far more bloodthirsty. But while almost everybody else's chauvinistic lapses were forgiven or glossed over after the war, this was not the case for Lissauer and his *Haßgesang*. The obituary published in *The Times* after Lissauer's death bears this out: "In post-War Republican Germany Lissauer, on account of the then discredited 'Hymn of Hate,' which seemed to Germans of that period to embody all the false doctrines which had led them to defeat, fell into disrepute. He was attacked as a warmonger, and this led to a libel case, in the course of which he said he regretted that his name was inseparably connected with the 'Hymn of Hate'" (11 December 1937). This ongoing association is related to the way in which the debate around the *Haßgesang* soon evolved into a discussion about racial characteristics and Lissauer became the object of intensified hostility from anti-Semitic quarters. It was insinuated that his poem was a calculated attempt to gain personal advantage from the wave of patriotism. The anti-Semitic journal *Hammer* even considered the sentiments expressed by Lissauer "as un-German as possible" (1914, no. 300: 668). Notably, the *Hammer* also mentioned that Lissauer displaced anti-Semitic stereotypes onto the English: "It appears strange, though, that Mr. Lissauer reproaches the English for certain characteristics, which especially appertain to another race, too, e.g. mercantilism and greed" (1914, no. 300: 668). It cannot be said whether this was an intentional move on Lissauer's side to bolster up the kaiser's internal truce and at the same time relieve the German Jews from racist attributions. However, the kaiser's declaration that he knew no parties anymore, but only Germans, had raised hopes in Lissauer and others that the war would finally bring about full equality for German Jews. That the "idea of the unity of Germany has nowhere been expressed more provocatively and effectively" (Albanis 2002: 232) than in Lissauer's poem can be understood as an expression of this hope.

Lissauer's description of the waters that separate England and Germany as being "thicker than blood" reminds of his view expressed in the *Kunstwart* that race was of less importance than spatial and, hence, social and cultural affiliation. It might even be said that, with this phrase, Lissauer advocated an alternative conception of *völkisch* thought: for him, it is not *blood and soil,* but *soil, not blood.* Yet, while more open definitions of Germanness and "race" had been possible during the early days of the *völkisch* movement, as has been shown with regard to Lagarde, for example, a biological definition of race became increasingly the ultimate criterion for an individual's affiliation to the German or Jewish people (see Puschner 2001: 51–76).

Against this background, it is no surprise that a poem written by a Jew that expressed a concept of the nation in which "race" was of subordinate importance would enrage anti-Semites. Their reaction was hostile. They saw the *Haßgesang* as proof of a Jewish predisposition for hatred and revenge (see Albanis 1998: 207–209). Albanis describes the further development: "Lissauer's poem unleashed a discussion of the compatibility of Jewish and Christian beliefs with hatred, in which neither side wanted to be seen as the disturber of the peace. The discussion was conducted on theological, as well as on ethical and, plainly, racial grounds, but it was questions of race which prompted the strongest defence on the Jewish part" (2002: 242). In their defense against anti-Semitic prejudices, Jewish writers were anxious "to prove that Lissauer was not a 'proper' Jew and that his writings were not influenced by his Jewish heritage" (Albanis 1998: 210). Even factions of the German Jewry championing assimilation distanced themselves from Lissauer "in order to dissociate themselves from the idea of fostering hatred and revenge" (ibid.: 207). One example is Binjamin W. Segel's article in the Jewish journal *Ost und West*: "His [Lissauer's] approach to life and his sentiments are as distant from Jewishness as ever possible" (1915: 16). As a result of the discussion sparked by the *Haßgesang*, Lissauer "became something of a pariah for the Jews" (Albanis 2002: 242).

In view of these facts, Albanis's assertion that the "effect of the poor reception of the 'Haßgesang' was Lissauer's increased affiliation with Judaism" (ibid.: 234) needs to be reexamined. It is certainly correct that Lissauer's identity came under fire from his contemporaries, but not from anti-Semites alone. *All* sides strongly scorned the sentiments expressed in the *Haßgesang*, finding them improper for either a German or a Jew. Moreover, Anti-Semites and Zionists alike, though for wholly different reasons, mocked Lissauer's claim to Germanness. As a result, Lissauer repeatedly had to defend his position between Germanness and Jewishness in public.

The first time Lissauer explained his views on his position between Germanness and Jewishness after his experiences with the reactions to his *Haßgesang* was an autobiographical sketch published in the journal *Die Literatur* in November 1918. Anti-Semitism in Germany had increased over the course of World War I and continued to do so after the German defeat and the treaty of Versailles. In this changed social climate, it was impossible for Jews to merge as seamlessly into German society as Lissauer had hoped for at the time of the *Kunstwart* debate. Nevertheless, he continued to advocate his claim to Germanness, while making concessions to his Jewish background: "I have always felt myself to be principally German, without suppressing my Jewishness. In spite of the fact that my religious tendencies, which gradually grew clearer within me, ... lead me far away from Judaism and Christianity, I have not left Judaism" (1918: 269).

Later in the article, Lissauer even stated that he had begun to realize "how strong Jewish elements from far away are at work inside myself" (ibid.: 270). The change in comparison to his statements in the *Kunstwart* is significant: from 1918 on, whenever Lissauer defended his claim to Germanness in public, he also acknowledged and referred positively to his "Jewishness," a category whose general relevance he had doubted in 1912. Yet, here and elsewhere it remained unclear what exactly he meant by his "Jewishness" or what these "Jewish elements" might be; the more so as he stressed their origin from far away and emphasized his increasing alienation from Judaism. Obviously, these terms continued to have only very little personal meaning to him.

"Borderline Germans in Spirit"

Under the changed circumstances in the Weimar Republic, Lissauer was forced to find new ways of advocating his claim to Germanness. In 1924, he elaborated on his position between Germanness and Jewishness in his book *Zum eigenen Leben* (On My Own Life). Therein, he emphasized that his "life so far has almost exclusively served German literature and German history" (1924: 6). That "once again, the Jews are supposed to have poisoned the wells" had left him with a sense of "deep humiliation" (ibid.: 6), and awakened a sense of solidarity in him: "Today, especially, it would be treason to abandon Judaism" (ibid.: 4). Yet, this was a political decision at the core that did not lead to a change in Lissauer's cultural or religious attachments. For in the same context he stressed that the only reason he had not converted to Protestantism was "that such a conversion was rewarded with advantages" (ibid.: 4). Furthermore, his deep affiliation with Germanness remained unchanged: "All the more strongly I feel the obligation to persist and, to the extent of [my] power, to give, on my part, an example of a Jew serving the German cause with utter commitment" (ibid.: 6).

In the changing social and political climate around the mid-twenties, Lissauer drew closer to the association that represented German Jewry politically, the *Centralverein*. This is no surprise, because Lissauer was "acutely political where contemporary anti-Semitism was concerned" (Albanis 2002: 271), and the *Centralverein* was a natural, if not the only, political ally left for him, since the liberal parties were continually losing their influence over the years of the Weimar Republic. In a special issue of the *C.V.-Zeitung* about the contribution of German Jews to German culture published in August 1927, he made a significant statement, titled *Persönliches Bekenntnis* (Personal Avowal), stressing its political nature: "I speak of these matters not as an artist, but for the purpose of political clarification and in political self-defense" (1927: 466). In his essay, he described several attacks from both anti-Semites and Zionists, triggered by his assimilationist stance, and, again, defended himself against any attempt to deny his affiliation with Germanness. He then coined a new metaphor, "borderline Germans," for the position of the

German Jews within German society: "Yes, we are borderline Germans, but the border on which we are settled is located in the spirit and invisible, yet nevertheless real and existing" (ibid.: 468). He explained his metaphor further: "We observe that those parts of a nation that live at its borders avow themselves with special fervor to their nation and their language ... and at all times they expressed the sentiments of broad parts of the nation" (ibid.: 467f.). These remarks contain several points geared toward advocating the German Jews' claim to Germanness. Firstly, the main idea behind his choice of the term "borderline Germans" was that it placed the German Jews *within* the borders of the German nation. Secondly, what first seems to be a concession to the "otherness" of the German Jews, Lissauer's placing them at the borderline, was effectively turned into a positive trait, since it rendered them *passionate* Germans. Thirdly, they were attributed the ability to express the feelings of the majority of the nation even better than others, thus helping the nation to understand itself and unite behind a common idea. To emphasize his thought, he listed, among others, Theodor Storm from Holstein and even the Silesian writer Gustav Freytag as prominent examples for fellow "borderline Germans" (ibid.: 468).

In November 1932, Lissauer published an article in the *C.V.-Zeitung* entitled *"Grenzdeutsche" des Geistes?* (Borderline Germans in Spirit). By then, the Nazis had come very close to seizing power. Though Hitler had lost the presidential election of 1932 to Hindenburg, the Nazis had become the strongest party in the *Reichstag* and the Prussian parliament in the same year, winning considerably more than a third of the votes. With the next election to the *Reichstag* close at hand, the anti-Semitic threat had grown even more. In Lissauer's article, his usage of the term "borderline Germans" reflects the changed social realities: "Borderline Germans. This explains that they differ in some respects from the other Germans and that they experience and defend their Germanness with exceptional fervor, like other borderline Germans, simply because it is disputed and contested" (1932: 455).

Lissauer's concession that German Jews differed "in some respects from the other Germans" can be interpreted as a reaction to the strength that anti-Semitism had gathered by then. In this climate, compromises had to be made even when defending the German Jews' claim to Germanness. But Lissauer again turned his admission of the German Jews' "otherness" into something of a feint. For he used it not only to make his main point, which was that they were experiencing and defending "their Germanness with exceptional fervor," but also to establish a connection between their disputed national affiliation and their status of "borderline Germans." Thus, he implied that as soon as "race" ceased to be the defining criterion of nationhood and their affiliation was undisputed, the German Jews would naturally turn into "heartland Germans." In this way, Lissauer continued to advocate the assimilated Jews' claim to Germanness, with a new metaphor, yet essentially from the same stance as in 1912.

Twenty years after the essay in the *Kunstwart*, Lissauer's article in the *C.V.-Zeitung* was also written as a contribution to a debate about the place of Jews in German culture, triggered this time by an anti-Semitic essay by the literary historian Josef Nadler. Once more, Lissauer promoted language, culture, and soil/territory as more important than race. He even went further in his arguments than in the *Kunstwart*. While in the latter he described German Jews as being in an "intermediate state" (1912: 7) that required self-education to Germanness, the notion of their status as "borderline Germans in spirit" reshaped the assimilated German Jews into champions of Germanness, as important as those Germans that defended the German nation and its values at its external borders.

Yet, even though Lissauer's main arguments were still more or less the same as in his *Kunstwart* essay, both articles differ greatly in another respect. While Lissauer had been able to address the broad German public in the context of the *Kunstwart* debate, he now only preached to the converted, with little hope of convincing anyone else. And while he had promoted his convictions with enormous self-assurance and considerable optimism in the *Kunstwart*, he now argued defensively in a tone of bitterness and pessimism. For as he had predicted in the *Kunstwart* debate, he had come under fire from both anti-Semites and Zionists while fighting a war on two fronts against attributions aimed at imposing a Jewish identity on him. Drawing on his experience, he exposed the hypocrisy of Nadler's anti-Semitic arguments: "Professor Nadler requests us to choose 'between two wishes.' But, in reality, there is no choice. If one chooses Germanness, one is reproached for mimicry and concealment of one's Jewishness, as by Professor Nadler; if one does not conceal one's Jewishness, one is unable to choose 'between two wishes.' It is like walking through a hail of bullets" (1932: 455).

After the Nazis' rise to power, the situation grew even worse for Lissauer. Living in Vienna since 1924, he was not exposed to the same degree of persecution and suffering as Jews in Nazi Germany, but was effectively exiled. He also lost all possibilities of publishing in Germany, except for Jewish journals. Ostracized as the author of the infamous *Haßgesang*, Lissauer was even refused access to the publishing houses, journals and newspapers of the German exile. His anti-Semitic enemies gloated. In December 1933, for example, the journal *Deutsches*

Volkstum published an article permeated with anti-Semitic slurs about Lissauer. Its author, Fritz Diettrich (1933), not only fell back upon the established anti-Semitic reading of the *Haßgesang* as proof of a Jewish predisposition for hatred. Diettrich also disparaged Lissauer's whole literary work as Jewish "subversion wrapped up in a German coat" (ibid.: 1008). A further essay by Diettrich (1934) that argued on the same line appeared in the *Berliner Börsen-Zeitung*. The Zionist newspaper *Jüdische Rundschau* commented on both articles (5 December 1933: 5; 24 July 1934: 5). Even then, it treated Lissauer like a treacherous enemy to whom the Zionists refused to lend support, aid, or even encouragement. Instead, both articles were used as an opportunity to distance themselves from Lissauer again, to discredit his assimilationist stance with marked self-satisfaction, and to advise other assimilation-oriented Jews to draw their lesson from Lissauer's experiences.

Yet, even under enormous pressure, Lissauer was not prepared to give up his claim to a true German identity: "My attitude toward Germanness has never been in any doubt, and it would be ridiculous to doubt it, too" (1933: 237). Still, his position between Germanness and Jewishness had certainly become more complex over the years, as an article in the Viennese Jewish journal *Die Wahrheit* illustrates: "We believe the term 'assimilation' to be imprecise; because non-Zionists fall into four groups, at least: Those who have assimilated completely into the surrounding nation and got baptized; those who have been baptized but have remained conscious of their connection with Judaism; those who never abandoned Judaism, but completely assimilated into the surrounding nation; those who have a sense of belonging to the surrounding nation and yet affirm the Jewish elements of their character" (1935: 2).

In this article, Lissauer once more made clear where his affiliations lay and listed himself among those "who have a sense of belonging to the surrounding nation." He remained a firm advocate of assimilation into a culturally defined *Deutschtum* until his death. Yet, at this stage in time, Lissauer had already acknowledged that at least for the moment he was fighting a losing battle. Acting as a "representative of all German Jews, who suddenly did not belong to a *Volk* anymore" (Heuer 1985: 691), he expressed the inner sufferings and the crisis of identity originating from their situation in his last volume of poetry, *Zeitenwende* (Turn of an Era) (Lissauer 1936a). One of his poems, *O Volk, mein Volk!* (O People, my People!) speaks of the contradictory position of an individual not allowed to define his own cultural identity and national affiliation.

O people, my people! To which people do I belong?
Like a pannier filled with the rocks of history
I carry two peoples' burden.
To the Germans a Jew in German disguise
To the Jews German, traitorous to Israel
Do you hear the rattle, giving an alert from afar?
Leprous due to two people's fault!
The Millenium's gale hollowly blowing around me
I cower far up the wild pass of time
Scratching the grey scab of world history
on me, infirm due to the hatred between peoples. (Lissauer 1936a: 23)[3]

Confronted with conflicting narratives of race, the only place left for Lissauer was at the top of the pass that separated the spheres of Germanness and Jewishness. He was now forced to languish in the no man's land directly *on* the borderline. Both ways down were barred to him—the road to Germanness by racial exclusion, that to Jewishness not only by the rejection he experienced from Zionist quarters, but even more so by his own self-concept.

Conclusion

From statements like those in his article in *Die Wahrheit,* in which Lissauer (1935: 2) listed himself among those who "affirm the Jewish elements of their character," some scholars have argued for a "shift [toward Jewishness] that took place in Lissauer's identity" (Albanis 2002: 217; see Brändle 2002). Albanis (2002: 270) even speaks of Lissauer's "conversion" to Jewishness, stating that "he emphatically turned to Judaism" (ibid.: 271). The author seems to be conflicted only concerning the question of whether this "meant an admission to a long-hidden and deep-felt affiliation or was newly adopted" (ibid.: 270). That Rainer Brändle (2002: 16) even embarked on a search for those "Jewish elements" in Lissauer's poems and plays raises not only the question of Lissauer's personal identity but also of how to define "Jewishness" or "Jewish substance" (Lissauer 1936b: 254) in an author's work.

It is of paramount importance to note Lissauer's own position on these matters. He questioned the existence of a specific "Jewish spirit" (1932: 454) in his article on Nadler, and argued that even Nadler himself had difficulties with defining what he meant by this concept. As late as September 1936, Lissauer voiced doubts about whether it was generally possible to infer a writer's "race" from his works or subject matter. Using Friedrich Hebbel's play *Judith* as an example, he declared that it expressed the *Jewish* nature "in an incomparably strong way" (1936b: 254). Yet, no one would ever have questioned Hebbel's Germanness because of his successful artistic composition of "Jewish" subject matter. Therefore, the choice of topics from Jewish history alone was, quite obviously, no evidence for an author's affiliation with Jewishness or a sign of his Jewish identity. Yet, despite Lissauer's stated positions on these matters, Brändle (2002: 166–191, 219–237) interprets the fact that Lissauer (1928; 1931) wrote plays about Moses and Jeptha in this way exactly, thereby imposing more of a Jewish identity on Lissauer than his published statements allow. To me, that is much more of a problem than my perception that Brändle's readings of the plays are not convincing.

What is more, Lissauer altogether doubts "that something definite might be said about the Jewish spirit at all" (1936b: 254). Although he allowed for the possibility that a "Jewish substance" was at work in Jewish writers, he emphasized that, if so, it was "to a different extent" in different people (ibid.). Concerning his own works, he stated: "As far as I am able to say something about them anyway, the Jewish substance emerges more strongly at times, less at others, then again not at all, and even about these facts opinions have differed and continue to differ most widely" (ibid.: 255).

In her analysis, Albanis (2002: 253–254) recognizes that Lissauer's psalms "do not deal with specifically Jewish themes." In her earlier study, the author is even more precise when she states: "The God in Lissauer's psalms is neither a Jewish nor a Christian God, but rather a German God or a God of cultural inspiration" (ibid.: 220). Against this background, it would not only be wrong to interpret Lissauer's psalms as a sign that he was moving toward Judaism or developing a Jewish identity, as Brändle's (2002: 159–165) readings suggest. Instead, such a view would reproduce the racist disregard of Lissauer's own perception of his identity. The same is true of attempts to exonerate him on the assumption that he might have (re)discovered a Jewish identity for himself. For even if Lissauer "was under no illusion about the fact that he was considered a Jew by others, he would not let this dictate his personal cultural identity" (Albanis 2002: 277). As has become apparent from his own statements, he continued to feel "principally" (1918: 269), if not "exclusively" (1924: 4) German until his death. Even in his religious beliefs he never developed any affiliation with Judaism. There is little reason to attribute a Jewish identity to him, except for his descent. To use this as an argument forbids itself in light of the fact that Lissauer's own concept of nationhood was based on culture and language instead of race and blood.

It is true, however, that Lissauer became part of the *Schicksalsgemeinschaft* ("community of fate") of assimilated German Jews as a result of the rise of anti-Semitism, and that he associated himself with its *political* association, the *Centralverein*, in order to defend himself against racial ostracism and later persecution. Yet, Lissauer never changed his cultural affiliation or gave up his claim to Germanness. "Walking through a hail of bullets" (1932: 455) coming from anti-Semites and Zionists alike, made his thoughts on his position between Germanness and Jewishness and his stance on assimilation certainly more complex. While he had advocated a concept of *Deutschtum* ("Germanness") based on *völkisch* thought but open to the inclusion of racial minorities before World War I, the subsequent rise of anti-Semitism rendered it impossible for him, as a Jew, to take part in *völkisch* endeavors to revitalize Germanness. Lissauer was thus forced into an ever more defensive position and had to reassess his aims and methods. From around the mid-twenties onward he advocated the claim to Germanness not only for himself, but for the whole "community of fate" of assimilated German Jews, which he had become part of. To him, however, this was not a change in affiliation or identity, but nothing more—and nothing less!—than a political necessity at a time, when the narratives of "race" endangered his personal identity and social position.

Arne Offermanns was born in 1972 in Elmshorn, Germany. After vocational training he worked as a wholesaler until 2004. He then studied German and English language and literature at the University of Hamburg. He graduated in 2010 and received the University of Hamburg's Joseph Carlebach Prize.

Notes

1. Unless otherwise indicated, all translations from German are by the author.
2. "Wir lieben vereint, wir hassen vereint, // Wir haben nur einen einzigen Feind: // Den ihr alle wißt, den ihr alle wißt, // Er sitzt geduckt hinter der grauen Flut, // Voll Neid, voll Wut, voll Schläue, voll List, // Durch Wasser getrennt, die sind dicker als Blut. // … // Nimm du die Völker der Erde in Sold, // Baue Wälle aus Barren von Gold, // Bedecke die Meerflut mit Bug bei Bug, // Du rechnetest klug, doch nicht klug genug. // … // Dich werden wir hassen mit langem Haß, // Wir werden nicht lassen von unserm Haß, // Haß zu Wasser und Haß zu Land, // Haß des Hauptes und Haß der Hand, // Haß der Hämmer und Haß der Kronen, // Drosselnder Haß von siebzig Millionen, // Sie lieben vereint, sie hassen vereint, // Sie haben alle nur einen Feind: // England."

3. "O Volk, mein Volk! Welch Volk ist denn nun mein? // Wie eine Kiepe voll Geschichtsgestein // Schleppe ich zweier Völker Last. // Dem Deutschen Jude, deutsch getarnt, // Dem Juden deutsch, treulos an Israel, —// Hört Ihr die Klapper, welche weithin warnt? // Aussätzig von der beiden Völker Fehl! // Dumpf um mich bläst Jahrtausendwind, // Ich kauere hoch am wilden Zeitenpaß // Und kratze mir den grauen Grind // Weltgeschichte, siech vom Völkerhaß."

References

Albanis, E. 1998. "Ostracised for Loyality: Ernst Lissauer's Propaganda Writing and its Reception." *Leo Baeck Institute Year Book* 43: 195–224.

———. 2002. *German-Jewish cultural identity from 1900 to the aftermath of the First World War: A comparative study of Moritz Goldstein, Julius Bab and Ernst Lissauer.* Tübingen.

Bauer, O. 2000. *The Question of Nationalities and Social Democracy.* Trans. J. O'Donnell. Minneapolis, MN.

Brändle, R. 2002. *Am wilden Zeitenpass. Motive und Themen im Werk des deutsch-jüdischen Dichters Ernst Lissauer.* Frankfurt am Main.

Diettrich, F. 1933. "Der ‚deutsche Barde' Ernst Lissauer." *Deutsches Volkstum* 15 (December): 1007–1009.

———. 1934. "Ernst Lissauer, der Literaturagent." *Kritische Gänge (Literaturblatt der Berliner Börsen-Zeitung)*, 22 July.

Friedländer, F. 1933. "Für Deutschtum und Judentum." *C.V.-Zeitung*, 29 June: 249.

Goldstein, M. 1912. "Deutsch-jüdischer Parnass." *Der Kunstwart* 25, no. 11 (March): 281–294.

———. 1957. "German Jewry's Dilemma: The Story of a Provocative Essay." *Leo Baeck Institute Year Book* 2: 236–254.

Haarmann, H., W. Huder, and K. Siebenhaar. 1983. *"Das war ein Vorspiel nur …": Bücherverbrennung Deutschland 1933; Voraussetzungen und Folgen.* Berlin.

Heidler, I. 1998. *Der Verleger Eugen Diederichs und seine Welt (1896–1930).* Wiesbaden.

Heuer, R. 1985. "Lissauer, Ernst." In *Neue Deutsche Biographie. Bd. 14: Laverrenz – Locher-Freuler*, ed. Historische Kommission bei d. Bayerischen Akademie d. Wissenschaften. Berlin, 690–691.

Hiller, K. 1913. *Die Weisheit der Langeweile: eine Zeit- und Streitschrift*, vol. 1. Leipzig.

Der Kunstwart. 1912. "Vorbemerkung." Vol. 25, no. 13 (April): 6.

Lagarde, P. de. 1913. *Deutscher Glaube, deutsches Vaterland, deutsche Bildung. Das Wesentliche aus seinen Schriften ausgewählt und eingeleitet von Friedrich Daab.* Jena.

———. 1924. *Schriften für das deutsche Volk*, vol. II. Munich.

Lissauer, E. 1907. *Der Acker.* Vienna.

———. 1912. "Beitrag im Sprechsaal." *Der Kunstwart* 25, no. 13 (April): 6–12.

———. 1913. *1813. Ein Cyklus.* Jena.

———. 1914. *Worte in die Zeit.* Göttingen.
———. 1918. "Autobiographische Skizze." *Das literarische Echo* 21, no. 4 (November): 270–273.
———. 1924. *Zum eigenen Leben.* Chemnitz.
———. 1927. "Persönliches Bekenntnis." *C.V.-Zeitung,* 5 August: 466–468.
———. 1928. *Das Weib des Jeptha.* Berlin.
———. 1931. *Der Weg des Gewaltigen.* Chemnitz. Gesellschaft der Bücherfreunde zu Chemnitz.
———. 1932. "'Grenzdeutsche' des Geistes?" *C.V.-Zeitung,* 4 November: 453–455.
———. 1933. "Der deutsche Jude und das deutsche Schrifttum." *C.V.-Zeitung,* 22 June: 237–238.
———. 1935. "Das Schicksal des deutschen Judentums in Briefen." *Die Wahrheit,* 22 February: 1–2.
———. 1936a. *Zeitenwende. Gedichte 1932/36.* Vienna.
———. 1936b. "Gegenwart und Zukunft der jüdischen Literatur." *Der Morgen* 12, no. 6 (September): 254–255.
Mosse, G. L. 1971. *Germans and Jews: The Right, the Left and the Search for a "Third Force" in Pre-Nazi Germany.* London.
Nicosia, F. R. 2008. *Zionism and Anti-Semitism in Nazi Germany.* Cambridge.
Nimni, E. J. 2000. "Introduction for the English-Reading Audience." In *The Question of Nationalities and Social Democracy,* ed. O. Bauer; trans. J. O'Donnell. Minneapolis, MN: XV–XLV.
Puschner, U. 2001. *Die völkische Bewegung im wilhelminischen Kaiserreich: Sprache – Rasse – Religion.* Darmstadt.
Schwadron, A. 1916. "Wie aus einem Juden ein Deutscher ward (Nachgewiesen an Ernst Lissauer)." *Der Jude* 1, no. 7 (October): 490–492.
Segel, B. W. 1915. "Erziehung zum Hass." *Ost und West* 15, no. 1–5 (January–May): 13–22.
Sieg, U. 2007. *Deutschlands Prophet: Paul de Lagarde und die Ursprünge des modernen Antisemitismus.* Munich.
Valentin, H. 1937. *Antisemitenspiegel. Der Antisemitismus. Geschichte, Kritik, Soziologie.* Vienna.
Wistrich, R. S. 1982. *Socialism and the Jews: The Dilemmas of Assimilation in Germany and Austria-Hungary.* Rutherford, NJ.
———. 2012. *From Ambivalence to Betrayal: The Left, the Jews, and Israel.* Lincoln, NE.
Wittner, O. 1913. "Ernst Lissauer. Eine Studie." *Die Tat* 5, no. 1 (April): 66–89.

 5

THE JEWISH CEO AND THE LUTHERAN BISHOP
The Impact of German Colonial Studies on Young Jewish and Christian Academics' Cultural Narratives of Race

Lukas Bormann

This chapter deals with the influence of the German empire's colonial policies on the mindset and attitude of aspiring Christian and Jewish intellectuals. The emergence of institutions for colonial research (Ruppenthal 2007), the history of the most important colonial actors, as well as the question of the relationship between colonial politics and National Socialist policies of living space (*Lebensraum*) and extermination have all been well researched (Ebner 2009; Zimmerer 2011). The effect of colonial activities on racial anti-Semitism (Sarè, 2011) and on the views of educated Jewish and Christian Germans (Davis 2012; Perraudin 2011; Seemann 2011) have been occasionally discussed. However, the question of what consequences colonial politics had for the relationship between Judaism and Christianity, and accordingly between Jewish and Christian Germans, has been barely investigated. This chapter will use as examples a successful Jewish business executive and a Lutheran bishop in order to study the intellectual and cultural influence of German colonialism and thus understand how colonial studies' placing of value on different groups of people impacted the development of cultural narratives about Jews in Germany.

When in 1879 Wilhelm Marr (1879b: 4) began his anti-Semitic publications, he insisted that his enmity against Judaism was not religious, but "sociopolitical." Marr (1885: 39) was convinced that Protestants, Catholics, and even foremost agnostics, or "free thinkers" as he called them, should be able to join this movement. In these years of the sociopolitical phase of anti-Semitism, conservative critics of anti-Semitism coined the saying: "anti-Semitism is the socialism of stupid lads" (Anonymous 1910).

In 1910 the Protestant and moderately anti-Semitic weekly *Staatsbürgerzeitung* drew attention to the ongoing change in anti-Semitic discourse. An anonymous author, presumably someone on the editorial board of the paper, penned an opinion piece with the provocative title: "Is anti-Semitism still justified?" (ibid.). The author stated that the former anti-Semitic sociopolitical fight against Jews had lost its importance and instead was increasingly becoming a fight against two European developments: the international orientation of European societies, which he called "internationalization," and the cultural and racial mixture, which he called "bastardization," both of which were cast by the author as supported mainly by Jewish individuals, groups, and organizations.

This opinion piece of the *Staatsbürgerzeitung* looking back on the previous years of the anti-Semitic discourse reflected an ongoing change in anti-Semitic thinking. The mostly sociopolitical anti-Semitic narrative about Jews had its high point during the Berlin anti-Semitism debate between 1879 and 1881 and then shifted into an increasingly cultural anti-Semitic narrative of race around 1900. According to Veronika Lipphardt (2008: 64–66) this cultural narrative of race, organized around the key topic "bastardization," gleaned some of its main arguments from medicine, biology, and anthropology. In these years so-called race research became an established discipline in medicine and biology. Lipphardt (ibid.: 36) describes how in the following years a "bio-historical narrative of race" was developed. The double apex of scientific publication on the topic was reached in 1910–1913 and 1926–1927, when the publications of the two authors to be discussed in this chapter, Friedrich Blach and Hans Meiser, were published. Despite the fact that only a few researchers in biology and medicine were eager to draw cultural or political conclusions from biological or medical observations (ibid.: 19), many results were discussed in cultural, social, and even political debates concerning the impact of race on society. The new disciplines of anthropology and ethnology provided additional arguments for this discourse about race. In Germany these new scholarly approaches were deeply connected to colonial studies, which developed between 1880 and 1911, starting with lectures about colonial topics and established with the founding of the *Handelshochschule* Berlin in 1906 and the Hamburg Colonial Institute in 1908 (van der Heyden 2002; Ruppenthal 2007). One of the leading figures in German anthropology was Eugen Fischer (1874–1967) (Roller 2002: 133). Fischer (1913: V) saw himself as a pioneer in the new scientific discipline of "anthropo-biology." The prestigious Humboldt-foundation of the Royal-Prussian academy of sciences, the predecessor of the *Alexander von Humboldt-Stiftung* and the *Deutsche Forschungsgemeinschaft,* funded Fischer's research on a population in former Southwest Africa, understood as a stable mixed racial population, the so-called Rehoboth Bastards-people (Fischer 1913). The members of this population not only happened to be from mixed origin, Boer and indigenous African, but had built a stable and independent society separated from both indigenous and Boer populations (Fischer 1909: 1048). Fischer not only published the results of his prestigious research in two volumes in 1913, but immediately after finishing his field studies in Africa in 1908 and before publishing his scholarly research, he began to publish popular articles in newspapers about the political implications of his studies, reaching a broad interested readership, especially in the more educated parts of the German society (1909; 1910; 1911). Fischer (1913: V) emphasized his scientific approach, but in fact, as shown by many scholars, his conclusions clearly contradicted the results of his research (Ha 2009: 212f.; Campt 2004: 39–41). Fischer's research indicated that the state of health of the mixed population was very good and no signs of degeneration could be observed. However, instead of drawing the appropriate conclusion—namely, that mixed marriages have no negative impact on the health of the population and should be allowed—Fischer (1913: 303) argued that "every patriot educated in anthropology" should reject mixed marriage. He (ibid.: 300–304) added an appendix entitled "The political significance of the bastards," within which he drew moral, cultural, and political conclusions unrelated to his research but based on his racial and cultural ideology. He thus constructed a new narrative of race, the scholarly record of the morally and socially degenerated mixed racial people (Ha 2009: 212f.). His proposal was that these mixed populations be trained to function as a "useful working class," but should always be separated from the German or European population, "because *every* drop of blood from colored races *harms, incurably harms* our people's body" (Fischer 1909: 1051; emphases in original). His results also had an impact on the discussions about mixed marriage in the Reichstag in 1912 (Missionsausschuss 1912; Grentrup 1914; Hedrich 1941; Becker 2004) and were used to back the later "Rhineland bastards" campaign (Campt 2004: 37–50). Fischer's research and his popular publications supported the general public assumption of race as a fixed and unchangeable entity determined by origin. This entity was seen as vulnerable to losing its purity in the process of reproduction, and hence as something that can be damaged through the generations by the process of mixture through contact with other racial entities. Tina Campt states (2004: 26) that Fischer's research intensified a scientific discourse about "race as a biologically immutable category of human difference" and about "the threat of racial mixture." This idea of race was very useful in casting the European races, particularly the German and the Anglo-Saxon, as immutably superior to African races, when racial mixture was avoided.

However, the idea elicits problems in connected ideological systems, such as in the conviction that Christianity is superior to every other religion, particularly to nature worship, but also to Islam and Judaism. What can the significance of conversion and mission be, for instance, when not belief but an unchangeable and vulnerable entity called race has a conclusive impact on human development? The basic idea of conversion defined by Saint Paul was that it is an act of "new creation," breaking down all barriers between nations, gender, and races, even for such disdained ancient populations as Barbarians and Scythians (Col 3:11). Committed to this Christian theological assumption, the conservative Protestants and the Catholic party *Zentrum* opposed laws forbidding mixed marriage (Grentrup 1914: 46). This debate about mixed marriage was the first instance in which racial ideas openly, and on official and even legal levels, contradicted the Christian ideas of a universal Christianity based on baptism.

A result of this idea of an unchangeable but vulnerable racial entity as the core of the cultural narrative of race, was that the anti-Semitic and related national and colonial debates became increasingly racial, partially in good faith, since the basic ideas were seen as scientific facts, and partially in contradiction to the idea of Christian mission, since the racial narrative challenged the fundamental universalistic principles of the Christian religion. Forced by this scholarly racial narrative, branches of the anti-Semitic movement started to criticize the Christian denominations, because they saw in Christianity a "half-Semitic religion" (Volland 1993: 75). In 1919 Theodor Fritsch (1852–1933), the radical anti-Semitic author of the influential "Handbook on the Jewish Question," stated that there was no real difference between Judaism and Christianity as long as Jews were allowed to convert to Christianity. Fritsch stated (1919: 19): "The baptized Jew secretly remains a member of the Hebrews' great covenant of blood and has the duty to serve Jewish special interests everywhere and at all times."

It is in this atmosphere determined by anthropological, cultural, theological, and legal discourses about race and racial mixture that the two young academics dealt with in this chapter grew up. Both were proud of German colonial expansionism, and learned that mixed populations were a topic of scholarly debate that had an impact on the social and cultural life of society. However, both were committed to a different set of values, namely Jewish self-confidence on the one hand, and Christian universalism on the other, and both felt compelled to contribute to this discourse about the cultural narratives of race on Judaism and Christianity.

Friedrich Samuel Blach (1884–1969) and Hans Meiser (1881–1956)

Friedrich Samuel Blach was born in Stralsund, an old trade city on the Baltic Sea, to a leather trader from an old Prussian Jewish family. Besides trading activities, the life of the city was dominated by the institutions of state administration and the Prussian garrison stationed there. In 1914 the population of the city numbered about 36,000, with a tiny Jewish minority including about 180 official members of the Jewish Synagogue (Schiel 1996: 11; Wilhelmus 1996: 55–66). Stralsund was peopled by civil servants and members of the military staff, both of which were seen as the foundation of the Prussian authoritarian and militaristic state. The workers' movement and the Social Democrats had no significant influence on the cultural and political life of the city. Blach was the first of his family to complete higher education. In 1902 he began his study of law at the Universities of Berlin, Würzburg, and Greifswald. Between 1906 and 1910 he also attended lectures in colonial studies at the newly founded institutions for colonial studies in Hamburg and Berlin. It seems quite probable that Blach considered a career as a state employee in the German colonies or the colonial administration. The latter was a part of the state service in which, writes Christian Davis (2012: 4), "men designated as 'Jewish' by their peers played prominent roles in Germany's colonial project, as administrators, financiers, publicists, and political and extraparliamentary advocates."

The main ambition of colonial studies was to train students to increase the economic value of the colonies and their populations. Karl Rathgen (1856–1921), from the Hamburg Colonial Institute, introduced a key term of German colonial politics: "*Inwertsetzung*" (valorization) (Fischer 1981: 43). This process of valorization was applied to natural resources as well as to the population. In the words of Rathgen (1908: 43): "Precisely the natives' low level of civility compels us in the direction of a fatherly, welfare-oriented gov-

Figure 5.1. Friedrich Samuel Blach, ca. 1929.

ernment." This caring government was grounded on the economic assumption: "In terms of economic value, the negro is the most valuable asset" (Rathgen 1910: 281). Therefore, the "education for labor" was seen as the most important aim of the colonial training of indigenous peoples (Rathgen 1900: 140). These ideas of Rathgen were adopted by State Secretary of the Colonial Office Bernhard Dernburg (1865–1937), who stated: "The natives are the main subject of colonization ... and the manual labor of the natives is the most important asset of the colonies" (Zeller 2008: 105). Therefore a twofold process was to be implemented on the colonized population: disciplining as well as education and training.

The lectures held at the German colonial institutes included ones on general anthropology, as well as racial studies in particular, such as "politics of race," "separation of races," and "mixture of races" (Ruppenthal 2007: 191–193). The institutes employed some indigenous teachers in African and Asian languages, but in their daily life followed a "strict separation of races" between these individuals, their German colleagues, and students (ibid.: 192). In 1909 the topic of the annual exam at the Hamburg Colonial Institute was: "The bastards and the question of mixed marriage in southwest Africa" (ibid.: 219), perhaps inspired by discussion of Fischer's research in South West Africa.

Inspired by the lectures he had heard on the subject of colonial studies, Blach wrote his book *The Jews in Germany* during his last year at university in 1910, in which he employed methods learned in his colonial studies to analyze the situation of Jews in Germany and proposed the methodological training of German Jews to increase their social and economic value within the German society. Despite his ambitious goals, Blach became a lawyer on the isle of Rügen, a position that he later described as "defending chicken thieves and poachers" (Blake 1993: 3). In 1914 he closed his practice and joined the German army as a chief sergeant. His son Peter described his father's most important act of heroism in the war, but not without a touch of irony (ibid.: 3). During the battle of Tannenberg in 1914, to show his heroic spirit, Blach attacked Russian cavalry in an absolutely hopeless situation and came close to death after he was butchered by five bayonets and his skull split by a sword. Severely wounded, he was left for dead, but when the area was reconquered by German troops they found him alive. After a year of hospitalization he was honored with the Iron Cross and made a lieutenant, an event significant to him because very few Jews were accepted as officers in the German army.

After the war he made a significant career change. There is no known information as to why this Jewish lawyer and hero of the Great War was promoted to director of an important public utility company in Berlin, the Charlottenburg Water Company. It is clear that in 1918 he became a very influential manager and member of the executive board of this company, occupying a mansion in Berlin's Grunewald district, and accruing two cars, many domestic servants, and an English governess for his two children. His private family life is chronicled in detail by his brother in law, the German Jewish writer Hans Sahl (1980; 1991: 31–37; 2008: 89–91). Blach's son Peter described his father as a conservative lawyer who was appalled by his son's admission of his ambition to become a writer, since for the elder Blach writers were "people roughly on a level with pimps, communists, and other deadbeats" (Blake 2003: IX). Peter decided to become an architect instead, a decision that his father accepted. In 1933 Blach lost his position as director of the Charlottenburg Water Company in response to political pressure applied by the new National Socialist administration. He left Germany between 1936 and 1938 for New York and began a new, much more modest life as an employee of a New York bank (Hambrock 2003: 706).

Hans Meiser (1881–1956) was born in the city of Nuremberg. His father was a merchant, and it is often noted in scholarship that Meiser learned in this environment to be careful in decision-making, always considering loss and profit (Simon 1960: 404). He attended the Royal Old School, founded by Philipp Melanchthon, a leading figure of the Protestant Reformation, but the attempt by the city of Nuremberg to return to the school's original name (Melanchthon School) was repeatedly rejected by the Catholic state of Bavaria. Meiser learned to be obedient to his Catholic king, but the Protestant church taught him that God demands only obedience to, but not love or sympathy for, the authorities (Bezzel 2008: 125f.). He began studying economics in Munich, and then took theology in Erlangen, Berlin, and Halle.

In Berlin he may have encountered the ideas of Karl Heinrich Plath (1829–1901), a leading missionary and professor of missionary studies. Plath was a strong supporter of German Colonial politics and introduced the psychology of nations and of race into his lectures on missionary studies (Raupp 1994: 721f). He wrote the infamous book "What Shall We Christians Do with Our Jews!?" which proposed solving the so-called Jewish question with methods of the psychology of nations, which included racial theories (1881). Meiser began his career as a minister in 1905, but more importantly became a minister of social work in the Lutheran church in 1909. He was confronted with the life of the poor, orphaned, and homeless. During the Great War he served as an army chaplain until 1915 and then led a social institution for Protestant unmarried female deaconesses in Munich. During the so-called soviet republic in Munich, which lasted from 7 April to 2 May 1919, the red guards took hostages, and in their search for a representative of the conservative Protestant church the revolutionary guards decided to arrest Meiser (Simon 1960: 408). His deaconesses successfully pled for his release, the day after which the remaining ten hostages were executed at the courtyard of the *Luitpoldgymnasium*.

In 1922 Meiser was appointed as director of a newly founded institution: the seminary of Pastoral training of the Protestant church in Nuremberg. He occupied this position until 1928, when he was appointed as a senior church official in Munich. Living in Munich and Nuremberg in these years meant witnessing the birth and

Figure 5.2. Hans Meiser around 1928 (Landeskirchliches Archiv der Evangelisch-Lutherischen Kirche in Bayern [LAELKB] BS Bi 5: 46).

early period of the Nazi movement, which was founded and consolidated in these two cities of Bavaria. In 1933 Meiser was named bishop of the Lutheran church in Bavaria, a position he held until his retirement in 1955.

Blach's book *The Jews in Germany: Written by a Jewish German* was printed in 1911 by the publisher Karl Curtius, owner of the small, but renowned eponymous publishing house. The book examines a single central idea: how the Jewish and Christian Germans might be merged into a single folk, the Germans, a goal that the author calls a utopia. The book is divided into two main parts discussing the behavior of the Jews and the behavior of the Christian majority. In the first part Blach gives an overview of the participation of the Jews in economy (described as mostly traders, very successful, intelligent, always looking to profit), in politics (construed as mostly liberal, even communist, with only a few conservative nationalistic Jews), in culture, and in social life. The author paints the Jews with characteristics deemed negative from a conservative and nationalistic point of view and, as he suggested, the characteristics should thus be changed as quickly as possible. The twenty-first-century reader will recognize the most well-known anti-Semitic stereotypes in this section of the book. He claims that all Jews

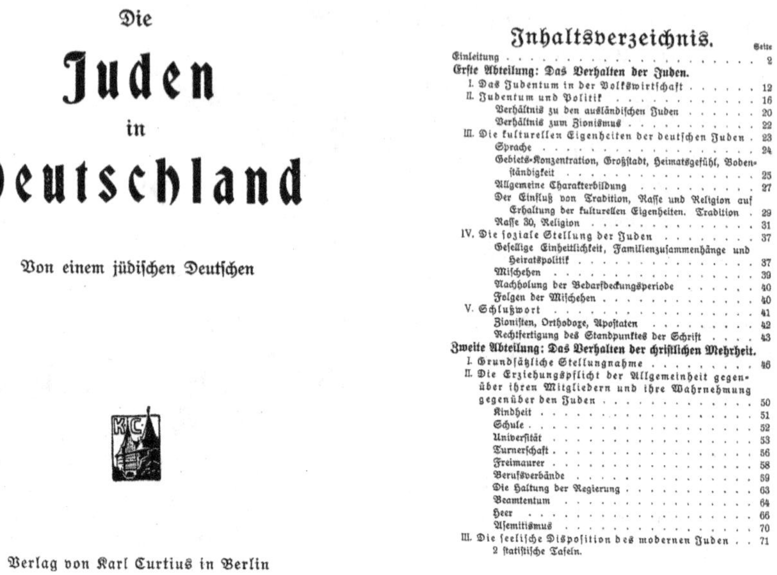

Die

Juden

in

Deutschland

Von einem jüdischen Deutschen

Verlag von Karl Curtius in Berlin

Inhaltsverzeichnis.

Figure 5.3. Cover and table of contents of Friedrich Blach's *The Jews in Germany* (*Die Juden in Deutschland*), Berlin, 1911.

have to work hard to improve their "good Jewish characteristics" and use them for the good of their fellow Germans, but not in service of such movements as Communism or Zionism. He argues that every Jew should fight against the bad characteristics, offensive to Germans, such as speaking with a Yiddish accent or loyalty to non-German, especially eastern European, Jews. Blach proposes assimilation as the only way for German Jews to be fully part of the German community. Some might choose baptism, he suggests, but the majority of Jews will never accept Christianity and thus mixed marriages will be the most convenient way for German Jews to become integrated in German society (1911: 35–45). The author also states: "The Zionists call assimilation suicide," but he insists that this sort of suicide, which entails becoming German in a full sense, will be a "free joyful suicide" (ibid.: 42).

The second section discusses proposals for the behavior of the Christian majority, which should accept Jews in all assemblies, groups, and informal communities. The author asks Germans to educate the Jews to be good Germans, while acknowledging the racial barriers that he identifies between Jews and Germans. Considering these, he proposes mixed marriage to overcome the barriers between Jewishness and Germanness, and suggests that Jews should seek to marry Germans. Such intermarriage is necessary in order to reach the utopia of a German society in which German Jews view themselves and behave not primarily as Jews but as Germans: nationalist, proud, truthful, strong, intelligent, altruistic, brave, always looking to profit not themselves but Germany. Thus the Jewish and the German race, the text demands, must be mixed to reach a Jewry that will become more and more German in terms of racial criteria. For Blach it was very important that the children produced by these mixed marriages remain Jewish, because they would be both Jews in a full sense and also more German than the Jewish part of their parents. The final result was conceived of as a German Jewry that could not be distinguished by racial categories from German Christianity or Germans as such.

The book was broadly received and very hotly debated. In the Berlin Jewish community a lecture was given about the topic, of which several reviews were published in Jewish and non-Jewish papers. The radical anti-Semitic publication *Semi-Kürschner* (1913: 218) criticized Blach for his attempt to build a population of "Jewish Germans" and rejected his ideas. The moderately anti-Semitic *Staatsbürgerzeitung* (Stegemann 1911) published three lengthy articles on the book, which concluded that Blach did not want to turn Jews into Germans, but Germans into Jews, a suggestion that the articles rejected. Writing from a Zionist perspective, Bruno Blau (1911: 32) considered the book an attempt to show the inferiority of Jewishness. The Zionist weekly *Jüdische Rundschau* (Anonymous [M. J.] 1911: 50f., 64f.) insisted that Jews and Germans were deeply disconnected and their cultures were based on totally different racial conditions. The anonymous author claimed Blach's ideas would lead to the "destruction of the Jewish race," since the only real solution for the Jewish question is Zionism. Fritz Baum criticized Blach for his lack of familiarity with Jewish history and rejected his ideas from a more conservative non-Zionist point of view (1911: 130). Ludwig Geiger (1911), the well-known scholar and cohead of the Central Association of German Citizens of Jewish Faith, published a lead article in the most important mainstream Jewish monthly, *Allgemeine Zeitung für das Judentum,* in April 1911. First he noted that Blach had been totally unknown before publishing the book. Geiger accepted some of its proposals, especially improvement of the behavior of those who were perceived as too "Jewish," but rejected its main idea of merging German and Jewish-Germans through intermarriage. In Geiger's view, Blach's utopia would exterminate the culture of the German Jewry in its entirety.

The reviews were mostly critical, but illustrate that Blach's booklet drew attention to a main issue in the self-understanding of German-Jewish relations, and German Jewry itself, between 1900 and 1930. Most

German Jews loved their country, German culture, German ideals, the language, and even the German way of life, but felt rejected and discriminated by the German majority. Most of them were also proud to be German Jews and did not want to convert to Christianity. Some modern scholars denote the views of the small group of German Jews who shared the views of Blach as "Only-Germans": German-nationalistic Jews who wanted to be German without becoming Christians and thus reduced Jewishness to a religious denomination without social, political, and ethnic meaning (Hambrock 2003: 44–46). Some followed Blach's ideas and founded the National-German Jews movement led by Max Naumann, which claimed about 2 percent of the Jewish voters in Berlin in 1930 (Nachama 2001: 152).

Meiser's "The Christian Congregation and the Jewish Question" (1926)

At the core of German nineteenth- and twentieth-century anti-Semitism lay the idea of something unchangeably Jewish seen as dangerous and contagious to political, economic, social, and cultural life. The biological idea of race was very conducive to defining this immutable entity in scientific terms. Anthropology was important for connecting biology to culture and race to society, and such anthropologists as Fischer claimed that research in race was important not only for discovering causes and cures for genetic diseases and for health more generally, but also mattered culturally, ethically, socially, and politically. However, anti-Semites did not wait for scientific proofs. They were convinced that Judaism was an immutable evil in all respects, not only racially, and so "hidden" Jewishness was identified as the most dangerous aspect of Judaism. This assumption also affected their understanding of the Old Testament as a part of the Christian Bible and even of Christianity as such, which was clearly founded by Jews, who, in the view of anti-Semites such as Marr and Fritsch, inserted some of this unchangeable, dangerous, and contagious entity into Christianity. Thus in addition to being overwhelmingly active against Jews and what they understood as Jewishness, certain aspects of aggressive anti-Semitic propaganda were also directed at elements in Christianity they considered "Jewish," protesting against the reading, teaching, and preaching of the Old Testament. They also criticized what was construed as Jewish in the New Testament, opposed conversion and baptism of Jews, and Christians with Jewish roots occupying positions of influence in the church. These versions of anti-Semitic propaganda questioned the fundamental Christian confession of the universality of Christianity—that is, the conviction that people of all races are equal as Christians. However, even the most conservative circles of the churches, which were far from opposing anti-Semitism, such as the Greifswald professor of theology Eduard von der Goltz (1925: 9), opposed growing pressure from anti-Semites in their conviction "that the universality of Christianity is above all differences of races" (cf. Seeberg 1922: 30).

Nevertheless, the pressure of racist groups inside and outside of the church was growing in some regions. One site of such conflicts was Nuremberg, where Julius Streicher founded the infamous weekly newspaper *Der Stürmer*. In 1925 *Der Stürmer* had a print run of between two and three thousand and the *Streicher*-group was part of Hitler's National Socialist party (Bormann 2009: 194). The Protestant weekly *Evangelisches Gemeindeblatt* had about ten thousand subscribers. The conflict between the Protestant church and the *Streicher*-group escalated in 1925 when Ernst Cahn (1875–1953) was invited to Nuremberg to give a lecture on "the foundations of ethics of profession" during an event of the *Evangelisch-sozialer Kongress*, a more liberal part of the Protestant church (cf. Cahn 1924: 17). A member of the Calvinist *Deutschreformierte Gemeinde*, Cahn was a prominent lawyer in Frankfurt am Main and held a professorship of economics. The *Streicher*-group planned to protest against a "Jewish" speaker at the event. In fact, Cahn was not religiously Jewish, but one of about 500,000 partially Jewish people in Germany, most of them Christians (Cohn 1988: 350). The Nuremberg Nazis tried to portray him as one of the five hundred baptized Jews involved in a conspiracy that sought control of the Protestant church.

Figure 5.4. Headline of *Der Stürmer: Nuremberg weekly to struggle for the truth*, July 1925: "500 Jews as dictators of the Protestant church."

After this controversial event, the Protestant leaders of Nuremberg asked Meiser to write a piece about the church and the Jewish question, which was published in 1926. It was clear that the main goal of the essay was the consideration of partly Jewish Christians and baptized Jews. Meiser worked very carefully, ordering material and books from the Protestant Press Association. The sources suggest that Meiser also consulted the books of Carl Heinrich Plath and Friedrich Blach, mentioned previously. In fact, Meiser used the argument of Plath's book as an outline and Blach's book as main material to construct a view of Judaism more modern than Plath's. About a third of his article consists of Blach's ideas. Meiser adopted the former's notion that the Jews should merge with the German people, but he opposed Blach's proposal of mixed marriages. Instead he adopted Plath's argument that only baptism was able to provide full integration in the German population. Moving beyond Plath he stated that baptism was more powerful than race and able "to refine the race of the Jews" (Meiser 1926: 406). He argued that Jews who were baptized should be considered German in a full sense, which even included race.

Meiser's writing was deeply rooted in the biohistorical racial narrative, but when he was faced with the conflict between the narrative of race as unchangeable and the Christian narrative of new creation through baptism, he chose the Christian narrative. The single known critical comment stems from *Der Stürmer*. In several articles of October 1926 it criticized the leading ministers of the church, labeled them "Lutheran Orthodoxy," and tried to convince young Protestant students that the church should forbid the baptism of Jews, because, the argument ran, baptized Jews were enemies of Christianity. A more sophisticated article with the title "Christian and Antichrist" was included in the same edition, and was framed as the reply to a letter by a young student of theology, who asked whether the anti-Semites were enemies of Christianity. *Der Stürmer* answered by claiming that anti-Semites were true supporters of Christianity, because they recognized the "deadly enemy" of the church, the Jewish race.

Conclusion

Blach was influenced by colonial studies in Hamburg and Berlin, which included the discourse about gains and losses caused by "mixed populations," "mixed marriages," and "racial mixture." He wanted to contribute to a future German Jewry that could no longer be distinguished from the non-Jewish majority.

Blach's reflections were particularly influenced by the academic debate in German colonial studies concerning the valorization (*Inwertsetzung*) of a colonial population for the purpose of the colonizers. He entered the debate about Jews in Germany accepting the underlying premises of the otherness, or even in some respects inferiority, of the Jews, seeing them as a population that should be educated and trained by the dominating German population according to the nationalistic and imperialistic aims of a unified German nation composed of both German Jews and non-Jewish Germans. Blach felt the contradictory implications of this concept: on the one hand, he pled for the education of German Jews to become Germans, while on the other he shared the category of race as something unchangeable and felt compelled to also deal with the challenge of the widespread assumption of biological determinism implied by the category of race. As one of many steps toward this ambition he proposed mixed marriages between non-Jewish Germans and German Jews to build up a mixed population with an increasingly non-Jewish ancestry to improve the racial constitution of German Jewry. Yet he also urged the avoidance of baptism, which he accepted only as a last resort toward integration into the non-Jewish German majority.

Meiser was influenced by studies in Christian mission in Berlin, which included "psychology of nations" and racial theories. In this context missionaries were trained with the understanding that the non-Christian indigenous population was to some degree determined by race. This concept was seen as helpful for a better understanding of the successes and failures of Christian mission. However, the category of race and its implications contradicted the idea of baptism as an unparalleled powerful force superior to all biological categories, including race. As a Christian he combined the narrative of the Christian mission with the Jewish question in his proposal of an anti-Jewish, but also antiracial narrative of Jews. He argued that baptized Jews should be acknowledged not only as Christians, but also as Germans in a full sense, a proposition that was significant at this time. Meiser contested the central anti-Semitic conviction that everything Jewish was invariably dangerous because it was biologically determined. He thus challenged the biological narrative of race that had dominated German cultural debate over race and Jewishness since the *Berliner Antisemitismus Streit.*

Blach and Meiser were familiar with the cultural narrative of race, which asserted the existence of something "unchangeable," and was defined by origin and seen as dangerous and contagious. The idea of something "unchangeable" was the invariant core of the many variants of colonial, anti-Semitic, and racial narratives of nineteenth- and early twentieth-century Germany. The category of race was seen in the scholarship of this period as a factual matter with many implications for the defining, analyzing, and solving of research questions, particularly in colonial studies. This category was used without hesitation as an underlying assumption, or even axiom, for further research in new and different cultures. The application of the category of race as a paradigm also for the understanding, analyzing, and handling of the relationship between different groups within their own society was seen by many young German academics, Jewish and non-Jewish, as an unavoidable, and for some even as an attractive and promising, endeavor. Finally, even those who criticized it in some respects often worked within its presuppositions and accepted it as an epistemic system.

However, both authors were moved by their deeper convictions about Jewishness on the one hand, and about Christianity on the other, to challenge the idea of the "unchangeable." They sought to open the cultural debate concerning their Jewish and Christian communities to members of society with diverse cultural and religious backgrounds. Finally, both failed intellectually and politically. The intellectual flaws of their argument resulted from contradictions that are unavoidable when racial categories in cultural and social discourses are used. They were defeated in their opposition to the radical racial activism of the NSDAP, which established its dominance over culture and society in Germany after the seizure of power by the National Socialist movement in 1933, silencing both Blach and Meiser.

Lukas Bormann is professor for New Testament at the Philipps-University Marburg. Before this he held chairs at Friedrich-Alexander University of Erlangen-Nuremberg, the University of Bayreuth, and Brunswick University of Technology, and was researcher and lecturer at the universities of Hildesheim and Frankfurt. His main expertise lies in the New Testament and the history of ancient religions. Since 2009, his research includes the history of protestant mentality in the twentieth century in transnational perspective and also the views of scholars and clergies on both contemporary and ancient Judaism.

References

Anonymous. 1910. "Ist der Antisemitismus noch berechtigt? (Ein Brief)." *Staatsbürgerzeitung*, 8 December, no. 287.
Anonymous (M. J.). 1911. "Ein neuer Vorschlag zur Auflösung des Judentums." *Jüdische Rundschau*, vol. 16: 50f., 64f.

Baum, F. 1911. "Ein neuer Vorschlag zur Auflösung der Juden im Deutschtum." *Kartell-Convent-Blätter* 16, no. 8: 130–132.
Becker, F., ed. 2004, *Rassenmischehen—Mischlinge—Rassentrennung. Zur Politik der Rasse im deutschen Kolonialreich*. Stuttgart.
Bezzel, H. von. 2008. *Löhe und seine Zeit. Einsegnungsunterricht 1908*. Neuendettelsau.
Blake, P. 1993. *No Place like Utopia: Modern Architecture and the Company We Kept*. New York and London.
Blau, B., 1911. "Review of F. Blach." *Zeitschrift für Demographie und Statistik der Juden* 7, no. 1: 32.
Bormann, L. 2009. "Der 'Stürmer' und das evangelische Nürnberg (1924–1927): Zur Entstehung von Hans Meisers Artikel aus dem Jahr 1926 'Die evangelische Gemeinde und die Judenfrage.'" *Zeitschrift für bayerische Kirchengeschichte*, vol. 78: 187–212.
Cahn, E. 1924. *Christentum und Wirtschaftsethik*. Gotha and Stuttgart.
Campt, T. 2004. *Other Germans: Black Germans and the Politics of Race, Gender, and Memory in the Third Reich*. Ann Arbor, MI.
Cohn, W. 1988. "Bearers of a Common Fate? The 'Non-Aryan Christian Fate-Comrades' of the Paulus Bund, 1933–1939." *Leo Baeck Institute Yearbook*, vol. 33: 327–366.
Davis, C.S. 2012. *Colonialism, Antisemitism, and Germans of Jewish Descent in Imperial Germany*. Ann Arbor, MI.
Deutscher Wirtschaftsverlag. 1930. *Reichshandbuch der deutschen Gesellschaft. Das Handbuch der Persönlichkeiten in Wort und Bild*. 2 vols. Berlin.
Ebner, T. 2009. "Staatsform—Bio-Macht—'Rasse'. Lebenswissenschaftliche Kontinuierungen vom deutschen Kolonialismus bis zum nationalsozialistischen 'Volkskörper.'" In *Gemachte Differenz. Kontinuitäten biologischer "Rasse"-Konzepte*, ed. AG gegen Rassismus in den Lebenswissenschaften. Münster, 166–201.
Fischer, E. 1909a, "Das Rehobother Bastardvolk in Deutsch-Südwestafrika." *Die Umschau*, vol. 13: 1047–1051.
———. 1909b. "Beobachtungen am Bastardvolk in Deutsch-Südwestafrika." *Korrespondenzblatt der deutschen Anthropologischen Gesellschaft*, vol. 40: 75–77.
———. 1911. "Zum Inzuchts- und Bastardierungsproblem beim Menschen." *Korrespondenzblatt der deutschen Anthropologischen Gesellschaft*, vol. 42: 105–109.
———. 1913. *Die Rehobother Bastards und das Bastardierungsproblem beim Menschen. Anthropologische und ethnographische Studien am Rehobother Bastardvolk in Deutsch-Südwest-Afrika*. Jena.
Fischer, H. 1981. *Die Hamburger Südsee-Expedition. Über Ethnographie und Kolonisation*. Frankfurt.
Fritsch, T. 1919. *Handbuch der Judenfrage*. Hamburg.
Geiger, L. 1911. "Die Juden in Deutschland." *Allgemeine Zeitung des Judentums. Ein unparteiisches Organ für alles jüdische Interesse*, 7 April, vol. 75: 157–158.
Goltz, E. von der. 1925. *Christentum und Rassenfrage*. Königsberg.
Grentrup, T. 1914. *Die Rassenmischehen in den deutschen Kolonien*. Paderborn.
Ha, K. N. 2009. "'Bastarde' als Problem der deutschen Eugenik und 'Rassenhygiene' im 20. Jahrhundert." In *Gemachte Differenz. Kontinuitäten biologischer*

"Rasse"-Konzepte, ed. AG gegen Rassismus in den Lebenswissenschaften. Münster, 203–238.

Hambrock, M. 2003. *Die Etablierung der Außenseiter. Der Verband nationaldeutscher Juden.* Colonge, Weimar, and Vienna.

Hedrich, K. 1941. *Der Rassegedanke im deutschen Kolonialrecht. Die rechtliche Regelung der ehelichen und außerehelichen Beziehungen zwischen Weißen und Farbigen.* Tübingen.

Lipphardt, V. 2008. *Biologie der Juden. Jüdische Biowissenschaftler über "Rasse" und Vererbung (1900–1935).* Göttingen.

Marr, W. 1879a. *Vom Sieg des Judenthums über das Germanenthum vom nicht confessionellen Standpunkt aus betrachtet.* Bern.

———. 1879b. *Wählet keinen Juden! Der Weg zum Siege des Germanenthums über das Judenthum. Ein Mahnwort an die Wähler nichtjüdischen Stammes aller Confessionen.* Berlin.

———. 1885. *Lessing contra Sem. Allen "Rabbinern" der Juden- und Christenheit, allen Toleranz-Duselheimern aller Parteien, allen "Pharisäern und Schriftgelehrten" tolerantest gewidmet.* Berlin.

Meiser, H. 1926. "Die evangelische Gemeinde und die Judenfrage." *Evangelisches Gemeindeblatt Nürnberg*, no. 33–35: 394–397, 406f., 418f.

Missionsausschuss. 1912. *Die Rassenmischehen in den deutschen Kolonien, das Internationale Institut für missionswissenschaftliche Forschungen und die Ansiedlung von Katholiken in den Kolonien. Verhandlungen des Missionsausschusses des Zentralkomitees der Katholikenversammlungen Deutschlands.* Freiburg.

Nachama, A. 2001. *Juden in Berlin*, vol. 1. Leipzig.

Perraudin, M., and J. Zimmerer, eds. 2011. *German Colonialism and National Identity.* New York.

Plath, C. H. C. 1881. *Was machen wir Christen mit unseren Juden!?* Nördlingen.

Rathgen, K. 1900. *Welche sittlichen und sozialen Aufgaben stellt die Entwicklung Deutschlands zur Weltmacht unserm Volke?* Göttingen.

———. 1908. *Beamtentum und Kolonialunterricht.* Hamburg.

———. 1910. "Die Neger und die europäische Zivilisation." *Jahrbuch für Gesetzgebung, Verwaltung und Volkswirtschaft im Deutschen Reich* 34: 279–305.

Raupp, W. 1994. "Plath, 'Carl Heinrich Christian.'" *Biographisch-Bibliographisches Kirchenlexikon*, vol. 7: 720–723.

Roller, K. 2002. "Der Rassenbiologe Eugen Fischer." In *Kolonialmetropole Berlin. Eine Spurensuche*, eds. U. van der Heyden and J. Zeller. Berlin, 130–134.

Ruppenthal, J. 2007. *Kolonialismus als "Wissenschaft und Technik". Das Hamburgische Kolonialinstitut 1908 bis 1919.* Stuttgart.

Sahl, H. 1980. *Hausmusik. Eine Szenenfolge.* Bad Homburg.

———. 1991. *Die Wenigen und die Vielen. Roman einer Zeit.* Hamburg

———. 2008. *Memoiren eines Moralisten.* Munich.

Sarè, C. K. 2011. "Abuses of German Colonial History: The Character of Carl Peters as a Weapon for Völkisch and National Socialist Discourses: Anglophobia, Anti-Semitism, Aryanism." In *German Colonialism and National Identity*, eds. M. Perraudin and J. Zimmerer. New York, 160–172.

Schiel, E. 1996. *Mein lieber Sohn und Kamerad. Stralsunder Briefe aus dem Ersten Weltkrieg.* Kückenshagen.

Seeberg, R. 1922. *Antisemitismus, Judentum und Kirche.* Berlin.

Seemann, M. 2011. *Kolonialismus in der Heimat. Kolonialbewegung, Kolonialpolitik und Kolonialkultur in Bayern 1882–1943*. Berlin.
Simon, M. 1960. "Hans Meiser, bayerischer Landesbischof, 1881–1956." In *Lebensläufe aus Franken* von Pölnitz. Würzburg, 404–417.
Stauff, P. 1913. *Art. Blach, Friedrich. Semi-Kürschner oder literarisches Lexikon der Schriftsteller, Dichter, Bankiers, Geldleute, Ärzte, Schauspieler, Künstler, Musiker, Offiziere, Rechtsanwälte, Revolutionäre, Frauenrechtlerinnen, Sozialdemokraten usw. jüdischer Rasse und Versippung, die von 1813–1913 in Deutschland tätig oder bekannt waren*. Berlin.
Stegemann, H. 1911. "Die Juden in Deutschland." *Staatsbürgerzeitung*, 7 April.
van der Heyden, U., and J. Zeller, eds. 2002. *Kolonialmetropole Berlin. Eine Spurensuche*. Berlin.
Verlag der Deutschen Wirtschaft, ed. 1930. *Art. Blach, Friedrich, Reichshandbuch der deutschen Gesellschaft. Das Handbuch der Persönlichkeiten in Wort und Bild*, vol. 1. Berlin, 143.
Volland, A. 1993. *Theodor Fritsch (1852–1933) und die Zeitschrift "Hammer."* Mainz.
Wilhelmus, W. 1996. *Juden in Vorpommern*. Schwerin.
Zeller, J. 2008. *Bilderschule der Herrenmenschen. Koloniale Reklamesammelbilder*. Berlin.
Zimmerer, J. 2011. *Von Windhuk nach Auschwitz? Beiträge zum Verhältnis von Kolonialismus und Holocaust*. Berlin.

PART III

GERMANY AND TRANSNATIONAL OTHERNESS

 6

RACE AND ETHNICITY IN GERMAN CRIMINOLOGY
On Crime Rates and the Polish Population
in the *Kaiserreich* (1871–1914)
Volker Zimmermann

On 15 January 1890 the first prosecutor in Gleiwitz in Upper Silesia sent a report to the Ministry of Justice in Berlin in which he expressed his opinion of the Polish population in his region in no uncertain terms: "It is to be hoped," he wrote, "that in the course of time German culture will be able to reduce the criminality that forms part of the [Polish] national character" (Becker 2002: 328).[1] With this missive, the prosecutor was conveying two messages to Berlin: firstly, that Poles, seen by many German contemporaries as members of a different race (Conrad 2006: 145–149), were more prone to criminal behavior than Germans, and secondly, that they could better themselves if they overcame their "national character" through assimilation with the culturally more highly evolved Germans.

This attitude of the first prosecutor in Gleiwitz must surely have had far-reaching consequences for the quality of law enforcement in this region of Prussia, which was home to a large Polish community; given his comments, it might be expected that, as a high-level representative of the German justice system, he acted more stringently in his region against the Polish segment of the population than against its German residents. Moreover, he was not alone in his appraisal of the situation—many of his colleagues shared his opinion that Poles were backward and more likely to engage in crime, while Germans were more civilized and less prone to criminal behavior. Such views are illustrated by reports emanating from other public prosecutor offices at the end of the nineteenth century.

Prejudices relating to the Poles' alleged criminal tendencies were by no means uncommon at this time. These preconceptions hardened toward the end of the nineteenth century; it was a trend that, for example, found expression in the high-profile coverage of crimes committed by Poles in conservative nationalist newspapers (Johnson 1995: 78–83). The prejudicial stereotype of the "thieving Pole" is widespread even today. It may well have its origin in discussions on how an allegedly disproportionate number of Poles were engaged in criminal behavior at the time of the German Empire.

One of the central functions of negative stereotyping is to stabilize the positive social identity of one's own group through the act of shutting out other groups. This observation applies to interethnic relations as much as to any other variety of intergroup relations (Tajfel 1974; Cinnirella 1997). It can also be observed as a form of social categorization in constructing national self-images and images of the Other as part of the process of German nation building in the course of the nineteenth century; the discursive inclusion of ethnic Germans and exclusion of the allegedly culturally backward Poles helped establish the self-perception of the Germans as a highly developed nation in terms of culture (Pleitner 2001). Given this background, the criminalization of Polish people should be understood as having also contributed to the consolidation of a German group identity through negative stereotyping of the Other.

This development may have had a connection with the conscious or unconscious colonial self-image of German society in the nineteenth century. After all, over the last few years, historians have been at pains to point out that the German Empire should not be interpreted simply as a nation-state, but also as a continental empire. In this context, German mastery over the Poles living mostly in the eastern provinces of Prussia should be understood as a form of colonialism (Ther 2004; Kopp 2012). For anyone adopting this point of view, American and British "race and crime studies," which include discussions on the criminalizing effect of "colonial" practices, provide inspiration for the analysis of how the Polish minority was treated. As a consequence, there is a need to analyze criminal policies and the treatment of colonized peoples in the discourses of colonial and postcolonial societies, including—among other issues—the construction of allegedly backward "immoral" and "uncivilized" populations. A further important factor in colonial perspectives on race and crime is the strict surveillance of such populations, most notably by the justice system, the police and the military (Gabbidon 2010: 181–197).

According to considerations on the construction of Others in postcolonial theories, ethnically based Othering served (and indeed still serves) to ground the hierarchization of society, the process through which the hegemonic practices of dominant social groups and/or elites are consolidated (Thomas-Olalde and Velho 2011; Heitzeg 2011). This social hegemonization was reinforced by the criminalization of sectors of the population defined as Other—which ultimately had the effect of making such groups appear to people belonging to the dominant social echelons not just as alien, but as actually dangerous. In this way, existing social hierarchies were conferred additional legitimacy.

"Experts" in a wide variety of disciplines played an important role in providing the scientific basis for this Othering. Thus, "race" and "nationality" (in the sense of ethnicity) became central arguments in German criminological studies. Authors often used these terms synonymously, but even where they did not—when they explicitly mentioned differences between (biological) "racial" and (cultural) "ethnic" concepts—the effect was the same: both categories served as social constructions to reinforce identities and mark distinctions and hierarchies of power between different groups in society (Brückweh 2015: 278; Hall, McClelland, and Rendall 2000: 46).

Yet, as important as questions relating to criminalizing stereotypes in German-speaking countries during the nineteenth century may be, there exists little historical research to date on the subject. Despite an increase in the prominence of race and crime studies over the past decades, particularly in the United States and Great Britain (Greene and Gabbidon 2009), few historians have engaged rigorously with this topic specifically in connection with Slavic populations (like Johnson 1995: 78–83, 147–151; Zimmermann 2006; 2014). Neither the field of criminal history nor the very extensive German-, English-, and Polish-language literature on the history of the Polish minority in Prussia and the German Empire have mentioned this topic any more than in passing (like Becker: 327–328).

Some historians have focused their attention on the situation of Polish labor in the Ruhr region and have also dealt with the topic of the criminalization of this group (Kleßmann 1978: 74–82). A particularly informative study of this subject is Bastian Pütter's published Master's thesis, which includes a short analysis of the relevant general criminological discourses (2006). Pütter deploys the assertion that it was precisely the concept of the "cultural nation"—as opposed to the nation-state—that positively compelled the marginalization of ethnic minorities. He supports his case by analyzing the starkly stereotyping press reports, thus revealing the discursive practice of criminalization of Polish immigrants to the Ruhr Valley.

The discussion to follow will pursue the issue of the criminalization of Poles in the German Empire in a number of stages: after making some introductory remarks on the importance of race as a criminogenic factor in nineteenth-century criminological texts, it will show how people at the time used crime statistics to interpret the rates, types, and trends in crimes allegedly committed by Poles. The analysis will then assess the German criminological literature of the time, which proposed a variety of interpretations of high crime rates in the eastern regions of the Empire. A regional case study of the Prussian province of Posen, based on documents obtained in the region's archives, will be used to illustrate ways in which these statistical data might be explained from the perspective of today. The chapter will conclude by considering the manner in which, in the context of the German Empire, the stigma of criminality had any connection with a specific racial or ethnic narrative.

Race as an Indicator of Criminal Tendencies in Late Nineteenth- and Early Twentieth-Century Criminology

One of the most important European figures to deal with the topic of race and crime in the nineteenth century was the Italian physician and psychiatrist Cesare Lombroso. In five editions of his most popular book *L'Uomo delinquente* (The Criminal Man), published over the course of twenty years, he identified a number of different criminal types. In particular, he attributed the crimes of convicted individuals to their inherited physical and mental dispositions, thus establishing the idea of the "born criminal." Although many scientists, initially at least, rejected this theory, some of Lombroso's arguments were to become very influential, particularly in the longer term.

Many studies have shown how in the late nineteenth century narratives on criminality, shaped by bourgeois norms and codes of behavior, influenced ideas on crime and its perpetrators. These narratives led to the creation of a negative counterpart to "normal" society by appeal to the above-mentioned scientifically defined criminal Other. Yet the interpretation of crime by criminologists also changed as time went on: whereas initially people spoke of "fallen" individuals, later criminals often ended up being categorized as "disabled" (Becker 2002). As a result, crime and the struggle against it were no longer characterized as a moral and ethical issue, but a medical and anthropological one, a shift for which Lombroso and his Italian Positivist School of criminal law and anthropology essentially bore shared responsibility.

Lombroso's theories and influence have been thoroughly researched by a number of authors (Gibson 2002; Wetzell 2000). As Mary Gibson has described, Lombroso employed the concept of race in the fifth edition of his study *L'uomo delinquente*. He suggested that certain races were more disposed to criminal acts because of their supposed physical and mental backwardness, "degeneration," and lack of morals. Lombroso was especially interested in the particular proclivity toward crime he observed in southern Italy, a region he defined as racially different from the northern parts of the country because of the (biological or racial) influence of Africa and the Orient. But he also discussed other groups, ranging from "Gypsies" to Afro-Americans (Gibson 2002: 97–126).

Other Italian criminologists—Enrico Ferri and his student Alfredo Niceforo, for example—also considered race to be a central concern of the study of crime. While Ferri was more interested in sociological and economic arguments, Niceforo explained high crime rates in the southern Italian province of Nuoro on the basis of alleged similarities between Nuorese and African skulls (Gabbidon 2007: 12). Thus, Italian criminology—at least during its early development—formed a very substantial thread in European discussion on the connection between race and crime. These authors quickly became influential among criminologists in other countries. While it is unsurprising that Lombroso's German disciples, such as Alfred Kurella, who will be discussed at length later, agreed with this atavistic conception, it is notable that even critics of biological theories were beginning to consider the importance of race as an explanatory factor in criminology.

At this time, interpretation of the term "race" varied among authors. Franz von Liszt, one of the most influential German criminologists of the nineteenth century, argued, for example, that "race should be considered to be absolutely the most important of all social groupings. It is race which first determined how social relations were first formed and how societies' earliest social development occurred. ... It seems to me beyond all doubt that the formation of criminality is also determined by racial influences" (1903: 211).[2] Significantly, Liszt distanced himself from biological determinist theories—he was primarily interested in the sociological causes of crime and used the term "race" in a sense that suggested cultural diversity. Nevertheless, like some of his contemporaries, he at least acknowledged the importance of the idea of race or ethnicity in the study of crime. Although many authors continued to question this point of view (Galassi 2004: 201–203), it was a perspective that gradually began to gain ground in criminology.

This trend was also driven by discussions on the alleged connection between race and crime in the United States (Schmidt 2007: 136–138). Alongside Lombroso—who deemed the "primitive, wild instincts" of the "Negroes" (Schmidt 2007: 136) responsible for America's high murder rate—German authors too were among those inspired by these considerations. Some of them pointed to the importance of what they considered differing negative biological influences on the criminal disposition of "Negroes." This scholarly faction stood in contrast to American sociologists like William E. B. Du Bois, who related higher crime rates to environmental influences such as economic circumstances (1899).

Thus, authors adopting biological arguments contributed to the establishment of the debate on the alleged connection between race and criminality. One of them, Paul Näcke, saw an individual's "racial biological structure" as harboring "in itself one of the roots of crime,"[3] but at the same time—in a similar manner to the Gleiwitz lawyer quoted at the beginning of this article—believed in the possibility of "improvement" through assimilation (Näcke 1906). Authors independently turned their attention to other states such as the Russian Empire (Weinberg 1905–1906), a country regarded by Liszt as a useful laboratory for the examination of the possible link between race and crime, due to the ethnic diversity of its inhabitants (1906: 212).

Jews and "Gypsies" were particularly suspicious in the eyes of large sections of social elites and of the German population. The alleged tendency of Jews to commit specific types of crime, such as usury and fraud—or even "ritual murder"—had been a subject of discussion for centuries (Vyleta 2007: 40–69). Yet more widespread was a discourse dedicated to so-called *Zigeunerkriminalität* (Gypsy crime), a discussion that also had a long tradition. Criminologists, journalists, judges, the police, and many more described "Gypsies" as born criminals whose sole ambition was to be vagabonds and thieves (Engbring-Romang 2007; Lucassen 1997). This frequent stigmatization of Jews and "Gypsies" in interpretations of crime was not a phenomenon limited to Germany, of course.

For the purposes of our case, the shift in which discussions on race and crime became more influential in the last decades of the nineteenth century in European countries is very important. It lays bare the transnational character of the trend and positions it within the discursive context of the newly established science of criminology. This in turn points to the emergence of a German variant of this discussion—grounded on the specific claim of a greater disposition to criminality among the Polish population in Prussia. One motor for the emergence of this discourse was the publication of the first official crime statistics of the German Empire.

German Crime Statistics and the Polish Population of the *Kaiserreich*

Crime statistics for the German Empire, published by the Imperial Office of Statistics (Kaiserliches Statistisches Amt), exist from the year 1882 onward (Kriminalstatistik 1884). If we want to take a closer look at these figures, we would do well to bear in mind the peculiarities of the data (Galassi 2004: 90–97). For instance, they record the number of individuals convicted for crimes (*Verbrechen*) and misdemeanors (*Vergehen*) against Imperial Law, but do not include the number of offenses actually committed. What this means is that we know the figures neither for undetected offences, nor for crimes that went unreported or were not registered by the police for other reasons. The mix of offences included in crime statistics also varied as laws changed, police postings moved, and the focus of police attention shifted.

Another point to be considered, for example, is the temporal and regional differences obtaining between each specific area under analysis. Such differences will include varying local political and socioeconomic factors, as well as differing understandings of right and wrong common in the local population of the time. The latter factor is particularly difficult to study fruitfully. In this context, figures on numbers of convictions might also be influenced by the willingness of the population, victims, the police, and authorities to report crimes—particularly for crimes referred to as *Antragsdelikte,* which could only be prosecuted upon an official complaint being made by the individuals affected by them. It is thus clear that we are not dealing with objective figures in these crime statistics, but rather with the outcomes of a variety of discourses and social processes involving the interaction of a variety of individuals.

An additional limitation is that crime statistics for the German Empire did not distinguish between German- and Polish-speaking offenders. Although they reveal the number of convicted offenders in the different regions of the Empire, giving their gender, religion, age, and occupation, they reveal nothing about their national background—that is, whether a person was of Polish or Danish descent, for example. In any case, they do not inform us whether a convicted offender regarded himself as a "Pole" or a "Dane" living in the German Empire or as simply a subject of the *Kaiser.* Thus, the formation of a connection in social discussions between ethnicity and a propensity to criminality was entirely dependent on the consultation of other data.

Yet, for all their limitations, crime statistics remain a central point of reference for this analysis. This is largely because they formed the basis of contemporary interpretations of criminality that will be considered in the fourth part of this chapter. At the time, only statistics of actual convictions were seen as reliable "indicators of the reality of crime." Therefore, the term "crime rate" (*Kriminalitätsziffer*) was then considered synonymous with "rate of convictions" (*Verurteiltenziffer*) (Melchers 1992: 3). Furthermore, the published crime statistics are the only printed source that both provide comprehensive data over time and also give a breakdown for each of the various administrative districts of Prussia. This geographical breakdown of offenses contained in the data is of particular interest. In the very first publication of the statistics, giving the figures for 1882, the Imperial Office of Statistics comments: "In this, the first year in which we have processed [the data] … we have not yet commissioned maps to be drawn up to show crime distributions. … It may, however, be said at this early stage that in all probability any such maps would show a quite consistent downward trend in crime levels as one moves from East to West" (Kriminalstatistik 1884: 60).[4] This text, in identifying an east-west gradient in terms of crime statistics (Johnson 1995: 147–151), was making implicit hints about the Polish population of the Empire: after all, the Prussian eastern provinces contained a large number of Polish-speaking inhabitants. According to the census of 1890, in which people stated their native language, this Polish population amounted to approximately three million people. It is impossible at this point to evaluate how accurate these language statistics were (Belzyt 1998). It was, however, precisely these data that made it possible in the first place to construct any ethnic qua criminal Other. Following the publication of these statistics, the number of authors who made a connection between the large number of Poles living in the east of the Empire and the high crime rates in these regions was to increase rapidly.

In the eyes of such authors, their suspicions were corroborated by the statistics emanating from particular administrative districts (*Regierungsbezirke*) that contained higher proportions of Poles among their inhabitants. Thus, the administrative district of Bromberg in the province of Posen, with over 2,000 convicted offenders out of 100,000 inhabitants of the age of criminal responsibility, topped all figures by a large margin. It was followed by the administrative district of Gumbinnen in the province of East Prussia (which was also home to a substantial Lithuanian population) with about 1,800 convicted offenders, the administrative district of Posen with 1,700 convicted offenders, closely succeeded by four other eastern administrative districts, all of which contained large Polish populations.

Thus, in 1882 the seven administrative districts of the German Empire with the highest conviction rates were all located in the eastern Prussian provinces. The national average across the Empire was about 1,000 convicted offenders per 100,000 inhabitants of the age of criminal responsibility. Twenty years later, in 1902, the Imperial Office for Statistics analyzed the crime rates in terms of regional distribution by administrative district from 1882 onward. This revealed that the Prussian eastern provinces remained at the top in terms of overall crime. The

Bromberg	2 083	Lübeck	1 055	Wiesbaden	912	Düsseldorf	735
Gumbinnen	1 790	Neckarkreis	1 037	Arnsberg	906	Hessen	734
Posen	1 685	Hamburg	1 034	Fürstenthum Lübeck	898	Lüneburg	711
Marienwerder	1 665	Donaukreis	1 032	Bayern	885,1	Stargard	708
Danzig	1 655	Deutsches Reich	1 028	Ober-Elsaß	885	Lippe	700
Königsberg	1 593	Mittelfranken	1 023	Sachsen-Weimar	881	Lothringen	698
Oppeln	1 499	Hannover	1 011	Jagstkreis	872	Schleswig	692
Schwarzburg-Rudolstadt	1 484	Schwaben	1 002	Karlsruhe	858	Oberhessen	688
Bremen	1 407	Oberfranken	1 000	Sachsen-Altenburg	854	Osnabrück	676
Schwarzburg-Sondershausen	1 406	Sachsen-Coburg-Gotha	995	Vörrach	852,4	Mosbach	660
Berlin	1 350	Stettin	994	Offenburg	852	Stade	659
Pfalz	1 326	Mannheim	991	Herzogthum Oldenburg	848	Koblenz	650
Niederbayern	1 295	Württemberg	987	Magdeburg	845	Trier	622
Oberbayern	1 267	Heidelberg	986	Aurich	834	Sigmaringen	621
Breslau	1 183	Konstanz	975	Baden (Groß.)	827,4	Baden	615
Bayern	1 146	Schwarzwaldkreis	974	Oldenburg (Groß.)	827	Waldeck	612
Anhalt	1 135	Frankfurt	963	Freiburg	815	Bielefeld	611
Dresden	1 123	Cassel	954	Rheinhessen	812	Mecklenburg-Strelitz	605
Unterfranken	1 096	Potsdam	947	Liegnitz	798	Mecklenburg-Schwerin	597
Leipzig	1 090	Reuß älterer Linie	940	Erfurt	792	Sigmaringen	574
Zwickau	1 088	Reuß jüngerer Linie	930	Stralsund	785	Aachen	557
Sachsen (Kgr.)	1 073	Sachsen-Meiningen	925	Elsaß-Lothringen	774	Minden	475
Cöslin	1 067	Braunschweig	924	Waldshut	760	Münster	468
Oberpfalz	1 058	Hildesheim	917	Unter-Elsaß	754	Schaumburg-Lippe	424
Preußen	1 056	Merseburg	915	Cöln	751		

Figure 6.1. Total number of crimes and misdemeanors against Imperial Laws in 1882 (broken down by administrative districts). Convicted offenders per 100,000 inhabitants of the age of criminal responsibility (Kriminalstatistik 1884: 60).[5]

most common offences were crimes against property such as theft. For petty theft, which was widespread in rural regions, it became evident that the higher the percentage of Polish within the general population, the higher the crime rate seemed to be. In connection with violent crime too, and in particular with physical assault, higher-than-average figures were also recorded. In this category as well, district-specific analysis showed that localities with a large Polish population (as revealed in language statistics) were disproportionately affected (Kriminalstatistik 1904: II.34).

To many observers, the assumption that responsibility for the high conviction figures in the eastern provinces might be found in local Polish populations seemed plausible enough at first glance. Taking this assumption a little further, the apparent dominant tendency toward deviant or criminal behavior in the eastern provinces was perceived to be the result of their populations' supposed ethnic otherness. In this regard the following rule seemed to apply: the more detailed and differentiated the data collection became, the more aggressive were "experts" in asserting a connection between "race" or "nationality" and criminality. Thus it is hardly surprising that findings that contradicted the general impression of Poles as possessing a heightened tendency to criminality were rarely discussed more closely. Yet notably, rates both for serious economic crime and for sex offences in the eastern provinces were below the national average.

Furthermore, although in later decades the eastern regions retained their position at the top of crime tables, from the turn of the century on figures for theft dropped at a higher-than-average rate in the east as compared to other parts of the Empire. At the same time, in the west of the Empire, especially in Rhineland and Westphalia, the number of convictions rose. Thus, after the turn of the century, rates of statistically registered crime "migrated" to a certain extent from east to west. These general trends can be observed up until the outbreak of World War One (Kriminalstatistik 1914).

However, developments in the period from 1882 to 1914 should be also considered in light of observations relating to the preceding decades. In the few recent criminal history studies that make mention of the east-west gradient discussed above, that gradient is understood as being temporary (Schwerhoff 1999: 60–61), and no detailed consideration is made of the various types of offences included in the figures. Statistics over a longer time period are needed in order to ascertain whether the phenomenon is exclusively a turn-of-the-century effect. For this reason, I have consulted earlier data for Prussia, as integrated crime statistics for all German states exist only from 1882 on. This earlier data includes contemporary Prussian materials dealing with crime statistics as well as overviews of the prison population for the period from the 1850s to the 1870s (Triest 1863; Valentini 1869; Verhältniss 1857; Aschrott 1884; Illing 1885; Engel 1865).

A comparison of this material with the crime statistics collated by the German Empire from 1882 on exhibits an almost identical pattern: the eastern provinces were, at least from the 1850s on, at the top of the rankings. The geographical distribution of cases of physical assault or theft, for one, was the same as at the end of the nineteenth century. For instance, a study on crime in Prussia in the 1850s published in the *Zeitschrift des Königlichen Preussischen Statistischen Bureaus* (Journal of the Statistical Office of Royal Prussia) commented, "the noticeably lower level of criminal activity in the West in comparison with the East cannot be denied" (Triest 1863: 189).[6]

So the high crime rates recorded in the eastern provinces were clearly not a temporary phenomenon. Crime experts would have been able to find purported evidence linking Poles with a higher-than-average rate of criminality dating at least as far back as the middle of the nineteenth century. In addition, religion will have lent further weight to this theory, as it was well known that in the eastern provinces a higher-than-average number of offenders were Catholic, something that was also true of almost the entire Polish-speaking population (Verhältniss 1857). But was this ethnic distinctiveness of the eastern provinces an ongoing theme of contemporary discourses? To answer this question it is worth taking a look at the period's official and scholarly literature on criminality.

Contemporary Explanations for
High Crime Rates in the Eastern Provinces

There was nothing new about the negative stereotypes attached to Poles at the end of the nineteenth and the beginning of the twentieth century. Indeed, the cliché of the "uncivilized" Poles was common all the way back to the partitions of Poland at the end of the eighteenth century. While positive images of freedom-loving Poles prevailed in the first half of the nineteenth century among German liberals, after 1848 negative heterostereotypes of at least those Poles that lived in Prussia increased as a result of growing national tensions during the course of the German nation-building process. These stereotypes often went hand in hand with autostereotypes that stressed the Germans' moral and civilizing superiority over the Poles (Kosman 1996; Pleitner 2001). For example, the term *Polnische Wirtschaft* (a "Polish state of affairs") was in widespread pejorative use. In fact, right up until a few years ago it was sometimes used to describe political or economic structures that simply do not work (Orlowski 1996).

It is striking, however, that for a long time it was not just the statistics that omitted to distinguish between Polish- and German-speaking criminals. On initial observation, this also appears to be true of most authors writing on crime up until the end of the nineteenth century. Between the 1850s and 1890s, even in the light of the already (by the middle of the century) noticeable east-west gradient in crime statistics, any question of the nationality or race of offenders rarely appeared — on condition, that is, that the cases did not involve Jews or "Gypsies." Many authors cited instead economic and social deprivation as the main explanation for crime in the eastern provinces well into the 1880s (Triest 1863; Verhältniss 1857; Aschrott 1884; Illing 1885; Engel 1865).

Thus criminal law reformer Hermann von Valentini, in an exposition published in 1869, addressed in detail the issue of the Prussian "*Verbrecherthum*" (criminal world). His work discussed criminality in the eastern provinces, and in particular in the province of Posen. Although he shared the opinion of many of his contemporaries that there was a large cultural gap between Germans and Poles in these regions, in his view there was no substantial "criminal impulse" ("*verbrecherischer Sinn*") among the local population. For him the frequent occurrence of crimes against property would seem to indicate material and intellectual wants. He thought it no wonder that, given the "tragic conditions" suffered in the province, so many crimes against property were to be seen (1869: 33–34). And one can see his point: many localities in the eastern provinces suffered miserable living conditions. For example, wages were markedly lower than in other parts of Prussia. This affected the rural and industrial workforce, both of which consisted mostly of Poles (Stöwesand 1910: 134–153). In addition, the average life expectancy in areas inhabited by Poles was also lower (Johnson 1995: 174–177).

Alfred Kurella, medical director of the provincial lunatic asylum at Brieg in Lower Silesia and the most ardent advocate of Lombroso's ideas, was one of the first to break with this mode of thinking (Zimmermann 2006: 135–144). In his 1893 work *Naturgeschichte des Verbrechers* (Natural History of the Criminal) he echoed Lombroso's ideas and discussed the alleged criminogenic "racial" predispositions of the Polish inhabitants of Prussia in his chapter on "Heredity and Biological Factors in Criminal Dispositions." Kurella argued that the Poles were "degenerate" due to their historical underdevelopment, and that low wages, unhygienic housing, and bad nutrition were a hindrance to their development. In such conditions, "sympathetic feelings, modesty, sincerity, self-control are neither developed nor inherited; the population must degenerate, as is so often the case in the eastern provinces of Prussia with their terrifyingly high and growing criminality" (1893: 172–173).[7]

Although Kurella recognized the role played by material and social deprivation, his argumentative approach was clearly biologicalistic. Initially, his ideas found no great resonance and most authors remained unconvinced that the eastern provinces' high crime rates could be deemed a sign of degeneration. Perhaps the best-known example of such authors is Gustav Aschaffenburg, head physician of the observation department for mentally ill criminals in Halle an der Saale, who rejected Kurella's arguments and stressed economic deprivation as a central reason for the high crime rates in the eastern provinces (Aschaffenburg 1903: 201, 204). This view supported calls for stronger social prophylaxis, such as the construction of poor houses and schools, and the introduction of workers' insurance. As Aschaffenburg put it, while "racial configurations" could not be influenced, "economic hardship" and alcohol problems, in contrast, could be actively tackled (ibid.: 45).

In the last decade of the nineteenth century, and in the wake of the publication of the aforementioned crime statistics—which enjoyed considerable popularity among scholars as well as in the press—regional studies of criminality began to emerge. This professionalized research, with its fascination for statistics, placed the general issue of crime in the eastern provinces, and in particular within the Polish population, on the agenda. It is hardly a coincidence that this interest was increasing during a period in which Prussian policies of Germanization and settlement were pouring fresh fuel on the German-Polish national struggle (Blanke 1981; Grabowski 1998; Jaworski 1986). A paradigm shift occurred in the discussion on crime during this time, and the question of race or nationality was allocated greater importance.

A particularly radical example of the instrumentalization of criminology as evidence for an alleged racial predisposition to crime is provided by retired Breslau district court judge Paul Frauenstädt. In 1906 he published a study on selected areas of the eastern provinces in the *Zeitschrift für Sozialwissenschaft* (Journal for Social Science). He concluded that, in cases of grievous physical assault and theft, areas whose population contained a Polish majority almost always exhibited more disturbing statistics than did regions with a mainly German population (1906: 574). In his conclusion he referred to the aforementioned statistical evidence that crime in the Rhineland and in Westphalia had increased since the turn of the century. This, Frauenstädt argued in line with his earlier claims, was a result of Polish migrant labor, as "in every place into which the Poles infiltrate and gain a foothold, an immediate worsening of conditions can be seen" (ibid.: 582).[8]

Since Frauenstädt made no secret of his anti-Polish attitude in other passages of his article, it is clear that what we are dealing with here is primarily a politically motivated text. But such opinions were defended by authors with more scholarly aspirations, and not only by those whose studies shared Frauenstädt's nationalist motivations. Thus Frauenstädt can hardly be regarded as an isolated case (Gau "Ruhr und Lippe" 1901; Schulze 1909: 88–89; Rüdin 1906). Although there were indeed authors who discussed the topic in a more neutral manner (Galle 1908; Blau 1903), all considered it necessary to debate the question of nationality or race. Even if most continued to reject Kurella's argument appealing to degeneration, negative stereotypes certainly influenced their analysis.

For example, one study considered the possibility of Poles being responsible for the high rate of physical assault in the province of Posen: "The Pole is described by all experts on the region as obsequious and scheming. Well-built and very agile, he is lively and easily peeved, lawless with a violent temper" (Stöwesand 1910: 86).[9] It was thus only natural that Polish people resorted to physical violence in arguments, and references to supposed "Kenner des Landes" (very roughly, "experts on the country") were considered enough by the author to legitimize such a claim. In light of such ethnically based ascriptions of criminality, it is clear that a shift had occurred: the new discipline of criminology was now helping to establish the nationality or race of an offender as an analytical category to be included in the study of his criminality. In commentaries on crime statistics by the Office of Imperial Statistics from the turn of the century onward there are increasing references to

Polish criminals. Even moderate authors called for the inclusion of nationality in the collation of crime statistics, declaring that this question ultimately demanded further investigation (Stöwesand 1910: 176; Galle 1913: 169).

How did Polish minority authors deal with this issue? An example is provided by the 1908 Polish-language study titled *O przyczynach występków i sposobie ich zwalczania* (The Causes of Crime and Ways to Conquer It), which conceded that there was a higher crime rate in the Polish population due to their "lower cultural level," particularly among the working class, but which stressed the economic destitution of the eastern provinces (Stark 1908: 22–23). The study called for an improvement in education and economic conditions. The 1905 article *Polacy w świetle niemieckiej statystyki kryminalnej* (The Poles in German Crime Statistics) considered several issues, highlighting the tense political situation in terms of its adverse effect on overall statistics in relation to crime (Sygma 1905: 126).

This latter example indicates a potentially important factor in the causes of higher crime rates in the Prussian eastern provinces as recorded in crime statistics: the extent to which the national struggle—fought out between state authorities, the judiciary, and the police, as well as the national press on the one side and the Polish national movement on the other—influenced both rates of conviction and how crime was analyzed. Regional studies may be expected to be especially useful in identifying any such possible connection, since the conflict took place under the particular conditions that obtained at the time in the eastern provinces.

Crime in the Prussian Province of Posen

Due to its demographic makeup and high crime rate, the province of Posen proffers an ideal case for a regional study in the history of criminality in the area. The province consisted of the administrative district of Posen, hosting a Polish population of around 70 percent in 1910, and the administrative district of Bromberg, whose Polish population was approximately 52 percent. Crime rates in both these administrative districts were consistently high.

Records also show that levels of poverty in the province of Posen were particularly high in areas containing a large Polish population. Nevertheless, crime statistics for precisely this province also expose the shaky foundations upon which ethnically charged discourses on criminality were based. For instance, in the district of Bromberg, economically deprived areas with large German populations also suffered high conviction rates. Thus, even adhering to the logic of the period's discourse on the causes of crime, it was evident that it was not nationality or race but social circumstance that was largely responsible for much of the crime that occurred at the time (Stöwesand 1910: 68).

This becomes clear in the light of the substantial general decline in overall crime around the turn of the century in the eastern provinces of Prussia, which went hand in hand with a faster-than-average decline in the number of property crimes for the same region. This can be attributed to two factors: firstly, improved economic circumstances, and secondly, the increasingly successful "organic work" of the Polish national movement, which aimed at encouraging self-reliance in social and national matters (Hagen 1972; Trzeciakowski 1999).

Economic hardship might therefore go some way toward explaining the high rates of theft at the time. To put it another way, any improvement in the economic situation may certainly help us to understand the decline of such rates. Yet such factors will not necessarily explain the high figure for violent crimes that, in contrast to property crimes, did not show any decline as the nineteenth century drew to a close. This topic leads us back to the question of German-Polish antagonism. As a 1903 study of crime in the province of West Prussia surmised: "But it is quite natural that, in places where two nationalities confront one another in considerable numbers, frequent frictions should occur between the two leading to the commission of crimes, especially when on both sides national hatred is unfortunately enflamed. And it is no doubt the Poles more than the Germans who break the law in this regard, because it is the former who feel that they are being suppressed by the latter" (Blau 1903: 126–127).[10] In the province of Posen there are indeed statistics that show a higher incidence of violent crimes in areas with a mixed population. It seems likely that this national conflict could have contributed to the higher crime rate in a variety of ways. A sample of records from Berlin and Posen archives also show that the higher figures on physical assault may have been the result of disputes between Poles and Germans.[11] This suspicion is further substantiated by police reports, as well as the monthly situation reports that were submitted by the individual administrative districts.

To cite one example, in 1872, on the occasion of a by-election for the Prussian parliament in a village in the province of Posen, a fight broke out between Poles and Germans, leaving many injured.[12] The cause was evidently the Germans' refusal to accept the election result. It can thus be presumed that this and similar confrontations could in no way always be ascribed to the actions of Poles who felt themselves under

German suppression. In the province of Posen—as elsewhere—such incidents were not recorded separately as political crimes, but rather as ordinary offences. In cases of serious physical assault, the police and the legal system intervened, and if their action resulted in a conviction, the assault would be included in crime statistics. However, if the crime was a minor physical assault—in such cases the offence was classified as an *Antragsdelikt*—a legal trial occurred only if those involved had a personal interest in initiating such a process and one or more offenders were then convicted.

It seems certain, however, that the high rates of violent crimes in the eastern provinces were due to more than just physical disputes between Poles and Germans. The impact of this national antagonism is much more likely to have appeared in other ways, such as in discrimination against Poles in court. The fact that a particularly large number of convictions were documented in these areas could, after all, be due to the law enforcement authorities in other parts of the Empire having been less strict in their enforcement of the law. It would therefore seem a useful exercise to take a look at how well native Polish speakers were represented in the judiciary and the police force.

An 1896 report by the Higher Regional Court for the Imperial Ministry of Justice makes clear that, almost without exception, Polish defendants were brought before German lawyers and judges.[13] There had always been a paucity of Polish judges in the province of Posen. For example, out of a total of 242 trial judges in 1883, only 30 were Polish (Wilhelm 2010: 189–190; Ormond 1994: 456–469). Furthermore, in a secret directive issued in 1896, the Ministry of Justice decreed that civil servants of Polish nationality should "as a rule" be posted to "purely German" areas.[14] The provincial administration in Posen showed particular zeal in this matter, a circumstance that irritated even the Ministry for Justice in Berlin, as it was concerned to avoid social conflict and wanted its directive to be enforced discreetly in order to avoid any political discussion on the matter.[15] Thus it seems that the periphery in Posen was sometimes more zealous than central powers in Berlin.

The situation in relation to the police was similar: sometimes "Polish" gendarmes, a category that often included German gendarmes married to Polish women, would be posted to areas largely populated by Germans (Jessen 1991: 322). Furthermore, from 1876 on, German became the only officially accepted language in court, thus requiring the use of interpreters (Wilhelm 2010: 135–137). A study of the files of the Higher Regional Court of Posen, held in the State Archive of Poznań, reveals one possible influence of national-related conflict on judicial practice that took a different form.[16] The *Deutscher Ostmarkenverein* (German Society of the Eastern Marches) had called for a toughening up of procedures, demanding that the Higher Regional Court hand down harsher punishments to Poles convicted of (political) defamation. The offence mentioned is important here because defamation, like minor physical assault, constituted an *Antragsdelikt*. Since any such toughening up of procedures could be expected to cause the crimes of defamation and minor physical assault to have a greater impact on general crime statistics, it seems reasonable to assume that national-related conflicts could have had a more or less direct influence on contemporary crime statistics.

In addition, the increased attention paid to the Polish-speaking population by the Prussian police is of significance—and it was well known that such police attention intensified as the national conflict between Germans and Poles deepened. It may have been this, and not higher crime rates, that led to the more concentrated presence of gendarmes in rural areas and of police officers in the city of Posen as compared to the rest of the Empire from the end of the nineteenth century on (Jessen 1991: 357–358). A citizen of the *Kaiserreich* whose native language was Polish could thus expect to be subjected to more intrusive and systematic surveillance from the police. Nevertheless, it is difficult to produce empirical evidence to prove a connection between criminality and/or criminalization motivated by nationalism on the one hand, and higher crime rates in areas with large Polish populations on the other.

The foregoing findings should be understood to be preliminary, and have yet to be confirmed in more detailed case studies.[17] Nonetheless, questions emerge on a number of levels relating to the consequences of heightened social and police vigilance, as well as the effect of that vigilance on the data collected at the time. We are left with a cluster of possible explanations for the high crime rates obtaining in the eastern provinces of Prussia. The influence of German-Polish antagonisms on both crime figures and their interpretation should in any case be much clearer by now.

Conclusion

According to contemporary statistics, rates of crime in the Prussian eastern provinces had been markedly higher than in other parts of Prussia, not only since 1882, but for the previous decades as well. This trend affected two categories of crimes in parallel: namely violent offences (meaning mostly physical assault) and crimes against property (mostly theft). The currently available evidence suggests that the cause of high crime rates in the eastern provinces can be found in the interplay of economic and social destitution on the one hand, and national antagonisms on the other. National-related conflict in particular played an increasingly important role in crime figures from the last third of the nineteenth century onward. Quite apart from the fact that this struggle often took on violent form for both Germans and Poles, it also had a massive influence on how criminality was attributed.

This development was connected with a shift in German national identity and in its view of its own crime policies. After all, the newly formed *Kaiserreich* had introduced overall crime statistics to get a comprehensive picture of crime within its territory. But in the east in particular the new statistics revealed the problem as allegedly having an ethnic or "racial" background. Many believed they had identified the reason for the statistically verified east-west gradient in crime rates that the statistics provided. Their explanation—the assumed nexus between high crime rates and the geographical distribution of Poles—serves as clear proof that a growing process of Othering was being practiced by a number of legal officials and criminologists. This Othering should be seen in interplay with the social structures mentioned above, especially the social and economic inequality between the dominant ethnic Germans and a minority population labeled as alien.

Due to these conditions, people were becoming increasingly concerned with questions of "us" and the "other"—that is, with discourses and practices of inclusion and exclusion. In keeping with this labeling process, the attribution of criminality to the Other was a logical consequence of this pattern of thinking (in our case, the portion of the population experienced as foreign happened to be Polish, though "Gypsies," Jews, and other groups were also often treated similarly). Tellingly, the fact that other areas of Germany (parts of Bavaria, for example) also had high levels of criminal convictions was of no, or only marginal, importance in most contemporary authors' interpretation of crime. There are clear parallels to be drawn here with other countries: in addition to the discussion on Afro-Americans cited above, there are also similarities with the alleged comparative propensity among Irish immigrants to Great Britain to commit crime (Swift 1989; 2005; Summers 2009).

In the German Empire, diffuse stereotypes portraying the Poles as immoral and backward were given official confirmation and corroboration on the basis of statistical data on crime and by the criminology that relied on these data. A number of German authors of the newly established science of criminology—in particular Alfred Kurella—played a key role in this development. This was especially so due to the fact that, in line with an increasing trend toward undertaking regional studies in criminology and crime statistics, several of them simultaneously chose to focus precisely on the eastern provinces of the German Empire. In contrast to the intellectual traditions of the preceding decades, in which higher crime rates in the east had been interpreted as mainly the result of economic and social hardship, some authors began establishing race or nationality as a category in their analysis of the causes of crime. In doing so, they became part of a transnational trend in criminology—irrespective of whether they were advocates of Cesare Lombroso or not.

In other words, where the "racial" or "national" background of offenders had previously barely been an issue, it was to become a concern from the end of the nineteenth century on. Although the discussions about the extent to which race and nationality should be seen as a criminogenic factor were complex, many authors of such criminological studies, as shown above, continued adamantly to reject any claim that such considerations might be the cause of any heightened tendency toward criminality. Furthermore, several authors used the terms "race" and "nationality" synonymously—and quite vaguely—to describe cultural differences between parts of the population of the Empire, so that the term "race" was often used in a sense other than its meaning in racial anthropology.

However, issues of race or nationality were to exert an ever greater influence on German criminology, simply because they became an increasing part of discussions—whether an author was arguing along racial lines or not. Thus criminologists established the idea of a difference that allegedly existed between Germans and ethnic Others in relation to criminal behavior. On the one hand, even moderate authors were swayed by traditional stereotypes and, on the other, they began reinforcing those stereotypes with what they purported to be scientific evidence.

In the long run a growing number of official representatives of the Empire and a (probably large) portion of the German population appeared to have internalized a specific narrative of a backward and potentially criminal Slavic Polish population living in the "Wild East" (Kopp 2012), which was seen as a danger to the newly founded *Kaiserreich* and its hard-working and law-abiding ethnically German citizens.[18] From then on it would only be a small adjustment to revise their previously held positions, as was shown by the remarkable example of prominent German criminologist Gustav Aschaffenburg, who argued at the beginning of the twentieth century against racial determinism in criminology, but by 1923 wrote of the "inherent degeneration of the [Slavic] race" in the (former) eastern provinces as an important cause for high crime rates in these regions (Galassi 2004: 202).

Thus it can be seen that the characterization of German mastery over the Polish minority as a colonial relationship might well be considered a fruitful approach in analysis of ethnically based criminalization in the *Kaiserreich*. The way in which backwardness and behavioral deviancy was ascribed to the Polish portion of the population strongly suggests a colonial pattern of interpretation at the time. Walther Stöwesand's unexplained figure of the *"Kenner des Landes"* speaks volumes, as it made connections between already existing narratives containing racial or national stereotyping and seemingly objective data and analysis. Thus both imaginative and aesthetic narratives on the one hand and "scientific" approaches such as criminological interpretations of crime statistics on the other suited each other very well. This process of criminalization, whose motor was provided by "experts"—mostly statisticians, criminologists, and administrators of justice—had the effect of contributing further to the social marginalization of the Polish population of the Empire.

This process also may have substantially reinforced social hierarchies in the *Kaiserreich* and hegemonic practices in the form of social (police) control. Furthermore, some lawyers would have felt the need to take sides in the national conflict between Germans and Poles in the eastern provinces. It would seem credible that all this would in turn have had the direct effect of putting Poles at a disadvantage in court proceedings, but this supposition can only really be proven on the basis of detailed regional studies. In any case it is true to say that, since crime rates function as indicators of social temperature (Schwerhoff 1999: 9), the east-west gradient charted in contemporary crime statistics indicates an unhealthy state of affairs. This assessment, however, has much less to do with the state of the relevant crime figures in themselves than it does with the way in which those statistics were collated and interpreted.

Translated by Carly McLaughlin and Jaime Hyland

Volker Zimmermann is research assistant at the Collegium Carolinum (Research Institute for the History of the Czech Lands and Slovakia) in Munich and extraordinary (*außerplanmäßiger*) professor for contemporary history and eastern European history at Heinrich Heine University in Düsseldorf. From 2000 to 2006 he worked as research assistant at the Institute for Culture and History of the Germans in Eastern Europe at Heinrich Heine University and from 2006 to 2010 he taught at Charles University in Prague. He has published a number of monographs, anthologies, and articles on German and central European history (especially Czech and Czech-German history).

Notes

1. "... zu hoffen, daß es der deutschen Kultur mit der Zeit gelingen wird, die in dem Volkscharakter [der Polen] liegende Neigung zur Kriminalität zu vermindern."
2. "Als die wichtigste soziale Gruppe kommt in erster Linie die Rasse in Betracht. Die Rasse ist es, die die Bildung und die erste gesellschaftliche Entwicklung des gesellschaftlichen Lebens bestimmt hat. ... Es erscheint mir ganz zweifellos, dass auch die Gestaltung der Kriminalität durch Rasseneinflüsse bestimmt wird."
3. "Rassenbiologische[n] Struktur"; "in sich eine Wurzel des Verbrechens."
4. "Es ist in diesem ersten Jahre der Verarbeitung ... noch nicht angezeigt, Kartenbilder der Kriminalität zu entwerfen. ... Es darf aber schon jetzt gesagt werden, daß aller Wahrscheinlichkeit nach dieselbe eine ziemlich regelmäßige Abnahme der Kriminalität von Osten nach Westen zeigen würden."
5. "Verbrechen und Vergehen gegen Reichgesetze überhaupt im Jahre 1882 (nach Verwaltungsgebieten). Verurteilte auf 100.000 Einwohner im strafmündigen Alter."
6. "... die im Westen des Staates wahrnehmbare geringere verbrecherische Thätigkeit, in Vergleichung mit dem Osten desselben, wohl nicht in Abrede stellen."
7. "... sympathische Gefühle, Schamhaftigkeit, Ehrlichkeit, Selbstbeherrschung nicht entwickeln und vererben, die Bevölkerung muss degenerieren, wie es in den östlichen Provinzen Preussens mit ihrer erschreckend hohen, erschreckend wachsenden Kriminalität so oft der Fall ist."
8. "Überall wo das Polentum eindringt und festen Fuß faßt, zeigt sich sofort eine Verschlechterung der kriminalistischen Verhältnisse."
9. "Der Pole wird von allen Kennern des Landes als gefallsüchtig und ränkeliebend geschildert. Von kräftigem Körperbau und großer Gewandtheit ist er lebhaft und leicht reizbar, zügellos und jähzornig."
10. "Es ist aber ganz natürlich, daß, wo sich zwei Nationalitäten in erheblicher Stärke gegenüberstehen, vielfach Reibungen zwischen beiden entstehen, die dann zu Verbrechen führen, zumal wenn, auf beiden Seiten leider, der Nationalitätenhaß entfacht wird. Und es wird dabei gewiß mehr von den Polen als von den Deutschen delinquiert, da sich jene diesen gegenüber als die Unterdrückten fühlen."
11. For example, the Archiwum Państwowe, Poznań (State Archive Poznań, subsequently APP), Oberlandesgericht Posen (Higher Regional Court Poznań) 1826–1919, Sygn. 120: Upkeep of Public Peace and Order, 1888–1919, pp. 1–8, 18, 246–247.
12. Geheimes Staatsarchiv Preußischer Kulturbesitz, Berlin (Secret State Archives Prussian Cultural Heritage Foundation, Berlin, subsequently GStA), I HA Rep. 77 Tit. 427 Nr. 1^{III}, Ministerium des Innern, II. Abteilung (Ministry of the Interior, II. Department): Papers concerning the security situation and the administration of the security police in the Grand Duchy of Posen; specifically in the administrative district of Posen, pp. 176–177.

13. Minister of justice to the president of the Higher Regional Court on 19 October 1896 and report by the president of the Higher Regional Court of 9 November 1896. APP, Oberlandesgericht Posen 1826–1919, Sygn. 1, pp. 17–25.
14. Minister of justice to the president of the Higher Regional Court of Posen on 10 November 1897 [confidential]. APP, Oberlandesgericht Posen 1826–1919, Sygn. 8, pp. 1–3.
15. Minister of Justice to the president of the Higher Regional Court of Posen on 9 December 1897 [confidential]. APP, Oberlandesgericht Posen 1826–1919, Sygn. 8, no page numbers.
16. APP, Oberlandesgericht Posen 1826–1919, Sygn. 2, pp. 1–15, 170–186, 199–201; APP, Oberlandesgericht Posen 1826–1919, Sygn. 9: Reports warranted by the justice minister and to be filed with him in special circumstances, pp. 5–13; 29–40.
17. Such a detailed study is planned as part of my research project "Die Kriminalität der Anderen. Ethnische Zuschreibung von Kriminalität am Beispiel der preußischen Ostprovinzen und der böhmischen Länder (1871 bis 1914)" (The Crimes of Others: Ethnically based ascription of criminality in the eastern provinces of Prussia and the Bohemian Lands [1871 to 1914]).
18. Here comparisons with other states are also revealing—for example with Victorian England, where murder was interpreted as not being in keeping with "English identity." This implied that it was "outsiders" or "others" (not necessarily ethnic others) who were responsible (Wiener 2004).

References

Aschaffenburg, G. 1903. *Das Verbrechen und seine Bekämpfung. Criminalpsychologie für Mediciner, Juristen und Sociologen. Ein Beitrag zur Reform der Strafgesetzgebung*. Heidelberg.

Aschrott, P. F. 1884. "Betrachtungen über die Bewegung der Kriminalität in Preußen während der Jahre 1872 bis 1881." *Jahrbuch für Gesetzgebung, Verwaltung und Volkswirtschaft im Deutschen Reich* 8: 185–223.

Becker, P. 2002. *Verderbnis und Entartung. Eine Geschichte der Kriminologie des 19. Jahrhunderts als Diskurs und Praxis*. Göttingen.

Belzyt, L. 1998. *Sprachliche Minderheiten im preußischen Staat 1815–1914. Die preußische Sprachenstatistik in Bearbeitung und Kommentar*. Marburg.

Blanke, R. 1981. *Prussian Poland in the German Empire, 1871–1900*. Boulder, CO.

Blau, B. 1903. *Kriminalstatistische Untersuchung der Kreise Marienwerder und Thorn. Zugleich ein Beitrag zur Methodik kriminalstatistischer Untersuchungen*. Berlin.

Brückweh, K. 2015. *Menschen zählen: Wissensproduktion durch britische Volkszählungen und Umfragen vom 19. Jahrhundert bis ins digitale Zeitalter*. Berlin.

Cinnirella, M. 1997. "Ethnic and National Stereotypes: A Social Identity Perspective." In *Beyond Pug's Tour: National and Ethnic Stereotyping in Theory and Practice*, ed. C. C. Barfoot. Amsterdam, 37–51.

Conrad, S. 2006. *Globalisierung und Nation im Deutschen Kaiserreich*. Munich.

Du Bois, W. E. B. 1899. *The Philadelphia Negro: A Social Study*. Philadelphia, PA.
Engbring-Romang, U. 2005. "Zur Kriminalisierung der Zigeuner." In *Diebstahl im Blick? Zur Kriminalisierung der "Zigeuner,"* ed. U. Engbring-Romang. Seeheim, 19–37.
Engel, [E.]. 1865. "Die Frequenz der Strafanstalten für Zuchthausträflinge in der preussischen Monarchie während der Jahre 1858 bis mit 1863." *Zeitschrift des Königlich Preussischen Statistischen Bureaus* 5, nos. 11/12: 278–318.
Frauenstädt, [P.]. 1906. "Die preußischen Ostprovinzen in kriminalgeographischer Beleuchtung." *Zeitschrift für Sozialwissenschaft* 9: 570–583.
Gabbidon, S. L. 2007. *Criminological Perspectives on Race and Crime*. New York.
Galassi, S. 2004. *Kriminologie im Deutschen Kaiserreich. Geschichte einer gebrochenen Verwissenschaftlichung*. Stuttgart.
Galle, J. 1908. "Untersuchungen über die Kriminalität in der Provinz Schlesien." *Der Gerichtssaal* 71/72, nos. 1/2: 42–117, 321–357.
———. 1913. "Kriminstatistik für das Jahr 1909." *Der Gerichtssaal* 80: 168–174.
Gau "Ruhr und Lippe" des Alldeutschen Verbandes, ed. 1901. *Die Polen im Rheinisch-westfälischen Steinkohlen-Bezirke. Mit einem statistischen Anhang, einer Sammlung polnischer Lieder und 2 Karten*. Munich.
Gibson, M. 2002. *Born to Crime: Cesare Lombroso and the Origins of Biological Criminology*. Westport, CT.
Grabowski, S. 1998. *Deutscher und polnischer Nationalismus. Der Deutsche Ostmarkenverein und die polnische Straż 1894–1914*. Marburg.
Greene Taylor, H., and S. L. Gabbidon. 2009. *Encyclopedia of Race and Crime*, 2 vols. Los Angeles, CA.
Hagen, W. W. 1972. "National Solidarity and Organic Work in Prussian Poland, 1815–1914." *Journal of Modern History* 44, no.1: 38-64.
Hall, C., K. McClelland, and J. Rendall. 2000. "Introduction." In *Defining the Victorian Nation: Class, Race, Gender, and the Reform Act of 1867*, eds. C. Hall, K. McClelland, and J. Rendall. Cambridge, 1–70.
Heitzeg, N. A. 2011. "Differentials in Deviance: Race, Class, Gender, and Age." In *The Routledge Handbook of Deviant Behavior*, ed. C. D. Bryant. New York, 53–59.
Illing, [J.]. 1885. "Die Zahlen der Criminalität in Preußen 1854–1884." *Zeitschrift des Königlich Preussischen Statistischen Bureaus* 25: 73–92.
Jaworski, R. 1986. *Handel und Gewerbe im Nationalitätenkampf. Studien zur Wirtschaftsgesinnung der Polen in der Provinz Posen 1871–1914*. Göttingen.
Jessen, R. 1991. *Polizei im Industrierevier. Modernisierung und Herrschaftspraxis im westfälischen Ruhrgebiet 1848–1914*. Göttingen.
Johnson, E. 1995. *Urbanization and Crime, Germany 1871–1914*. Cambridge et al.
Kleßmann, C. 1978. *Polnische Bergarbeiter im Ruhrgebiet, 1870–1945. Soziale Integration und nationale Subkultur einer Minderheit in der deutschen Industriegesellschaft*. Göttingen.
Kopp, K. 2012. *Germany's Wild East: Constructing Poland as Colonial Space*. Ann Arbor, MI.
Kosman, M. 1996. "Zbrodniarze i nieudacznicy? Uwagi o nowych pracach o dziejach stereotypów polsko-niemieckich i charakterze narodowym, ze szczególnym uwzględnieniem okresu rozbiorów (1772–1815)." *Przegląd zachodni* 52, no. 1: 121–135.

Kriminalstatistik für das Jahr 1882, ed. Reichs-Justizamt and kaiserliches Statistisches Amt. Berlin, 1884; reprint Osnabrück, 1973.

Kriminalstatistik für das Jahr 1902, ed. Reichs-Justizamt and kaiserliches Statistisches Amt. Berlin, 1904; reprint Osnabrück, 1976.

Kriminalstatistik für das Jahr 1912, ed. Reichs-Justizamt and kaiserliches Statistisches Amt. Berlin, 1914; reprint Osnabrück, 1977.

Kurella, H. 1893. *Naturgeschichte des Verbrechers. Gründzüge der criminellen Anthropologie und Criminalitätspsychologie für Gerichtsärzte, Psychiater, Juristen und Verwaltungsbeamte.* Stuttgart.

Liszt, F. von. 1903. "Die gesellschaftlichen Faktoren der Kriminalität. Vortrag am 21.9.1902 auf der Petersburger Tagung der I.K.V." *Zeitschrift für die gesamte Strafrechtswissenschaft* 23: 203–216.

Lucassen, L. 1997. "'Harmful Tramps': Police Professionalization and Gypsies in Germany, 1700–1945." *Crime, Déviance, Société* 1, no. 1: 29–50.

Melchers, A. 1992. *Kriminalstatistik im 19. Jahrhundert. Ein Beitrag zur Geschichte der Kriminalsoziologie und ihrer Methodik.* Frankfurt am Main.

Näcke, P. 1906. "Rasse und Verbrechen." *Archiv für Kriminal-Anthropologie und Kriminalistik* 25: 64–75.

Orlowski, H. 1996. *"Polnische Wirtschaft". Zum deutschen Polendiskurs der Neuzeit.* Wiesbaden.

Ormond, T. 1994. *Richterwürde und Regierungstreue. Dienstrecht, politische Betätigung und Disziplinierung der Richter in Preussen, Baden und Hessen 1866–1918.* Frankfurt am Main.

Pleitner, B. 2001. *Die "vernünftige" Nation. Zur Funktion von Stereotypen über Polen und Franzosen im deutschen nationalen Diskurs 1850 bis 1871.* Frankfurt am Main et al.

Pütter, B. 2006. *Kriminalität und Kriminalitätsdiskurs: Die Ost-West-Migration im westfälischen Ruhrgebiet vor 1914.* Munich.

Rüdin, E. 1906. "Zur Mehr-Kriminalität des polnischen Elements." *Archiv für Rassen- und Gesellschafts-Biologie* 3, no. 6: 919–920.

Schmidt, D. 2007. "Zahl und Verbrechen. Kriminalstatistiken im internationalen Dialog." In *Die Internationalisierung von Strafrechtswissenschaft und Kriminalpolitik (1870–1930). Deutschland im Vergleich*, eds. S. Kespers-Biermann and P. Overath. Berlin, 126–139.

Schulze, F. 1909. *Die polnische Zuwanderung im Ruhr-Revier und ihre Wirkungen.* Munich.

Schwerhoff, G. 1999. *Aktenkundig und gerichtsnotorisch. Einführung in die historische Kriminalitätsforschung.* Tübingen.

Stark, T. 1908. *O przyczynach występków i sposobie ich zwalczania.* Poznań.

Stöwesand, W. 1910. *Die Kriminalität in der Provinz Posen und ihre Ursachen.* Stuttgart.

Summers, V. 2009. "'A Source of Sad Annoyance': The Irish and Crime in South Wales, 1841–81." *Immigrants & Minorities* 27, no. 2/3: 300–316.

Swift, R. 1989. "Crime and the Irish in Nineteenth-Century Britain." In *The Irish in Britain, 1815–1939*, eds. R. Swift and S. Gilley. London, 163–182.

———. 2005. "Behaving Badly? Irish Migrants and 'Crime.'" In *Criminal Conversations: Victorian Crimes, Social Panic, and Moral Outrage*, eds. J. Rowbotham and K. Stevenson. Columbus, OH, 106–125.

Sygma, R. 1905. "Polacy w świetle niemieckiej statystyki kryminalnej." *Ruch chrześcijańsko-spoleczny. Dwutygodnik poświęcony sprawom spolecznym i gospodarczym* 4, nos. 5–6: 97–102, 121–126.
Tajfel, H. 1974. "Social Identity and Intergroup Behaviour." *Social Science Information* 13, no. 2: 65–93.
Ther, P. 2004. "Deutsche Geschichte als imperiale Geschichte. Polen, slawophone Minderheiten und das Kaiserreich als kontinentales Empire." In *Das Kaiserreich transnational. Deutschland in der Welt 1871–1914*, eds. S. Conrad and J. Osterhammel. Göttingen, 129–148.
Thomas-Olalde, O., and A. Velho. 2011. "Othering and its Effects: Exploring the Concept." In *Writing Postcolonial Histories of Intercultural Education*, eds. H. Niedrig and C. Ydesen. Frankfurt am Main, 27–51.
[Geh. Justizrath, Berlin] Triest. 1863. "Beiträge zur Criminal- und Strafanstalts-Statistik Preussens. Teil II." *Zeitschrift des Königlichen Preussischen Statistischen Bureaus* 3, no. 7: 169–192.
Trzeciakowski, L. 1999. "Wielkopolski program samomodernizacji – kształtowanie się nowoczesnego społeczeństwa." In *Samomodernizacja społeczeństw w XIX wieku. Irlandczycy, Czesi, Polacy*, eds. L. Trzeciakowski and K. Makowski. Poznań, 65–105.
Valentini, H. von. 1869. *Das Verbrecherthum im Preussischen Staate. Nebst Vorschlägen zu seiner Bekämpfung durch die Gesellschaft und durch die Reform der Strafvollstreckung.* Leipzig.
Verhältniss der katholischen zur evangelischen Konfession in Beziehung auf die in den letztverflossenen Jahren vor den Schwurgerichten des Preussischen Staats verhandelten Verbrechen. Ein Beitrag zur Criminal-Statistik, beachtenswerth für Katholiken und Evangelische. Münster, 1857.
Vyleta, D. M. 2007. *Crime, Jews and News: Vienna 1895–1914.* Oxford et al.
Weinberg, R. 1905–1906. "Physische Degeneration, Kriminalität und Rasse." *Monatsschrift für Kriminalpsychologie und Strafrechtsreform* 2: 720–730.
Wetzell, R. F. 2000. *Inventing the Criminal: A History of German Criminology, 1880–1945.* Chapel Hill, NC, et al.
Wiener, M. 2004. "Homicide and 'Englishness': Criminal Justice and National Identity in Victorian England." *National Identities* 6, no. 3: 203–214.
Wilhelm, U. 2010. *Das Deutsche Kaiserreich und seine Justiz. Justizkritik—politische Strafrechtsprechung—Justizpolitik.* Berlin.
Zimmermann, V. 2006. "'Der Einfluss des slavischen Elements'. Zeitgenössische Erklärungen für die Kriminalität im Osten des Deutschen Kaiserreichs." In *Die Deutschen und das östliche Europa. Aspekte einer vielfältigen Beziehungsgeschichte. Festschrift zum 65. Geburtstag von Prof. Dr. h.c. Detlef Brandes*, eds. D. Neutatz and V. Zimmermann. Essen, 131–147.
———. 2014. "Prowincja Poznańska jako ostoja przestępczości? O kryminalizacji polskiej ludności w Prusach i Cesarstwie Niemieckim w długim wieku XIX." In *Życie na skraju—marginesy społeczne wielkiego miasta*, eds. Z. Galor, B. Goryńska-Bittner, and S. Kalinowski. Bielefeld, 97–128.

7

Narratives of Race, Constructions of Community, and the Demand for Female Participation in German-Nationalist Movements in Austria and the German Reich

Johanna Gehmacher

In the early twentieth century, German Nationalist parties (Dostal 1995; Ohnezeit 2011) and *völkisch* organizations (Puschner 1996) participated in the development and popularization of the highly versatile concept of a "community of the people" (*Volksgemeinschaft*) (Bruendel 2004; Thamer 1998). While the term initially included a range of (also antihierarchical and emancipatory) meanings, German Nationalists increasingly claimed its use during the 1920s, and translated it into a concept of exclusionary categories. This chapter examines German Nationalist understandings of community in the context of contemporary political strategies and concepts. It takes the example of German Nationalist women's arguments for female political participation to illuminate their transformation and their interaction with categories such as *Volk* (people) and race. Analyzing the differences between the employment of the concept of a "community of the people" in Austria and Germany, it demonstrates the broader implications of gender as an analytical category as well as the importance of a comparative approach. This chapter will introduce and substantiate two key assumptions. First, the constructions of the boundary of a community, a people, or a nation—that is, the definition of who belongs to an imagined group and who is an outsider—are inextricably tied up with negotiations of participation within this entity. Therefore, arguments, such as the demand for female political participation, implicitly or explicitly refer always to the construction of the community as a whole. Second, the dissemination and transformation of an ideological concept (such as race) is always wed to metaphoric language of some kind. The development of a cultural or political concept inevitably entails a process of negotiation, in which one verbal image substitutes and contests the other. The meaning of the developing concept shifts slightly with each of these substitutions and contestations. For an analysis of the transformation of a specific concept, it is particularly helpful to address the ensuing surplus of possible meanings, or, in other cases, the reduction of a nuanced concept to one narrow term. It is the gap of meaning in all these "translations" that allows the concept of time to enter discourse analysis.

Narratives of Race

During the second half of the nineteenth century race became a powerful and popular concept that ranged far beyond the scientific context. Given its enormous tenacity over political shifts and fissures and its disastrous consequences, its efficacy seems to be self-evident. However, I suggest that its remarkable career as a *political* concept is rather surprising, and does need explaining.

At first glance, race in fact seemed to have only limited potential to become a main paradigm in political discourse. In contrast to other political ideas of the nineteenth and early twentieth centuries (like liberalism, conservatism, or socialism), race was a mongrel idea descended partly from natural science, and partly from agricultural stock breeding knowledge, and thus did not open much opportunity for political agency. It suggested a way of describing differences, but implicated no specific political perspective. As a potential practice, race must have been a rather humiliating idea for nineteenth- and early twentieth-century citizens. The fact that race-breeding initiatives like Willibald Hentschel's "*Mittgart*"-settlement, designated to produce a racial elite through the temporary marriage of one thousand women to one hundred men, had difficulties finding female participants (Puschner 2000: 175) reflects the reservations and even outrage triggered by the idea that humans could—and needed to—be reared like animals. So why and how could race become so popular? How did its dissemination spread from rather narrow scientific and pseudo-scientific circles to different fields of practice, such as politics and popular culture? In other words: how was race embedded in broader discursive contexts and social practices, and how should we deal with its diverse and even contradictory articulations? Discussing the example of political racism within German Nationalist parties in interwar Germany and Austria, I will argue that in German-speaking countries the fluid and inconsistent term "*Volksgemeinschaft*" was established as one of the channels through which the concept of race could be disseminated, and thus made acceptable, in a wider public.

Researching different forms of early twentieth-century political racism in Austria and Germany primarily means addressing anti-Jewish ideologies and activism. Modern anti-Semitism became the prevalent form of racism in east and central Europe, as it turned long-lasting religious and social prejudices into a racist ideology. Thus anti-Semitism can be described as a specific way of constructing inner outcasts in the face of recurrent crises in modernizing societies, and differs significantly from other forms of racism (Rürup 1987; Volkov 1978). The transformations of anti-Jewish sentiments and exclusionary practices during the nineteenth and early twentieth centuries should not only be reflected as an avenue to the dark side of modernization (Bauman 1998), but must also be understood as an example for the flexibility of anti-Semitism as a concept, as well as for its ability to take on different forms of differentiation and strategies of exclusion.

Constructions of Community and Transformations of the Concept of *Volksgemeinschaft*

The idea of a German *Volksgemeinschaft* is one of the crucial concepts with which anti-Semitism began to interact after the turn of the century. The overdetermined and highly symbolic connotations of the term cannot fully be translated into English. While *"Volk"* in the language of the time already referred to a group that is bound together by ideas of shared features and a sense of group membership, the meaning of *"Gemeinschaft"* added a specific quality. *Gemeinschaft* was used as an idealized, yet somewhat vague concept in opposition to "society." While society was associated with all the ambivalences of modernity, *Gemeinschaft* promised a community free from alienation, exploitation, and social conflict. The comparison of the two concepts goes back to the German sociologist Ferdinand Tönnies (1887), but has only later been formulated as ideologically contrasting. The term *Volksgemeinschaft* can therefore probably best be characterized by its strange doubling of the affirmation of belonging. This can be read as a semantic reference to modern societies' inability to ever fully grant social integration—their cohesion is rather built on incessantly changing promises.

Volksgemeinschaft became a widely spread notion during and after the First World War. Virtually all German and Austrian political parties, including the Social Democrats, adopted it for their different purposes (Bruendel 2004; Thamer 1998: 375ff; Heinsohn 2007). It has been argued convincingly that *Volksgemeinschaft* was a core term of interwar political language, which had to be addressed in some way by those seeking to gain political influence (Heinsohn 2010: 124). Notwithstanding its broad dissemination (and changing definitions), the concept became more and more connected to nationalist and *völkisch* ideologies. Commonly used in nationalist propaganda, the term *Volksgemeinschaft* increasingly came to signal an anti-Semitic stance. It also figured prominently in political discourses among right-wing women's groups, a fact that requires rigorous gender-based analysis (Gehmacher 1998a; Heinsohn 2000; 2002; Puschner 2000; Süchting-Hänger 2002; Streubel 2006; Schöck-Quinteros and Streubel 2007; Zettelbauer 2005). Eventually, *Volksgemeinschaft* emerged as a key term of National Socialist propaganda in the late 1920s—one of the many concepts the Nazis appropriated from other movements. After the National Socialist seizure of power it became a fundamental propagandistic instrument for the integration of the masses in the new regime (Haug 1980; Thamer 1990; Steinbacher 2007). The National Socialist propaganda of the *Volksgemeinschaft* particularly addressed populations who had either long been the clientele of political opponents (such as the workers), or whose formal participation was actually restricted by the National Socialist state—as was the case for women. If the use of *Volksgemeinschaft* thus indicates a tension between the need for integration on the one hand, and suspicion (e.g., against the political opposition) and marginalization (e.g., of women) on the other hand, it is worth asking for *specific* cases in which the term occurs.

The question of the way in which to engage with the ideological concept of *Volksgemeinschaft* in a historiographical context has been subject to recent and vivid theoretical discussion. Important historians of National Socialism have criticized the descriptive use of the term, thus leaving it sorely undertheorized (Mommsen 2007; Steuwer 2010). Critics caution that as an *analytical* concept, *Volksgemeinschaft* makes class differences within the NS society invisible. Other critics like Michael Wildt (2011) suggest that the ideological concept of *Volksgemeinschaft* needs to be analyzed (and thereby deconstructed) precisely because of its high propagandistic effect during the NS period—which implies to research the ways the concept works rather than to use it as an analytical tool. Responding to Ian Kershaw (2011), who explores the potentials and limitations of the concept, Wildt proposes an analysis of the way in which *Volksgemeinschaft* changed from a term of rather general use into an anti-Semitic and exclusionary rhetoric. Studying this transformation, he suggests, can make visible the steps by which ordinary Germans (and Austrians, we should add) came to accept and even support the exclusion and murder of the Jewish population (and other groups of the society). If this approach proves useful, an analysis of the development of the concept of *Volksgemeinschaft* may also further understanding of the dissemination and cultural appropriation of the concept of race. It will, however, be necessary to distinguish carefully between the development of a scientific concept and the analysis of a term so prominently used in the sources (for recent research on National Socialism that focuses on the concept of *Volksgemeinschaft*, see Steinbacher 2007; Bajohr and Wildt 2009; Schmiechen-Achermann 2011; for recent discussion on the concept, see Steber and Gotto 2014; Steber et al. 2014).

This chapter will focus on parties and organizations that helped the Nazis come to power—especially the German Nationalist parties *Deutschnationale Volkspartei* (German National People's Party, DNVP) in Germany and the *Großdeutsche Volkspartei* (Pan-German People's Party, GDVP) in Austria and the *völkisch* movement in which they were rooted. How did they use the notion of *Volksgemeinschaft*? Which different meanings does the term carry in different contexts? How and why does its meaning change, and how is it connected to the notion of race?

Struggles for Female Participation

To explore the interacting developments of concepts of community and narratives of race I will focus on arguments about women's political participation after the introduction of women's suffrage in the newly founded republics. I thereby not only want to show that a focus on the category of gender can contribute significantly to the analysis of political discourses and strategies. But I also argue that scholarship on political history that omits a gender perspective misses central aspects of its subject. I will take discourses on gender issues, such as female suffrage and higher education for girls, as examples, as I assume that the functionality and the transformations of the ideology of the *Volksgemeinschaft* can be observed particularly well in a context rife with tension and ambivalence surrounding the issue of integration.

In Germany and Austria, universal suffrage was implemented after the First World War (Bader-Zaar 2009). In both countries this implementation entailed formal political equality for women. The new situation was characterized by both big hopes and fears. Female suffrage became a symbol for the profound change both for those who welcomed the new political system, as well as for those who rejected the republic. It was introduced in Austria and Germany during a time in which these societies suffered from economic depression and considerable damages to national self-esteem—a situation that has been characterized as a severe crisis of modernity (Peukert 1987; Hanisch 1995). The political elites were confronted with the challenge of integrating the newly enfranchised female population—who, importantly, formed the majority of the electorates—into their activities on a practical and symbolic level. In the early phases of the new republics, most parties in fact did address women as voters. However, only the Social Democrats included them into their party structures in larger numbers (Gehmacher 2009; Hauch 1995; Riescher 2012). Right-wing and nationalist parties found the task most challenging, because their male followers often experienced the perceived national humiliation as a threat to their masculine identity. Although a number of German Nationalist women demanded equal participation in all political decisions, party leaders seldom saw the integration of women as an issue of major importance. I suggest that *Volksgemeinschaft* was one of the concepts that allowed parties to mediate between their male self-conception and the seemingly contradictory necessity to include women. Both in Germany and Austria, German Nationalist women organized their own structures within, and at the margins of, their respective parties. These German Nationalist women's organizations employed the term *Volksgemeinschaft* with remarkable frequency (Gehmacher 1998a; 1998b; Heinsohn 2000; 2002). It is thus worth asking how they appropriated and employed the concept to claim participation in their parties and in the broader political arena.

Analyzing these strategies can deliver relevant insights into the ways the ideological concept of *Volksgemeinschaft* worked. At the same time, such analysis can also shed light on the way in which *Volksgemeinschaft* as a political term played an important part in the dissemination and popularization of the concept of race. In the following, I will introduce the most relevant parties for this discussion by sketching the political contexts of their activities and by illustrating the way in which they used the ideology of the *Volksgemeinschaft* in their programs and propaganda. Drawing on research on women's nationalist organizations in Germany and female German Nationalism in Austria, I will then highlight some aspects of the marginalized integration of women into those parties. Finally, I will discuss two exemplary texts from women's nationalist organizations in both countries in greater detail.

German Nationalism in Postwar Germany and Austria

The German National People's Party (DNVP) in Germany and the Pan-German People's Party (GDVP) in Austria were both founded postwar, unifying a couple of smaller parties. While the DNVP was launched by a number of right-wing politicians in November 1918, the Austrian GDVP began as a union of former German Nationalist and German Liberal members of parliament in 1919, and was formally transformed into an independent party in August 1920. Both remained heterogeneous and in ongoing need of internal integration. The German nationalists in Germany as well as the Austrian German Nationalists combined nationalism with hierarchical concepts of society, and called for the revision of the peace treaties. The parties most obviously differed in their relation to the countries they were based in: while the German party affirmed the identity and legitimacy of their own nation, the Pan-Germans in Austria rejected any idea of an *Austrian* nationalism, instead envisioning a union with Germany. However, these principles were complicated by the two parties' actual political strategies. In Germany, the DNVP fluctuated between fundamental opposition against the state they denounced as the Weimar system, and phases of more constructive participation in political decision making. Between 1925 and 1928, the party cooperated in several governments on different levels (Heinsohn 2010; Ohnezeit 2011). In Austria, German Nationalists gathered in the GDVP formed a rather pragmatic bourgeois coalition with the governing (catholic) Christian social party for more than a decade, while rejecting the idea of an independent Austrian state ideologically (Ackerl 1967; Dostal 1995).

In the early 1930s, both parties aided the National Socialists ascent to power in their respective countries. In 1931, the DNVP and the extreme right association *Stahlhelm* formed an alliance with the National Socialists that was dubbed *Harzburger Front*. They eventually coalesced with the NSDAP in January 1933 (Sturm 2011). In Austria, the GDVP had continuously ruled together with the Christian Social Party between 1921 and 1932. However, in May 1933 the party formed an alliance with the Austrian National Socialists, a terrorist organization that was formally prohibited only a couple of weeks later (Pauley 1988: 86, 107).

In spite of their similar political goals and comparable historical role, the two parties differed significantly in crucial aspects reflecting differing political constellations in their countries. In Austria, the main ideological divide opened between the (catholic) Christian Socials and the (secularly oriented) Social Democrats, who were nearly equally strong, and militantly opposed to each other. The Pan-Germans represented a secular middle-class clientele and thereby filled an ideological gap left by the two bigger parties. The Pan-German program and propaganda covered a heterogeneous spectrum of bourgeois beliefs and *Weltanschauungen*, anticlerical attitudes, racist anti-Semitism, and *völkisch* nationalism. In Germany, the political spectrum was much more diverse. Among the reasons for this diversity is the confessional split between protestant and catholic regions as well as the economic development (which had created a much more independent middle class than in Austria). Moreover, in Germany the ties to the former monarchy were much stronger, while Austria had faced a more severe break with the old aristocratic elites. For all these reasons the German DNVP was just one among several conservative or nationalist "right-wing" parties. Most obviously, the German DNVP described itself as a Christian (i.e., protestant) party that wanted to restore "German glory," and decried the loss of the former monarchist system. In contrast, the Austrian GDVP promoted more secular models of life in its strictly catholic country, even integrating anticlerical positions into their propaganda. Moreover, the Austrian party did not share its German counterpart's nostalgia for the lost monarchy. After the fall of the Habsburg monarchy, Austrian German Nationalists vehemently demanded the integration of Austria into a greater German Reich. Due to this refusal to acknowledge Austria as a legitimate state they relied more on *völkisch* (i.e., ethnic and racist) concepts of community than nationalists in Germany (Ackerl 1967; Dostal 1995; Heinsohn 2010; Ohnezeit 2011).

Racist Anti-Semitism and the Concept of *Volksgemeinschaft*

As a term, *Volksgemeinschaft* often remained highly ambiguous. It could address a German state, a German nation or *Volk*, or an Aryan race. It was this ambiguity that made the concept so attractive in Austria. *Volksgemeinschaft* became a key concept of the Austrian GDVP's program. Passed at the 1920 party convention, the text conceived of *Volksgemeinschaft* as an anti-individualistic alternative to both "liberalism" and "Marxism": "Liberalism has loosened the solidarity among the people, Marxism has totally dissolved it. ... Therefore we hold the idea of *Volksgemeinschaft* against individualism."[1] The program of the GDVP situated *Volksgemeinschaft* in a paradoxical time structure: on the one hand, it was presented as an ideal concept for the future, while on the other hand it appeared as something that had already existed in the past and was now lost. This temporal paradox called for a plausible explanation why *Volksgemeinschaft* was lost and how it should be reconstructed. This was achieved by the construction of an external enemy. *Volksgemeinschaft* was thus constructed both as a lost state of social harmony and as a remedy against the disintegrating effects of modernity with a firm connection to anti-Semitic ideologies. The prominence of anti-Semitism was proclaimed at the party-congress in 1921: "The dominance of the Jewry is based on the destruction of the *Volksgemeinschaft*. The chains of Jewish power can therefore ... only be blasted by an anti-Semitism of action through law and self-help."[2] As one of the party founders, Josef Ursin (1863–1932), pointed out, the party had two political issues: unification with Germany and solving what he called the "Jewish question" (Die Verhandlungen des zweiten Reichsparteitages 1921: 61). In terms of concrete policy, *Volksgemeinschaft* therefore had two core goals: first, the inclusion of all ethnic Germans (whatever their national citizenship was) into a future ideal community, and second, the exclusion of all Jews (if they were Austrians or not) from that community. This programmatic position was accompanied by exclusionary statutes that denied "non-Aryans" membership in the GDVP. The GDVP was the only parliamentary party in Austria to formally exclude Jews. Still in Austria, anti-Semitism was a much broader phenomenon that had its roots in the late nineteenth century. Many cultural and sports clubs (among them the most prominent of the alpine clubs, the *Deutsch-Österreichischer Alpenverein* and the influential German Nationalist students' organizations) combined their German Nationalist tendencies with overt anti-Semitism, and barred Jews from their organizations (Achrainer 2012; Aicher 2012; Weidinger 2012). The increase of open violence against Jews in the late 1920s and in the early 1930s must be interpreted in that context.

The GDVP in Austria can be characterized as a party representative of the broad heterogeneous milieu of anti-Semites and German Nationalists in parliament. It linked the ideology of the *Volksgemeinschaft* with racist anti-Semitism on a programmatic as well as on a practical level and found most of their voters in the middle classes. Many supporters were university trained and of secular orientation. The situation in Germany was more complex. While anti-Semitism was an important issue in the DNVP in Germany, it had varying and disputed meanings. The DNVP, too, held the battle against what they considered a "fatal Jewish dominance" as part of their agenda (Deutschnationale Volkspartei, Grundsätze 1920). Still, there were recurrent statements that the "Jewish question" should not be put forward too openly and that such positions should be expressed more discreetly by referring to the cultural code of *völkisch* "Germanness." A controversy about the relevance of racist anti-Semitism in the party's agenda and the inclusion of members with Jewish background led to the split-off of the more radical anti-Semites and the founding the *Deutschvölkische Freiheitspartei* in 1922 (Bergmann 2012: 194). However, with the *Völkischer Reichsausschuß* a strong anti-Semitic fraction, which also counted a number of women members, remained inside the DNVP (Süchting-Hänger 2002: 270–274). It has been argued, though, that other, more conservative fractions in the party used anti-Semitism strategically to integrate the *völkisch* groups, but that they saw their main goal in the destruction of the democratic republic (Bernd 2004: 403ff.; cf. also Breuer 2010: 254; Striesow 1981: 448). Their anti-Semitism aimed at what they called the "Jewish spirit" (*jüdischer Geist*), which in their opinion could be observed in Jews as well as in non-Jews. Thus they were prepared to include conservative Jews whom they saw as the most effective propagandists for their nationalist and antidemocratic cause in their party (Bernd 2004: 405).

The German DNVP also linked anti-Semitism and *völkisch* ideology, yet the word *Volksgemeinschaft* did not have the same importance in the party's propaganda as with groups in Austria. "Fatherland" was the term used most frequently in the early years. This can probably be interpreted in the context of a broader use of the term *Volksgemeinschaft* in the political arena: in Germany, the term was closely linked with the concept of national unity during the First World War, and especially with the Social Democrats parliamentary consent with the war bonds in 1914 (Bruendel 2004). This stood in stark contrast with the connotations of the term in Austria. Consequently, its most important use to political parties in Germany was in imagining the overcoming of class difference. In the DNVP, *Volksgemeinschaft* remained a disputed concept throughout the 1920s (Heinsohn 2010: 134).

Demands for Female Participation and the Concept of *Volksgemeinschaft* in Germany

Despite their party's reservations, *Volksgemeinschaft* was a central term in the principles of women's agitation in Germany. Thus, the first case study will examine a program the party's women's organization approved in 1920 and published in 1922 as "principles of German Nationalist women's agitation" (*Grundsätze deutschnationaler Frauenarbeit*). The document provided guidelines for propaganda and organization. The first paragraph directly addressed the concept of *Volksgemeinschaft*: "As a member of the German *Volksgemeinschaft*, the German Nationalist woman pledges to the idea of the organic state as it is asserted by the DNVP on a Christian basis. ... She considers all questions of public life, including women's questions, not from an individualistic angle, but from a holistic perspective."[3] The importance of the concept was reaffirmed in the last paragraph, where German Nationalist women confessed their willingness to serve their people and the homeland with all their strength. Here, they also expressed their hope for the rejuvenation of the people (*Volkserneuerung*) and for a deeper *Volksgemeinschaft* (Grundsätze deutschnationaler Frauenarbeit 1922: 297).

While these formulations sound rather submissive, in fact they point to the central German Nationalist argumentation for women's equal integration into the political arena. The program mentions women serving the homeland and thereby addressed the link between women's war service and political rights; this was an argument in an election appeal shortly after the war. This previous pamphlet stated that women had won the right of political participation only through their wartime commitment. Now, women were greeted as "equal collaborators at the resurgence of the people."[4] Set against this background, references to duties and service in the principles of women's organization both concealed and named the question of women's rights, which remained an extremely conflicted issue within the party. In fact, in many of their publications German Nationalist women proclaimed that the community of the people could be restored only with the full participation of women. In other words: the ideal goal of the restored *Volksgemeinschaft* could only be reached by full integration of German women. Kirsten Heinsohn demonstrates that this argumentation was brought forward both from a perspective of gender differences and from an egalitarian perspective. She argues, for instance, that the theorist Magdalene von Tiling (1877–1974) deduced political rights from women's familial duties (Heinsohn 2010: 129f.). On the other hand, Heinsohn shows that Käthe Schirmacher (1865–1930) or Sophie Rogge Börner (1878–1955) contended that there was no principal difference between men and women, and therefore the *Volksgemeinschaft* could only be completed if all men and women were integrated on equal terms (ibid.: 127).

The 1922 "principles" make further reference to women's inclusion in their formulation of a position counter to individualism. This position directly addressed conservative critiques that condemned the women's movement as selfish and "individualistic." In contrast, German Nationalist women presented themselves as committed to the whole of the people's community (Grundsätze deutschnationaler Frauenarbeit 1922: 295). This meant that women were responsible for the *Volksgemeinschaft* as a whole—and not just for themselves or their families. Nationalist and *völkisch* women used this claim of broader responsibility as the main argument to present their cause as the legitimate successor of the women's movement. In their opinion, the movement had become irrelevant because it only addressed the women's question instead of considering the nation in its entirety. In other words: nationalist and *völkisch* women claimed that they had taken a substantial step beyond addressing isolated issues, and stood instead for a full political program.

Women's use of the term *Volksgemeinschaft* to argue for equal rights can be interpreted as ambivalent. On the one hand, it might have been promising to link women's rights agendas to this comprehensive entity, which also served as a utopian container of all the *völkisch* movement's hopes. On the other, it showed the German Nationalist women's reluctance to tie their demands to the more realistic concept of the state, which might plausibly have caused further conflict. Therefore, the preference for the imaginary concept of the *Volksgemeinschaft* can be read as sign of uncompromising demand, but also as an indication of the women's relative weakness within their party.

How can *völkisch* women's rhetoric be linked with narratives of race? There has been some controversy about how important the category of race was to right-wing women's conception of the *Volk* during the Weimar republic. Andrea Süchting-Hänger observes a radicalization of *völkisch* positions in the publications of the *Ring nationaler Frauen*, a major nationalist women's organization at the time, in her dissertation about conservative women's associations (2002: 300f.). However, Christiane Streubel, who discusses radical female nationalists, disagrees with Süchting-Hänger's analysis. Streubel maintains that in the ongoing debate among the *Ring*, whether race or culture (*Blut* or *Geist* in contemporary terminology) should constitute the *Volk*, the conceptions based on *Geist* prevailed (2006: 349f.). Nonetheless, she concedes that concepts based on race coexisted with more cultural definitions of *völkisch* belonging. Streubel concludes that ideological differences between right-wing women's groups often faded against a main interest that united them: women's integration into "people, public and state" (*Volk, Öffentlichkeit und Staat*) (ibid.: 351f.). Examining the characteristics and relevance of narratives of race, the most important conclusion appears to be that paradoxically the concepts of race and culture were translated into one another again and again. While this seemed to confirm that they were rendered as synonyms, the constant repetition disclosed a difference that always remained between them.

Equal Education and the Narrative of Race: The Austrian Case

The Gordian knot of cultural and racist argumentations also provides the background for my case study of the Austrian GDVP. The focus is on a text by Maria (Mizzi) Schneider (1898–1979) (Gehmacher 1998a: 213–221; Gehmacher and Hauch 1995), a university-trained teacher who was member of Parliament for the GDVP from 1930 on. Schneider had reached her position due only to strong support by the Austrian liberal women's movement (Pint 1988: 108f.). In her 1923 article "*Eine Volksgemeinschaftsaufgabe*" (A duty for the community of the people), she addressed an agenda characteristic of the liberal women's movement: access to higher education for girls and women (Simon 1993). Higher education remained an important issue for the GDVP women over the course of time. Major protagonists like Emmy Stradal (1877–1925), a board member of the party, not only expressed their agreement with the liberal women's movement's demands concerning questions of education, but formed coalitions with women of other parties to work toward these goals (Gehmacher 1998a: 92–103). German Nationalist women were even willing to give up their programmatic demand for separate schooling for girls and boys if coeducation promised a swift and direct way for improving girls' education. GDVP women collaborated with Social Democratic women toward coeducation and the installation of female teachers at the state funded schools—a move that sparked heavy critique from within their own party (ibid.: 86–88; see also Hauch 1995: 210ff.). Seeking to calm the inner-party debate, Maria Schneider reformulated the issue of female education in a racist anti-Semitic way: "As girls secondary schools are flooded by subjects of a foreign race it is a national duty to support the children of the own people."[5] Her call is particularly interesting because of its ideological substitution of one difference with another. In her article, Schneider refused to discuss the contested question of coeducation, and shifted the focus to another difference closer to her party's core ideology: the difference of race. Implying that the separation of Jewish and non-Jewish students was a much more important issue than the separation of boys and girls in school, she proposed that female university students should tutor German girls in secondary schools for free. The tutelage would strengthen the community of women belonging to the *Volk*, regardless of their class status. In her opinion, the cooperation would help university students to understand that the ultimate goals of the women's movement were neither higher education nor suffrage, but a rejuvenation of the whole *Volk* that would finally also serve women. The *Volk*, however, was a racial community to her and excluded all those members of the Austrian population that were not considered Aryan.

It is obvious that Schneider, who owed much to the liberal women's movement, demonstrated respect for the feminist agenda of her time, and tried to make one of its main issues acceptable to the GDVP in the face of obvious resistance. Using the concept of the *Volksgemeinschaft*—a concept of central importance for her party—she claimed that girls' education should be a core agenda of the GDVP. The reference to *Volksgemeinschaft* was, however, not just strategic. In fact Schneider reformulated the central agenda of the liberal women's movement along racist lines. Without the anti-Semitic introduction, her text could also be read as an idealistic call for female education and solidarity across class boundaries. The racist anti-Semitic framing makes clear that help was to be provided only for girls of their "own race." Schneider legitimized her integration of a feminist agenda and all the concessions made to facilitate girls' secondary education by stating that these policies would empower members of the Aryan race.

Schneider's text illustrates how the ideology of the *Volksgemeinschaft* worked in its last consequence: as an imaginary solution of social conflict by the exclusion of an imaginary Other. Wolfgang Fritz Haug has shown the operation of this ideology in his analysis of the National Socialist use of the term. He argued that a program calling for the solution of class conflicts in spite of the obvious economic reality of exploitation must soon turn out to be illusionary. The illusion that capital owners and workers will be reconciled eventually can only be maintained if each is split into two groups. The ideological construction of a division between productive and exploitative capital[6] and "honest workers" and "destructive agents of the revolution" allowed binding together the positive and negative representatives of both classes. As a consequence, harmony between productive capitalists and honest workers within the *Volksgemeinschaft* appeared endangered by a destructive coalition of revolutionaries and exploitative capitalists. To set this ideologically constructed threat to work, however, the unlikely cooperation of negative forces had to be made plausible. This was accomplished by conjuring up the phantom of a worldwide Jewish conspiracy. Put another way, the ideology of *Volksgemeinschaft* was stabilized by the invention of a Jewish counter community (Haug 1980). Elsewhere I have shown how *völkisch* youths found similar ways to address gender conflicts sparked by the political transformation and the economic crisis after World War I. By employing the figure of the seducing and/or raping Jew—who was construed as poisoning German girls—they translated fear of, and aggression against, the other sex into a conflict of "race." From a female as well as from a male perspective the feared other was no longer a desirable and/or dangerous man or woman but the other "race" against which German youth had to stand together in a sisterly way. Narratives of race thus seemed to have sidelined gender conflicts (Gehmacher 1992). In all these cases, seemingly irreconcilable differences (between classes, between women and men) within the *Volk* were both addressed and rendered irrelevant through the ideological construction of an even deeper rift between "races." Only by the exclusion of imaginary Others the *Volk* could be transformed into a community. This can also be observed in Schneider's text, where the contested mixing of girls and boys was rendered irrelevant by the insertion of a difference of "race" that required segregation. The versatile concept of *Volksgemeinschaft* served as a metaphorical bridge to link a gender issue with the issue of race.

Conclusion

To understand the development of racist concepts in the contexts of German and Austrian German Nationalist parties it is extremely helpful to engage a gender-based analysis. It can demonstrate the ways in which concepts of a "community of the people" were translated into narratives of race. The struggle for women's access to higher education as well as to the political arena in German Nationalist contexts are excellent examples. Concepts of equal female participation were highly contested in both the Austrian GDVP and the German DNVP. In both parties women's strategies to construct and perform a community that was to include them on equal terms were similar in many respects. In both cases, women used the vague and multifaceted term *Volksgemeinschaft* to argue for their integration. Both referred to an ideological concept of community that was either explicitly racist or did not exclude a racist translation of the community they constructed. And both argued that the national strength and/or racial purity their party demanded was only to be established if women were integrated on equal terms.

However, the comparison between the Austrian and German discourses makes visible some differences. The first is that German Nationalist women in Austria were less in fear of contact with the Social Democrats, as well as with the women's movement. The second is that German Nationalists in Austria saw the class conflict as a major political problem and that women could demonstrate their political importance by promising solutions of this conflict. The main difference, however, is that German Nationalists in Austria did not address the existing state, but put forward a concept of *Volksgemeinschaft* defined by race. The Austrians could not translate citizenship into nationality and vice versa, thus investing the concept of *Volksgemeinschaft* with greater importance. When women in Austria employed the term for their demands, they aimed at the core of German Nationalist ideology in Austria. Other than in Germany, the party program and many texts adopting the notion of *Volksgemeinschaft* clearly show a racist meaning that indicates the ubiquity of racist anti-Semitism in Austrian political discourses. In Germany, on the other hand, the DNVP addressed the German state as the entity they wanted to improve and strengthen, while the notion of the *Volksgemeinschaft* denoted merely the potential quality of that entity. When women in Germany employed the term, it often marked an ideological detour to formulate their actual demands toward the German state, but did not necessarily mean this demand was to be included in the hegemonic discourse of their party.

In both cases, *Volksgemeinschaft* was an illusionary concept, which could be made plausible only by inventing a counter community that was to be excluded. This was exactly where race entered the concept of *Volksgemeinschaft*, helping to keep both "communities" apart from each other discursively. Consequently, *Volksgemeinschaft* was an important gateway for the politicization of the biological concept of race. Still, I do not understand this process as a linear, teleological development, but would rather turn my attention to effects of simultaneity and coexistence of the concepts. This way, we can make visible fluctuating translations that remained open for rather different political realizations, as long as they were proposed in a pluralistic political context.

The concept of *Volksgemeinschaft* integrated rather different, if not conflicting, political groups into its exclusionary policy, as illustrated by the discussion of the German Nationalist women in Germany and Austria, who both used the concept of *Volksgemeinschaft* to argue for women's equality. The different meanings inherent in its use by German and Austrian German Nationalist women makes clear that the imaginary concept could come to factual relevance only if it also translated the power structure of a state into the real. This occurred in Germany in 1933, when the National Socialists took power and made apparent that they would translate *Volk* into an exclusionary concept of race.

Johanna Gehmacher is professor at the Institute for Contemporary History, University of Vienna. Her main issues in research and teaching are: gender and nationalism, theory of auto/biography, and social movements in the twentieth century. She currently heads a research project on the biography of the feminist and German Nationalist activist Käthe Schirmacher. (https://schirmacherproject.univie.ac.at/). One of her recent publications is: "A Case for Female Individuality: Käthe Schirmacher—Self-Invention and Biography," in Joy Damousi, Birgit Lang, and Katie Sutton's *Case Studies and the Dissemination of Knowledge* (2015).

Notes

1. "Das 'Salzburger Programm' der Großdeutschen Volkspartei, 1920," in Österreichische Parteiprogramme 1868–1966, ed. K. Berchtold (Vienna,

1967), 439–482: "Der Liberalismus hat den Zusammenhalt des Volkes gelockert, der Marxismus hat ihn vollends aufgelöst. ... Deshalb stellen wir dem Individualismus den Gedanken der Volksgemeinschaft gegenüber." Translation by the author.
2. *Die Verhandlungen des zweiten Reichsparteitages der Grossdeutschen Volkspartei, Wien, Saal der Bäckergenossenschaft 27. und 28. Juni 1921* (Vienna, 1921), 172: "Auf die Zerstörung der Volksgemeinschaft ist die Herrschaft des Judentums gegründet. Die Fesseln der Judenherrschaft kann daher ... nur ein Antisemitismus der Tat sprengen, der im Wege der Gesetzgebung und der Selbsthilfe die Volksgemeinschaft wieder herstellt." Translation by the author.
3. "Grundsätze deutschnationaler Frauenarbeit, April 1922," in Heinsohn (2010: 295–297, 295): "Als Glied der deutschen Volksgemeinschaft bekennt sich die deutschnationale Frau zum organischen Staatsgedanken, wie ihn die Deutschnationale Volkspartei auf christlicher Grundlage vertritt. ... Sie betrachtet alle Fragen des öffentlichen Lebens und somit auch Frauenfragen nicht vom individualistischen Standpunkte, sondern vom Standpunkte der Gesamtheit aus." Translation by the author.
4. Wahlaufruf der Deutschnationalen Volkspartei. Werbeblatt Nr. 10 (UB Rostock, Nachlass Käthe Schirmacher 344/043): "Wir begrüßen die Frauen als gleichberechtigte Mitarbeiter an der Wiederaufrichtung unseres Volkes." Translation by the author.
5. Dr. Mizzi Schneider, "Eine Volksgemeinschaftsaufgabe," *Deutsche Zeit*, 1. Juni. 1923: "Angesichts der fürchterlichen Überschwemmung der Mädchenmittelschulen mit Fremdrassigen ist es geradezu eine nationale Pflicht, die Kinder des eigenen Volkes zu unterstützen." Translation by the author.
6. The German propagandistic terms *"schaffendes Kapital"* and *"raffendes Kapital"* had additional connotations of something creative on the one hand and the image of someone grubbing money on the other hand.

References

Ackerl, I. 1967. "Die Großdeutsche Volkspartei 1920–1934." PhD dissertation, University of Vienna.

Achrainer, M. 2012. "Alpine Vereine." In *Handbuch des Antisemitismus. Judenfeindschaft in Geschichte und Gegenwart vol. 5: Organisationen, Institutionen, Bewegungen*, ed. W. Benz. Berlin and Boston, MA, 16–20.

Aicher, M. 2012. "Deutschnationale Studentenverbindungen in Österreich." In *Handbuch des Antisemitismus. Judenfeindschaft in Geschichte und Gegenwart*, vol. 5: *Organisationen, Institutionen, Bewegungen*, ed. W. Benz. Berlin and Boston, MA, 189–191.

Bader-Zaar, B. 2009. "Women's Suffrage and War: World War I and Political Reform in a Comparative Perspective." In *Suffrage, Gender and Citizenship: International Perspectives on Parliamentary Reforms*, eds. I. Sulkunen, S.-L. Nevala-Nurmi and P. Markkola. Newcastle upon Tyne, 193–218.

Bajohr, F., and M. Wildt, eds. 2009. *Volksgemeinschaft. Neue Forschungen zur Gesellschaft des Nationalsozialismus*. Frankfurt am Main.

Bauman, Z. 1998. "Das Jahrhundert der Lager?" In *Genozid und Moderne*, vol. 1: *Strukturen kollektiver Gewalt im 20. Jahrhundert*, eds. M. Dabag and K. Platt. Opladen, 81–99.
Bergmann, W. 2012. "Deutschnationale Volkspartei." In *Handbuch des Antisemitismus. Judenfeindschaft in Geschichte und Gegenwart*, vol. 5: *Organisationen, Institutionen, Bewegungen*, ed. W. Benz. Berlin and Boston, MA, 191–197.
Bernd, H.-D. 2004. "Die Beseitigung der Weimarer Republik auf 'legalem' Weg. Die Funktion des Antisemitismus in der Agitation der Führungsschicht der DNVP." PhD dissertation, Fernuniversität Hagen.
Breuer, S. 2010. *Die radikale Rechte in Deutschland 1871–1945*. Stuttgart.
Bruendel, S. 2004. "Die Geburt der 'Volksgemeinschaft' aus dem 'Geist von 1914'. Entstehung und Wandel eines 'sozialistischen' Gesellschaftsentwurfs." *Zeitgeschichte-online*: *Fronterlebnis und Nachkriegsordnung. Wirkung und Wahrnehmung des Ersten Weltkriegs* (May), www.zeitgeschichte-online.de/md=EWK-Bruendel.
"Deutschnationale Volkspartei, Grundsätze 1920." In *Deutsche Parteiprogramme*, ed. W. Mommsen. Munich, 1960, 534–543.
Dostal, T. 1995. "Die Großdeutsche Volkspartei." In *Handbuch des politischen Systems Österreichs. Erste Republik 1918–1933*, eds. E. Tálos et al. Vienna, 195–206.
Gehmacher, J. 1992. "Antisemitismus und die Krise des Geschlechterverhältnisses." Österreichische Zeitschrift für Geschichtswissenschaften 3, no. 4: 424–448.
———. 1998a. *"Völkische Frauenbewegung". Deutschnationale und nationalsozialistische Geschlechterpolitik in Österreich*. Vienna.
———. 1998b. "Men, Women, and the Community Borders: German-Nationalist and National Socialist Discourses on Gender, 'Race' and National Identity in Austria." In *Nation, Empire, Colony: Historicizing Gender and Race*, eds. R. R. Pierson and N. Chaudhuri. Bloomington and Indianapolis, IN, 205–19.
———. 2009. "Wenn Frauenrechtlerinnen wählen können.... Frauenbewegung, Partei/Politik und politische Partizipation von Frauen – begriffliche und forschungsstrategische Überlegungen." In *Wie Frauenbewegung geschrieben wird. Historiographie, Dokumentation, Stellungnahmen, Bibliographien*, eds. J. Gehmacher and N. Vittorelli. Vienna, 135–180.
Gehmacher, J., and G. Hauch. 1995. "Eine 'deutsch fühlende Frau' Die großdeutsche Politikerin Marie Schneider und der Nationalsozialismus in Österreich." In *Frauenleben 1945. Kriegsende in Wien*. Vienna, 115–132
"Grundsätze deutschnationaler Frauenarbeit, April 1922." In K. Heinsohn, *Konservative Parteien in Deutschland 1912 bis 1933. Demokratisierung und Partizipation in geschlechterhistorischer Perspektive*. Düsseldorf, 295–297.
Hanisch, E. 1995. "Einleitung. Das politische System Erste Republik. Zwei Erklärungsversuche." In *Handbuch des politischen Systems Österreichs. Erste Republik 1918–1933*, eds. E. Tálos et al. Vienna, 1–7.
Hauch, G. 1995. *Vom Frauenstandpunkt aus. Frauen im Parlament 1919–1933*. Vienna.
Haug, W. F. 1980. "Annäherungen an die faschistische Modalität des Ideologischen." In *Faschismus und Ideologie 1*, eds. W. Behrens et al. Berlin, 44–80.
Heinsohn, K. 2000. "Im Dienste der deutschen Volksgemeinschaft: Die 'Frauenfrage' und konservative Parteien vor und nach dem Ersten Weltkrieg." In

Nation, Politik und Geschlecht. Frauenbewegungen und Nationalismus in der Moderne, ed. U. Planert. Frankfurt am Main and New York, 215–233.

———. 2002. "'Volksgemeinschaft' als gedachte Ordnung. Zur Geschlechterpolitik der Deutschnationalen Volkspartei." In Geschlechtergeschichte des Politischen. Entwürfe von Geschlecht und Gemeinschaft im 19. und 20. Jahrhundert, eds. G. Boukrif et al. Hamburg, 83–106.

———. 2007. "Kampf um die Wählerinnen: Die Idee von der 'Volksgemeinschaft' am Ende der Weimarer Republik." In Volksgenossinnen. Frauen in der NS-Volksgemeinschaft, ed. S. Steinbacher. Göttingen, 29–47.

———. 2010. Konservative Parteien in Deutschland 1912 bis 1933. Demokratisierung und Partizipation in geschlechterhistorischer Perspektive. Düsseldorf.

Kershaw, I. 2011. "'Volksgemeinschaft'. Potenzial und Grenzen eines neuen Forschungskonzepts." Vierteljahreshefte für Zeitgeschichte 59, no. 1: 1–17.

Mommsen, H. 2007. "Forschungskontroversen zum Nationalsozialismus." Aus Politik und Zeitgeschichte no. 14–15: 14–21.

Ohnezeit, M. 2011. Zwischen "schärfster Opposition" und dem "Willen zur Macht". Die Deutschnationale Volkspartei (DNVP) in der Weimarer Republik 1918–1928. Düsseldorf.

Pauley, B. F. 1988. Der Weg in den Nationalsozialismus. Ursprünge und Entwicklungen in Österreich. Vienna.

Peukert, D. J. K. 1987. Die Weimarer Republik. Krisenjahre der Klassischen Moderne. Frankfurt am Main.

Pint, J. 1988. "Die österreichische Frauenpartei 1929–1934." MA thesis, University of Vienna.

Puschner, U. 2000. "Bausteine zum völkischen Frauendiskurs." In Nation, Politik und Geschlecht. Frauenbewegungen und Nationalismus in der Moderne, ed. U. Planert. Frankfurt am Main and New York, 165–181.

Puschner, U., et al., eds. 1996. Handbuch zur "Völkischen Bewegung" 1871–1918. Munich et al.

Riescher, G. 2012. "Politisches Vertrauen. Weibliche Abgordnete in der Weimarer Republik." In Staat in Unordnung? Geschlechterperspektiven auf Deutschland und Österreich zwischen den Weltkriegen, eds. S. Krammer et al. Bielefeld, 47–59.

Rürup, R. 1987. "Die 'Judenfrage' der bürgerlichen Gesellschaft und die Entstehung des modernen Antisemitismus." In Emanzipation und Antisemitismus. Studien zur "Judenfrage" der bürgerlichen Gesellschaft, ed. R. Rürup. Frankfurt am Main, 93–119.

"Das 'Salzburger Programm' der Großdeutschen Volkspartei, 1920." In Österreichische Parteiprogramme 1868–1966, ed. K. Berchtold. Vienna, 1967, 439–482.

Schmiechen-Ackermann, D., ed. 2011. "Volksgemeinschaft": Mythos, Wirkungsmächtige soziale Verheißung oder soziale Realität im "Dritten Reich"? Propaganda und Selbstmobilisierung im NS-Staat. Paderborn.

Schneider, M. 1923. "Eine Volksgemeinschaftsaufgabe." Deutsche Zeit, 1 Juni.

Schöck-Quinteros, E., and C. Streubel, eds. 2007. Ihrem Volk verantwortlich. Frauen der politischen Rechten (1890–1933). Organisationen–Agitationen–Ideologien. Berlin.

Simon, G. 1993. *Hintertreppen zum Elfenbeinturm: höhere Mädchenbildung in Österreich – Anfänge und Entwicklungen*. Vienna.
Steber M., and B. Gotto, eds. 2014. *Visions of Community in Nazi Germany. Social Engineering and Private Lives*. Oxford et al.
Steber, M., et al. 2014. "Volksgemeinschaft und die Gesellschaftsgeschichte des NS-Regimes." *Vierteljahrshefte für Zeitgeschichte*. 62, no. (July) 3: 433–468.
Steinbacher, S. 2007. "Einleitung." In *Volksgenossinnen. Frauen in der NS-Volksgemeinschaft*, ed. S. Steinbacher. Göttingen, 9–26.
Steuwer, J. 2010. Conference report, "German Society in the Nazi Era: 'Volksgemeinschaft' between Ideological Projection and Social Practice," London, 25–27 March. In *H-Soz-u-Kult,* 28 May, http://hsozkult.geschichte.hu-berlin.de/tagungsberichte/id=3121.
Streubel, C. 2006. *Radikale Nationalistinnen. Agitation und Programmatik rechter Frauen in der Weimarer Republik*. Frankfurt am Main and New York.
Striesow, J. 1981. *Die Deutschnationale Volkspartei und die Völkisch-Radikalen 1918–1922*. Frankfurt am Main.
Sturm, R. 2011. "Zerstörung der Demokratie 1930–1933." *Informationen zur politischen Bildung* 261: 1–9.
Süchting-Hänger, A. 2002. *Das "Gewissen der Nation". Nationales Engagement und politisches Handeln konservativer Frauenorganisationen 1900 bis 1937*. Düsseldorf.
Thamer, H.-U. 1990. "Nation als Volksgemeinschaft." In *Soziales Denken in Deutschland zwischen Tradition und Innovation*, eds. J.-D. Gauger and K. Weigelt. Bonn, 112–128.
———. 1998. "'Volksgemeinschaft.' Mensch und Masse." In *Erfindung des Menschen. Schöpfungsträume und Körperbilder 1500–2000*, ed. R. van Dülmen. Vienna, 367–386.
Tönnies, F. 1887. *Gemeinschaft und Gesellschaft. Abhandlung des Communismus und des Socialismus als empirischer Culturformen*. Berlin. Die Verhandlungen des zweiten Reichsparteitages der Grossdeutschen Volkspartei, Wien, Saal der Bäckergenossenschaft 27. und 28. Juni 1921. Vienna.
Volkov, S. 1978. "Antisemitismus als kultureller Code." *Leo Baeck Institute Yearbook* XXIII: 25–45.
Wahlaufruf der Deutschnationalen Volkspartei. Werbeblatt Nr. 10. University Library Rostock, Käthe Schirmacher papers 344/043.
Weidinger, B. 2012. "Deutsche Burschenschaften in Österreich." In *Handbuch des Antisemitismus. Judenfeindschaft in Geschichte und Gegenwart vol. 5: Organisationen, Institutionen, Bewegungen*, ed. W. Benz. Berlin and Boston, MA, 140–145.
Wildt, M. 2007. *Volksgemeinschaft als Selbstermächtigung. Gewalt gegen Juden in der deutschen Provinz 1919 bis 1939*. Hamburg.
———. 2011. "'Volksgemeinschaft'. Eine Antwort auf Ian Kershaw." *Zeithistorische Forschungen / Studies in Contemporary History* 8, no. 1: 3. http://www.zeithistorische-forschungen.de/16126041-Wildt-1-2011.
Zettelbauer, H. 2005. *"Die Liebe sei Euer Heldentum". Geschlecht und Nation in völkischen Vereinen der Habsburgermonarchie*. Frankfurt am Main et al.

8

IN THE CROSSHAIRS OF DEGENERACY AND RACE
The Wilhelmine Origins of the Construction of a National Aesthetic and Parameters of Normalcy in Weimar Germany

Lara Day

This chapter examines ongoing narratives of race, degeneracy, and deviance present in the architect and writer Paul Schultze-Naumburg's (1869–1949) writings of the Wilhelmine and Weimar period, exemplified by his books *Die Kultur des weiblichen Körpers als Grundlage der Frauenkleidung* (1901) and *Kunst und Rasse* (1926), to question the presumed homogeneity of the *entartete Kunst* discourse. It argues that perceptions of deviance were not simply used as contrasts to Germanhood but tried to establish traditionalism and purity as parameters of normalcy. It posits that the continuity of thought visible in Schultze-Naumburg's writing represented the continuity or development ideas of broader cultural parameters, which were tested and optimized in the so-called *Trutzgau* Weimar. His published work—37 books, over 230 articles, and countless lectures—ranging from art and architectural pedagogy, practice, and criticism to cultural and racial theory, made him one of the most widely read German authors of the first half of the twentieth century. Renowned during his lifetime, his racial and eugenic writing prompted his relegation in postwar German historiography, which ignored his impact and central position in the cultural and architectural landscape of German modernism. This essay examines his role as a specific cultural catalyst of radical nationalist and racist art and architectural history and theory, and traces his trajectory through Wilhelmine, Weimar, and National Socialist Germany. Beyond the fine arts, Schultze-Naumburg helped formulate the conceptions of the anti-Semitic, pro-*Heimat,* and antiurban, *völkisch* mind frame that would be transformed into the blood and soil rhetoric of the emerging National Socialist ideology. Schultze-Naumburg's historical stature and sociocultural prominence were recognized throughout his life, and history's subsequent repression of his figure is based on the nefarious and fanatical potency of his ideas and not on his erstwhile importance.

While this investigation does not propose a clear teleology between *fin de siècle* and National Socialist ideology, it asks which Wilhelmine and Weimar discourses shaped National Socialist conceptions of art and the body. The discussions surrounding National Socialist art and cultural policies were by no means predetermined or monolithic—the struggle between Rosenberg and Goebbels, and Hitler's response are well documented—and so this investigation proposes that instead of focusing on the fate of individual artists, the relationship of art to the body, the collective *Volkskörper* should be reconsidered. In an ideology celebrating the body as eternal, the art produced by the collective emerged as the only true indication (and thus diagnostic tool) of the racial state of its producers and its audience. By considering Schultze-Naumburg's influential texts on the body this chapter traces his shift from *Milieutheorie* (sometimes called *Umwelttheorie*), which proposes all humans have the capacity to be influenced and bettered by environment and education, to a blood and soil–based *Volksgemeinschaft*. Beginning with his involvement in the anticorset movement and women's fashion, as exemplified in *Die Kultur des weiblichen Körpers als Grundlage der Frauenkleidung* (1901), it culminates in his *Kunst und Rasse* (1926), and although the methods used—such as the juxtaposition of *Beispiel* and *Gegenbeispiel* (example and counterexample)—are not innovative, their ends are. One unanticipated end is the influence on, or at the very least deep resonance with, Hitler's race theory, which claimed autonomy from history, culture, and theory, and assumed that *only* art made race visible effectively, just as Schultze-Naumburg proposed (Groys 2004: 3).

Using art as a diagnostic tool, Schultze-Naumburg analyzed the form and physiognomy of art and buildings as indicative of the producing artist and his *Volk*'s cultural state, in a radical shift away from *fin de siècle Lebensreform* ideal of art's redemptive potential. Art and art production thus moved from a position of influence with a pedagogical imperative, to one of a mirror of its audience, which was expected to recognize it by visceral instinct. Over the span of his career, Schultze-Naumburg developed an approach to the body that depended on visual narratives and identified characteristics imbued with the ability to communicate about the individual's racial makeup, which determined his mental and physical state and ability. While his *Lebensreform* and *Heimatschutz* writing proposed the physiognomy of houses as direct illustrations of the poor taste and cultural degeneracy of their builders, his Weimar writing favored the topic of the polluted *Volkskörper*, which he argued must be purged of undesirable elements. Schultze-Naumburg's understanding and use of physiognomy within the framework of *Milieuthe-*

orie is laid bare in the second volume of his infamous *Kulturarbeiten*, published in 1902:

> Inherent in form lies a peculiar faculty of expression, of the sort in which any change in form, no matter how minute it appears, results in a marked change of the expression. The skill of reading the form can be much increased. The following observations illustrates this; in principle singular individuals of the same race resemble each other quite closely. All have noses, eyes, ears, arms, and legs arranged in the same manner. Still we know no person looks exactly like another, and can identify the different expressions of individual forms, although at first glance they vary only very slightly in "type." This skill, to read the forms, is the result of training our sense of face by the systematic education of observational [skills]. (1902a: 126–128)

While *Kunst und Rasse* is infamous for such juxtaposition of reproductions of modern art with photographic portraits of patients with a variety of syndromes and diseases, Wilhelmine reform writings in which this subject matter and rhetoric were developed are less known. This chapter will examine Schultze-Naumburg's early writing to identify some of the themes that came to inform, underpin, and guide the discourses of degeneracy and race in 1930s Weimar. Ideas of degenerate versus healthy art were projected not only into geographically remote areas—in which the "true *Negerkunst*" was seen to blossom (Hesse 1995)—but onto the past. Like conceptions of a highly valued Indigenous *Stammeskunst* (Haag 2014; forthcoming), the art of ancient Greece was held aloft as healthy, as it and the Nordic emerged as paradigms of virtue.

When Hitler pronounced that "the only truly immortal talent within all of human endeavor and achievement is art," at the 1936 *Kulturtagung* of the NSDAP party congress in Nuremberg, Schultze-Naumburg's influence on art and architectural criticism and the architecture of the Third Reich was waning (Hitler 1936: 115). Hitler's understanding of art as an eternal value, to be transmitted not only by the body of the artist, but through the *Volkskörper* and inherited by generations to come, suggests a new conception of the role of the corporeal. Boris Groys identifies this as the creation of an "ahistorical identity—not the political identity of a people or nation, not the cultural ideas of its *Geist*, but the hidden identity of purely instinctual, purely visceral reactions" (2004: 33). Schultze-Naumburg's early writing engages with and seeks to elicit just such responses. The trained landscape painter turned autodidactic architect (like so many of the generation among them most famously Peter Behrens and Henry van de Velde), widely read critic and founding member of the *Werkbund*, was at the center of discussions of reform in the arts and crafts, in architecture, and, more broadly, of life itself (the *Lebensreform* movement). His biologistic eugenic and racial polemics are rooted in the pushback against social and moral degeneracy perceived in the visible changes to the landscape, understood as the results of industrialization and urbanism. The core of the *Lebensreform* movement was the desire for sweeping social change, which would "realize itself by the summation of individuals' self-education and self-improvement" (Krabbe 1974: 7).

These were also the tenets of *Milieutheorie* that Schultze-Naumburg promoted in his writing of the Wilhelmine period, and that were diametrically opposed to the conception he championed in his post–World War I writing, which considered human potential as determined by blood and inheritance, and cast those perceived unfit (by their blood and inherited traits) as static and harmful to the collective. Paul Betts's suggestion that "as soon as *Kultur* itself became a distinctly material and biological concept, as soon as the national 'community' became coterminous with the so-called national body, the expanded visual and medical domain of hygiene … became intensely political" (2004: 55) is particularly relevant in light of the individual's subjugation to the collective for the greater good. In Schultze-Naumburg's writing, the individual, temporal body is considered a link in the eternal chain of the *Volkskörper,* a conception first made possible by the popularization of science, and the move of biologic concepts into popular print journalism. The optimization, or *Aufartung,* of the race was the long-term goal, shared with the discourses of eugenics permeating writing across European political and disciplinary spectra. The outcome of Wilhelmine eugenic and racial theories was undetermined and discussed as a revolutionary and exciting scientific advance. Kevin Repp's argument that "'progressive evolutionism' followed many, forking paths into the twentieth century, some of which did not end in disaster, and [of which] many more were left untaken" (2000: 312) is illustrated particularly well by the women's reform clothing movement championed by Schultze-Naumburg alongside a host of writers and artists, such as Anna Muthesius and Alfred Mohrbutter, whose careers make apparent the disconnect between their shared cause and his eventual political affiliation.

Schultze-Naumburg's writing on women's reform clothing bridged the gap between the scientific medical literature of the nineteenth century and the popular journalism of the emerging *Lebensreform* movement, by proposing artistic practice based on an aesthetic determined by function and "natural health." The crucial equation of beauty with *Leistungsfähigkeit* elevated beauty to the criterion for the "dis/qualification of the norm" (Haug 1986: 147) and, in its identification of reason and function as central to all design understood to be "natural" and "good," resonates with the other strands of the *Lebensreform*. Despite this correlation, Schultze-Naumburg explicitly encouraged the differentiation of this cause, bemoaning public perception that considered: "women's clothing, emancipation, cycling, the organization for the reform of women's clothes, smoking and free love, as pretty much one and the same" (1901a: 139; 1902–1903: 91). Othmar Birkner identifies clothing reform as a key to all-encompassing reform, in a climate in which the woman was rediscovered as the idol of "national renaissance," elevating the question from mere superficial fashion to one of national importance (1977: 52–53). Schultze-Naumburg's advocacy for *Körperkultur* and *Körperfreudigkeit* functions as an opposite to the growing fear of degeneration, decline, and destabilization. The Wilhelmine period was a time of the rehabilitation of the body and the corporeal, and as such one of the *Lebensreform*'s most revolutionary impulses, and, as Klaus Wolbert suggests, its most decisive and lasting effect on the conception of modern man (2001: 339).

The title *Die Kultur des weiblichen Körpers als Grundlage der Frauenkleidung* sums up its proposal of reforming women's dress design by reconsidering the female form. Building upon popular medical texts (albeit without citation), Schultze-Naumburg singled out the corset, and fashion dependent on its use, as absolutely hazardous to women's, and by extension the nation's, health. The book drew upon a wealth of source material from the medical community and accorded with a burgeoning trend in popular journalism. Sabine Welsch names the wide availability of the commercially produced corset beginning in the 1840s as the unifying factor in the movement for women's clothing reform (1996: 8). The discussion of the corset in the medical community began much earlier, as in, for example, Thomas Soemmering's "Über die Schädlichkeit der Schnürbrüste" (1787), which is cited by writers throughout the nineteenth and twentieth centuries as a first declaration of war on the corset (Welsch 1996: 7). Georg Forster's frustrated question in 1798 whether "the continued use of *Schnürbrüste* [is] determined by the tainted taste of men, who, due to their slavish devotion to habit, still see the cone shape as an ideal of beauty, which while impossible to achieve in nature, is certainly within any tailor's reach" (as cited in Welsch 1996: 7) describes the discrepancy between scientific knowledge and fashion. The physicians Heinrich Lahmann (1860–1905) and Gustav Jaeger (1832–1917) expanded on the earlier work of such writers as Forster, providing the scientific theories upon which the movement was built, in Jaeger's *Die Normalkleidung als Gesundheitsschutz* (1880) and the journal *Prof. Dr. G. Jaeger's Monatsblatt. Organ für Gesundheitspflege und Lebenslehre.*

The heyday of reform fashion came between 1900 and 1905, after wide-ranging discussions about the dangers of the corset by artists, suffragettes, pedagogues, and physicians, visible for example in the founding of the *Allgemeiner Verein zur Verbesserung der Frauenkleidung* in Berlin in 1896, which gave rise to a series of lectures, exhibitions, journals, and contests. An audience and market for the topic was manifest in such journals as *Kraft und Schönheit,* founded in 1901, and *Schönheit* (1903), edited by Karl Vanselow. Wolfgang Krabbe describes the latter as an organization, which "did not conceive of itself as a mouthpiece of nudism, but was one of the apologists of the rediscovered phenomenon of *Leiblichkeit* (corporeality), with which it interacted under the auspices of aesthetics," a trait he argues it shares with Schultze-Naumburg's *Kultur des weiblichen Körpers* (Krabbe 1974: 94). The latter was included in the *Literaturverzeichnis* of a pamphlet published by the *Verein zur Verbesserung der Frauenkleidung* in 1904, alongside titles by Henry van de Velde and Heinrich Pudor (Frecot, Geist, and Kerbs 1972: 51). The book was a catalyst for the abolition of the corset and for artists to take ownership of an antifashion, the *Reformkleid.* It helped establish Schultze-Naumburg's name in wider popular discourse, in part by his publication of sections of this book in a variety of other journals and edited volumes, including in the undated *Weibliche Körperbildung und Bewegungskunst nach dem System Mensendieck,* in which he argued, "as a matter of fact, clothing can be elevated to a true art and become a manifest expression of the representational" (n.d.: 147).

Die Kultur des weiblichen Körpers als Grundlage der Frauenkleidung was published in 1901 by Eugen Diederichs's publishing house. Diederichs was committed to the cause of the so-called *Körperkulturbewegung* (Ulbricht and Werner 1999: 185), and a personal friend of Schultze-Naumburg. He identified the publication of *Häusliche Kunstpflege* as the beginning of his publishing house's "artistic culture" (ibid.). It first appeared in September 1899 (Imprimatur 1900), was in second edition by that Christmas (Heidler 1998: 251), and went on to sell 14,635 copies by 1930. Irmgard Heidler suggests that Schultze-Naumburg's practical bent ensured its immediate popularity (1998: 251). The correspondence between Schultze-Naumburg and Diederichs around this volume and the move of the latter's publishing house to Jena in 1903 strengthened his connection with the circle surrounding Schultze-Naumburg and his *Heimatschutz* friends (Werner 1996: 224). Diederichs soon counted many members of the *Kunstwartkreis* among his authors, perhaps due to the economic success of *Die Kultur,* which sold 12,910 copies by 1914–1915 (Jäger 2001: 393). Within the publishing house the closest second that year was the Werkbund's *Die Durchgeistigung der deutschen Arbeit*, which sold 7,575 copies, and third was Hermann Muthesius's *Stilarchitektur und Baukunst* (1910), which sold a mere 119 copies (ibid.).

One hundred and forty-nine pages long, *Die Kultur* is divided into two parts: "The first, which considers the precondition, namely the female body in its relationship to clothing, and the second, which draws conclusions and applies them to the clothing itself" (Schultze-Naumburg 1901a: ii),[1] and includes 133 illustrations. By claiming that the German *Modeideal* was natural and opposed to foreign influences, those unwilling to adopt it were deemed hostile to the nation *and* nature, not to mention all notions of practicality and beauty (Adamek 1982: 215). By conceiving of illnesses as an acute danger to the nation, a new *Körpergefühl* and health were identified as the basis of social reform (Weipert 2006: 159). Schultze-Naumburg's equation of aesthetics and function availed itself of the momentum of the *Lebensreform*'s push for a shared and unifying national ambition. In addition to his discussion of the detrimental effects of the corset on the female anatomy, Schultze-Naumburg took a stringent position on footwear that distorted and damaged the foot for fashion's sake. Although this section comprises only sixteen pages, the topic was included in an advertising pamphlet published by Diederichs, which promised this "further topoi of our physical self-mutilation" would be "exhaustively discussed."[2] In fact, Schultze-Naumburg names the feet as a site of body mutilation second only to the waist. The rhetoric used in the discussion alludes to the public's perceived ignorance: "One does not know what an ugly distorted, not to mention a beautiful normal, foot looks like, and cannot admit this ignorance, instead becoming aggressive and agitated, and, in order to vindicate oneself, asserts all sorts of unfounded things" (1901a: 122).[3] He invokes a sense of responsibility with moral implications: "The truly ethical person does not cripple himself" (ibid.: 134),[4] and his overview of the history of footwear and the representation of feet in the arts draws predictably on examples from classical Greek and Roman sculpture.

This section of *Die Kultur* draws heavily on the essay "Der Fuss," first included in the essay collection *Kunst und Kunstpflege* (1901), in which it stood alongside pieces such as "Das Korsett," "Kultur des menschlichen Körpers," and "Menschliche Schönheit" (1901b). In the latter essay, Schultze-Naumburg's language and rhetoric resonate deeply with that used in *Die Kultur*: "How is it possible that no one notices that all the women, all the girls around us have such disfigured bodies? Is it merely wanton, negligent ignorance, that they worship the '*elegante façon*' and desire no knowledge of the wretched body which is underneath, and yet exhibits itself everywhere with such brash explicitness?" (ibid.: 108–109).[5] Schultze-Naumburg's ambition to cast light on these disfigured bodies resulted in *Die Kultur*'s illustrations, which consist of photographs of female nudes and sculpture, paintings, and etchings, and are, in their explicitness, perhaps the most influential aspect of the book. Schultze-Naumburg explains that his intention was *not* to create an amusing picture book, and that only those images strictly necessary to create the visceral understanding crucial to the development of new ideas of the body and clothing were included (1901a: 6).[6] While the publications of the nudist strand of the *Lebensreform* movement certainly introduced a wider swathe of the population to nude photographs, the sheer volume of Schultze-Naumburg's photographs and his explanation that the large number of images were necessary to train the reader's eye, so used to the "tradition of deformed bodies," to recognize the true shape of the body, seems contrived.

Many of the images he employs seem, as Kirsten Weiss puts it, "unnecessarily racy," which she attributes to their nature as "obviously erotic images" (2008: 41), and not as Schultze-Naumburg attests to "increase the viewing from mere observance to logical examination" (1901a: 6).[7] Weiss agrees here with Diethart Kerbs's suggestion that the book's immediate popularity was due in part to the generous inclusion of nude photographs (1999: 222). While Weiss's point that many of the photographs do not include titles, date, or authors is accurate, her supposition that "Schultze-Naumburg took the rest [many] of the photographs himself on his trips to Italy, judging from the dark hair, olive skin, and toga costumes of most models" (2008: 41) remains unsubstantiated. Beyond the sheer number, the subject matter is rife with titillating potential. While Schultze-Naumburg uses classical sculpture and canonical nudes and odalisques as a matter of course, he includes such highly stylized nudes as illustration 49, of a woman with her fluttering dress suggestively unbuttoned, one arm extended and her forearm resting on flowing hair (1901a: 54). His preface includes the disclaimer: "The fact that primarily the female body is discussed, will result in superficial judges, who do not recognize the moral severity of the question, pigeonholing the book with the class of prurience. I will have to bear this" (ibid.: 47).[8] Schultze-Naumburg goes so far as to attest that this volume is intended as a "scientific and aesthetic examination of a female body," and that "if the individual is unable to deactivate the sexual from his perception, that is merely an unintentional and irrelevant side effect" (ibid.: 6–7).[9] And yet his text belies his protest, proposing such *fin de siècle* ideals as: "Only breasts, that are so firm and plump that they mock the very concept of needing external support, qualify as beautiful" (ibid.: 39),[10] a line repeated exactly in the later article "Zur Reform der Frauenkleidung" (1902–1903: 83).

A further aspect of note is his explicit celebration of a very specific female body type, namely of the slender, narrow-hipped, tall woman. Correlating aesthetic with functionality is another opportunity for the establishment of "good" taste: "Slender is beautiful only if it is an evenly slender body, not the unmotivated narrowing at a single spot, which is unfounded both anatomically and aesthetically, and was created by the misconceptions and perverse tastes of a time that should be behind us" (1901a: 112–113; 1902–1903: 91).[11] Indeed, while this first citation is rather subtle, Schultze-Naumburg uses nonconforming body types to illustrate perversion itself: "after all this caricature of the woman, with her abnormally wide hips must please a perverted taste" (1901a: 107–108).[12] Still, as Michael Hau points out, within his body aesthetics, Schultze-Naumburg maintained a distinction between the norm and the average, because he believed the behavior as well as the appearance of the majority of the people did not correspond to his aesthetic norms, which he claimed were equivalent to hygienic norms (Hau 2003: 39).

The illustrations are so numerous that many are discussed in only passing, as in this single example of a series of photographs—"our illustrations 24, 25, 28, 31, 32, 33, 34, 37, 38"—used solely in illustration of his argument that "the most beautiful shape of the breast is without question the perfectly smoothly rounded, which blends evenly into the body without allowing a crease to be created under or between them" (1901a: 47).[13] In such illustrations and in his assessment of the female body purpose, Schultze-Naumburg is more honest than in his initial caveat: "Certainly a woman's bosom is not something to be denied or hidden by clothing. By its beauty, her body is intended to arouse the desire of man" (ibid.: 142).[14] The lack of engagement with actual art historical analysis of such elements as line, composition, or rhythm, makes immediately obvious that these texts are the projection of a political ambition onto the visual arts.

This type of image was familiar to many *fin de siècle Bildungsbürger*, due in large part to the efforts and publications of a separate yet related subgroup of the reform movement. The *Nacktkultur* or *Freikörperkultur* movement proposed nudity as the solution to social ills. Johannes Guttzeit (1853–1935) was a pioneer of the *Nacktkultur* movement, alongside Heinrich Pudor,[15] Richard Ungewitter, the infamous *Kohlrabiapostel* Karl Wilhelm Dieffenbach (1851–1913), and of course the painter Hugo Höppner, known as Fidus (for more on *Freikörperkultur* and its proponents, see Wedemayer-Kolwe 2004). The latter studied with Dieffenbach, who published the two-volume *Ein Beitrag zur Geschichte der zeitgenössischen Kunstpflege* (1895), and was instrumentally involved in the propagation of *Freikörperkultur* in Germany by his paintings and illustrations. Fidus's *Lichtgebet* is perhaps the best-known example of a powerful idealized figure as an expression of the new *Lebensgefühl* and the belief in a better, happier, healthier state of being in the new century. Beyond fostering a reconsideration and acceptance of the nude human figure, the movement had moral and social ambitions (Viehöfer 1988: 35). The main proposition of *Freikörperkultur* was a "less inhibited attitude toward the physical," which, it was assumed, would create a harmonious accord of body, *Geist* (spirit), and soul (Krabbe 1974: 94). A characteristic it shared with the other strands of *Lebensreform* was the conviction that a return to a pure, ancient way of life on the land would free its members from the shackles of fashion. Inspired by the texts of Nietzsche, Lagarde, and Langbehn (Viehöfer 1988: 35), Pudor celebrated the healing power of the earth and a religious, erotic convergence with nature (Frecot, Geist, and Kerbs 1972: 48), anticipating *Blut und Boden* rhetoric. He imagined the Nordic-Aryan as the agent of the future, describing his physiognomy: "Golden hair, blue eyes, red lips, white teeth and a velvety russet body—that is the color chart of the body of the future human in Europe" (Pudor 1893: 10, as cited in ibid.: 49). This "color chart" illustrates his, and by extension the movement's, belief not only in physiognomy as indication of race and worth, but in the potential for a form of *Aufartung,* or improvement of the race, central to this *völkisch* variation of clothing reform. While Schultze-Naumburg lacked Pudor's specific vision, he too saw the cultivation of the body as the precondition for a well-developed, balanced personality, and body culture (*Körperkultur*) as a necessary complement to and not replacement for the culture of the mind (*Geisteskultur*) (Hau 2003: 46–47).

Gegenbeispiele: Constructing an "Other" to the German Body

The construction of potential foreign influences, foils, or "others," is most saliently illustrated by Schultze-Naumburg's descriptions of human folly: "The Botocudo inserted wooden blocks into their lower lip to be more beautiful, Chinese women transformed their feet into lumps; certain tribes love filing their teeth to sharp points. Anthropological museums document even stranger human impulses. They flit past the viewer's gaze like fevered dreams. The central questions, primarily concerned with the causes of these events, find no answers other than the resigned admission that a self-destructive bent runs parallel to all human drive for progress" (1901a: 94; 1902–1903: 83).[16] He concludes that a population is in control of its ascent or descent, and its state is visible in its aesthetic choices and production. The specific examples of Botocudo and Chinese are paired with the undefined group of "certain tribes." Schultze-Naumburg combines the trope of Social Darwinist self-determination with a fatalistic shrug at the essentialist urges of humanity, apparently bound not only by the desire to better itself but by its self-destructive opposite. By claiming that aesthetics supersede the superficial pursuit of individual determination and are crucial to the loss or gain of social mores, Schultze-Naumburg invests his cause with utmost national importance: "It is a mistake to believe that the sense of beauty can arise from an accidentally beautiful race (by which accident?). In fact the reverse is true, the sense of beauty begets the beautiful race. Our race still wants to be short and fat, that is why it is" (1902–1903: 118).[17] Entering rhetorically into an implicit union with his audience, he places the responsibility for "our" race's shortcomings firmly with the reader. Appealing to national pride and responsibility, Schultze-Naumburg presents two options: to be fat and short or, presumably emerging from the self-destructive bent, to be beautiful. These are merely the superficial side effects of a problem that Schultze-Naumburg makes much more dramatic: "We can no longer depend on the existence of a reservoir of healthy bodies in the *Volk*, from which to replace that frivolously ruined. Today the damage there is as bad as in our social circles. For this reason an enemy has arisen from the dominant woman's fashion, which is comparable in its danger to alcohol, whose devastating effects threatens to overturn all our proud hopes for the future of our species, begging the question whether the *Kultur der neuen Zeit* will ever be consummated" (1901a: 141).[18]

Shifting biological processes out of their disciplinary context, Schultze-Naumburg avails himself of the *Lebensreform* arguments of the natural and intuitive, again placing the onus on the reader: "Immediately responding with distaste when confronted with a detrimental influence to the body is a symptom of healthy senses, and it is certainly not a good sign if they no longer do. ... Thus a healthy person cannot stand the constriction of his ribcage and the soft tissues beneath it and is immediately uncomfortable" (ibid.: 102).[19] The innately "natural" response to these states is juxtaposed with the perverse throughout the book.

Schultze-Naumburg points to Parisian fashion houses as the origin of the corset throughout his book, just as France is identified as the foreign influence responsible for the perceived descent in German art, despite the Parisian *sans ventre* corset's firm establishment in Germany by 1900. Sabine Welsch deems it the most detrimental corset, because its creation of the ideal S-shaped figure was achieved by elongating the torso, in the process displacing hips, buttocks, and breasts while constricting the stomach (1996: 10). Othmar Birkner's argument that the corset was considered as "*corpus delicti* of the assassination of French fashion on the German '*Völkerfrühling*,'" encompasses some of the drama associated with this debate (1977: 52). To make the connection between French fashion and the corset, Schultze-Naumburg used not only the sketches often published in fashion magazines, but a range of examples from the fine arts.

Pointing to two sculptures, both of which "were exhibited a couple of years ago at the Paris Salon and garnered a great deal of attention," he acknowledges "it was doubtlessly the intention of the artist to express the beauty of the human body" (1901a: 92).[20] This good intention is used as a straw man in his ensuing argument: "We definitely see the corset figure type: the compressed rib cage, the abdomen forced forward, the heavy accumulation of fat around the hips" (ibid.).[21] Suggesting "it takes a very large degree of alienation of the sense of the beauty of the human body for a sculptor to celebrate such a form" (ibid.),[22] he implies a deep estrangement of French artists from the natural human figure. The focus on the French origin of the corset has persisted in German scholarship, visible in Sabine Merta's proclamation that historical protests were aimed primarily against a fashion "dictated by Paris, which used the body of a woman like a sculpture, to be molded at will" (2003: 384).

Schultze-Naumburg puts great emphasis on artistic responsibility, bemoaning current artistic production, explaining "there is a large number of those who are very taken with just this distortion, this caricature of the human body with its tight waist and all the rest, and who are very fond of our modern Parisian fashion, because it is the only one they can imagine" (1901a: 93).[23] Thus the visual arts are overwhelmed with "a blatant delight in the tight waist" (ibid.).[24] He identifies this as a matter of innate preference: "No one creates that which does not appeal to him. ... If the will to create the beautifully developed human body were innate to artists, they would achieve apotheosis everywhere and thus be the best teachers" (ibid.).[25] While he suggests that personal preference is expressed in artistic creation, the citation as a whole does not endow the artist with the prophetic and truthful intensity that would come to define his place in Weimar and National Socialist society. Instead, Schultze-Naumburg suggests artists "too must be guided, so that they may follow the leaders as a herd, since among painters and sculptors spiritual leaders are just as rare as in the rest of humanity" (ibid.).[26] He appropriates a position as the voice of reason for both the wider populace and his fellow artists. The movement exhibited a similarly nationalist agenda, pitting Germany against France, as that iterated in the realm of the fine arts by the *Protest Deutscher Künstler,* led by Carl Vinnen in 1911.

Using the method of direct comparison introduced by his *Kunstwart* articles and *Kulturarbeiten,* Schultze-Naumburg presented not only titillating photographs—used in both his positive and negative examples—but examples of ancient Greek sculpture, which exemplify the ideal female form. The positive example, or *Beispiel,* of the ideal human form used in *Kultur* is usually described as "entirely identical with the forms of antiquity" (Schultze-Naumburg 1901a: 53).[27] Wojciech Kunicki points out that Schultze-Naumburg did not conceive of the classical past as a humanist lesson, but instead as a practical point of reference for the artists, who should be committed entirely to the single beautiful object: the human body (Kunicki 1988: 208). He also draws attention to the use of the classical tradition as a signifier of a class, in this case the *Bildungsbürgertum,* whose ambition was to reclaim a position of political and cultural prominence (ibid.: 209).

Extrapolating from his understanding of human anatomy ruled by laws of functionality, Schultze-Naumburg assigned a normative meaning to that ideal form he considered "natural" and/or "healthy" and "beautiful," concluding that an "aesthetic defect is the visible indication of failing utility" (1901a: 31).[28] This was not a novel position, but fits into the pattern by which *fin de siècle* popular hygienic literature commonly "presented an aestheticized version of the ideal human body, espousing the bodily norms of Greek and Roman antiquity," in which beauty was regarded as "the expression of healthy and normal organic functioning and ugliness as a sign of disease" (Hau 2003: 33).

An example of this pervasive philhellenism, with which Schultze-Naumburg was intimately familiar, is Robert Mielke's juxtaposition:

> Germany: more a painterly than a sculptural disposition; lyrical, heartfelt disposition, that is turned toward contemplative enjoyment and cheerful quiescence. These are characteristics, which also belonged, in a different combination, to the ancient Greeks, which permits the conclusion that German art could if it developed undisturbed experience a similar artistic flowering as the Greek. That was truly Greek; ours, now approaching, will be truly German; the former was carried as much by the totality of the *Volk,* as ours will be now. Modern art is eminently *volkstümlich*; it follows the migration of the countryman into the city, takes its place by the smoking chimney stacks, and conversely returns to the countryman's table. (1891: 27)

In 1900 the physician Carl Heinrich Stratz published the article "Die Vergewaltigung des weiblichen Körpers" and the heavily illustrated book *Die Frauenkleidung*. Like Schultze-Naumburg, Stratz felt he had a mission to educate the wider public in the aesthetic norms of the human body. His text lists a range of illnesses and irreducible deformations and depended on photographs and sketches to illustrate the corset's effects on bones, skin, muscles, and organs as well as body shape. While photographs illustrated the anatomic disfigurements, such as a protruding stomach, depressed lower ribcage, and shifted organs, the text described the loss of blood supply to liver, pancreas, gall bladder, uterus, intestine, and lower parts of the lungs, and significant pathological results including ulcers, digestive troubles, bilious complaints, fatigue, and trouble with menstruation (Stratz 1900: 144, as cited in Welsch: 1996: 15). Stratz's positive examples, again like Schultze-Naumburg's, drew on sculptural examples from Hellenic antiquity. The use of statues of Hercules and Apollo to illustrate "the masculine ideals of beauty and strength," and Venus to give "form to feminine ideal," was a common trope (Hau 2003: 33).

Ludwig Bartning reviewed the book for the *Kunstwart* unfavorably, chiding such criticism of reform clothing as "partially more detrimental to health, partially uglier" than the corset, and including a special note alongside the text establishing Schultze-Naumburg as the *Kunstwart's* preferred expert on the matter: "The readers of the *Kunstwart* know that Schultze-Naumburg has fought for better women's clothing for years. His book on the topic is forthcoming. Naturally, a good book by another author on this topic would be very welcome to him, and to the *Kunstwart*, as kindred spirit. It is all the more disappointing to encounter arguments in Stratz's book that force us into the opposition, and discussion, since these falsities are presented with a doctor's authority and the authority of a man, who has gained considerable public influence as an expert on this topic" (1901: 266–267).

As Bartning's review illustrates, Norbert Borrmann's suggestion that *Kultur des weiblichen Körpers* was Schultze-Naumburg's most influential book, alongside the *Kulturarbeiten* series (1989: 18), is apt. In addition to its immediate contribution both to the discussion at hand it lifted Schultze-Naumburg to a more prominent position in popular journalism. More noteworthy and problematic are Borrmann's attempts to place Schultze-Naumburg's work in the scientific rather than the salacious realm. He suggests that the latter explored an interest in anatomy by auditing four semesters of Hans Virchow's lectures in Berlin, citing the *Lebenserinnerungen*, which recall "assiduously sketching the dissected corpses" and recognition of the "odd incongruity between the current state of women's clothing and the actual form of the human body" (Schultze-Naumburg, *Lebenserinnerungen, Seitensprünge*, 39, as cited in Borrmann 1989: 18).[29] This may be influenced by Bartning's interpretation of the book as an example of Schultze-Naumburg's extraordinary foresight: "Thirty years ago he anticipated what has now become the literal reality of European women's clothing" (1929: 14–15). Bartning casts Schultze-Naumburg as an innovator, the first to make a strong, cogent case, since until his book "even doctors commented in a relatively vague and indecisive manner" (ibid.: 15).

Indeed the book includes such exemplary descriptive passage on the alignment of hip and leg bones and their effect on birth, in which Schultze-Naumburg concludes "'wide hips' are indicative neither of heightened parturition, nor of any other physiological advantages, but rather the opposite" (1901a: 31).[30] Putting aside the statements' rather tenuous relationship to scientific research, his appropriation of medical authority is made particularly noteworthy by his ensuing connection of these "findings" to aesthetics and race: "When oriental peoples celebrate wide hips as beautiful, in contrast to the Nordic-Aryans, then taste is developed along a racial type, of which it is impossible to prove, that it is higher and has greater developmental potential" (ibid.).[31] While it is evident that his interest in and use of the topic served his political agenda, it may have had its origins in rather more practical considerations. The mass of writing in cultural and arts criticism, philosophy, and the broader humanities has been well established, but it was only after 1850 that the genre of popular sciences emerged in German journalism, straddling the dry transmission of knowledge and superficial trivialization, and, as Andreas Daum points out, often pursued by failed academics trying to make a living (1996: 205–206).

Ursula Volbert suggests that the title, or more aptly the inclusion of the word *"Kultur,"* attempted to link this new subject matter to the successful *Kulturarbeiten* series (2001: 34). This suggestion seems plausible, not in terms of the series of which only two volumes were published before *Kultur des weiblichen Körpers*, but as an addition to the series of articles upon which it was based, published in *Der Kunstwart* in 1901. The whole series' influence will probably have helped the books ongoing republication in the Weimar Republic, when the immediate issue here at hand—the widespread use of the corset by German women—was no longer relevant. In turn-of-the-century popular discourse however, the topic was timely. This subject matter also allows for a brief examination of Schultze-Naumburg's prolific publication practice, since, drawing on *Die Kultur*, he published a range of articles on the topic in which he reused entire sections, tailoring each article only very slightly to its audience. One such example is the short article "Zur Reform der Frauenkleidung," published in the *Frauen-Genossenschafts-Blatt* in which Schultze-Naumburg omits all mention of national origins of offending women's clothing, omnipresent in the book (1902–1903: 83). This is of particular note, since the article's other passages are rife with unaltered self-citations, but would have been less interesting to the presumably fairly homogeneous readership of women more interested in practical advice. The article was published in two parts, of which the latter deals almost exclusively with the implementation of corset-less dresses and the alternatives, which Schultze-Naumburg discusses at length. He strikes a chatty tone, avoiding any implication of blame: "At fourteen or earlier the mother put the corset onto her daughter, with the best intentions, simply not knowing any better" (ibid.), and mourning the state of fashion as: "A confession of failure, a hideous mark of our culture and irreconcilable with the intellectual enlightenment of the twentieth century" (ibid.). Maximilian Harden invited Schultze-Naumburg to write on the topic in his journal *Die Zukunft* in 1902, strengthening Schultze-Naumburg's position as the movement's spokesman, and eliciting cautious optimism in the success of the cause: "Those publicly denying the need of a reform are becoming fewer" (1902b: 204).

As Heinrich Tessenow's rather late review of 1908 illustrates, the book continued to be well received:

> In this book Schultze-Naumburg teaches very congenially, first the internal structure of the human body and then, using photographs of a large number of women's bodies, which have developed freely and naturally, illustrates the way in which especially the Greek and the best new artists consider such human bodies sacred. The photographs and drawings in the book aptly illustrate the text, and the book in its entirety is such, that one must expect every reader to become its grateful devotee—as long as he is not inherently opposed to all innovation—and will take on the campaign against the terrible disfigurement of women's bodies perpetrated by our national dress. (206)

The book's appeal is not lost on more recent scholarship, in which it is touted as "fresh and lively in tone, with a good dose of polemic and not lacking humor" (Kerbs 1999: 222). In 1915, Schultze-Naumburg grouped the movement in with the reform movement more broadly, and specifically with the *Heimatschutz*:

> No movement can develop in the very depths of a people, without a general cohesion with the inner developments of the people, and it is no coincidence that those thoughts, which coalesced under the name "*Heimatschutz*," were contemporary to those ideas hoping to create a new people's ethos. So men arose who examined the threatening physical de-

> generation of the people with fear and demanded that a new lineage be developed through physical exercise and competition. The women and girls forced into tight French corsets were pointed out, and it was demanded that they too grow up in free and healthy corporeal beauty, to be able to be the mothers of strong men. Much laziness and self-consciousness, much ugly prudery was dispensed with, and the body became a source of joy again, as it was to all the great peoples. (21–22)

This need to push back against perceived degeneracy was present in much popular journalism, such as the article in *Kraft und Schönheit*, which announced in 1914: "We see the physical degeneration of a large part of our race and want to work against it in every possible way."[32]

Excerpts of *Die Kultur* were republished in the Weimar Republic, under the title "Der ethische Wert der Körperpflege," in the Swiss journal *Werbeschrift für Körperkultur* (Schultze-Naumburg 1925: 32–33). The piece bemoans the lack of an appropriate women's fashion as well as the attitude toward cleanliness and *Körperpflege*, something that might initially seem outmoded for a publication date of 1925. Nonetheless, by 1929, in his very flattering review of Schultze-Naumburg's career, Hans F. K. Günther acknowledged: "Another Nordic trait is the *sense for a well-kept demeanor*—we remember Schultze-Naumburg's once so subversive, now almost forgotten book on clothing the female body and the 'demeanor' of the houses he built" (274). Across the Atlantic, in *The New Republic*, Lewis Mumford credited Schultze-Naumburg's work as an accelerant to the German *Jugendbewegung* and the "active culture of the body" (1932: 280). Mumford extolls:

> It was a present-day Nazi reactionary, Dr. Schultze-Naumburg, who thirty years ago published a remarkable book upon human physical development, illustrated by a handsome array of photographs of naked women, beautiful or deformed: the book went through numerous editions and gave a deep impulse both to the culture of the body and its comely display. The New Germany utilized all the latent good of the old Germany: but in ten years, through its powerful élan, through its sense of spiritual release, it did more to embody all these formative elements than the old Germany had done in forty-five. (Ibid.)

The following year, in response to "the rigid pronouncements the National Socialists made in terms of public displays of eroticism," Diederichs's publishing house purged its warehouse and with "this revision [at the end of 1933] Schultze-Naumburg's richly illustrated *Die Kultur* (1901), disappeared from the list of revenues (Triebel 2004: 116). Florian Triebel argues that this cut "had nothing to do with revenue, though the numbers dipped from 349 in 1924 to 0 in 1931, and of the total 1,420 copies sold between 1924–1933, only 601 were sold in 1933" (ibid.: 416).

Schultze-Naumburg's 1901 position is one of almost unbridled optimism, which, unlike the cultural pessimism usually cited as the defining *fin de siècle* experience *and* a root cause for National Socialism (Schwarz 2003: 228), assumes society is in constant linear progress and is representative of his social circle. He presumes that his work will educate his reader and convince them of his goal: "There are people who seek to establish an inner necessity by looking to the circumstances of the past. Indeed, even the Roman woman of the decadence wore corsets. By the same logic one could condone the inquisition, witch trials and torture. We strive, after all, to continue to develop to a higher state and not get caught in the misconceptions of the dark Middle-Ages" (1901a: 108). The hopeful and matter-of-fact attitude proposes an alternative modernity, assumed to be happier and healthier than the present and is in no way reactionary. As Edward Dickinson points out, this school of thought was "characterized by a distinctive … belief that things are doable, [and] that anything can be done" (2004: 2), promising propagandistic potential and resonance among the *Bildungsbürgertum*. Schultze-Naumburg's erstwhile student, and later friend and champion, Ludwig Bartning gave a speech in his role as professor at the *Vereinigte Staatsschulen Berlin* in 1931 in which he recalled the development of the past decades: "A transformation of the woman, which could hardly have been greater, took place before our eyes. Her dress and body were newly created. Women are more beautiful, than they ever were … the racial formation of human facial features has been newly explored and moved into the focus of general interest" (Bartning 1931: unpaginated).

Constructing the *Volkskörper*

After the ousting of the corset, Schultze-Naumburg left the discussion of women's fashion, but continued to use and develop his rhetoric of the corporeal, in biologistic and racial narratives. Schultze-Naumburg recalls his shift away from a *Milieutheorie*-motivated *Volkspädagogik* seeking to awaken and rally the masses: "My entire structure began to shake, when I was forced to realize that hoping an inherited trait might be changed in some way by persuasion, is a lost cause."[33] In the unpublished manuscript "Mein baukünstlerisches Vermächtnis," Schultze-Naumburg dates this shift: "I spent decades considering these strange apparitions in architecture, and, caught in the delusional pedagogy of the nineteenth century, thought the cause of all evil could be identified in incorrect architectural education. I only became familiar enough with the laws of sociology and anthropology to understand the root causes during and after the First World War. ... Now everything was clarified, simplified, and illuminated in light of the natural sciences' method of approach."[34] As only those of German blood may be *Volksgenossen,* Schultze-Naumburg concluded that only German blood enabled education and insight: "And yet today there is more hope than ever that man will take his fate into his own hands. Essentially, the possible measures are composed of two modes: the curtailing of multitudinous procreation of the unfit, in particular the criminals, drinkers, idiots, and those afflicted with genetic physical or mental illness, while the number of children of the able should be encouraged in every possible way" (1926b: 387–388).[35] As Daniela Bohde argues, the intertwining of his eugenics, which incorporated a readiness for violence, and his conception of physiognomy, was never content to merely "read" the physiognomy, but always proposed "shaping" it (2012: 88). In *Kunst und Rasse* Schultze-Naumburg's describes his "life-long goal" as "the examination of our country's physiognomy, determining in which way it is exhibited in the buildings and designs of the people, to examine the expression within it, and by comparing it to the work produced in other epochs, to establish conclusions regarding those populations and their spiritual and corporeal compositions" (1927: 123).[36] He strengthens the particular point of the centrality of this theme to his corpus by explaining that "the original plan to spend a chapter of my *Kulturarbeiten* on the revision of racial considerations had to be relinquished, since the topic would far have outstripped the scope of a single chapter" (ibid.: 10).[37] It is noteworthy that an albeit secondary objective may have been to establish himself as a progenitor of this discourse.

His *Kunst und Rasse* explicitly dismisses *Milieutheorie*: "When the environment is stronger than the human, he will also conform *to it,* but not by a change to hereditary disposition, but primarily by individual assimilation. Selection for the purpose of assimilation has—unfortunately—not yet been used intentionally. The unbridled overestimation of education and the corresponding misunderstanding of hereditary disposition is simply a part of nineteenth century gospel and its underlying falsities" (ibid.: 154).[38] The book grapples with this paradigm shift: "Only two avenues remain to explain the shift in valuation of human physiognomy. The first examines the environment or temporal determinants of the environment, the other the humans populating this world. The former conceives of humans merely as a malleable wax, which can be molded in any direction, and is kneaded by an exterior destiny. The latter recognizes each individual as a genetic carrier of specific traits, born with them and passed on to their progeny" (ibid.: 153).[39] The book's rhetoric makes clear that he ascribes to the latter avenue, but the ideological concepts established in his early *Heimatschutz* writing were subsumed into his racialized art history.

In 1918 Schultze-Naumburg cofounded the *Nordischer Ring* and joined the *Deutsche Nationale Volkspartei,* and, having completed building the Cecilienhof in Potsdam, recentered his life entirely in Saaleck. The surrounding communities of Naumburg, Weimar, and Jena provided close contact with such writers as Hans F. K. Günther, Richard Walther Darré, and the *völkisch* self-proclaimed literature critic Adolf Bartels. While the former became a close friend only in the Weimar Republic, the latter was a member of the *Kunstwart* circle and well known to Schultze-Naumburg from his *fin de siècle* involvement in the journal. Bartels produced texts with a distinct biologistic bent: "Healthy art is always possible; for beside the sick—otherwise existence itself would be impossible—there are always healthy elements in the *Volk,* indeed they preponderate. … *Heimatkunst* accompanies this German Ur-feeling, it desires the entirety of Germany, the union over the plurality, in this plurality the unity" (1924: 10). Having described the ambition, Bartels goes on to describe its foils: "Absolute fidelity is its main ambition, fidelity in the recognition of natural character and the soul of the *Volk.* A strong trend of thought opposes the *Heimat* artists: the backlash to the flattening, cookie-cutter effects of the opinions of the liberal bourgeoisie and its vacuous *Reichssimpelei,* as well as the internationalism of social democracy" (ibid.: 11). In *Kunst und Rasse,* Schultze-Naumburg echoes Bartel's "natural character," in his phenotypical argument that "man has the ability … to project a part of his inner being onto his buildings and the construction of his natural landscape. All these projects, even the smallest and most insignificant, carry a certain expression on their forehead, and we can read it, much like the expression on a human face. It unerringly reveals the type and being of its creator" (1927: 123).[40]

Günther and Darré became close personal friends and regular guests at Saaleck, and exerted great influence on Schultze-Naumburg's emerging racial theories and sensibility. Paul Ortwin Rave identifies Günther's work as the origin of the "National Socialist doctrine of visual arts," which, he argues, "cumulated in the demand that every figural artistic representation correspond to the canon of Nordic racial theory" (1987: 22–23). Günther's first work, *Ritter, Tod und Teufel. Eine Wesensart des nordischen Menschen* (1922), was indebted to the works of Gobineau, Le Bon, and Chamberlain, and "hoped to awaken the *Volksgenossen*'s racial perception" (Hoßfeld 2001: 47). His *Rassenkunde des Deutschen Volkes* was commissioned by the publisher J. F. Lehmann in Munich, and printed in 1922 to great acclaim: the first edition sold out within two months, by 1929 it was in its thirteenth edition, and sold over 500,000 copies by 1945 (ibid.). Lehmann emphasized the quality of illustration, and produced the book as an illustrated guide, which suggested browsing a magazine, rather than reading a treatise. Gustav Blume calls the book "doubtlessly one of the most effective weapons of National Socialism," and identifies Günther as the "last and at the same time the most important of the harbingers of National Socialism" (1948: 85). Schultze-Naumburg recalls: "[In 1922] Gradually I came to see that nothing could be expected from such people. I began to be suspicious of my conceptions of the educability of the human race … I sought deeper understanding and found it only in the analysis of *Rassenkunde* and the teachings of heredity" (1941: 21).[41]

Kunst und Rasse was published two years after *Rasse und Stil* and exhibits a similar rhetoric, holding Jews and Freemasons responsible for cultural decline, tied to the negative influences of the metropolis, conceived as a breeding ground of racially inferior populations. A central issue driving public consumption of these ideologies remained the fear of the destruction of familiar and treasured aesthetic benchmarks, by such impulses as Expressionism and Dadaism, without viable alternatives or replacements. The book's writerly approach too is similar, lacking specialist vocabulary, or abstract theoretical musings, and is thoroughly illustrated with photographs by which the reader is encouraged to train his or her eye to recognize the stereotypes pointed out by the text. Schultze-Naumburg gives it significant credit: "It ascertained the legitimacy of a chain of thoughts, I'd been entertaining for a long time, but for which I was lacking the notional conception" (ibid.),[42] and implies suggesting an exchange of ideas: "Rarely did I encounter such a rigorous intellectual exchange, which was by no means restricted to a narrow subject area" (ibid.). A brief review published in the *Annalen der Philosophie und philosophischen Kritik* in 1928 provides the context in which Schultze-Naumburg's work was considered. He is included under the subheading *Ästhetik – Philosophie der Kunst*, and alongside Walter Benjamin's *Ursprung des deutschen Trauerspiels* (1928), Paul Ernst's *Der Weg zur Form* (1928), and Johannes Volkelt's *System der Ästhetik* (1927). A journalist, denoted by his initials J. J., comments drily, that the book "attempts to show the reflection of the artist's race in his work," and that "the development in architecture of the last century, as well as sculpture and painting, show that we are situated in dramatic racial decline" (J. J. 1928: 94).

Despite his lack of training in *Rassenkunde,* anthropology, or ethnography, within Nordic circles Schultze-Naumburg assumed a patriarchal role as the authority on all things *Kunst und Rasse*. This central position is illustrated in the dedications inserted by Günther into his *Platon als Hüter des Lebens* (1928), his *Rassengeschichte des hellenischen und des römischen Volkes* (1929), and Darré's *Neuadel aus Blut und Boden* (1930), completed during a stay at Saaleck. Indeed, Darré and Schultze-Naumburg's friendship extended to the latter's wife introducing Darré to his second wife Charlotte Vietinghoff-Scholl (Bramwell 1985: 47). This *völkisch* context informed Schultze-Naumburg's tone and the political ends of his art and architectural writing, but the discussion's content, the Nordic, was also shared with a community of German-speaking art historians such as Wilhelm Pinder (1878–1947), "the great public art historian between the wars in Germany" (Boyd Whyte 2013: 19), whose literary career resembles Schultze-Naumburg's in its emphasis on the production of accessible texts, published for consumption by the masses, in his case in the *Blaue Bücher* series. Perfectly illustrating the continuity of his popularity after the Second World War is the republication of his *Deutsche Burgen und feste Schlößer aus allen Ländern deutscher Zunge* (1913) as *Deutsche Burgen und feste Schlößer* in 1957.[43] While nationalist *Kunstimperialismus* was not a novel approach and is exemplified best by Goethe's panegyric to the Strasbourg Cathedral, these writers, like Schultze-Naumburg, considered the artist's ethnicity or blood—i.e., membership of a *Volk* or *Rasse*—as the determining factor, or "style," produced.

In his 1926 article "Die internationale Kunstausstellung in Dresden in rassenhygienischer Betrachtung," Schultze-Naumburg proposed "an art that is disconnected from life is unthinkable, and the reality is that every art truthfully mirrors the purpose in life of the Volk, by whom it is created" (1926a: 440).[44] With this premise, he describes the exhibit as:

> a true hell of subhuman beings ... if the exhibition indeed presents an objective representation of the state of our *Volkskörper* and the condition of its environment, there are hardly words to describe the horror of the test results in an appropriately drastic way. I see three options: either the material presented here is in fact an expression of the nature or entirety of the German *Volk*. Then Germany seems ripe for decline or to resignation from the cultural sphere of the white *Völker*. Or the exhibition is the expression of a cycle [that] for reasons that cannot be examined here only allows a small fraction of the *Gesamtwesen* to be expressed ... or, finally, the *Volkskörper* is physically and spiritually oriented differently and is healthier; it is only the contemporary arts that focus exclusively on phenomena of decline and degeneration." (Ibid.: 441)[45]

Availing himself again of statistics, albeit without data or real discussion, Schultze-Naumburg casts the exhibition as a litmus test of the population as a whole: "Like many phenomena, the arts too reflect a significant racial decline, both in terms of the ratio of the creative race within the total composition, and in terms of the definition of the types themselves" (ibid.: 442).[46]

He joined the NSDAP in 1930, perhaps at the behest of his friend Wilhelm Frick, the first NSDAP minister in the Weimar Republic. In 1930 Frick invited Schultze-Naumburg to take on the directorship of Weimar *Künstlerische Lehranstalten*, and also instated the Germanist Hans F. K. Günther, who first rose to prominence with his *Rassenbuch des deutschen Volkes* in 1922, as professor of social anthropology at the University of Jena (Lützhoft 1971: 39). Frick and Schultze-Naumburg developed the decree "*Wider die Negerkultur für das Deutsche Volkstum*" issued on 5 April 1930. This decree was the first iteration of a policy of *entartete Kunst*, and resulted in Germany's first twentieth-century *Bildersturm* in October 1930, in which Schultze-Naumburg "cleansed" the collections of the Weimar university and *Schloßmuseum*. As Frick's consultant on the arts (*Kunstberater*), Schultze-Naumburg helped define and develop the emerging arts, cultural, and pedagogical policy of the NSDAP in Thuringia, resulting ultimately in the National Socialist "degenerate art" exhibitions beginning in 1937.

Both *Kunst und Rasse* and this edict seek to construct a physical portrait of positive racial attributes of the German populace in opposition to the deviant other, based on continuities in the use of race and degeneracy in constructions of a national art and aesthetic proposed by such Wilhelmine texts as *Die Kultur*. Peter Walkenhorst calls the shift in the spread and public acceptance of radical nationalist interpretive paradigms a "historical quantum leap" (2007: 333). As the defining difference between the Wilhelmine radical nationalist *Schreibtischtäter*, who did not question the state monopoly on violence, and perhaps more importantly, expected the government or military to implement measures against cultural and ethnic minorities, Walkenhorst points out the Weimar Republic's new nationalists' readiness (and at times determination) to put their thoughts into violent action (ibid.: 338). Bazon Brock's work comes to the same conclusion and emphasizes the disinterest and dismissal of empty words and theories by the National Socialists, determined to put their ideas into practice and realize utopias by whatever means (1990: 16).

If the arts were conceived of in the Wilhelmine period as a tool of national unification and economic betterment, as Hildegard Brenner points out, in the Weimar Republic they became the medium best suited to illustrating the degeneracy and sins of the *Systemzeit* (1963: 37)—this term was used retrospectively by the National Socialists to describe the Weimar Republic. This development is clearly visible in Schultze-Naumburg's idealistic vision of the German *Volkskörper*, which was constructed in opposition to and at the expense of "the other," the non-Germans who could not possibly measure up. While Schultze-Naumburg explored this new discourse by the analysis of art and architecture, and Günther wrote on literature in *Rasse und Stil*, Richard Eichenauer discussed music in *Musik und Rasse* (1932) (Dümling 1993). The development and introduction of these ideas shaped the cultural criticism before and after 1933. In the arts, it meant the dismissal of the wide range of "isms," and a push toward a singular artistic concept, which could function as the final and eternal unifier for the proposed thousand-year *Reich* only by virtue of its singularity (Brock 1990: 16). The aesthetic counterworld Schultze-Naumburg constructed addressed dreams, desires, anxieties, and cultural and political criticism, and was cast as a possible future waiting to be realized. *Lebenskunst* and the fine arts were figured as palingenetic defenses against decadence and degeneration.

Kunst und Rasse was followed by *Der Kampf um die Kunst* in 1932, *Rassegebundene Kunst and Kunst aus Blut und Boden* in 1934, and *Nordische Schönheit: Ihr Wunschbild im Leben und in der Kunst* in 1937. These, it should be noted, are only his publications relating to race-bound art; his wider record included an additional thirty books, over two hundred articles, and countless lectures. *Rassegebundene Kunst* (1934) identifies art as the crucial vehicle of illustration of the racial *Zielbild* of the new National Socialist state: "No other term is as definitive of the entire Weltanschauung of the new state, as the concept of blood and soil. But only the arts can make visible the racial *Zielbild*" (26).[47] Inherent in this citation, tying art inextricably to the theories of blood and soil, and in the establishment of National Socialist ideology and the Third Reich, is the need to differentiate the new state from previous governments of Germany. Establishing this division, particularly between the Third Reich and the Weimar Republic, was crucial in establishing the Third Reich at once as a progression and as the return to a purer Germany. This past Germany, imagined as the ideal racial utopia, free from conflict and strife, could be reclaimed, it was suggested, by overcoming the current degenerate elements pervading social, political, and cultural life.

Ostensibly, National Socialism wrought change by revamping existing hierarchies and systems, including some extant factors and excluding others. Its combining of evolutionary Social Darwinism with the return to a bygone age is a characteristic contradiction inherent to the movement's ideology and propaganda. This inconsistency becomes apparent in the examination of individual instances of propaganda in which unclear messages emerge, and it is by no means clear that the appropriation of medieval sculpture or the Greek nude, for example, constitute improvements on the original. Schultze-Naumburg presents "blood and soil" as the single most important term in the creation of this new worldview. While this argument is in part self-serving and perhaps an attempt to enter the main stream of the emergent policy discourse, it captures the propagandistic power of the blood and soil rhetoric, in redefining the population and reimagining the *Volksgemeinschaft*. Ian Kershaw suggests that this people's community, established by the exclusion of undesirable elements, replaces the hierarchy of class with that of racial purity (2010). This new hierarchy introduces a new equality within German society and created the illusion that, as long as bloodlines permitted, in the new *Reich* anything was possible.

Lara Day is an art and cultural historian who studied at the University of Edinburgh's Edinburgh College of Art, and the School of History, Classics and Archaeology. She has written on twentieth-century German art, architecture, and culture, on such topics as the artist Anselm Kiefer and collective guilt, and the Wilhelmine *Heimatschutz* movement. She is currently preparing an intellectual biography of Paul Schultze-Naumburg for publication. She works for Artsy.net in Berlin.

Notes

1. "Den ersten, der die Voraussetzung, den weiblichen Körper, in seinen bei der Kleidung in Frage kommenden Beziehungen behandelt, den zweiten, der die Schlussfolgerungen auf die Kleidung zieht." All translations are by the author unless stated otherwise.
2. "Verlag Eugen Diederichs: Paul Schultze-Naumburg *Die Kultur des Weiblichen Körpers als Grundlage der Frauenkleidung*," Deutsches Literatur Archiv Marbach, A: Eugen Diederichs Verlag / Florentiner und Leipziger Anfänge, HS. 1995.0002. Undated: 2.
3. "Man weiß nicht, wie ein hässlicher verkrüppelter, geschweige den wie ein schöner und normaler Fuss aussieht, gesteht sich diese Unwissenheit aber auch nicht ein, sondern wird vor allen Dingen heftig und erregt, und behauptet dann in den Tag hinein alle möglichen haltlosen Dinge, um sich selbst zu rechtfertigen."
4. "Der wahrhaft ethische Mensch verkrüppelt sich selbst nicht. Er erwirbt sich das Gefühl für die richtige Form seines Körpers bei der Pflege, die er ihm angedeihen läßt, und er beachtet es sofort, wenn an einem Teile seines Körpers eine Mißhandlung vor sich gehen soll."

5. "Wie ist es denn möglich, daß niemand wahrnimmt, wie all die Frauen, all die Mädchen um uns herum verunstaltete Leiber haben? Ist es denn lediglich fahrlässige Unwissenheit, daß sie die 'elegante façon' anbeten und keine Ahnung von dem jämmerlichen Leibe haben wollen der darunter steht und der sich doch überall mit solch aufdringlicher Deutlichkeit darbietet?"
6. "Ein amüsantes Bilderbuch soll es nicht sein. Ich habe dem Buche die Illustrationen beigegeben, die unentbehrlich waren, um jene plastischen Anschauungen zu erzeugen, die zum Aufbau ganz neuer Ideen vom Körper und mithin von der Kleidung notwendig sind."
7. "Die große Fülle von Bildern … sind mit überlegter Absicht ausgewählt … um die an die Entstellung des Körpers durch unsere übliche Tradition gewöhnten Augen durch immer neue Bilder zur anschaulichen Erkenntnis der wahren Form des Körpers zu erziehen. Ich habe dabei wie schon in verschiedenen anderen Schriften, das System angewendet, Beispiel und Gegenbeispiel direkt nebeneinander zu setzen, um das bloße Betrachten zum logischen Schauen zu steigern."
8. "Das es sich hier vorwiegend um weibliche Körper handelt, wird von oberflächlichen Beurteilern, die den sittlichen Ernst der Frage nicht erfassen vermögen, das Buch in die Klasse der auf die Lüsternheit spekulierenden Schriften gerechnet werden. Ich werde das ertragen müssen."
9. "Es handelt sich hier um eine wissenschaftliche und aesthetische Betrachtung eines weiblichen Körpers, und wenn dabei der Einzelne das Sexuelle aus seiner Empfindung nicht ausschalten vermag, so ist es doch nur eine zufällige Begleiterscheinung, auf die es bei der Gestaltung des Problems nicht ankam."
10. "Denn nur Brüste, die so fest und prall sind, daß sie der Idee, sich von fremder Hilfe tragen zu lassen, spotten können, haben Anspruch auf Schönheit."
11. "Schlankheit ist nur dann schön, wenn sie eine ebenmäßige Schlankheit des ganzen Körpers bedeutet, nicht die unmotivierte Enge an einer einzigen Stelle, die in keiner Weise weder anatomisch noch aesthetisch begründet ist und nur durch Irrtümer und perversen Geschmack einer Zeit entstanden ist, die hinter uns liegen muss."
12. "Allerdings muss die Karikatur der Frau mit ihren abnorm breiten Hüften einem perversen Geschmack doch wohl gefallen. Es wäre sonst gar nicht zu verstehen, aus welchen Gründen die Sitte aufgekommen ist, sich 5 und 6 Unterröcke auf den Leib zu binden."
13. "Die schönste Form der Brüste ist zweifellos die vollkommen gleichmäßig gerundete, die ebenmäßig in den Körper verläuft, wie unsere Abb. 24, 25, 28, 31, 32, 33, 34, 37, 38 es zeigen, ohne unter oder zwischen ihnen eine Falte aufkommen zu lassen."
14. "Gewiß ist der Busen des Weibes nichts, was von der Kleidung verleugnet oder versteckt werden soll. Ihr Körper ist bestimmt, durch seine Schönheit das Begehren des Mannes zu reizen."
15. Thanks are due to Matthew Jefferies for drawing my attention to the fact that the *völkisch* reactionary Pudor was regarded by many of the *Lebensreform* circle as a bit of a ridiculous fringe figure, and thus should be considered as illustrating the far end of the spectrum.

16. "Schon manche Tollheit hat die Menschheit in den fünftausend Jahren, die wir zur Not an Kulturdokumenten übersehen können, begangen. Die Botokuden haben sich Holzklötzchen in die Unterlippe gesteckt zur Verschönerung, die Chinesinnen ihre Füße zu Klumpen entwickelt; gewisse Völkerschaften lieben es, sich die Zähne spitz zu feilen. Anthropologische Museen erzählen von noch seltsameren Trieben der Menschheit. Wie Fieberträume ziehen sie dem Blick des Beschauenden vorüber. Das große Fragezeichen, das wir vor alledem machen, um zu erfahren, aus welchen tiefsten Ursachen es geschieht, findet keine andere Beantwortung als die resignierte Bestätigung, daß eben neben all den Trieben der Menschheit, die nach Höherentwicklung drängen, immer solche nebenher gehen, die auf Selbstzerstörung zielen."
17. "Es ist ein Irrtum zu glauben, daß in einer zufällig (durch welchen Zufall?) schönen Rasse der Schönheitssinn entstünde. Umgekehrt, der Schönheitssinn erzeugt sich die schöne Rasse. Unsere Rasse will immer noch kurz und dick sein, darum ist sie's."
18. "Wir dürfen uns nicht mehr darauf verlassen, im 'Volke' einen Fonds von gesunden Körpern zu besitzen, der ersetzen kann, was oben leichtsinnig verdorben wird. Die Verkrüppelungen sind heut dort genau so schlimm wie in unseren Gesellschaftskreisen. Darum ist uns in der herrschenden Frauentracht ein Feind erwachsen, der sich an Gefährlichkeit wohl mit dem Alkohol messen kann, dessen verheerende Wirkung all unsere stolzen Hoffnungen für die Zukunft unseres Geschlechts über den Haufen zu werfen droht, so daß einem Zweifel kommen, ob die 'Kultur der neuen Zeit' sich je vollendet."
19. "Es ist ein Zeichen von Gesundheit, wenn die Sinne eines Menschen sofort auf eine dem Körper schädliche Einwirkung durch Unlustgefühl reagieren, und es ist durchaus kein günstiges Symptom, wenn sie es nicht mehr thun. Wenn einem ganz gesunden Menschen eine Speise widersteht, so kann er sicher sein, daß sie seinem Körper nicht zuträglich ist. Der Säufer hat diese Empfindung gegen den Alkohol verloren, da sein eigenes Prinzip, so weit es im Unbewußten liegt, auf Selbstvernichtung ausgeht. So ist auch einem ganz gesunden Menschen jede Beengung des Rippenkorbs sowie der darunter liegenden Weichteile unerträglich und ruft sofort Unbehagen hervor."
20. "Beides sind Arbeiten, die vor einigen Jahren in Paris im Salon ausgestellt waren und viel Beachtung fanden. In beiden war es ja zweifelsohne die Absicht der Urheber, die Schönheit des menschlichen Körpers zum Ausdruck zu bringen."
21. "Man sieht hier (Abb.92) durchaus den Typen der Korsettfigur: den zusammengepressten Rippenkorb, den vorgetriebenen Unterleib, die starken Fettansammlungen um die Hüften. ... Noch auffallender ist die Deformierung bei Abb. 94."
22. "Es gehört schon thatsächlich ein starkes Entfremden des Sinnes für die Schönheit des menschlichen Körpers dazu, wenn ein Bildhauer eine solche Form verherrlicht."
23. "Es [gibt] eine reichte Anzahl von solchen, denen eben dieses Zerrbild, diese Karikatur von Menschenleib mit der engen Taille und all das andere

ganz ungemein gefällt und die unsere modern 'Pariser' Kleidung wunderschön in Ordnung finden, weil es die einzige ist, die sie aus dem Leben in ihre Vorstellung aufnehmen."
24. "Sehe man sich doch um in der bildenden Kunst—überall wird man ein unverhülltes Vergnügen an der 'engen Taille' entdecken."
25. "Es bildet Niemand etwas, was ihm nicht gefällt. Oder er will, daß ihm nicht Gefallende verhöhnen und bildet es zur Karikatur. Würde der Wille zum herrlich entwickelten Menschenleib in den Künstlern stecken, so würden sie ihn eben überall zur Apotheose bringen und so zu den besten Erziehern werden. Leider ist dem nicht so. Die Künstler sind genau solche Menschen, wir die übrigen auch, mit ihrer Kurzsichtigkeit, ihren Vorurteilen und ihrer geistigen Unfreiheit."
26. "Sie müssen genau so ins Schlepptau genommen werden, damit sie als Herde den Führern nachlaufen, den auch unter den Malern und Bildhauern sind die geistigen Führer genau so selten wir unter der übrigen Menschheit."
27. "Eine vollkommene Identität mit den Formen der Antike."
28. "Der ästhetische Fehler [ist] der sichtbare Anzeiger für den Zweckmäßigkeitsfehler."
29. "Dabei fleißig nach der sezierten Leiche zeichnete ... sonderbarem Mißverhältnis die damalige Frauenkleidung zu der wirklichen Form des menschlichen Körpers geraten war."
30. "Man sieht aus alledem, daß bei Lichte besehen die 'breite Hüfte' weder auf erhöhte Gebärfähigkeit noch auf sonstige physiologische Vorzüge hinweist, sondern eher auf das Gegenteil."
31. "Wenn orientalische Völker im Gegensatz zu nordische-arischen die breite Hüfte als schön besingen, so hat sich der Geschmack am Rassentypus gebildet, von dem man aber in keiner Weise beweisen kann, daß er der entwicklungsfähigere, höhere sei."
32. "Was wir wollen," *Kraft und Schönheit* 14, no. 1 (1914): 1, as cited in Kai Buchholz, "Lebensreformerisches Zeitschriftenwesen," in Buchholz et al., *Die Lebensreform*, 51.
33. Paul Schultze-Naumburg, "Kulturarbeiten," in *Lebensbekenntnisse*, 117, as cited in Gerhard Kratzsch, *Kunstwart und Dürerbund* (Göttingen, 1969), 434.
34. Schultze-Naumburg, "Mein Baukünstlerisches Vermächtnis," unpublished manuscript, NL Schultze-Naumburg, Germanisches National Museum Nuremburg, 12.
35. "Und doch besteht heute mehr Aussicht als je, daß der Mensch sein Geschick in die Hand nimmt. Im wesentlichen bestehen die *möglichen Maßnahmen* aus zwei Arten: Die Hemmung der allzu zahlreichen Fortpflanzungen der Untauglichen, also vor allem der Verbrecher, Trinker, Idioten und mit erblichen körperlichen oder geistigen Krankheiten Behafteten, während die Kinderzahl der Tüchtigen in jeder nur irgend zu Gebote stehenden Weise zu fördern wäre."
36. "Eine Lebensaufgabe des Verfassers war es, die Physiognomie unseres Landes, wie sie in den Bauwerken und den übrigen Gestaltungen der Menschen sichtbar wird, auf den ihre innewohnenden Ausdruck zu untersuchen und aus dem Vergleich mit den Werken anderer Epochen Rückschlüsse auf

die Bevölkerung und ihre geistige und körperliche Zusammensetzung zu ziehen."
37. "Der ursprüngliche Plan, ein Kapitel meiner "Kulturarbeiten" in deren Neubearbeitung dieser Rassenbetrachtung zu widmen, mußte jedoch aufgegeben werden, da das Thema weit über den Rahmen eines einzelnen Kapitels hinausgewachsen wäre."
38. "Wo die Umwelt stärker ist als der Mensch, passt er sich auch *an sie* an, aber nicht durch Veränderung der Erbanlage, sondern vor allem durch individuelle Anpassung. Auslese zum Zweck der Anpassung ist bisher—leider—kaum bewußt angewandt worden. Die maßlose Überschätzung der Erziehung und dementsprechende Verkennung der Erbanlagen gehört nun einmal mit zum Evangelium des 19. Jahrhunderts und seinen grundlegenden Irrtümern."
39. "Als Erklärung für die Wertveränderung der Physiognomie der Menschen bleiben nur zwei Möglichkeiten. Die eine sucht sie in der Umwelt oder den umweltbestimmenden Zeitumständen, die andere in den diese Welt bevölkernden Menschen. Jene erblickt in den Menschen nur ein nach allen Richtungen hin formbares Wachse, welches von einem außerhalb stehenden Schicksal geknetet wird; diese erkennt in den einzelnen Menschen Erbträger von gegebenen Eigenschaften, die mit ihnen geboren werden und welche sie auch ihre Nachkommen mitvererben."
40. "Auch in seinen Bauwerken und in der Umgestaltung der natürlichen Landschaft ... besitzt der Mensch ein Mittel, einen Teil seines Selbst sozusagen in die Außenwelt zu projizieren. All diese Werke, auch die kleinsten und unbedeutensten, tragen einen bestimmten Ausdruck an ihrer Stirn, und wir können in ihnen lesen, wie in dem Ausdruck eines menschlichen Gesichts. Er verrät uns in unbestechlicher Weise Art und Wesen des Urhebers."
41. "Ich sah allmählich ein, daß von so gearteten Menschen nichts zu erwarten sein würde. Ich wurde langsam mißtrauisch gegen meine eigenen Vorstellungen von der Erziehbarkeit der Menschen ... ich suchte nach besserer Erkenntnis und fand diese allein in den Deutungen der Rassenkunde und der Erblichkeitslehre."
42. "Es brachte mir die Bestätigung für die Richtigkeit einer Gedankenkette, die ich schon seit langem hegte, für die mir aber doch die begrifflich haltbaren Vorstellungen fehlten."
43. Both books were published by the Langewiesche Verlag in Cologne, which also published his: *Die Bildwerke des Naumburger Doms; Bürgerbauten Deutscher Vergangenheit* (1957); *Deutscher Barock* (1951); *Rembrandts Selbstbildnisse* (1950); *Der Bamberger Dom* (1949); *Der deutsche Park, vornehmlich des 18. Jahrhunderts* (1926).
44. "Eine vom Leben losgelöste Kunst ist undenkbar und tatsächlich spiegelt jede darstellende Kunst getreu den Lebensinhalt des Volkes, das sie hervorgebracht."
45. "Eine wahre Hölle des Untermenschen, die sich hier vor uns ausbreitet ... zeigte die Ausstellung in der Tat ein objektives Bild von dem Zustand unseres Volkskörpers und den Zuständen seiner Umwelt, so gäbe es kaum ein Wort, das das Grauenhafte dieses Prüfungsergebnisses drastisch genug

zu bezeichnen vermöchte. Ich sehe drei Möglichkeiten: Entweder ist das hier gebotene Material tatsächlich ein Ausdruck des Wesens der Gesamtheit des deutschen Volkes. Dann scheint allerdings Deutschland reif zum Untergang oder doch zum Ausscheiden aus dem Kulturkreis der weißen Völker. Oder die Ausstellung ist die Lebensäußerung eines Kreises, der aus Ursachen, die hier nicht untersucht werden können, nur einen Teilausschnitt aus dem Gesamtwesen zum Wort kommen läßt. … Oder endlich: der Volkskörper ist körperlich und geistig anders orientiert und gesunder; nur die Kunst von heute befaßt sich in einseitiger Einstellung mit Verfalls— und Entartungserscheinungen."

46. "Wie so viele andere Erscheinungen erzählt uns auch die Kunst von einem starken rassischen Niedergang sowohl hinsichtlich des Verhältnissatzes der schöpferischen Rassen in der Zusammensetzung der Gesamtheit als auch hinsichtlich der Ausprägung der Typen selber."

47. "Kein anderer Begriff ist für die gesamte Weltanschauung des neuen Staates so richtunggebend wie Blut und Boden. Das rassische Zielbild sichtbar machen kann uns aber allein die Kunst."

References

Adamek, U. 1982. *Reformkleidung als Fortschritt? Zur Entstehung einer Reformierten Kinderkleidung um die Jahrhundertwende.* Marburg.
Bartels, A. 1924. *Heimatkultur, Heimatdichtung, Heimatkunst.* Leipzig.
Bartning, L. 1901. "Wie man über Frauenkleidung schreibt." *Der Kunstwart* 14, no. 19: 266–269.
———. 1929. *Paul Schultze-Naumburg: Ein Pionier Deutscher Kulturarbeit.* Munich.
———. 1931. "Was ist lehrbar in der Kunst?" Berlin.
Betts, P. 2004. *The Authority of Everyday Objects.* Berkeley, CA.
Birkner, O. 1977. "Der Neue Lebensstil." In *Der Werkbund in Deutschland, Österreich und der Schweiz,* ed. Lucius Burckhardt. Milan, 52–53.
Blume, G. 1948. *Rasse oder Menschheit?* Dresden.
Bohde, D. 2012. *Kunstgeschichte als Physiognomische Wissenschaft. Kritik einer Denkfigur der 1920er bis 1940er Jahre.* Berlin.
Borrmann, N. 1989. *Paul Schultze-Naumburg. 1869–1949. Maler, Publizist, Architekt. Vom Kulturreformer der Jahrhundertwende zum Kulturpolitiker im Dritten Reich. Ein Lebens- und Zeitdokument.* Essen.
Boyd Whyte, I. 2013. "Nikolaus Pevsner: Art History, Nation, and Exile," *RIHA Journal* 75, October: 1–33.
Bramwell, A. 1985. *Blood and Soil: Richard Walther Darré and Hitler's "Green Party."* Bourne End.
Brenner, H. 1963. *Die Kunstpolitik des Nationalsozialismus.* Hamburg.
Brock, B. 1990. "Kunst auf Befehl?" In *Kunst auf Befehl?* eds. B. Brock and A. Preiß. Munich.
Daum, A. 1996. "Das Versöhnende Element in der neuen Weltanschauung." In *Vom Weltbildwandel zur Weltanschauungsanalyse,* eds. V. Drehsen and W. Sparn. Berlin.

Dickinson, E. R. 2004. "Biopolitics, Fascism, Democracy: Some Reflections on Our Discourse About 'Modernity.'" *Central European History* 37, no. 1: 1–48.
Dümling, I., ed. 1993. *Entartete Musik: Dokumentation und Kommentar zur Düsseldorfer Ausstellung von 1938*. Düsseldorf.
Forster, G. 1789. "Über die Schädlichkeit der Schnürbrüste." In *Göttinger Taschenkalender* (Göttingen, 1789), cited in S. Welsch, 1996, *Ein Ausstieg aus dem Korsett*. Darmstadt.
Frecot, J., J. F. Geist, and D. Kerbs. 1972. *Fidus 1868–1948*. Munich.
Groys, B. 2004. "Das Kunstwerk Rasse." In *Reden zur Kunst- und Kulturpolitik 1933–1939*, ed. R. Eikmeyer. Frankfurt am Main, 24–39.
Günther, H. F. K. 1929. "Schultze-Naumburg und der Nordische Gedanke." *Die Sonne* 6, no. 6: 269–278.
Haag, O. 2014. "Idealized Race. The Function of Idealized Indigeneity in German Imperial Discourses. Bibliographic Part." PhD dissertation, University of Edinburgh.
———. Forthcoming. "Idealized Australian Aboriginality in German Narratives of Race." In *The Persistence of Race from the Wilhelmine Empire to National Socialism: Re-Examining Constructions and Perceptions of Cultural Narratives of Race in German History, 1981–1945*. New York.
Hau, M. 2003. *The Cult of Health and Beauty in Germany*. Chicago, IL.
Haug, W. 1986. *Die Faschisierung des Bürgerlichen Subjekts*. Berlin.
Heidler, I. 1998. *Der Verleger Eugen Diederichs*. Wiesbaden.
Hesse, A. 1995. *Malerei des Nationalsozialismus: Der Maler Werner Peiner 1897–1984*. Hildesheim.
Hitler, A. 1936. "Die Rede des Führers," Nuremberg, 11 September, in *Reden zur Kunst- und Kulturpolitik 1933–1939*, ed. Eikmeyer, 99–116.
Hoßfeld, U. 2001. "'Er war Schultze-Naumburgs bester Freund'. Eine Lebensskizze des Hans F. K. Günther." *Schriftenreihe Saalecker Werkstätten* 3: 43–61.
J. J. 1928. "Kunst und Rasse by Paul Schultze-Naumburg." *Annalen der Philosophie und philosophischen Kritik*. 7: 94.
Jäger, G., ed. 2001. *Geschichte des Deutschen Buchhandels im 19. und 20. Jahrhundert*. Frankfurt am Main.
Kerbs, D. 1999. "Vestigia Terrent." In *Jahrbuch des Archivs der Deutschen Jugendbewegung*. Burg Ludwigstein, 219–232.
Kershaw, I. 2010. "Volksgemeinschaft: Potential and Limitations of the Concept," keynote lecture at GHI London, 10 March.
Krabbe, W. 1974. *Gesellschaftsveränderung durch Lebensreform*. Göttingen, 1974.
Kunicki, W. 1988. "Paul Schultze-Naumburg. Voraussetzungen einer Biologischen Aesthetik." In *Traditionen und Traditionssuche des Deutschen Faschismus*, ed. Hartung et al. Posnan, 205–217.
Lützhoft, H. J. 1971. *Der Nordische Gedanke in Deutschland 1920–1940*. Berlin.
Merta, S. 2003. *Wege und Irrwege zum Modernen Schlankheitskult*. Wiesbaden.
Mielke, R. 1891. *Die Revolution in der Bildenden Kunst*. Berlin.
Mumford, L. 1932. "Notes on Germany." *New Republic* 72: 279–281.
Pudor, H. 1893. *Nackende Menschen*, London, as cited in J. Frecot, J. F. Geist, and D. Kerbs, 1972, *Fidus 1868–1948*. Munich.
Rave, P. O. 1987. *Kunstdiktatur im Dritten Reich*. Berlin.

Repp, K. 2000. *Reformers, Critics, and the Paths of German Modernity: Anti-Politics and the Search for Alternatives, 1890–1914.* Cambridge.
Schultze-Naumburg, P. 1901a. *Die Kultur des Weiblichen Körpers als Grundlage der Frauenkleidung.* Leipzig.
———. 1901b. *Kunst und Kunstpflege.* Jena.
———. 1902a. *Die Kulturarbeiten II: Gärten.* Munich.
———. 1902b. "Die Neue Frauentracht." *Die Zukunft* no. 10: 204.
———. 1902–1903. "Zur Reform der Frauenkleidung." *Frauen-Genossenschafts-Blatt* no. 1/2: 82–91.
———. 1915. *Die Kulturarbeiten VII: Die Gestaltung der Landschaft durch den Menschen. I.Teil.* Munich.
———. 1920. "Gewand und Körper." In *Weibliche Körperbildung und Bewegungskunst nach dem System Mensendieck,* eds. F. Giese and H. Hagemann. Munich.
———. 1925. "Der Ethische Wert der Körperpflege." *Werbeschrift für Körperkultur* no. 1: 32–33.
———. 1926a "Die Internationale Kunstaustellung in Dresden in Rassehygienischer Beleuchtung." *Archiv für Rassen-u. Gesellschafts-Biologie einschließlich Rassen-und Gesellschafts-Hygiene* 18, no. 4: 440.
———. 1926b. "Rassenforschung, Vererbungslehre und Rassenhygiene." *Die Umschau* 30, no. 20: 387–388.
———. 1927. *Kunst und Rasse.* Munich.
———. 1934. *Rassegebundene Kunst.* Berlin.
———. 1941. "Hans F. K. Günther zum Geburtstag." *Volk und Rasse* 16, no. 2: 21.
———. 1989. *Lebenserinnerungen, Seitensprünge,* as cited in N. Borrmann, 1989, *Paul Schultze-Naumburg. 1869–1949. Maler, Publizist, Architekt. Vom Kulturreformer der Jahrhundertwende zum Kulturpolitiker im Dritten Reich. Ein Lebens- und Zeitdokument.* Essen.
Schwarz, A. 2003. "Bilden, Überzeugen, Unterhalten: Wissenschaftspopularisierung und Wissenskultur im 19. Jahrhundert." In *Wissenspopularisierung,* ed. C. Kretschmann. Berlin, 221–234.
Stratz, C. H. 1900. "Die Vergewaltigung des weiblichen Körpers." *Die Frauenkleidung,* Stuttgart, as cited in S. Welsch, 1996, *Ein Ausstieg aus dem Korsett.* Darmstadt.
Tessenow, H. 1908. "Paul Schultze-Naumburg 'Die Kultur des Weiblichen Körpers als Grundlage der Frauenkleidung.'" *Trierisches Jahrbuch für ästhetische Kultur*: 206.
Triebel, F. 2004. *Der Eugen Diederichs Verlag 1930–1949.* Munich.
Ulbricht, J., and M. Werner, eds. 1999. *Romantik, Revolution & Reform. Der Eugen Diederichs Verlag im Epochenkontext 1900–1949.* Göttingen.
Viehöfer, E. 1988. *Der Verleger als Organisator.* Frankfurt am Main.
Volbert, U. 2001. "Das Reformkleid der Jahrhundertwende." *Schriftenreihe Saalecker Werkstätten* no. 3: 31–42.
Walkenhorst, P. 2007. *Nation—Volk—Rasse. Radikaler Nationalismus im Deutschen Kaiserreich 1890–1914.* Göttingen.
Wedemayer-Kolwe, B. 2004. *"Der Neue Mensch": Körperkultur im Kaiserreich und in der Weimarer Republik.* Würzburg.
Weipert, M. 2006. *"Mehrung der Volkskraft": Die Debatte über Bevölkerung, Modernisierung und Nation 1890–1933.* Paderborn.

Weiss, K. 2008. "The Face of the German House: Modernization and Cultural Anxiety in Twentieth-Century Architectural Photographs." PhD dissertation, Massachusetts Institute of Technology.

Welsch, S. 1996. *Ein Ausstieg aus dem Korsett*. Darmstadt.

Werner, M. 1996. "Die Erneuerung des Lebens durch Ästhetische Praxis. Lebensreform, Jugend und Festkultur im Eugen Diederichs Verlag." In *Versammlungsort Moderner Geister. Der Eugen Diederichs Verlag—Aufbruch ins Jahrhundert der Extreme*, ed. G. Hübinger. Munich.

Wolbert, K. 2001. "Körper: Zwischen Animalistischer Leiblichkeit und Ästhetisierender Verklärung der Physis." In *Die Lebensreform. Entwürfe zur Neugestaltung von Leben und Kunst um 1900*, eds. K. Buchholz, R. Latocha, H. Peckmann, and K. Wolbert. Bonn.

PART IV

GERMANY AND COLONIAL OTHERNESS

 9

"The White Goddess of the Masses"
Stardom, Whiteness, and Racial Masquerade
in Weimar Popular Culture

Pablo Dominguez Andersen

In 1935, the popular fan magazine *Die Filmwoche* began a new serial contest entitled "Who Was It?" On a weekly basis, the contest presented the image of a well-known film star in one of his or her roles and promised attractive prizes for those readers able to identify the actor or actress in question. The third installment of the competition challenged its readers with a particularly tough nut to crack (see figure 9.1). The photograph showed a woman in blackface makeup, her eyes wide open, an exaggerated, widely grinning mouth, and large rings in both ears and nose. The identification of the actress so disguised was difficult not only because the photograph stemmed from a short scene in a film that was relatively unknown within the star's oeuvre. Beyond this, the challenge was particularly tricky because the character in which the actress was photographed was completely antithetical to her usual star persona.

The star in question was Henny Porten, an actress who, as a critic in the *Deutsche Filmzeitung* put it, "led the type of the well-rounded, blonde, motherly German woman to victory" (19 October 1928). To her contemporaries, Porten was *the* embodiment of an unambiguously white, German, and motherly femininity. By her signature blonde hair and buxom figure, Porten exuded a warm aura of simplicity and a down-to-earth popularity. In her films, she represented a femininity stereotypically characterized by its ability to suffer and to endure the most tragic strokes of fate. In 1924, an article in the magazine *Film-Kurier* accurately encapsulated her stock character as that of a "woman who, as an epitome of innocence, walks through life untouched by all temptations, whose beauty irradiates men, while she only loves the one for whom she makes the biggest sacrifices without hesitation" (8 November 1924). Such roles, which made her a favorite among pre–World War I audiences, turned her into the antithesis of modern femininity during the 1920s. As Weimar's New Women radically redefined exist-

Figure 9.1. Film star Henny Porten photographed in blackface makeup as part of a popular weekly quiz (*Filmwoche*).

ing definitions of gender and sexuality, the image of womanhood represented by Henny Porten remained conspicuously static, harking back to Wilhelminian gender ideals. Throughout her career, Porten stood in for a natural, innocent, simple, and nurturing type of femininity that contemporaries viewed as quintessentially German in opposition to the "Americanized" New Women of the 1920s. As a critic noted in the late 1920s, "she stayed the same all along, whether in her dress from 1914 or in the fashion of 1928, which does not suit her at all. She simply isn't a modern-day type of woman" (*Berliner Volkszeitung*, 3 October 1928).

Porten's popularity with German audiences was unsurpassed for a long time. Not only was she the first German film star, but her rise to fame in the 1910s coincided with the emergence of cinema as the central medium of mass cultural entertainment. By the 1920s, her name had become synonymous with the history of German cinema—a form of entertainment that developed from a cheap and ill-reputed sideshow amusement to a large-scale industry and an important factor of cultural life after the end of World War I. Porten's success story also ran parallel to the advent of the German star system. With Asta Nielsen, Porten was among the first actresses whose name was publicized and used as an advertising device to increase the appeal of the films in which she appeared. At a time when actors' names were usually neither mentioned within their films nor in the respective advertising, soon after her sensational first starring role in *Liebesglück einer Blinden* (The Blind Girl's Bliss of Love, 1911) Henny Porten became a household name.

In this essay, I investigate the understudied racial dimensions of Henny Porten's eminently white star persona to demonstrate the pervasiveness of racial and colonial thinking in German popular culture after 1918. Despite the fact that recent scholarship has finally established Germany's truncated colonial experience as a constitutive part of its fateful twentieth-century history, few scholars have explored the role that racial thinking and especially whiteness have played in German popular culture after 1918 (Nagl 2009; Eggers et al. 2005; Walgenbach 2005; Dietrich 2007; Krobb and Martin 2014). Porten's stardom shows that in Weimar society and culture, whiteness as a racial category was central to the production of German national identity. Within Porten's star persona and beyond, the representation of whiteness relied on, and harked back to, established colonial stereotypes of racial otherness. As I show in this essay, after World War I popular culture and especially star cinema became central discursive sites for the reformulation and dissemination of knowledge about whiteness and racial difference. Following Marcia Klotz's (2005) characterization of the Weimar Republic as a "postcolonial state in a still-colonial world," I understand Weimar Germany as a *postcolonial* state in a twofold sense: while the founding of the Weimar Republic coincided with the official end of German empire, colonial thinking continued to shape discourses of identity in the German metropole in a decisive manner. To analyze this phenomenon, I first demonstrate how Henny Porten came to embody an image of ideal whiteness offscreen and in her films. Secondly, I analyze the role that racial masquerade played in Porten's white star persona. As I demonstrate, Porten's donning of the racial masque ultimately served to stabilize her image as an ideal representation of white German womanhood.

• • •

In 1921, the famed journalist and writer Kurt Pinthus published an article titled "Henny Porten for President" in the widely read left-leaning weekly magazine *Das Tagebuch.* In it, the leftist Pinthus described Germany's most popular actress as a figure of national unification. According to Pinthus, presidents, politicians, playwrights, and statesmen failed to ignite the passion of the German people as a whole. Porten's overwhelming popularity, by contrast, stretched from the nation's metropolises to the most isolated and remote rural areas; transcending differences of age, class, and gender; and uniting Germans of the most different occupations and political affiliations: "Is there—or has there ever been—a person as famous and loved among the people in the German speaking countries as this blonde woman? ... Here is a figure that is more popular in Germany than the old Fritz or the Olympic Goethe. ... Here is a beautiful woman who, as a unification of Gretchen and Germania, has been erected by the nation [*Volk*] itself as an ideal image of this very nation [*Volk*]" (15 October). While the bitterly divided political parties of the Weimar Republic failed to find a man suited to represent the nation, Pinthus stressed, Porten was the single figure with which every German, independent of his or her background and worldview, was in love.

As Pinthus's account suggests, her contemporaries not only understood Henny Porten as a quintessentially German star, but as an embodiment of Germanness itself. As such, she became a figure of national unification at a point in time most Germans perceived as a moment of national crisis and defeat. But what exactly was so very German about Porten? Many accounts pointed to Porten's unmistakably German physique as the true source of her Germanness. As biographer Gustav Holberg rhapsodized in his early biography of the actress in a stereotypical manner, "the tall blonde woman with the magically immaculate silhouette, unfading blue eyes, classical neck and heavenly blonde hair has an inebriating presence. She represents the purest Germanic type in a truly classical pureness of form" (1920: 71). As this comment suggests, the star's physical whiteness was integral to her Germanness. Indeed, it was Porten's emphasized whiteness that gave her repeated coinage as *the* embodiment of the German woman its aura of naturalness and self-evidence.

In 1919, writer Kasimir Edschmid called Henny Porten "the white goddess of the masses" (Belach 1986: 80). Without a doubt, Henny Porten was an exceptionally white star. A semantic of light permeated characterizations of the actress. An interview article in the *Dresdener Neue Presse*, describing Porten's "white, neat hands" and her "high, white forehead," closed with an almost religious vision: "as I depart, her slender figure stands against the window, bathed in light" (14 December 1930). Porten's shining blondness was a pivotal characteristic of the actress, emphasized with an almost unbelievable pervasiveness and an often tiring redundancy. Commentators resorted to this rhetoric of whiteness and light to describe the actress herself as well as the roles that she impersonated on screen: "An atmosphere of cleanliness surrounds the female figures that she embodies. They are shining [figures of] lights [*Lichtgestalten*], predestined to defeat the dark" (*Illustrierter Film-Kurier*, 1924).

Many of Porten's films and photographs achieved a visual identification of the actress with glowing light, by use of extreme lighting and placing the actress before dark backgrounds. The use of makeup and white clothes added to the intensity of Porten's brightness. In film, the effect of this technique was that audiences in dark movie theaters must often have been literally blinded by the shining brilliance of Porten's image. Photographs used similar techniques to make the actress appear glowingly white. It is important to note in this context that photographically creating an image of immaculate whiteness was a complicated technical endeavor in the 1920s. As Richard Dyer emphasizes, orthochromatic film stock—the most widely used film material until about 1926—was insensitive to red and yellow, making both colors appear dark (1997: 91). The fact that skin tones of persons designated as white are often light red made the heavy use of white makeup necessary. Furthermore, orthochromatic stock's insensitivity to yellow made blonde hair appear dark, unless it was arranged as loosely as possible and specially lit. The trademark cinematic lighting style that was developed in Hollywood during the 1920s took this into account. It consisted of a primary or key light, a second, softer light (the fill), and a third light, called backlighting. The latter was particularly important in making blonde hair seem bright; it could also provide blonde women with a halo, underlining their supposedly angelic, saintly character. Chiaroscuro lightning, the technique common in German expressionist cinema (and later used in film noir), emphasized the contrasts between whiteness and darkness even more strongly. As all of these details make clear, Porten's whiteness was not as natural as many of her contemporaries liked to believe—on the contrary, it depended on the careful implementation of a whole range of technical procedures.

On star postcards, Porten was often photographed in front of a white background.[1] Usually wearing a white dress, her skin lightened by makeup, the actress almost merged with the shining background. The use of a soft-focus lens further added to the effect of dreaminess and peacefulness created by such images, making the star appear as an angelic, celestial, almost bodiless figure. Other photographs relied on heavy contrasts to emphasize the actress's whiteness. Set against dark backgrounds, the star appears to be glowing. Such images alluded to Christian iconography by giving the star a halo. Furthermore, Porten was often photographed with white objects loaded with iconographic meaning. One series of postcards depicted the actress at the side of a white horse. In many, Porten carried a bouquet of white flowers. Another series of publicity photographs staged Porten as a classical beauty. Wearing a simple tunic, her posture was statuesque; she seemed immobile, frozen in time. Carefully made up, her skin appeared plain, smooth, and almost polished. Such images suggested a feminine ideal based in Greek antiquity, commonly equated with ideal whiteness during the 1920s (Möhring 2004: 226–260; Painter 2010: 59–71).

Many promotional images combined several of these techniques; some managed to employ all of them (see figure 9.2), creating an image of Porten that coincides with Richard Dyer's characterization of the "angelically glowing white woman" (1997: 127) as the most extreme instance of an idealized representation of whiteness. As Dyer argues, referring mainly to the British Empire and the United States, this figure's circulation reached its apogee during historical moments characterized by a perceived destabilization of white hegemony. The apex of Henny Porten's popularity in Germany, stretching from the 1910s until the early 1930s, can be linked to several such moments of a perceived crisis of white superiority: the fear of racial contamination that surrounded the discussions about "mixed marriages" in the German colonies, ultimately leading to the rigidly racialized German citizenship law of 1913 based on the principle of *ius sanguinis* (El Tayeb 2001; 2005; Grosse 2000: 145–192); the country's defeat in World War I resulting in the forced end of the German colonial empire; the moral panic surrounding the alleged mass rape of white German women by Black soldiers deployed by the French army during the occupation of the Rhineland (Wigger 2007; Koller 2001; Campt 2005); the anxiety with which the German press detected the emergence of Black resistance movements such as Pan-Africanism or the fight for civil rights in the United States (Martin 2004); and finally, the celebratory and playful validation of Blackness and the "exotic" in Weimar popular culture, which many on the right attacked as a loss of "racial pride" and a call for "racial defilement" (Nagl 2009: 669–674).[2] In opposition to all of these unsettling developments, images of Porten conveyed an atmosphere of absolute peace and tranquility, a phantasy of pure, angelic, and virginal white femininity untainted by the perceived threats of Black sexuality and racial conflict.

In films starring Porten, the star's glowing whiteness constituted a central symbolic and narrative device. Its racial dimensions, while seldom made explicit, hid right underneath the narrative surface. *Anna Boleyn* (also known as *Deception*, 1921), for instance, one of Porten's most successful films, is of particular note in its use of white imagery. Directed by Ernst Lubitsch, the film was a spectacular historical costume drama set in the English court of the sixteenth century. One of the first large-scale Ufa productions after World War I, the film gained critical acclaim for its spectacular mass scenes, pompous scenery, lavish costumes, and the overall grandiosity of its production values. The

"The White Goddess of the Masses" • 215

Figure 9.2. Collection of Henry Porten star postcards (photo archive, Stiftung deutsche Kinemathek, Berlin).

film's significance to the German film industry's reemergence after World War I is perhaps best captured by the widely publicized visit of President Friedrich Ebert to the film set in Berlin-Tempelhof during the shoot. The film was also one of the few Porten films to gain popular and critical acclaim in the United States. Notably, a critic in the *New York Times* noted that Porten was "too heavy ... too old and too ponderous, possibly too Teutonic" to play the role of the tragic queen convincingly (18 April 1921).

Porten's starring role as Anna Boleyn matched the actress's usual typecasting as the innocent, suffering, and enduring motherly woman with an ultimately tragic fate. The film's story is well known: King Henry VIII (Emil Jannings) falls in love with Anna Boleyn. Anna rejects the king's forthright sexual advances, since she is in love with her childhood-friend Henry Norris. However, when Henry finally offers to divorce his wife, Queen Katherine, and marry Anna, she agrees. Anna's luck finds an abrupt end when she gives birth to a daughter instead of the expected son. While the furiously disappointed King Henry begins an affair with the court lady Johanna Seymour, Anna is innocently convicted for adultery. Her execution marks the end of the tragic narrative.

The film's depiction of whiteness foregrounds the tensions between race, gender, and sexuality that lie at the core of white representation. As Richard Dyer notes, heterosexuality is both central to whiteness and contradicts one of its fundamental paradigms. On the one hand, procreative sex between whites is necessary to ensure the prevalence and purity of the white race. On the other, in white representation, sexuality is associated with darkness. As Dyer fittingly sums up this contradiction, "to ensure the survival of the race, they have to have sex—but having sex, and sexual desire, are not very white: the means of reproducing whiteness are not themselves pure white" (1997: 26). But why is sex "dark" in white imagery? While ideal whiteness resides in the spiritual, and is thus noncorporeal, sexuality is a physical act. No matter how closely it complies with symbolic social norms then, within normative white imagery sexuality necessarily remains dirty and morally dubious because it is so clearly connected to the physical—thus the significance of both the immaculate conception in Christian mythology and the common symbolic transference of sexuality onto the "dark" racial Other in the imperialist imagination.

This ambiguity at the heart of white sexuality has different consequences for white men and women, both of which are visible in *Anna Boleyn*. In hegemonic texts, ideal white masculinity is compulsorily heterosexual. In other words, being sexually inactive usually puts white men's masculinity into question. At the same time, because of its dark connotations, active sexuality is likely to taint white men's whiteness. White women, on the other hand, are responsible for the reproduction of the white race. The reproduction of whiteness is the ultimate goal of the heterosexual union that marks the happy ending of so many hegemonic white narratives. At the same time, however, white women's whiteness is guaranteed by their innocence, spirituality, and morality, all of which basically impede the performance of the sexual act. "Their very whiteness, their refinement, makes of sexuality a disturbance of their racial purity," Dyer (1997: 29) writes about the construction of white women. This productive tension inherent in white sexuality is at work in most white heteronormative narratives. Its male and female characters oscillate constantly between the prerogatives of ideal whiteness and (an intrinsically dark) heterosexuality.

Anna Boleyn is caught between three conflicting forces: her love for Henry Norris—and thus, her own sexual desire—her responsibility to remain chaste and morally pure, and her reproductive obligation as an exceedingly white woman. An advertising booklet for the film emphasized the latter aspect: "Moved by her mission to give England the long-awaited male heir to the throne, she had renounced the happiness of her pure love and married the much older King Henry" (*Film und Brettl*, December 1920). Anna Boleyn is responsible for the reproduction of the white race in a very literal sense. As England's whitest woman, the king's and the nation's hopes rest on her. If she fails to bear the awaited son, the national/racial order, symbolically embodied by the royal family, faces the danger of extinction. When Anna finally gives in to the king's sexual urging, she succeeds in remaining immaculately white. The film achieves this by emphasizing that Anna merely tolerates the sexual act. Porten's appalled facial expression indicates that Anna understands sex with the king as a dreadful marital duty. Through her passivity and complete lack of sexual agency (and pleasure), Anna remains morally chaste despite her participation in the sexual act, thus coming close to an immaculate conception.

In the contrasting representations of its male and female characters, Lubitsch's film bears witness to the gendered dynamics of whiteness. King Heinrich is represented as ruthless, self-centred, brutal, and almost animalistic in his unsublimated carnal lust. In other words, he symbolically falls outside the parameters of whiteness. Anna, on the other hand, is virginal, innocent, benevolent, and morally pure, and thus the epitome of whiteness. As Richard Dyer points out, besides the basic dichotomy of white and nonwhite, different shades of whiteness serve to differentiate among the members of the white race (1997: 57). This subdivision serves to establish a hierarchy of increasing degrees of whiteness, which is often ordered along other categories of identity such as class or gender. Lower-class characters are usually darker than upper-class ones; women are whiter than men. In *Anna Boleyn*, the two main characters' moral connotations are symbolized accordingly. Through the use of clothing, makeup, and lighting, the king appears markedly darker than the queen throughout the film. During one particularly emblematic episode, Henry intrudes the nightly chamber of white-clad Anna hidden under a black hooded coat.

In her reading of Lubitsch's period films, Sabine Hake (1992a) stresses the extraordinary care and accuracy with which the director handled set design, costumes, and mise-en-scène. According to Hake, this emphasis resulted in a "'metaphysics of décor' that, while meant to support story and characters, often dominated all other cinematic elements" (ibid.: 132–133). As Hake notes, *Anna Boleyn* establishes a claustrophobic atmosphere of confinement through its dark and heavy interior settings. The film juxtaposes these constrictive spaces with the radiant whiteness of its main female figure. Throughout the film, Anna Boleyn is clad in a series of shiningly white dresses. More than once, the film's intertitles reference its protagonist's whiteness. As Anna tries on her white wedding dress, she happily exclaims, "Today I must be the fairest woman in England!" At another point in the film, a poem recited about the queen's beauty marvels at Anna, "whose breast is snow-white, whose neck is marble!" Typical of the feminine figures embodied by Porten, Anna Boleyn only obtains (and retains) her untainted whiteness through her fundamental passivity. Because she does not really act on her own behalf, she is never at risk of bringing guilt upon herself. Represented as a helpless puppet in the hands of ruthless and lusty men, Anna suffers constantly and tolerates innocently, and thus remains immaculately white. Anna's whiteness reaches its climax in her tragic martyrdom marking the film's end.

As several critics have noted, despite its historical and geographical distance to German politics of the day, Lubitsch's film negotiated questions of German national identity in the aftermath of World War I. Shortly after the German Revolution, the film provided an escapist return to the feudalistic world of monarchical authority. A contemporary review in the liberal *Tagebuch* well understood the film's nationalist tendency: "Undoubtedly, this maneuvering of thousands of film extras contains a Wilhelminian element. That's why some images seem reminiscent of snapshots from *Die Woche*. The street flooded with people, the entrance of the royal couple, the people's forced enthusiasm while waving with their handkerchiefs—all of this reminds us of the Wilhelminian age, and since the Germans still haven't mentally overcome it, this allusion to unconscious memories and the saturation with monarchistic imagery is clearly one element of the film's big success" (31 December 1920). The film's reception was rife with nationalist rhetoric. After the loss of World War I, monumental films like *Anna Boleyn* were to reverse the outcome of the war by forcing Germany's enemies to their knees on the cinematic world market. As Sabine Hake characterizes this interpretive framework, *Anna Boleyn* "gave new meanings to the nationalist, and, in fact, imperialist dreams of the old empire" (1992b: 74). The filmic representation of whiteness added a racial dimension to these nationalist aspirations. As such, it facilitated white German audiences' identification with the plot despite its "foreign" setting; at the same time, the latter allowed for the expression of a fantasy that otherwise might not have been publicly expressed as easily. At a moment of perceived crisis, national and racial fantasies of superiority and fears of national and racial decline were simultaneously negotiated in *Anna Boleyn*'s imagery. The virginally white figure of Anna Boleyn embodied by Henny Porten was the most emblematic expression of these fantasies.

Not all of Porten's films presented the star as a flawless embodiment of ideal whiteness. As the introductory photograph of Porten in blackface suggests, the quintessentially white and German star temporarily embodied racial difference in several of her films. In carnivalesque comedies like *Das Maskenfest des Lebens* (Carnival of Life, 1918), *Meine Tante, Deine Tante* (My Aunt, Your Aunt, 1927), *Liebfraumilch* (1928), or *Liebe im Kuhstall* (Love in the Cow Barn, 1928), Porten donned racial drag for comic effect. In such films, Porten turned into a "wild" Hungarian, an Indian princess, and a Black woman. The function of such metamorphoses, however, was usually to render the star all the more white at each narrative's end. In this last section, I exemplarily analyze Porten's blackface performance in the film *Meine Tante, Deine Tante* by situating it in the understudied history of German blackface.

Contrary to the belief expressed in a number of recent discussions of blackfacing in the popular German press (see *Süddeutsche Zeitung*, 10 January 2012), blackface has a long history in German popular culture, which cannot be separated from racist practices and thought. Historians date the emergence of modern blackface to the Wilhelmine period. As Jonathan Wipplinger writes, "blackface minstrelsy entered Germany around 1900, as American popular culture began its rapid ascent to becoming the transnational culture of the West" (2006: 92). Blackface's rise in Germany was connected to the growing popularity and presence of African American jazz and its cultural appropriations in Germany. According to Tobias Nagl, the first known instances of the practice called "negroing" (*negern*) occurred in the context of the cakewalk dancing craze during the Wilhelmine period (2009: 645). In the Weimar Republic, German blackface thus built on a cultural tradition.

As is well documented, the German fascination with jazz reached new heights during the 1920s (Partsch 2000; Wipplinger 2006; Weiner 1991; Kater 1988; Nagl 2009: 636–702). This popularity was an expression of a general cultural shift. An increasingly positive understanding and appropriation of Blackness characterized large parts of postcolonial German culture during the 1920s. Politically, Weimar negrophilia was a double-edged sword. On the one hand, it was laced with extant ideas of primitivism and as such reproduced stereotypes about a supposedly innate Black animality, wildness, and unsublimated sexuality. On the other hand, it markedly differed from the violent racism that had characterized the propaganda campaign of the "Black Shame on the Rhine." The aggressive and angst-ridden rejection of Blackness that erupted during the occupation of the Rhineland continued to flourish in the right-wing propaganda against the alleged racial contamination of white, German culture through so-called *Niggertänze*, "degenerate art," or "cultural bolshevism" in the later 1920s (Nagl 2009: 669–675). The increasing celebration of African American performers can be understood as a part of the general Americanization of German culture. The campaign against the "Black Shame," on the other hand, demonstrates that there was a hierarchy of different types of Blackness in the German public. Within this hierarchy, cultural phenomena that could be tied symbolically to the United States (like jazz) clearly stood above expressions of Blackness that were linked to Africa or other colonial or ex-colonial territories (like the Tirailleurs sénégalais).

Weimar blackface, then, like its American and European counterparts, must be situated between two poles. On the one hand, as Tobias Nagl states frankly, it was "a racist cultural practice through and through" (2009: 638). On the other, as a carnivalesque practice, it contained subversive elements that could at least potentially yield de-essentializing and denaturalizing effects. The critical discourse on American minstrelsy is organized around a similar dichotomy: while many critics have rightfully stressed how blackface theater has primarily served to ridicule African Americans and has historically perpetuated many of the degrading stereotypes claiming the innate racial inferiority of Blacks, recent theorists such as Eric Lott (1995) or W. T. Lhamon Jr. (1998) have suggested a more ambiguous and conflicted reading of blackface. Lott's seminal study *Love and Theft* carries minstrelsy's ambiguity in its title. While most prior critiques of blackface found racial aversion to be white minstrels' driving force, Lott emphasizes the constitutive role of cross-racial desire at the heart of blackface masquerade.

For Lott, American blackface is a fundamentally ambivalent cultural form: "Underwritten by envy as well as repulsion, sympathetic identification as well as fear, the minstrel show continually transgressed the color line even as it made possible the formation of a self-consciously white working-class" (1995: 8). Even if a proper historical comparison of American and German practices of blackface has yet to be undertaken, it seems suitable to apply Lott's and other American scholars' critical framework to the study of German blackface.

In Weimar film, blackface was a well-known and recurrent theme by the mid-1920s. Films such as *Die keusche Susanne* (The Innocent Susanne, 1926), *Die Blume von Hawaii* (Flower of Hawaii, 1933), *Die Tolle Lola* (Fabulous Lola, 1927), or *Die Boxerbraut* (The Boxer Bride, 1926) employed blackface either as a central narrative device or as a passing motive and simple means to create comic effects. In both cases, the respective films could draw on audiences' cultural knowledge of the functioning of, and the semantics implied in, blackface makeup. This knowledge was further disseminated in articles in the popular press that explained the technique of blackface to the German public. The article "White Negroes" in *Film Magazin*, for instance, simultaneously built on audiences' existing knowledge of blackface and presented it as a novelty in need of explaining (31 March 1929). The article illustrates how closely German audiences were acquainted with the rather complicated semantics of blackface. It opened with a report about an instance of Black blackface in a film that American director King Vidor was currently shooting with an all-Black cast in Hollywood ("Negroes aren't black enough!") and then recited several cases of the more common practice of blackening up white faces.

Despite the obvious pervasiveness of blackface in German culture, such articles often presented it as a purely American invention and practice. As a review of the Hollywood film *The Jazz Singer* in *Filmwoche* argued, "A white man hiding behind the mask of a Negro must be quite a sensation for American sensibilities: as we know, America has not yet moved beyond the race problem [*Rassenproblem*]; … what relevance must a film in which a white man performs as a negro singer [*Negersänger*] have over there! For old Europe, only a showpiece remains" (26 September 1928). The misguided idea that Europe or Germany had supposedly moved beyond the "race problem" while the United States was "still" wrestling with it, was not just falsified by German nationalists' indignant condemnation of American blackface films, such as *The Jazz Singer*. Rather, the prevalence of a whole range of specifically German appropriations of blackface minstrelsy in German popular culture shows that the Black/white dichotomy was as significant a site for the symbolic negotiation of German national and racial identity as it was in the United States. Furthermore, the article about "White Negroes" directly contradicted its own attempt to portray blackface as an American phenomenon by referring to Emil Jannings's blackface performance in the film *Othello* (1922) and including several images of popular heartthrob Willy Fritsch's blackface act in *The Boxer Bride*. Such articles served two related purposes. First they projected the racism inherent in blackface onto the United States while creating an image of Germany as a tolerant and open-minded society; at the same time, they further disseminated the existing knowledge about blackface among German audiences. As the article rightly observed, the audience's recognition that the performer underneath the black mask really was white was integral to the function of blackface minstrelsy. Such articles made this knowledge, necessary to ensure this recognition, available to its readers.

When Henny Porten's blackface performance in *Meine Tante, Deine Tante* first appeared on screen in early 1927, German negrophilia was at its peak. Josephine Baker's performances in Berlin had opened to enthusiastic reviews, Sam Wooding and his all-Black *Chocolate Kiddies* revue had toured Germany, and Paul Whiteman had successfully presented his attempt at a more respectable (read: white) version of "symphonic" jazz to Berlin audiences. In an ironic reversal of the "Black Shame" rhetoric, the avant-gardist intellectual Ivan Goll had proclaimed in 1926 that "the Negroes are conquering Europe ... and the old world calls on its failing strength to applaud them" (*Die literarische Welt*, 15 January).

On the other hand, many modernist's cultural enthusiasm for the revitalizing and invigorating effects of Blackness on old Europe were met with increased resistance from the strengthening nationalist, racist, and National Socialist forces. *Meine Tante, Deine Tante* was released only two weeks after the Leipzig world premiere of Ernst Krenek's modernist jazz opera *Jonny spielt auf*. Krenek's opera featured a German actor in blackface portraying the starring role of Jonny, an African American jazz musician who steals an expensive violin. Several performances of *Jonny spielt auf* had to be canceled due to nationalist riots and disturbances. In Munich, an angry crowd agitated by the ostensibly scandalous employment of a Black performer on a German stage could only be conciliated by the announcement that Jonny was played by a white German actor in blackface (Partsch 2000: 191; Nagl 2009: 671; Fichner 2005).

Essentially, *Meine Tante, Deine Tante* featured many of the themes that aroused the tempers in Krenek's scandal-ridden opera: in a chaotic series of masquerades and ensuing instances of mistaken identity, the film negotiated the relationship of, and the boundaries between, highbrow culture and mass entertainment, classical music and jazz, Germanness and Americanism, whiteness and Blackness. *Meine Tante, Deine Tante* also intertwined exoticism and sexuality in a manner with which German cinema audiences were by now highly familiar. Henny Porten played Helene, a poor music student who married her equally penniless fellow student Edgar (Angelo Ferrari).[3] The two desperately try to make ends meet by performing in cheap nightclubs and variety theaters. Their luck seems to turn, however, when Edgar gets an invitation from his rich uncle, Count Bodo von Bocksdorf, who is also a musician. The uncle's musical quintet has lost a member and Edgar is invited to come to his uncle's mansion in order to join the group and eventually become his uncle's heir. Unfortunately, the old-fashioned and rigorous uncle has a pointed dislike for women. Edgar decides to accept his uncle's offer and to conceal the fact that he is married. Soon, however, Helene follows Edgar to the mansion, dressed in male drag to disguise her female identity. As soon as she arrives at the mansion, however, "she turns everything upside-down: she jazzes up the venerable Beethoven so that the nigger cook becomes homesick and starts dancing until the old uncle's limbs start jittering" (*Filmwoche*, 2 March 1927).

Obviously, then, the uncle's mansion stands in for an outdated social order in dire need of modernization by Helene. The young woman introduces the world of Americanized jazz, titillating dances, and female sexuality to the count's conservative and asexual world. The count's lacking sexuality puts his masculinity into question. In order for him to shift from too white into a properly white male, he needs a healthy dose of exotic modernism, with which Helene provides him. Soon, the count falls for his nephew's wife and forgets about his opposition toward the female sex. Unaware of Helene and Edgar's relationship, the count even wants to marry the energetic woman. By behaving in a deliberately lavish manner, Helene knocks the nonsense out of Count Bodo. Finally, Bodo pays Edgar one million marks to marry Helene, to whom Edgar is already married. Through this plot, the film negotiated precisely those questions of identity that troubled the late Weimar Republic: Was modernization of German identity (in this case German masculinity) necessary? Were German men emasculated in their asexuality and lacking modernity? Should modernization of German identity be achieved by mimicking racial Otherness? And would German culture still be recognizable as such after this metamorphosis? The fact that these questions were posed in the context of Porten's star persona shows how far seemingly stable ideas of German identity had eroded by 1927.

Porten's blackface routine in *Meine Tante, Deine Tante* indeed caused quite a sensation. Despite its dramatic negligibility within the overall plot—Porten's minstrel act formed part of a short revue theatre scene at the beginning of the film—the scene was cited by most posters and advertisements for the film. A production photograph is the most expressive surviving evidence of Porten's racial masquerade (see figure 9.3). It shows Porten and her costar Angelo Ferrari clad in blackface minstrelsy's and "darky" imagery's typical signifiers of Black inferiority and primitivity. Both wear wigs to create the impression of "frizzy" hair, their skin is painted dark, and their mouths are exaggerated. Porten's grass skirt and large rings in her ears and nose serve to further emphasize her figure's supposed primitivity. The saxophones that both actors hold provide a loose association with jazz that emphasizes the music's supposedly primitive and childish roots. While jazz could also connote elegance, extravagance, and modernity in Weimar popular culture, the photograph employs it in a clumsy and infantile context.

A feature article in *Filmwoche* advertising *Meine Tante, Deine Tante* captures the sensation that Porten's short minstrel routine was intended to evoke:

> Is this really the beautiful, blonde, womanly Henny Porten, this creature that hops across the stage as a fat but unbelievably versatile nigger broad [*Niggerweib*], a hundred times more Negress [*Negerweib*] than Josephine Baker? The latter seems downright European by comparison with this figure; this most frizzy of all Negro heads; these impossibly rubbery [*wulstig*] lips; a loincloth, lanky sagging ear pendants and—a ring through her nose! Horror of horrors! And this "thing" puts a real nigger dance on the floor that lets the award-winning Charleston and Black-Bottom dancers from the last costume party hang their heads in shame. (2 March 1927)

To raise expectations for Porten's film, the piece exploited her racial masquerade as an outrageous sensation. Formulated in a racist rhetoric of aversion, the lines exhibit the feelings of disgust, horror, anxiety, and aggression that Porten's defilement through Blackness was to evoke. While the rhetoric is characterized by a voyeuristic lust for the supposedly grotesque and deviant, it primarily depicts the amount of loathing and hatred that Black femininity could arouse in postcolonial Germany's racist society. As Lola Young emphasizes, "the black woman, being neither white nor male, represents a double lack in the psycho-sexual colonial scheme: the antithesis of both whiteness and established notions of femininity and masculinity" (1996: 99). Bringing Porten into the vicinity of this figure constituted a disquieting transgression even in a comic context. The scandal was calculated, of course, the aim of its sensationalist presentation of Porten's blackface performance was

Figure 9.3. *Meine Tante, Deine Tante*, 1927 (photo archive, Stiftung deutsche Kinemathek, Berlin).

to lure audiences into the movie theatres. Here, all the negative emotions evoked in the advertising and the performance itself were to discharge in contemporary audiences' laughter about Porten's gruesome metamorphosis. After all, Porten's fans were safe in the knowledge that their star would return to her immaculate whiteness at the end of the film. Porten's racial masquerading fulfilled two opposing functions: On one hand, it allowed for the expression of transgressive desires in the context of Porten's otherwise highly conservative star persona. On the other hand, however, the star's juxtaposition with her own antithesis served to further strengthen Porten's association with ideal, white femininity. Porten's comic masquerades allowed her (and her audiences) to depart from the constrictive limitations of hegemonic norms, only to restore and restabilize the validity and alleged naturalness of these norms in the end.

It seems difficult to find any subversive or liberating dimensions in Porten's blackface performance. According to Eric Lott, blackface's ambivalence lies in the way that "minstrel performers often attempted to repress through ridicule the real interest in black cultural practices they nonetheless betrayed" (1995: 6). In comparison to some instances of modernist appropriations of Black culture during the 1920s, it seems hard to find any traces of this interest or admiration in Porten's minstrel performance. While films like *Meine Tante, Deine Tante* are indeed indicative of a widespread desire for racial otherness in the Weimar Republic, Porten's film merely cited this fascination in order to capitalize on it rather than really being a part of it. Like all blackface acts, Porten's is characterized by the simultaneity of aversion and desire. Indeed, the film's narrative cites contemporary views of Blackness and Americanism as invigorating and liberating cultural forces. However, the way in which the press marketed Porten's blackface act betrays that aversion and ridicule seem to have outweighed cross-racial desire as the performance's primary effects.

• • •

Henny Porten was Germany's first film star. Porten's glowing whiteness was essential to her star persona. In the postcolonial culture of Weimar Germany, this whiteness had numerous connections to racial discourse. As I have demonstrated, whiteness was far from an unmarked or empty category in Weimar popular culture (see also Decker 2014). A star like Porten enabled the German public to discuss the shape and boundaries of whiteness. Porten's staging as an angelically glowing white woman served to mitigate white German fears of national and racial decline at a moment of a perceived loss of white hegemony. Against such fears, images of Porten conveyed an atmosphere of undisturbed peace and unimpaired white superiority. Her staging as a white star served to underscore her Germanness by giving it a racial—thus seemingly natural—dimension. At the same time, Porten's star persona speaks of Weimar Germany's ongoing fascination with racial difference. In many of her comic roles, Porten came into contact with racial Otherness, oftentimes masquerading as a racial Other herself to create comic effects. Such masquerades, while clearly speaking of a desire for the racial Other, ultimately served to restabilize the boundaries of white German identity. Rather than yielding any destabilizing or counterhegemonic effects, Porten's blackface performance in *Meine Tante, Deine Tante* spoke of a widespread aversion and disgust toward Black femininity in Weimar Germany. As such, Henny Porten forms part of German blackface's still-understudied racist history.

Ultimately, a figure like Porten can only be understood properly when placed in the context of postcolonial Germany's racialized discourse of identity and difference. From this perspective, the end of the German empire in 1918 becomes a key point of reference for the study of popular culture after World War I. Race was an important interpretive framework for Weimar film critics and cinema audiences alike. Historians of German postcolonial popular culture, then, should further engage in its critical analysis. As Porten's star persona evidences, Germany's postcolonial popular culture remains yet to be thoroughly studied as a key site for the dissemination of racial thinking after the end of German empire.

Pablo Dominguez Andersen is a historian and digital communications specialist. He has published numerous essays on the history of film and popular culture, the politics of gender and sexuality, and the history of migration and racism. He is coeditor of *Masculinities and the Nation in the Modern World: Between Hegemony and Marginalization* and winner of the 2016 WerkstattGeschichte essay prize for his article *Mischen wir uns ein!* He works as a digital marketing manager for De Gruyter publishers in Berlin.

Notes

1. I am referring to the collection of star postcards in possession of the photo archive of the Stiftung deutsche Kinemathek, Berlin.
2. Throughout this essay, I capitalize the terms "Black" and "Blackness" to emphasize their status as political and self-reflexive concepts of collective identity used in an affirmative manner by subjects racialized as Other in racist societies. Because the term "whiteness" lacks such an affirmative political usage, I do not capitalize it.
3. Unfortunately, no copy of the film *Meine Tante, Deine Tante* has survived and the film must be considered lost. The following analysis is based on scat-

tered material such as press clippings, reviews, film stills, and other photographs, as well as promotional material. The plot summary is based on the article "Meine Tante, Deine Tante" (*Filmwoche*, 2 March 1927).

References

Belach, H. 1986. *Henny Porten: Der erste deutsche Filmstar, 1890–1960*. Berlin.
Campt, T. 2005. *Other Germans: Black Germans and the Politics of Race, Gender and Memory in the Third Reich*. Ann Arbor, MI.
Decker, R. J. 2013. "The Visibility of Whiteness and Immigration Restriction in the United States, 1880–1930." *Critical Race and Whiteness Studies* 9, no. 1 (November).
Dietrich, A. 2007. *Weiße Weiblichkeiten. Konstruktion von "Rasse" und Geschlecht im deutschen Kolonialismus*. Bielefeld.
Dyer, R. 1997. *White*. New York.
Eggers, M. M., et al., eds. 2005. *Mythen, Masken und Subjekte. Kritische Weißseinsforschung in Deutschland*. Münster.
El-Tayeb, F. 2001. *Schwarze Deutsche: Der Diskurs um "Rasse" und nationale Identität, 1890–1933*. Frankfurt am Main and New York.
———. 2005. "Dangerous Liaisons: Race, Nation and German Identity." In *Not So Plain As Black and White: Afro-German Culture and History, 1890–2000*, eds. P. Mazon and R. Steingrover. Rochester, NY, 27–60.
Fichner, W. 2005. "'Die Überfahrt beginnt': Schwarze Körper und Amerikanismus in Ernst Kreneks Zeitoper 'Jonny spielt auf.'" In *Leibhaftige Moderne: Körper in Kunst und Massenmedien 1918 bis 1933*, eds. M. Cowan and K. M. Sicks. Bielefeld, 292–304.
Grosse, P. 2000. *Kolonialismus, Eugenik und bürgerliche Gesellschaft in Deutschland, 1850–1918*. Frankfurt am Main and New York.
Hake, S. 1992. "Lubitsch's Period Films as Palimpsest: On Passion and Deception." In *Framing the Past: The Historiography of German Cinema and Television*, eds. B. A. Murray and C. Wickham. Carbondale, IL, 68–98.
———. 1992. *Passions and Deceptions: The Early Films of Ernst Lubitsch*. Princeton, NJ.
Holberg, G. 1920. *Henny Porten: Eine Biographie unserer beliebten Filmkünstlerin*. Berlin.
Kater, M. H. 1988. "The Jazz Experience in Weimar Germany." *German History* 6, no. 2: 145–158.
Koller, C. 2001. *"Von Wilden aller Rassen niedergemetzelt": Die Diskussion um die Verwendung von Kolonialtruppen in Europa zwischen Rassismus, Kolonial- und Militärpolitik, 1914–1930*. Stuttgart.
Klotz, M. 2005. "The Weimar Republic: A Postcolonial State in a Still-Colonial World." In *Germany's Colonial Pasts*, eds. E. Ames, M. Klotz, and L. Wildenthal. Lincoln, NE, 135–147.
Krobb, F., and E. Martin, eds. 2014. *Weimar Colonialism: Discourses and Legacies of Post-Imperialism in Germany after 1918*. Bielefeld.

Lhamon Jr., W.T. 1998. *Raising Cain: Blackface Performance From Jim Crow to Hip Hop*. Cambridge.
Lott, E. 1995. *Love and Theft: Blackface Minstrelsy and the American Working Class*. Oxford.
Martin, P. 2004. "Die 'farbige Front': Von der Angst Europas vor dem Aufstand der Kolonisierten." In *Zwischen Charleston und Strechschritt: Schwarze im Nationalsozialismus*, ed. P. Martin. Hamburg and Munich, 171–177.
Möhring, M. 2004. *Marmorleiber: Körperbildung in der deutschen Nacktkultur, 1890–1930*. Cologne.
Nagl, T. 2009. Die *Unheimliche Maschine: Rasse und Repräsentation im Weimarer Kino*. Munich.
Painter, N. I. 2010. *The History of White People*. New York.
Partsch, C. 2000. *Schräge Töne: Jazz und Unterhaltungsmusik in der Kultur der Weimarer Republik*. Stuttgart.
Walgenbach, K. 2005. *"Die weiße Frau als Trägerin deutscher Kultur". Koloniale Diskurse über Geschlecht, "Rasse" und Klasse im Kaiserreich*. Frankfurt am Main and New York.
Weiner, M. A. 1991. "Urwaldmusik and the Borders of German Identity: Jazz in Literature of the Weimar Republic." *The German Quarterly* 64, no. 4 (autumn): 475–487.
Wigger, I. 2007. *Die "Schwarze Schmach am Rhein": Rassistische Diskriminierung zwischen Geschlecht, Klasse, Nation und Rasse*. Münster.
Wipplinger, J. 2006. *The Jazz Republic: Music, Race, and American Culture in Weimar Germany*. PhD dissertation, University of Michigan.
Young, L. 1996. "Missing Persons: Fantasizing Black Women in *Black Skin, White Masks*." In *The Fact of Blackness: Frantz Fanon and Visual Representation*, ed. A. Read. London, 86–101.

 10

IDEALIZED AUSTRALIAN ABORIGINALITY IN GERMAN NARRATIVES OF RACE
Oliver Haag

> If one stands for the first time in the Australian jungle, under the primitive grass trees, sees for the first time lungfish or platypuses, or encounters Australian Natives in the wilderness, the impression of an archaic and primordial world comes to mind. ... These were not *Australneger* (Australian Negroes) but *Australarier* (Australian Aryans), or rather female Aryans, since it was women and very beautiful women at that; between 14 and 16 years. ... The girls were tall, slim and pretty without any trace of flat noses and thick lips; and—this was the most exciting—blonde hair. It was of course not the blonde that we know, yet still a very fair color. These girls were not half-blooded but authentic full-blooded Aranda and Loritja. They had a unique and lovely charm. A peculiar, almost secret appeal lay upon them, and in this moment I started to get interested in the Australian race.
> (Ross 1940: 249–250)

Thus writes Austrian author Colin Ross (1885–1945) in a German travelogue on Australia, first issued in 1930 and republished three times by 1941. A prolific author of travelogues and political commentary, Ross vigorously embraced National Socialism. A Nazi enthusiast deeply steeped in the conviction of (white) German superiority and simultaneously full of praise for the Aryan descent of Aboriginal Australians seems likely to surprise. Does it suggest malleability of the otherwise so calcified racial hierarchies existing during and before Nazism? This chapter traces what I call the idealization of Aboriginal Australians within a system of white supremacy by evaluating approximately 150 German-language publications on Aboriginal Australians issued between the 1870s and 1945.[1] It asks how to conceive racial idealization, and whether or not idealization constituted any systematic phenomenon or rather an exceptional case. When did it gather momentum, how did its narrative structure and frequency change, and what was its function? Aboriginal Australians made up only a small fraction of German writing about Indigenous peoples worldwide. Yet the number of reports—not all of them book-length studies, but mostly journal articles and short travel reports—merit closer scrutiny of conceptions of Australian Aboriginality in German discourses.

The first section shows the transnational character of such narratives, highlighting how much racial idealization was appropriated and incorporated into nationalist discourses. It also considers racial idealization and its function in imperial settings, arguing that idealization formed an integral part of upholding white supremacy in changing colonial conditions. The second part presents a qualitative and quantitative evaluation of German-language texts and concludes that the discourses of regaining the (former) German colonies stood in nexus with idealization of Aboriginal Australians.

The selection criteria for publications (1870s to 1945) rest on systematic sampling to avoid arbitrary inclusion of particular articles and genres. This means each journal consulted had all articles on Aboriginal Australians evaluated completely and that journals across different genres including social and physical anthropology, linguistics, religious studies, and missionary reports, as well as journals of popular culture, were considered.[2] This is to include as wide a range of imperial image production as possible. Monographs were consulted only if reviewed and/or advertised in one of the analyzed journals and if Aboriginal Australians figured as central to the text.

The qualitative approach is based on critical whiteness studies and aims at deconstructing textual whiteness as a normalizing and unmarked practice of the imperial contract (Frankenberg 1993; Moreton-Robinson, Casey, and Nicoll 2008). It retraces the function of idealization in imperialist discourse, which produced transnational claims to white superiority. In *Culture and Imperialism* Edward Said differentiates between imperialism as the discourses of colonial hegemony and colonialism as its practical implementation (1993: 9). Colonialism, or what Reinhard Wendt terms "formal imperialism," emerged as an effect of imperialist discourse (2007: 157–159, 235–236). Here I apply Said's differentiation to the various settings in which Aboriginal people were construed. Thus, discourses of imperialism, or what Susanne Zantop terms "colonial fantasies" (2007), are understood as having transcended formal colonialism, while colonialism is related to discourses about the actual German colonies.

The purpose of texts is certainly manifold, including reading for pleasure, education, and sensationalism. The hypothesis of this work suggests that the function of racial idealization serves to secure white hegemony, including racialized difference, in imperial settings. This focus on imperialism—here understood as the efforts of establishing white hegemony in (proto-) colonial contexts—does not mean to negate other purposes of meaning and text processing. Imperial texts could and did maintain whiteness, while not losing their entertaining and educating grip. Children's books and juvenile literature, for one, often did not mention any purpose of securing white leadership and regaining colonial rule. Although some texts rendered their colonial aim explicit, most were implicit in their imperial character. Texts, I will argue here, not only have explicit purposes but a hidden ideological force that, in an Althusserian sense, was perpetuated without being acknowledged. Louis Althusser has indicated that ideology interpellates social subjects as (normative) subjects (1971: 176). Subjects are already social subjects before their birth as subjects, normalized by ideology that is not recognized as political intrusion but as unquestionable social ordering. The power of ideology lies in its appearance of naturalness that remains fundamentally unknown to the interpellated subject. Ideology is a product of a (socioeconomic) structure that, as Stuart Hall has theorized, acts as social stabilizer (1983: 59, 66). The efficiency of ideology does not rest on its control from "above" but on its normalizing effects that appear unthreatening, if not comfortable. Qualitative methods try to retrace this ideological purpose that, this study argues, lay in the purpose of re-creating white hegemony in imperial order.

The sources have not only been analyzed with the tools of whiteness studies but also through content analysis that examines the intentions and contexts of texts (Krippendorff and Bock 2009). While the quantitative method provides a general frame to infer to broader tendencies, content analysis has grouped the texts according to frequency of themes: themes are ordered first by frequency (e.g., images of beauty as one of the most frequent tropes); followed by the specific time frame in which they emerged (e.g., descriptions of Aboriginal intelligence appeared with perceptible frequency after the loss of the German colonies); finally, contexts were identified in which the particular themes were most frequently embedded (e.g., efforts to regain the former colonies, stories of exploration and adventure).

Scholarship on German interest in Indigenous peoples, or those dubbed *Naturvölker* (lit. "people of nature"), has not systematically investigated imperial representations of Aboriginal Australians. Analytical engagement has focused on German discourses of Indigenous groups within the former German colonies, as well as North America and the South Pacific (e.g., Zantop 1997; Steinmetz 2007; Wildenthal 2001; Penny 2003; Berman 1998). Idealization of Indigenous North America in particular made up a firm part of German popular and juvenile culture (e.g., Feest 1999; Haible 1998; Calloway et al. 2002). Except in the cases of North America and so-called Polynesia, such studies of Indigenous representations have not made racial idealization their analytical focus. Idealization is often explicated as an expression of escapism and as a specifically German conception of noble-savage ideas projected—partly globally—into the Pacific and North America.

The contexts and intensity of idealization of Native Americans and Polynesians, however, do not translate equally into idealization of Aboriginal Australians. Kay Anderson and Colin Perrin argue that, in nineteenth-century racial discourse, Aboriginal Australians were classified as inferior not only to Europeans but to all other Indigenous races (2007: 18–39). On the grounds of their perceived inability to overcome the state of nature, the authors maintain, nineteenth-century racial theorists could not accommodate Aboriginal Australians within their view of human unity, and thus Aboriginal Australians served first as a trigger for the polygenist theory of innate human difference and subsequently, under monogenist evolutionism, as the lowest and immutable link of human development. Aboriginal Australians came to be considered throughout the Western world as the most "primitive" and "backward" race (Broome 2010: 130; Poignant 2004: 123, 217). This scaling among Indigenous groups corresponded to ideas of racial hierarchy that construed state-building groups and those considered similar to white cultures, such as the Ancient American cultures and Polynesians, as "more highly" developed than those groups assumed to lack any written culture, architecture, or military order, all accounting for "high culture" (Stocking 1968: 33, 55). A mixture of somatic references (skin color, so-called Caucasian facial feature and body height), literacy, and gender order influenced the scaling of Indigenous groups worldwide.

This scientific scaling eventually had an impact on popular culture (and vice versa). The images of Aboriginal Australians were never on par with what Hartmut Lutz calls "Indianthusiasm," the exalted German admiration of Indigenous North America (1985: 3). Likewise, while the trope of the beautiful Polynesians pervaded much German literature and art, there was no equivalent trope accorded to Aboriginal Australians in the late nineteenth and early twentieth centuries. Quite the reverse, as Jan Teagle Kapetasthus notes, Aboriginal Australians entered Western popular culture as "the ugliest people on earth" (2007: 33). Concepts of beauty thereby affected ideas of dignity and heroism. It would have been inconceivable for Karl May's Apache protagonist to act as a Wiradjuri warrior from New South Wales. The Australian case thus proffers an ideal means to show that German idealization was not restricted to the so-called highest-ranked Indigenous races. Instead, it emerged from discourses separate from the images of eighteenth-century noble savagery. This article will show that colonial politics affected the rise in idealized discourses of Aboriginal Australians or what Marcia Langton calls Aboriginality (1993: 34–35).

National Appropriations of a Transnational Discourse

Let us reconsider the chapter's opening vignette. It idealizes Aboriginal beauty not only through whitened norm-setting principles (the blonde hair, the lack of supposedly "Negroid" facial features) but also through their presumed Aryan origin. The former suggests an opposition of white and Aboriginal beauty (read as denigration of Aboriginal racial sovereignty), while the reference to Aryan origin exhibits (transnational) patterns of primitivism. David Bird has retraced how Australian nationalists, particularly those involved in the literary movement of the Jindyworobak, tried to construe a nativist Australian identity that exposed its uniqueness in Aboriginal heritage. Aboriginal Australians were praised not only for their cultural sovereignty, the author argues, but hailed as the "oldest" Aryan race and thus linked in phylogenetic commonality to settler Australians (2014: 71). Although different in context of its production, the metanarrative of Ross's German text is similar in proclaiming Aboriginal Aryanism. I shall call this metanarrative transnational primitivism.

Without describing any isomorphic analogy between Aboriginal Australians and contemporary "Aryans," Ross's reference to Aryan origin resembles concepts of archaic Caucasianness in nineteenth-century Australia. The establishment of an interracial genealogy "incorporate[d]," in Warwick Anderson's term, "Aboriginal Australians into the category [of whiteness] as distant relatives and object lessons" (2006: 193). Australian Aryanness, in Ross's writing, is equally understood as an expression of primitivism that construes Aboriginal Australians not as "cultureless savages" but, on grounds of their fictitious primitiveness, as the ancestors of humanity, hence "distant relatives." Aboriginal Australians are read as an epithet for phylogenetic origin, deemed both part of nature and a direct link to an archaic human past. Caucasians, Indians, Mongolians, and Aryans, Ross's text concludes, developed from this common origin. At the same time, idealized Aboriginality is suggested to the reader not merely as a form of racial origin, but also as authenticity qua racial purity, as shown through the appreciation of "full-bloodedness." This appreciation of Aboriginal purity aligns with ideas of racialized purity but also relates to ideas of cultural traditionalism. Like German ideas of Native American authenticity (Penny 2006: 798–819), Aboriginal authenticity permeated all German texts on Australia. Such ideas of primitivism were not a specifically German invention but firmly embedded in Western constructs of Aboriginality.

Primitivism projected views of Indigenous peoples as primordial and antithetical to white modernity in which pristine patterns of social contract were considered decipherable (Li 2006: 3–6; Street 1975: 10, 68, 129, 173). It acted as the central narrative category informing the construction of racialized Aboriginality from which, I argue, familiar meaning could be conferred upon a culturally estranged context. Authenticity, an epiphenomenon of primitivism, emerged with culture change instigated by interracial contact and prevails in expectations of "true" Aboriginality. Eva Marie Garroutte argues that colonial concepts of Indigenous authenticity are based on racialized primordiality and are never free of power relations (2003: 142). A product of power relations, primitivism does not dissolute racial difference but construes racial hierarchies: (idealized) primitivism very contradictorily dabbles in the primordiality of the spatially removed object (the Aboriginal Other) and the temporally removed object (the prehistoric European), merges the two, but never culminates in coalescence with the modern European subject. The promised glance onto the European past, by way of an Aboriginal present, does not forge common humanity but denies any commonality by establishing an insurmountable hierarchical past.

The following ethnographic texts provide an illuminating glimpse into the transnational structure of primitivism in both a German and a British Australian text on Aboriginal people. Baldwin Spencer (1860–1929), one of Australia's most renowned social anthropologists, in 1927 described the Aranda people as "near to death" when exposed to interracial contact; this contact, the author argues, led to an inevitable degeneration, for younger Aranda men rejected their traditions upon cultural contact. Spencer opens his study thus:

> Australia is the present home and refuge of creatures, often crude and quaint, that have elsewhere passed way and given place to higher forms. This applies equally to the aboriginal as to the platypus and kangaroo. Just as the platypus, laying its eggs and feebly suckling its young, reveals a mammal in the making, so does the aboriginal show us, at least in broad outline, what early man must have been like before he learned to read and write, domesticate animals, cultivate crops and use a metal tool. It has been possible to study in Australia human beings that still remain on the culture level of men of the Stone Age. (1927: viii)

The author continues his rather descriptive account with a discussion of Aranda character and physiognomy; the nature of the Aranda is seen as hospitable toward group members (sharing and caring for Elders), whereas their mental ability to think abstractly is considered relatively undeveloped. The author then acknowledges the grace of young Aranda women, which, he claims, fades in the early stage of adolescence:

> Naturally, in the case of the women, everything depends upon their age; the younger ones—that is, those between fourteen and perhaps twenty—have decidedly well-formed figures, and, from their habit of carrying on the head *pitchies* containing food and water, they carry themselves often with remarkable grace. As is usual, however, in the case of savage tribes the drudgery of food-collecting and child-bearing tells upon them at an early stage, and between twenty and twenty-five they begin to lose their graceful carriage; the face wrinkles, the breasts hang pendulous, and, as a general rule, the whole body begins to shrivel up, until, at about the age of thirty, all traces of an earlier well-formed figure and graceful carriage are lost, and the woman develops into what can only be called an old and wrinkled hag. (Ibid.: 36)

The concept of primitivism contained in Spencer's text bears a multitude of transnational traits. Mentioning humans in one breath with *awkward* Australian fauna, it creates Aranda people as an *awkward* part of nature, destined to disintegrate upon exposure to culture. As Gillian Cowlishaw has shown, the study's focus on culturally "intact" groups reflects the complicity of Australian anthropology in re-creating Aboriginal traditionalism (1988: 60). Spencer's conception of culture describes less a complete opposite to nature (Aboriginal Australians are credited with cultures) than one trapped in "savage" stage. The presumable Stone Age development leaves the Aranda people as a direct mirror into an archaic human past. This past, imbued with raw human behavior and immature reasoning, corroborates "civilization's" advantages: "civilized" humans are not exposed to extinction; "civilized" women do not undergo rapid physical deterioration; and "civilized" humans do not live in the stage of superstition.

In 1908 German anthropologist Erhard Eylmann (1860–1926) classified the South Australian Aboriginal nations, including the Aranda people, in a remarkably similar vein: the author contrasts Aboriginal people's filial love with their callousness, selfishness, and infantile behavior (1908: 34–45). This contrast of positive with negative character traits acts as a projection onto the evolutionist scale: the Aboriginal-as-child is seen as investing conditional virtues (filial love and occasional loyalty), partly developed in contrast to the full development in the adult stage of unconditional virtues (philanthropy read as sign for "civilized" love). Just like Spencer, Eylmann construes Aranda children and young adults as graceful yet rapidly deteriorating during adolescence: "[Many a face has something attractive]. The eyes are of striking beauty, overlapped by beautifully formed brows and long, dense lashes. I have otherwise seen such deep fairy tale eyes only in the Black Forrest. ... [In the older people] the mouth protrudes extremely, partly resulting from the thickness of the lips and the prognathism of the maxilla" (ibid.: 6, 9). Eventually, again like Spencer, Eylmann positions Aboriginal Australians, because of their instincts rather than intelligence, as akin to nature: "Also the extent and contents of the wealth of fairytales, songs, sagas, proverbs etc. allow conclusions about their great intellectual potential. As far as I can ascertain, such products of the people's spirit [*Volksgeist*] are more evident in most of the [Australian] tribes than among our fellow countrymen between the Weser and the Elbe. The instinct, the functional action without consciousness of its function is often noticeable. I think the white is superior in that he acts more often with consciousness and consideration and that he differentiates more sharply, that he can think" (ibid.: 57–58). The contradictory concession of intellect is steeped in the closeness of nature that is seen as accommodating Aboriginal Australians with instincts and artistic talents that are considered more developed than among Germans. The artistic gifts, Eylmann maintains, are related to talents in literature and foreign-language acquisition, but not to mathematics and (logical) thinking. Such artistic talents stood in contrast to white masculine reasoning, leading to both a feminizing and an infantilizing of Aboriginal Australians. The racialized and gendered paraphernalia of primitivism, visible in Eylmann's and Spencer's studies, are a Western product that developed its specificities in German discourse. Eylmann's idealizing traits engage in romantic description of Aboriginal physiognomy that is interspersed with analogies to German culture (the deep fairy tale eyes resembling those of the Black Forrest; the *Volksgeist* as the people's soul). Eylmann's proleptic reference to Aboriginal love for country resembles nationalist conceptions of a love for German soil: "The love for their home country (*Heimat*) is markedly great. It is possible to perceive a patriotic ethos among many elderly people. In his appreciation of the piece of land where he was born and raised the native completely resembles our peasants and small town dwellers: they too, knowing foreign country only by hearsay, cling with their full soul to their native clod" (ibid.: 35). The idyllic undertone of a people's rootedness in their *Heimat* reflects a specifically German nationalism that, inter alia, construed the individual's relation to the people (*Volk*) as linked to a commonly inherited landscape in which a people's soul had been inscribed (Jefferies 2003: 13, 208–216). Aboriginal Australians here became indigenized as born into, and intricately connected to, their respective lands. Nature as a landscape, George Mosse argues, was glorified in *völkisch* thought as a depository of archaism projected as a retreat from the scourges of urbanization and industrialization; both the primitive Germanic past and the (primitive = bucolic) German landscape became central nodes of German nationalism (1998: 15–16, 18, 26).

Eylmann's text is symptomatic for the national appropriation of transhistorical primitivism in German texts on Aboriginal Australians. It accommodates, I argue, cultural foreignness by domesticating racial narratives to familiar meaning. This domestication appears in references to the Black Forest and *völkisch* reverence of nature, but is embedded in the whitened metanarrative of primitivism. As Spencer's and Eylmann's texts exemplify, primitivism informs both subtexts and acts as the foil for including Aboriginal Australians into a concept of phylogenetic ancestry. Both authors engage in a description of Australian fauna as *awkward* and relate the seeming awkwardness to the Aboriginal inhabitants; the two authors describe these inhabitants as part of nature and as a direct mirror of a phylogenetic past that preconditions the view of monogenetic human origin, a theorem that replaced the polygenic views that prevailed in much of the nineteenth century.

Framing Idealization

Erhard Eylmann's study contains traces of idealization within a racialized context grounded in white normativity as its invisible marker. The physical idealization of Aboriginal women is markedly relative and positions Aboriginal beauty, though romanticized, in indirect relation to concepts of white beauty as epitomized through reference to the Black Forest. Aboriginal women are portrayed as implicitly less beautiful than white women, for their beauty is seen as withering exceptionally early. Part of Western rhetoric, this construction of female Aboriginality presupposed the construction of white femininity, for the "exceptional withering" rested notionally on a more endurable beauty which, as the norm-setting principle, remained the uncategorized white reference (Kapetas 2007: 33; Hollinsworth 1998: 63–65). White norms of beauty, in this event, act as synesthesia of European superiority. How can idealization, then, be theoretically conceived in relation to its racist (that is, hierarchical) structuring?

In a survey of German literary representations of Australia, Manfred Jurgensen identifies idealizing moments in what he deems otherwise overwhelmingly negative portrayals of the First Australians. The author explains this idealization as a markedly nonracist and nonfascist exception, exemplified by individual authors such as Colin Ross, who was influenced by Karl May's North American Noble Savage types

(Jurgensen 1992: 23, 37, 45, 74–75, 94). Presenting May's influence as if proven, the author does not engage further with the nature of such "positive" views. Colin Ross's publications are filled with endorsement of Nazism, rendering this author hardly an antifascist. Jurgensen's reading treats idealization as an exceptional entourage of *otherwise* racist discourse, instead of an *immanent part* of the very discourse. The equation of "positive" images with "nonracist" images is analytically incongruous, since both varieties, "negativity" and "positivity," form part of the same structure of racist discourse. Racist valence cannot logically be "part"-racist or "part"-positive.

Critical research into philosemitism has dismantled idealizing stereotypes about Jewish people as a practice of tolerance, which does not demolish but instead reinforces prejudice. Zygmunt Bauman recognizes philosemitism as part of the same repository that nurtures anti-Semitism (1998: 143). The seemingly positive clichés about Jewish people not only generalize idealizing attributes to an entire group, but reinvent the very group by "positive" definition. Both the racialized nature of the cliché and the asymmetrical power-relation in the process of defining the object of idealization render idealizing views a patronizing and colonizing practice, thus a fundamentally *non*-positive value judgment.

The method of the present study does not lie in the attempt to question "negative" accounts of colonialism, as Russel Berman (1998) pursues. Claiming that German colonial discourses ought to be conceived through the concept of space rather than race (suggesting that colonial space would not have been racialized), Berman argues that "broadbrush attacks on colonialism" (ibid.: 18) would not help in recognizing a seeming "openness" (ibid.: 204) of German colonial image production: "In this German case, however, the understanding of empire requires a deep revision. Although it can entail aspects of violent domination, it also allows for transgression, mixing, and plurality. To represent the colonial scene solely as a Manichaean segregation may be an adequate description of British imperialism, but as a general account it is a sorry misrepresentation and ultimately simply a political effect of a politicized anticolonialism, polemically distorting the scope of differentiation" (ibid.: 15).

Besides Berman's polemic dismissal of subaltern critique as mere "politics," his effort of constructing a distinct (that is, more diverse and humane) German colonial narrative rests on denying its racializing and whitened character. The rehabilitating effect in the phrasing, "it *can* entail *aspects* of violent domination," reduces the complexity of colonial violence to somatic violence and misconceives the Manichaean segregation in *any* (not merely British and French) colonial project that is premised on a relationship of asymmetrical knowledge production. This asymmetry, which builds on white hegemony, cannot be read as an expression of "diversity," for the complexity of colonial discourse is not identical with the process of racialization from which it originates. Although dynamic in nature, the racializing effects of colonial discourses are inherently oppositional in their placement of white races above people of color.

While judgments about human groups could be multidimensional, the central direction these judgments took was grounded in oppositional power relations, a Manichean allegory, in Abdul JanMohamed's sense, of white European superiority versus an Indigenous inferiority (1985: 63, 68). Images of Aboriginality, I argue, are both oppositional and ambivalent. This study applies three broad values to the direction of the different formations of racialized Aboriginality: idealizing, stigmatizing, and undirected (the final is neither idealizing nor stigmatizing in tendency, such as descriptive studies of cultural objects if unaccompanied by an overt statement of value). Erving Goffman conceives of stigma as a discrediting social attribute resulting from the incongruity between the virtual and actual social identity prescribed to the stigmatized object (1990: 3, 6). Applied to textual representation, stigmatizing traits are spatially re-created between what I term a prescribed racial space and a prescribed racial role, and evolve if the prescribed role does not converge with the prescribed space. The stigma appears not merely as racist but as overtly disparaging (and thus stands in contrast to what is often termed "positive" prejudice). In turn, idealizing principles were encapsulated in a racist hierarchy, with neither overt nor subliminal statements of racial hierarchy precluding idealizing views. The parameter to decipher idealizing traits is not the criterion of racial hierarchy but an enhancing direction of racial representation. To allocate a value direction, this analysis thus differentiates between stigmatizing inscriptions, which further disparaged the generally inferior position within the metanarrative of racial hierarchy, and idealizing views, which enhanced the generally inferior position *within* the metanarrative of racial hierarchy. Parameters include:

Inscriptions of racial and cultural character: According to Martha Mamozai, disparaging references manifested in German colonial literature as offensive body odor, dirtiness, laziness, insidiousness, and lasciviousness (1992: 134–135). The bipolar direction of these character values premises subtended values around axes of laziness versus industriousness, disloyalty versus loyalty, brutality versus gentleness, dirtiness versus cleanliness, courage versus cowardice, and strength versus weakness. All these ethnocentric devices act as instances of normative ordering of hegemonic whiteness but exhibit different directions in racist discourse, thus emerging as feasible analytical criteria for differentiating between idealizing and stigmatizing directions.

Inscriptions of the Aboriginal body: The colonial inscription of the racialized body is of an intrinsically gendered and sexualized dimension. The process of bodily racialization codifies the passivity and inferior status of the racialized object, resulting either in further denigration or in enhancing inscription. Aboriginal bodies, especially those inscribed with codes juxtaposed to ethnocentric traits, such as small physical size and "Negroid" appearance, were frequently stigmatized as abominable. On the other hand, bodies could be inscribed with codes of naturalness, beauty, and pride, resulting partly, although not necessarily, in a subtle eroticization of the Aboriginal body. Idealizing bodily inscriptions can thus be conceived of as a further enhancement of the Aboriginal body *within* the system of bodily inferiority, whereas stigmatizing bodily inscriptions can be understood as a further denigration of the Aboriginal body *within* the system of bodily inferiority.

Inscriptions of gender and sexuality: Closely related to the mechanism of the scripted body, racial discourse also imputes cultural norms to sexuality and gender, in which pathologizing views on sexuality and gender correspond to views of racial inferiority. Figures of effeminacy, Mrinalini Sinha shows, constituted a central part of imperial hierarchy (1995: 1–11). Traits of irrepressible hypersexual drives were inscribed in primitive sexuality to underpin the stigma of animalism. The process of gendered and sexualized inscription positions the normative inscriber as superior to the inscribed. Hegemonic scripting of white sexuality and gender operate as the norm-setting principle, with cultural codes again exhibiting a dichotomous direction of additionally degrading and enhancing traits *within* a system of racial inferiority.

Inscriptions of Aboriginal health: Similar to the scripting of sexuality and gender, cultural codes are inscribed in constructions of health and dis-ability. References to physical health and disease acted as an integral device to script racialized bodies, and the in-group was considered the epitome of utmost health. Disease transmission and a people's immune system formed important signifiers for scripting racialized health. Cultural codes of healthy norms can be understood as an enhancing scripting of health appearing *within* a system of racial hierarchy, while cultural codes of disease and pathology can be conceived of as an additionally downgrading scripting of health appearing *within* a system of racial hierarchy.

Inscriptions of intelligence, primitivism, and savagery: The most obvious inscription of Aboriginality is made by reference to intellectual capacity, which functions as a vector of white civilization, progress, and adulthood. Idealizing references to Aboriginal intelligence need to be theorized as patronizing endeavors that confirm the patronizer's own, seemingly superior, position of assessing intelligence. It is the direction instead of the mere process of ascertaining intelligence that exhibits analytical relevance, to differentiate between further downgrading and relative enhancement of Aboriginal intellect within a system of hierarchical intelligence. References to savagery and primitivism form an equally constituent part of the same system that re-creates the idea of imperial Aboriginality. Yet, as in the case of intelligence, primitivism and savagery had different connotations in different contexts, reflecting the ambivalence of European discourses about Aboriginal peoples. Savageness could be the basis of frenetic evil but, as Thomas Theye has delineated, could equally employ concepts of naturalness and innocence (1985: 12–14). The value direction of the denigration could point toward further denigration or enhancement *within* a system of racial hierarchy.

These five parameters do not imply they are unrelated to one another. Many texts were complex and accommodated many and contradictory values. In such cases, however, the quantitative part applies stigmatizing valorization, for idealizing elements do not reverse a text's principal direction of stigmatization.

From Stigmatized to Idealized Aboriginality

The evaluation of 150 German-language publications on Aboriginal Australians issued between the 1870s and 1945 reveals an ambivalent picture. Across all genres, in the entire period of publication, Aboriginal Australians were considered in evolutionistic scaling as one of the most primitive (that is, ancient) human races. None of the texts depart from ideas of Aboriginal cultures being stuck in Stone Age state. Value judgments, however, came to differ markedly between texts published before and after the loss of the German colonies in 1918–1919. With the gain of the first modern German colonies in Africa and the Pacific in the 1880s, texts on Australia largely stigmatized Aboriginal people as one of humanity's most "backward" races. As figure 10.1 shows, no German text issued until 1919 evinced unconditionally idealizing traits. Although stigmatization decreased slightly after the turn of the century, it remained the most frequent from of German Aboriginality. Aboriginal Australians were described across genres as "useless for work," as an impediment to settlement, as practicing infanticide, being outright hideous, and lacking intelligence.

An ethnographic text published in 1870 derided Aboriginal people as exceptionally "ugly because of their flat noses, the deep-lying eyes …

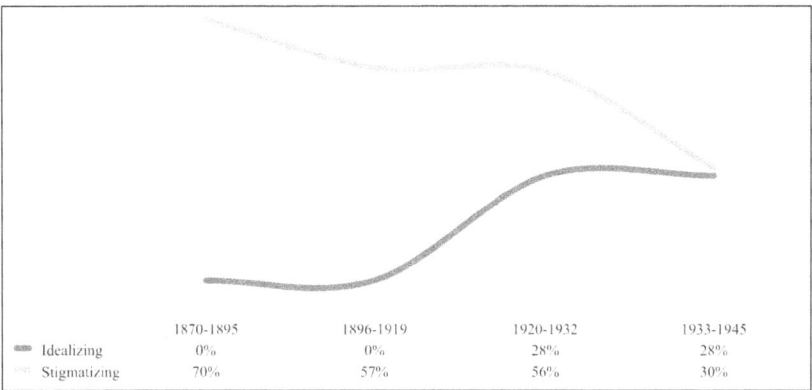

Figure 10.1. Value judgments of Aboriginal Australians in German publications, 1870–1945.

their dense, black, not woolly but shaggy hair, their exceptionally large mouths and thick protruding lips" (Andree 1870: 226). Texts described Aboriginal Australians also as brutish and dishonest in character. An ethnographic account from 1899 stated exemplarily: "the moral life of the Tasmanians is characterized by rawness and heartlessness ... lacking bravery in warfare" (Vierkandt 1899: 292). The text construes Aboriginal Tasmanians as excessively brutish on the one hand and lacking noble manners of manliness on the other. The effeminizing effect resulting from the paucity of warfare skills differentiates Aboriginal Tasmanians from energetic white males; the brutish behavior—virile in nature—is neutralized by reference to unmanly behavior in warfare. This stigmatization elicits a sense of absent culture and economic worthlessness (the status of hunter-gathering is contrasted with an advanced level of agriculture). The assumed paucity of material culture reflects the extremely inferior position that Aboriginal Australians occupied in the racial hierarchy. The presumed lack of intelligence—epitomized in the perceived dearth of material culture—permeated most publications preceding the 1920s. The following (representative) anthropological text from 1902 positions Aboriginal cultures on the brink between the "Paleolithic" and "Neolithic" stages of human development that had produced a "retarded" material culture: "this race is particularly interesting in what it is lacking ... the intelligence of the Australians is much lower than that of other savage people" (Semon 1902: 6–7).

This stigmatization was not specifically German, but its quantitative preponderance was unique in comparison to other Indigenous groups. Hardly any other Indigenous group was construed as so diametrically opposed to concepts of white civilization and discredited with such pertinacious fervor as Aboriginal Australians. An exception to this practice of stigmatization was, for example, the anthropologist Hermann Klaatsch (1863–1916), who, as Fiona Paisley and Corinna Erckenbrecht show, employed idealization in the context of anti-British propaganda (Paisley 2008: 205–210; Erckenbrecht 2010: 143, 150, 200–201). Such instances, however, were extremely rare and idealization was still ambivalent in having being expressed next to stigmatizing rhetoric. Exemplary of such ambivalent direction in pre-1919 colonial texts is an ethnographic travelogue published in a geographic journal in 1875. In it Aboriginal material culture is initially described as "original or rather Aboriginal" and its people as "good-natured," and some of their "womenfolk" as "pretty" (N. A. 1875: 183, 254). However, toward the end, upon engaging with the first interracial conflicts, Aboriginal people are portrayed as "thievish and lazy," juxtaposed to "industrious and God-fearing" settlers: "these low creatures of God's human family … must obtain their bread by the sweat of their brows; and no doubt it was with the intention of obtaining ours (as they thought so much more easily) that they were induced to make the attack upon us" (ibid.: 257). The text abruptly changes from idealizing to stigmatizing after a description of a violent colonial encounter, which is seen as entirely the fault of Aboriginal people.

This example demonstrates that Aboriginal stigmatization was frequent and embedded in concepts of what I call the possessed Indigene. Tolerance and colonialism form a reciprocal relationship. As David Theo Goldberg argues, the concept of tolerance in nineteenth-century colonialism presupposed a tolerance of Indigenous peoples in order to employ the practice of "education" (2004: 37). Idealizing views are an intricate part of the very principle of tolerance. In order to govern Indigenous subjects, they must first be tolerated (with the extent of toleration set by the colonizer). If Aboriginal people were deemed controllable—that is, integrated into colonial order and notionally possessed—they had to be idealized to uphold imperial hierarchies. Idealization thus formed if Aboriginal people were thought not to threaten white colonialism.

Texts concerned with an unstable colonial condition consequently had little room for idealization. In a German geographical journal article published in 1874, Aboriginal Australians were construed thus: "One moment they smile really friendly the next they are ready to murder someone callously. They interpret kindness as cowardice. Had the settlers not shown assertiveness and decisiveness right from the beginning, the settlement would have never succeeded.… Lying to someone—be he white or one of their own—is a particular joy for them, especially if they think they may benefit from the lie. If one asks them something, one can be sure to be told a lie" (N. A. 1874: 173–174). The trope of racially ingrained lying is a common stigmatization directed against Aboriginal people. The reproach of an "inborn" drive to lie, from which pleasure is thought to be derived, corroborates the superiority of white people as arbiters of universal truth regimes and justifies potentially violent measures as guarantors of successful colonization. Although violence against Aboriginal people is not explicitly vindicated, it is justified implicitly as a necessary means for effective settlement. The lying metaphor positions Aboriginal people as the actual source of violence (their lying entails violence), while projecting colonialism as an inherently peaceful project of human advancement (the human here read as confined to white humanity). The stigmatization of Aboriginal people does not merely serve to legitimize European colonialism (in contrast to a merely German colonialism) but also bears transnational whiteness that, as Aileen Moreton-Robinson, Maryrose Casey, and Fiona Nicoll argue, can "mobilize virtue when there is a perceived threat to its hegemony" (2008: ix). The virtue in this instance is peaceful human development (settlement), which is deemed to be under threat by its premodern counterpart. The settlement is described as neither Australian or German (Germans are not explicitly mentioned in the text) but implicitly as *white* (or European). Europeanness acts as a synonym for whiteness. As in most other texts, the stigmatization of Aboriginal Australians in this era was primarily one that held up white people, not explicitly Germans, as the superior opposite to Aboriginal people.

This trend in stigmatizing direction changed rather abruptly in the early 1920s. The first texts containing idealizing traits emerged in the 1920s and suddenly assigned a level of intellectual sophistication of material culture to Aboriginal Australians. What was previously regarded as "retarded," especially the production of boomerangs, became reinterpreted as a sign of mathematical knowledge. A 1919 text on boomerangs, though not outright in its stigmatization, belittled the artifact as a "toy" eliciting amusement: "the poor culture of Australia has left us modern humans a toy that always evokes amazement and amusement ... it is the boomerang, a simple piece of wood" (N. A. 1919: 96). A text published nineteen years later reinterpreted the boomerang in a markedly different light, not as a "simple toy" but as a sign of intellect that, along with Aboriginal laws, reflected the integrity of the Aboriginal social order. "However primitive the Aboriginal Australians might appear, they have created amazing things. How did they create the boomerang that requires complex mathematical formulas to come back in flight? Their taboos regulate social customs in a much more rigorous and strict way than our laws. No idea is more wrong than that of the timelessness and freedom of the 'savages'" (Johann 1938: 148–149). The text maintains the idea of utmost primitivism while departing from previous constructs of intellectual and moral inferiority—the boomerang preconditions sophisticated knowledge as much as the apostrophized term "savage" relates to (relatively) high moral standards. The text presents Aboriginal Australians in primitivist discourse, with references to semi-nakedness and hunting equipment—which remain part of the European reception of Aboriginal cultures to this day (Haag 2012)—but interprets the primitivism euphemistically as *relatively* sophisticated *for a* "primitive" culture. What I read as a sudden change in representations, I will argue, affected mainly the value judgments in assessing Aboriginal cultures, while the underlying narratives of primitivism and racial hierarchies remained stable.

This idea of primitivism is based on understanding of racial inferiority and thus different from—on first blush—similar concepts of German naturalness and primordiality as reflected in cultural pessimism or Germanic tribalism. Dirk Moses suggests that the German fear of a seemingly Jewish colonization fostered the idea of an anticolonial struggle against the imagined Jewish colonizer and construed German "tribes" as quasi-indigenous to German lands (2008: 29–30, 37). However, given the different racial hierarchies, both forms of idealized primitivism cannot be deracialized and read as parallel. The concept of German Indigeneity, in other words, does not explain the structure and function of idealized Aboriginality.

Instead increased idealization emerged from contexts of German colonial reclamation: the aforementioned article contains not only idealization but also indirect reference to colonial reclaim. It starts with a general description of Aboriginal cultures, moves to historic suffering, and eventually highlights contemporary injustice. The critique of the British colonization of Australia is implicitly contrasted with a (peaceful) German colonization in Africa. Idealization here occurred simultaneously with the rebuttal of German colonial guilt. The narrative structure of the bulk of post-1919 texts on Aboriginal Australians is structured within such a narrative context, beginning with a depiction of Aboriginal cultures as most primitive yet (relatively) sophisticated, followed by the enumeration of British Australian atrocities committed against Aboriginal Australians and often, although not necessarily, concluded by the sarcastic statement that the British had no right to reproach Germans with colonial guilt.

Post-1919 texts were influenced by the British *Report on the Natives of South-West Africa and Their Treatment by Germany,* released in 1918, which denounced German mistreatment of its colonial "subjects" and hoped to discredit German colonial rule (1918). The British argument of German colonial guilt, Roger Louis shows, had not emerged before the war and was subsequently used as a strategy to secure British dominance (1971: 27, 69–76). The treatise evoked many rejoinders that kept appearing until the demise of National Socialism. In 1919 the German Department of Colonial Affairs released the first official riposte to the British report. It uses arguments of racialized Indigeneity that were discernible in its British equivalent. Reversing the seed of colonial violence to the British, the German text opens by discrediting the British report as a mere polemic to denounce Germans as "exploiters and rapists of the highly developed, harmless and genuine Natives" and follows with a castigation of the British as the actual exploiters of the "peaceful tribes of Africa ... [misused] as cannon fodder against Germany" (Reichskolonialministerium 1919: 25, 4). The strategy of the German text is to highlight the success of German colonial "education." Like the British treatise, it follows the imperial logic of construing "good" and "bad" Indigenes, described as "peaceful" if conducive to the imperial project and as brutish if feared a threat to the project.

Apart from the efforts of construing German colonialism as successful racial "education," the German rejoinder enlists instances of British colonial violence committed beyond the former German colonies. Australia in particular is referred to as an epitome of British extermination policies: "As in other parts of Australia, the English have systematically and callously extirpated the Natives ... of Queensland" (ibid.: 180). The extension of the colonial critique to geographical contexts beyond the German sphere of influence led to a general increase in reports on Australia. Subsequent texts took up the morally charged rhetoric of a systematic British extermination of Aboriginal Australians. Although the supposed "fading" of Aboriginal Australians had been deplored in previous texts (resembling the dying race dogma), it was linked to "natural" and irreversible conditions rather than to a systematic policy of destruction. Although evolutionist logic prevailed (Aboriginal Australians continued to be seen as racially "weak" in an evolutionist setting), it turned into a more overtly politicized discourse aimed at linking their supposed extermination solely to British activity. Yet this guilt was characterized not as rooted in colonization (European colonization of Australia remained unquestioned) but in the "failed educational" principles of British colonialism.

The German counter-report, although actually focused on German colonies, triggered the subsequent production of texts on Australia and linked the description of Aboriginal Australians intricately to arguments of colonization, such as education and (just) white leadership. Post-1919 texts made frequent reference to the counter-report and what was termed the *Kolonialschuldlüge*. Issued in 1919 and influenced by the official rejoinder, the following article refers to rightful colonization, proposing that Aboriginal Australians had to be "educated" in proper labor to prevent their extinction—a protective policy explained to have been pursued by Germany but not Australia: "What, then, has Australia done in the interest of the Natives? The answer is striking: Nothing! It has worked systematically to eradicate the Native population of Australia … they are exterminated down to the last 150,000. … During the beginning of the colony, the Natives, bereft of their hunting grounds, were treated worse than dogs. They were shot for the smallest offences. … The conditions in Western Australia resemble slavery" (Kolbe 1919: 65). The harsh undertone of the critique marked a shift in German reports on Aboriginal Australians who, although not yet fully idealized, came to be construed as innocent victims of British aggression in a more undirected fashion. The counterpart to this aggression, the text explains, lay in the German policy of protecting Indigenous populaces from European influence, which was part of what Pascale Grosse dubs dissimilation (2000: 11, 26–29, 129, 135, 238). Primitivist protection became a central device of colonial revisionism—that is, the post-1919 arguments for regaining the former German colonies. To refute "colonial guilt," I argue, Aboriginal Australians had to be reimagined as subjects worthy of defense. The critique of Aboriginal mistreatment entailed idealization of Aboriginal people as respectable in their own tradition and construed Germans as the best protectors of primitivism. The concept of German defense drew on the metanarrative of childlike primitivism that predisposed a white adult figure to defend the otherwise "defenseless."

One of the first German texts to fully idealize Aboriginal cultures appeared in 1925 and praised Aboriginal people unconditionally for the first time, as "in their way culturally high standing. Childish and naive in their inner soul, they are exposed to the brutality of the Europeans. … With English colonization the suffering started … oppression and cruelty were particularly ruthless … and today the [Australian] government is smug about the moral and intellectual raising of the uncivilized natives" (Pfaff 1925: 67). The accompanying illustration (see figure 10.2) also presents Aboriginal people in a masculine yet primitivist fashion.

Figure 10.2. Australian throws his boomerang, *Feuerreiter* 1 (1925), 67.

Aboriginal manhood became increasingly portrayed in lines of whitened gender ideals. This stood in stark contrast to earlier visual representations. In a text published in the 1870s, for example, Aboriginal Australian men are gendered in markedly effeminate pose, in contrast to the norms of white masculinity (see figure 10.3).

The figure on the left visually translates the stigmatizing denotation of the text, which, though condoning "unnecessary" settler violence, portrays Aboriginal people as "retarded," their material culture as "low quality," and their physical shape as "ghastly" (Christmann 1870: 28–35). The 1925 text sharply departs from this stigmatizing direction by its stylization of a well-built and muscled body captured in the gracious movement of the hunt. In contrast to figure 10.3, the depicted person does not flee from, but instead opposes his potential prey. Idealization is here expressed in a relative sense (*in their way*) and draws on concepts of primitivism-as-childlikeness. The reference to British mistreatment that elicits idealization is relevant; British and Australian co-

Figure 10.3. Bee-hunting scene (Christmann 1870: 201).

lonial policies are castigated not only for exploiting Aboriginal people but also for disregarding their moral and intellectual customs; the text states that, based on extermination policies, Australians prided themselves on "raising" Indigenes. The failure of this policy is underlined by a reference to the high standing of Aboriginal cultures. This reference presents the British "raising" as unnecessary and destructive: the British "raising," the text says, led to the decay and extermination of a once "high-standing" culture. As this representative example shows, idealization does not work as romantic admiration of an "exotic" culture, which would not explain the sudden rise in idealized Aboriginality after the loss of the colonies. Instead, idealization operates as a vested political strategy to revile Entente colonialism.

Idealization culminated in frequency in the late 1920s and persisted throughout the 1930s and early 1940s. Texts came to exalt the natural beauty of Aboriginal people, admire their sophisticated art, and demonstrate the continuity of what was termed the oldest culture on earth. A journalistic text issued in 1935, for one, portrays Aboriginal Australians as extraordinary beautiful: "A human race has been planted into this nature that has the most beautiful and symmetric body type of all people of the world" (Job 1935: 24). This trend in an idealizing direction did not change in narrative structure during National Socialism and in *völkisch* texts. Ideologies of racial segregation, hierarchy, and racialized land relations that all aligned with National Socialism were included in, rather than posing a contradiction to, Aboriginal idealization.

For example, interspersed with references to National Socialist ideology, Hans Fischer's book *Menschenschönheit* likens Aboriginal hunting techniques to the skills of German javelin throwers (see figure 10.4): "The movement with which the kangaroo hunter hurls the spear from the boomerang clearly shows that a highly sophisticated technique has been devised for this endeavor, which is no less refined than that of our sportive javelin throwers" (1935: 46). The grace and naturalness of the bodies shown in figure 10.3 highlights ideals of racial beauty confined to a people's native land (part of racialized concepts of land that formed National Socialist and *völkisch* rhetoric).

Fischer's book revolves around human beauty and begins with European races, first and foremost Nordic Germans, and Indigenous populaces from around the world, but quite unsurprisingly excludes Jewish people and, less unsurprisingly, Europeans residing beyond Europe's shores (including settler Australians). This exemption of British settlers from ideas of beauty coalesced arguments of British colonial guilt with nationalist ideas of racialized land. Beautiful humans, the text stresses, could only be identified when living in their ancestral

Figure 10.4. Australians hunting kangaroos (Fischer 1935: 46).

lands, which plays out idealized Aboriginality as the nexus between a "traditional" people and its blood-based land. This form of beauty attached to a racially denoted land is mentioned implicitly in the text: "Certainly many a face seems strange to us … but the figures are appealing: the men are well-built, powerful yet smooth in their musculature, and the women often have an animal-like grace. One can tell that these creatures are well-created in their place and completely adapted to nature; the instinctive aversion towards these races is only justified if they cross our circles or, even more so, if their cultures are imposed on us as models" (ibid.: 42). The reference that Aboriginal subjects were "well-created *in their place*" bears out the importance attached to racial segregation and traditionalism in idealization: Aboriginal Australians were physically idealized as long as they remained within their racially confined lands ("if they cross our circles") and as long as they were not seen as meddling with German culture ("as long as their cultures are not imposed on us"). Moreover, the depiction of racial beauty posed a significant break from the past and informed deferring signifiers to (relative) morality and culture that were bound up with physiognomy. The Aboriginal body became partly aestheticized, thus loaded with cultural idealization—and thereby possessed as a narrative device in colonial reclaim. Primitivism not only acted as a flexible foil to domesticate racial exaltation to a nationalist opposition toward miscegenation and cultural mixing. It also proved flexible enough to permeate discourses of colonial reclaim as much as *völkisch* and National Socialist rhetoric that echoed a blood and soil tenet.

Such idealizing references, however, did not transcend racial boundaries but related within Indigenous cultures. Aboriginal people were portrayed as beautiful and sophisticated in their organic whole, and thus *within* Indigenous contexts. In relation to white culture, this sophistication was unmistakably relativized as infantile and underdeveloped. All texts ensured that idealization was limited and read within primitivist frames of white superiority over a childlike environment. An ethnographic text from 1939, for instance, reads: "the Australians are culturally in a transitional stage from the Paleolithic to the Neolithic, and thus at a level that analogous to European prehistory lies back millennia ... but one should not judge from this" (Tischner 1939: 1). This reference draws from the primitivist discourse that projected white European prehistory into a contemporary Aboriginal world. The idealization of Aboriginal Australians—certainly expressed more overtly here than under colonialism—rests on the construction of evolutionary stages of human development. The theoretical basis of this argument, Herbert Tischner's text shows, was neither new nor a specifically German invention. It springs from transnational primitivism and demarcates a racialized border between Aboriginal and white races: Aboriginal Australians remained on the lowest rung of racial ranking despite their idealization. The epithet of not being judgmental, however, seems rather specific to the era in which the text was produced. It functions as the ultimate expression of white leadership: in changing context of colonial loss, the "children-people" had, in Goldberg's sense, to be tolerated to uphold the imperial project.

The domestication of primitivism proved its malleability in different political and ideological climates. Idealization acted as a central way to secure white (German) leadership. In this, Aboriginal people could be idealized without change to their racial ranking. Aboriginal idealization worked beyond biological hierarchies as a separate category of racial construction. Aboriginality did not determine the status of racial hierarchy, which did not change during the entire period of German Empire between 1870 and 1945. Idealized Aboriginality did neither change the racial ranking within Indigenous groups—in all texts Aboriginal Australians remained the antipode in racial ranking to the North Americans, North Africans, and Polynesians. Racialized Aboriginality transcended classifications of race but informed racial stigmatization and idealization. While racial hierarchies remained constant throughout formal colonialism and colonial revisionism, Aboriginality produced representations of stratified race, unaffected in ranking but determined in "relative value."

Conclusion

This chapter has argued that the loss of the German colonies after the First World War triggered the augmenting idealization of Aboriginal Australians. The conceptual structure of idealized Aboriginality did not exhibit specifically German traits but remained elementary to transnational primitivism. Idealization, however, became specifically nationalized in appropriation, particularly after the loss of the German colonies. The specifically German interpretation of Aboriginality thus formed as a response to British suggestions of German colonial guilt. Nearly all considered texts are either implicitly or explicitly embedded in the context of colonial regain. Aboriginal Australians were idealized primarily in order to underpin the immoral failure of Entente colonialism. Idealized Aboriginality crystallized as a malleable concept to adapt to changing colonial conditions and transcended different ideological currents. It could be domesticated by the extremely racialized ideas of *völkisch* and National Socialist thought, without changing its direction. German texts hardly expressed a humane form of colonial narrative, as Berman's reading suggests. Such a reading not only reduces the different formations of racism to negativity but also overlooks the effect of cultural narratives on the construction of race and the dynamic nature of social prejudices. Instead of treating idealization as an opposite to racism and imperial rule, this study has proposed to understand racial idealization as an intricate means to secure white domination in national frames. It is expression of a claim to German superiority in a whitened world.

Oliver Haag teaches at the University of Barcelona and is visiting professorial fellow at Queen Mary's College, Chennai. Oliver has coedited a book on ego-histoire and Indigenous studies, *Ngapartji Ngapartji: Reciprocal Engagement* (Australian National University Press), and authored a special issue of *National Identities* (Routledge). His scholarship has appeared, among others, in *Continuum, Aboriginal History, Journal of New Zealand Studies,* and *Neohelicon*. He is coeditor of the bilingual *Australian Studies Journal* (*Zeitschrift für Australienstudien*).

Notes

1. For a complete bibliographic list, see Haag (2014).
2. They include *Afrika-Nachrichten, Afrika-Rundschau, Berliner Missionsberichte, Berliner Illustrirte Zeitung, Deutsche Kolonial-Zeitung, Die Gartenlaube, Illustrirte Zeitung, Evangelisch-Lutherisches Missionsblatt, Paideuma, Münchner Illustrierte Presse, Petermanns Geographische Mitteilungen, Rasse, Velhagen & Klasings Monatshefte, Verhandlungen der deutschen Gesellschaft für Rassenforschung, Westermanns Monatshefte, Zeitschrift für Ethnologie, Zeitschrift für Geopolitik, Zeitschrift für Morphologie und Anthropologie, Zeitschrift für Rassenkunde*, and *Zeitschrift für Vergleichende Rechtswissenschaft*.

References

Althusser, L. 1971. *Lenin and Philosophy and Other Essays*. London.
Anderson, K., and C. Perrin. 2007. "The Miserablest People in the World: Race, Humanism and the Australian Aborigines." *The Australian Journal of Anthropology* 18, no. 1: 18–39.
Anderson, W. 2006. *The Cultivation of Whiteness: Science, Health, and Racial Destiny in Australia*. Durham.
Andree, K. 1870. "Zur Kennzeichnung der Eingeborenen Australiens." *Globus* 18: 225–232.
Bauman, Z. 1998. "Allosemitism: Premodern, Modern, Postmodern." In *Modernity, Culture and "the Jew,"* eds. B. Cheyette and L. Marcus. Cambridge.
Berman, R. 1998. *Enlightenment or Empire: Colonial Discourse in German Culture*. Lincoln, NE, and London.
Bird, D. 2014. *Nazi Dreamtime: Australian Enthusiasts for Hitler's Germany*. London and New York.
Calloway, C., et al. 2002. *Germans and Indians: Fantasies, Encounters, Projections*. Lincoln, NE.
Christmann, Fr. 1870. *Australien. Geschichte der Entdeckungsreisen und der Kolonisation; Bilder aus dem Leben in der Wildnis und den Stätten der Kultur der neuesten Welt*. Leipzig.
Cowlishaw, G. 1988. "Australian Aboriginal Studies: The Anthropologists' Accounts." In *The Cultural Construction of Race*, eds. M. de Lepervanche and G. Bottomley. Sydney.
Erckenbrecht, C. 2010. *Auf der Suche nach den Ursprüngen. Die Australienreise des Anthropologen und Sammlers Hermann Klaatsch, 1904–1907*. Cologne.
Eylmann, E. 1908. *Die Eingeborenen der Kolonie Südaustralien*. Berlin.
Feest, C., ed. 1999. *Indians & Europe: An Interdisciplinary Collection of Essays*. Lincoln, NE, and London.
Fischer, H. W. 1935. *Menschenschönheit. Gestalt und Antlitz des Menschen in Leben und Kunst*. Berlin.
Frankenberg, R. 1993. *White Women, Race Matters: The Social Construction of Whiteness*. Minneapolis, MN.
Garroutte, E. M. 2003. *Real Indians: Identity and the Survival of Native America*. Berkeley, CA.

Goffman, E. 1990. *Stigma: Notes on the Management of Spoiled Identity*. London.
Goldberg, D. T. 2004. "The Power of Tolerance." In *Philosemitism, Antisemitism and "The Jews": Perspectives from the Middle Ages to the Twentieth Century*, eds. T. Kushner and N. Valman. Aldershot.
Grosse, P. 2000. *Kolonialismus, Eugenik und bürgerliche Gesellschaft in Deutschland 1850–1918*. Frankfurt and New York.
Haag, O. 2012. "Aboriginal Literature in Austria: A Discussion of Three Audiobooks." *Australian Aboriginal Studies Journal* 1: 51–64.
———. "Idealized Race: The Function of Idealized Indigeneity in German Imperial Discourses. Bibliographic Part." PhD dissertation, University of Edinburgh.
Haible, B. 1998. *Indianer im Dienste der NS Ideologie. Untersuchungen zur Funktion von Jugendbüchern über nordamerikanische Indianer im Nationalsozialismus*. Hamburg.
Hall, S. 1983. "The Problem of Ideology: Marxism Without Guarantees." In *Marx: A Hundred Years On*, ed. B. Matthews. London.
Hollinsworth, D. 1998. *Race and Racism in Australia*. Katoomba.
JanMohamed, A. 1985. "The Economy of Manichean Allegory: The Function of Racial Difference in Colonialist Literature." *Critical Inquiry* 12, no. 1: 59–87.
Jefferies, M. 2003. *Imperial Culture in Germany, 1871–1918*. Houndmills.
Job, E. 1935. "Australneger. Stiefkinder der Menschheit." *Durch alle Welt* 14: 26–29.
Johann, A. E. 1938. "Bumerang-Menschen: Die letzten Ureinwohner Australiens." *Die Koralle*: 148–149.
Jurgensen, M. 1992. *Eagle and Emu: German-Australian Writing 1930–1990*. St. Lucia.
Kapetas, J. T. 2007. "Lubra Lips, Lubra Lips: Reflections on My Face." In *Visibly Different: Face, Place and Race in Australia*, ed. M. Perkins. Bern.
Kolbe, F. 1919. "Australiens Anspruch auf die deutschen Südseekolonien." *Deutsche Kolonial-Zeitung*: 64–66.
Krippendorff, K., and M. A. Bock. 2009. *The Content Analysis Reader*. Los Angeles, CA.
Langton, M. 1993. "'Well, I Heard It on the Radio and I Saw It on the Television …': An Essay for the Australian Film Commission on the Politics and Aesthetics of Filmmaking by and about Aboriginal People and Things." Woolloomooloo.
Li, V. 2006. *The Neo-Primitivist Turn: Critical Reflections on Alterity, Culture, and Modernity*. Toronto.
Louis, R. 1971. *Das Ende des deutschen Kolonialreiches. Britischer Imperialismus und die deutschen Kolonien 1914–1919*. Düsseldorf.
Lutz, H. 1985. *"Indianer" und "Native Americans". Zur sozial- und literarhistorischen Vermittlung eines Stereotyps*. Hildesheim.
Mamozai, M. 1992. "Frauen und Kolonialismus—Täterinnen und Opfer." In *"Ein Herrenvolk von Untertanen". Rassismus—Nationalismus—Sexismus*, eds. A. Foitzik et al. Duisburg.
Moreton-Robinson, A., M. Casey, and F. Nicoll. 2008. *Transnational Whiteness Matters*. Lanham, MD.
Moses, D. 2008. "Empire, Colony, Genocide: Keywords and the Philosophy of History." In *Empire, Colony, Genocide: Conquest, Occupation, and Subaltern Resistance in World History*, ed. D. Moses. New York.

Mosse, G. 1998. *The Crisis of German Ideology: Intellectual Origins of the Third Reich*. New York.
N. A. 1874. "Die Eingeborenen am Lake Hope in der Colonie Südaustralien." *Globus* 25: 173–175.
———. 1876. "E. Giles' Reise durch West-Australien, 1875." *Mittheilungen aus Justus Perthes' Geographischer Anstalt* 22: 177–192, 254–261.
———. 1919. "Das Bumerang." *Kosmos* 16: 96.
Paisley, F. 2008. "Mock Justice: World Conservation and Australian Aborigines in Interwar Switzerland." *Transforming Cultures eJournal* 3, no. 1: 196–226.
Penny, G. H. 2003. *Objects of Culture: Ethnography and Ethnographic Museums in Imperial Germany*. Chapel Hill, NC.
———. 2006. "Elusive Authenticity: The Quest for the Authentic Indian in German Public Culture." *Comparative Study of Society and History* 48, no. 4: 798–819.
Pfaff, R. 1925. "Der Australier und sein Bumerang." *Der Feuerreiter* 1: 67.
Poignant, R. 2004. *Professional Savages: Captive Lives and Western Spectacle*. Sydney.
Reichskolonialministerium. 1919. *Die Behandlung der einheimischen Bevölkerung in den kolonialen Besitzungen Deutschlands und Englands. Eine Erwiderung auf das englische Blaubuch vom August 1918: Report on the natives of South-West Africa and their treatment by Germany*. Berlin.
Report on the Natives of South-West Africa and Their Treatment by Germany. 1918. London.
Ross, C. 1940. *Der unvollendete Kontinent*. Leipzig.
Said, E. 1993. *Culture and Imperialism*. New York.
Semon, R. 1902. "Australier und Papua." *Correspondenz-Blatt für Anthropologie* 33: 4–8, 11–14, 22–23, 32–34.
Sinha, M. 1995. *Colonial Masculinity: The "Manly Englishman" and the "Effeminate Bengali" in the Late Nineteenth Century*. Manchester.
Spencer, B. 1927. *The Arunta: A Study of a Stone Age People*. London.
Steinmetz, G. 2007. *The Devil's Handwriting: Precoloniality and the German Colonial State in Qingdao, Samoa, and Southwest Africa*. Chicago, IL, and London.
Stocking, G. 1969. *Race, Culture, and Evolution: Essays in the History of Anthropology*. New York.
Street, B. 1975. *The Savage in Literature: Representations of "Primitive" Society in English Fiction 1858–1920*. London and New York.
Theye, T. 1985. "Gesucht: Die Adresse des Schneemenschen." In *Wir und die Wilden. Einblicke in eine kannibalische Beziehung*, ed. T. Theye. Reinbek bei Hamburg.
Tischner, H. 1939. "Australien." In *Die Große Völkerkunde*, vol. 3, ed. H. A. Bernatzik. Leipzig.
Vierkandt, A. 1899. "Die Eingeborenen Tasmaniens." *Globus* 76: 189–292.
Wendt, R. 2007. *Vom Kolonialismus zur Globalisierung. Europa und die Welt seit 1500*. Paderborn.
Wildenthal, L. 2001. *German Women for Empire, 1884–1945*. Durham, NC, and London.
Zantop, S. 1997. *Colonial Fantasies: Conquest, Family, and Nation in Precolonial Germany, 1770–1870*. Durham, NC, and London.

Index

Aboriginal Australians, 1, 19, 230–234, 236–238, 243–248, 251–254
Aranda people, 230, 235, 236
Aboriginality, 231, 234, 235, 238, 240–242, 246, 251–254
activity (racial and gendered character), 48
aesthetics, 5, 46, 53–56, 58, 179, 180, 182, 184, 188
Africa, 8, 11, 46, 49–52, 78, 109, 110, 113, 133, 214, 219, 220, 222, 242, 246, 247, 253
African women, 49, 52
Africanism, 11, 214
African Americans, 219, 220, 222
Alexander the Great, 79
America, 3, 12, 59, 67, 130, 133, 146, 210, 219–223, 226, 232–234, 238, 253
United States, 59, 77, 131, 133, 214, 216, 220–222
Ancient American cultures, 233
Anglo-Saxons, 33, 110
anthropology, 7, 9, 10, 35, 44, 59, 109, 110, 113, 118, 132, 147, 192, 195, 196, 231, 236
anthropophagy, 11
anti-capitalism. *See* capitalism
antifascism. *See* fascism
antimodernism. *See* modernism
anti-Semitism, 3, 10, 15, 58, 93, 95, 98–100, 105, 108, 109, 118, 119, 121, 156, 160–163, 168
Berliner Antisemitismus Streit, 15, 121 (*see also* Berlin anti-Semitism debate)
Berlin anti-Semitism debate, 109 (*see also* Berliner Antisemitismus Streit)
architecture, 17–19, 114, 174, 176, 177, 192, 194, 195, 197, 233

Aristotle, 55
art, 17, 19, 53–57, 61, 174–176, 179, 182, 186, 193, 195–198, 202
Aryan, 3, 14, 19, 35–36, 57, 58, 65, 73, 74, 77, 83, 161, 162, 166, 167, 183, 188, 230, 234
Asians, 8, 113, 233, 234
assimilation, 8, 15, 55, 70, 90–95, 98, 99, 101, 102, 105, 116, 129, 134, 192
Assyria, 69
Athens, 72, 79
Aufartung, ideas of, 177, 183
Australia, 230, 234, 235, 238, 242, 245–248
Austria, 17, 80, 83, 154–163, 165, 166, 168, 169, 230
Austria-Hungary, 80
authenticity, 29, 230, 234, 235
avantgarde writing, 46, 47, 52–54, 58

backwardness, ideas of, 4, 5, 129, 130, 132, 146–148, 242
baptism, 102, 111, 116, 118–121
Bartels, Adolf, 193
bastardization. *See* miscegenation
Bauer, Otto, 92, 93, 157
Bavaria, 96, 114, 115, 146
Bildersturm, 196
biohistorical, 120
biologism, 1, 2, 4, 7–9, 14, 16, 33, 34, 47, 49, 53, 55–57, 65, 83, 95, 97, 109, 110, 118, 121, 131, 133, 134, 140, 149, 169, 177, 184, 191, 193, 253
biopolitics, 14, 15, 18, 45–48, 52, 57, 59
Blach, Friedrich Samuel, 15, 109, 112–118, 120–122
black beauty. *See* racial beauty
blackface, 18, 209, 210, 219–222, 224, 226, 227

blackness, 1, 12, 18, 30, 49–53, 59, 65, 77, 83, 133, 209, 210, 214, 218–224, 226, 227, 230, 237, 238, 242
blood and soil, 50, 55, 97, 174, 175, 197, 198, 253
Blut und Boden, 195, 197, 203
borderline Germans, 99–101
Brazil, 54
Britain, 16, 33, 59, 65, 81, 130, 131, 146, 214, 235, 239, 240, 244, 246–248, 250, 251, 254
England, 94–97, 105, 150, 217, 218
Bronze Age, 31

capitalism, 5, 92, 167
Catholic, 28, 76, 108, 111, 114, 138, 160, 161
Caucasian, concepts of, 233, 234
Celts, 72, 76, 80
Chamberlain, Houston Stewart, 65, 66, 69–73, 79, 82, 83, 193
Christaller, Hanna, 48, 50
Christianity, 12, 15, 57, 59, 72, 82, 97, 98, 104, 108, 111, 112, 114–122, 160, 161, 163, 213, 216
civilization, ideas of, 10, 67, 69–72, 75, 129, 130, 139, 236, 241, 244, 248
class, 70, 72, 93, 160, 161, 167, 168, 181, 218
cognitive mechanism, 37, 38
colonialism, 1, 8–15, 19, 44–52, 55, 58–60, 81, 108, 109, 111–114, 120–122, 130, 147, 148, 207, 211, 214, 220, 224, 226, 227, 231–233, 235, 239–241, 244–248, 251, 253, 254
colonial literature, 48, 49, 51, 52, 240
colonial studies, 15, 108, 109, 112, 120–122
colonies, 1–3, 12, 19, 44, 46, 48, 49, 51, 112, 214, 231, 232, 242, 247, 248, 251, 254
colonized peoples, 2, 8, 10–12, 48, 49, 113, 130
colonizer, 10, 239

concepts of community, 158, 161
conservatism, 4–6, 90, 108, 115, 117, 119, 129, 155, 161–165, 223, 226
continuity, 2, 17, 27, 174, 195, 251
criminalization, 130, 131, 145, 148
crime rates, 132, 133, 135–140, 142, 143, 145–148
crime statistics, 16, 131, 132, 134–142, 144–146, 148, 196
criminality, 129, 132–135, 137–141, 145–147, 150
criminologists, 16, 131–134, 146–148
cultural practice, 13, 220, 226
cultural space, 1–3, 5, 13, 29, 33, 46, 75, 79, 97, 108, 218, 235, 239, 240
culture, 3–15, 17–19, 31, 44, 45, 50, 52, 54, 55, 57, 72–74, 77, 78, 80, 81, 90–92, 94, 95, 99, 101, 104, 115, 117, 118, 122, 129, 130, 148, 155, 165, 175, 179, 183, 189, 190, 198, 211, 214, 219–221, 223, 224, 226, 227, 231–237, 242–246, 248, 250–253

Darré, Richard Walther, 193
Darwinism, 6, 7, 9, 39, 44, 66, 184, 197
decadence, ideas of, 18, 37, 70, 72, 73, 191, 197
decline, 18, 55, 65, 66, 68, 69, 71, 72, 74–76, 78, 79, 81, 82, 84, 143, 178, 194–196, 219, 226
degeneracy discourse, 17, 18, 49, 55, 65, 66, 69, 70, 73, 74, 77–79, 110, 132, 140, 141, 147, 174–178, 190, 195–197, 220, 235
architecture, 17–19, 114, 174, 176, 177, 192, 194, 195, 197, 233
entartete Kunst (degenerate art), 17, 174, 196
white hegemony, 18, 214, 226, 231, 232, 240
Der Kunstwart (journal), 90, 91, 94, 97, 98, 101, 179, 186–188, 193, 201
Der Stürmer (newspaper), 119, 120
Deutschtum, 15, 89, 94, 102, 105

Die Tat (journal), 95
disability, 132, 241
  mental illness, 140
DNVP (*Deutschnationale Volkspartei*), 158–163, 168
Du Bois, William E.B., 133
Dyer, Richard, 213, 214, 216, 217
dystopias, 47, 58

Eastern Provinces of Prussia, 16, 130, 136–145, 147, 148, 150
effeminacy, 241, 243, 250
Egypt, 69
Enlightenment, 2, 5, 72, 189
essentialism, 2, 57, 92, 184
ethnic concepts, 15, 35, 36, 65, 92, 94, 118, 130–138, 141, 142, 146–148, 150, 161, 162, 195, 196
  ethnicity, 35, 36, 131, 133, 135, 195
ethnology, 9, 35, 36, 38, 72, 109, 254
Eugen Diederichs (publisher), 94, 179, 180, 198
eugenics, 6, 14, 47, 54, 59, 70, 177, 192
Europe, 3, 4, 7, 9–12, 18, 28, 34–38, 47, 49–51, 54, 68, 71, 80, 92, 109, 110, 116, 132–134, 148, 177, 188, 220, 224, 233, 235, 238, 240, 242, 245–248, 251, 253
euthanasia, 74
evolutionism, 9, 19, 35, 177, 233, 236, 242, 247
extermination, 6, 108, 117, 247, 248
Eylmann, Erhard, 236–238

fascism, 4, 5, 46, 47, 58, 238, 239
femininity, 18, 209, 210, 214, 224, 227, 238
films, 18, 209–214, 216–219, 221–228
  cinema, 210, 211, 213, 218, 219, 223, 227
Fischer, Eugen, 59, 109, 110, 112, 113, 118, 251, 252
France, 12, 70, 77, 81, 184–186, 190, 214, 240
Franks, 76
Freikörperkultur (Nacktkultur), 182, 183

Frenssen, Gustav, 48
Frick, Wilhelm, 196

Gauguin, Paul, 54
gendarmes (police), 130, 144, 145
gender, 3, 17, 46, 49, 52, 58, 59, 111, 135, 154, 157, 158, 164, 167–169, 210, 211, 216–218, 227, 233, 237, 241, 250
German colonies, 2, 3, 12, 19, 46, 49, 112, 214, 231, 232, 242, 246–248, 254
German East Africa, 46
German nationalists, 17, 154, 160, 161, 168
German Southwest Africa, 46, 49, 50, 109, 113
  Deutsch-Südwest Afrika, 59, 60
German-Polish antagonism, 143–146
Germanen, 31, 37, 75
Germania, 37, 212
Germanic, concept of, 4, 14, 19, 31, 32, 34, 37, 76–78, 80, 212, 238, 246
Germanii, 37, 38
Germanness, 15, 44, 90, 91, 93–103, 105, 162, 212, 223, 226
Germans, 14, 31, 32, 36–38, 82, 94, 96, 99–101, 103, 108, 115–117, 121, 129, 130, 139, 143, 146–148, 162, 211, 212, 218, 246–248
Gobineau, Joseph Arthur Comte de, 9, 53, 60, 66, 68–73, 83, 193
Goebbels, Joseph, 175
Goths, 32, 33, 56, 76
Greek city-states, 16, 78
Greeks, 16, 32, 36, 60, 65, 72, 73, 78–80, 180, 186, 189, 198, 214
Grimm, Hans, 48, 50
Günther, Hans F.K., 55, 56, 61, 65, 69, 71–73, 83, 190, 193–197
"Gypsies", 133, 134, 139, 146

Haeckel, Ernst, 6
Halfmann, Waldemar, 76, 83
Hamitic races, 11

Haßgesang gegen England, 94–98, 101, 102
Hebbel, Friedrich, 103, 104
Heimat, notions of, 35, 193, 237
Heimatschutz, 19, 175, 179, 189, 193, 198
heredity, 7, 59, 140, 192, 194
heteronormativity, 217
heterosexuality, 57, 216, 217
historians, 7, 8, 19, 28–31, 101, 130, 131, 157, 195, 198, 219, 227
historiography, 33, 157
Hitler, Adolf, 65, 66, 68, 69, 71–74, 82, 83, 100, 119, 175, 176
Hobsbawm, Eric, 28, 29
Holy Roman Empire, 76, 77
humanity, 46, 53, 54, 184, 186, 234, 235, 242, 245

idealization, 1, 2, 8, 10–13, 16, 19, 156, 183, 214, 230–235, 237–242, 244–246, 248, 250–254
identity formation, 12, 13, 15, 16, 18, 44, 48, 52, 66, 67, 89–91, 93, 98, 101–105, 130, 146, 150, 159, 160, 176, 211, 218, 222, 223, 227, 234, 240
ideology, 5, 8, 16, 17, 27, 28, 30, 31, 34, 37, 45, 48, 58, 65, 66, 68, 71, 72, 90, 95, 110, 111, 154, 156–163, 165–169, 174, 175, 193, 194, 197, 232, 251, 253, 254
imperialism, 1, 7, 8, 12–14, 47, 48, 55, 59, 67, 72, 80, 121, 134–137, 141, 144, 195, 216, 219, 231, 232, 239, 241, 242, 244, 247, 253, 254
Indianthusiasm, 10, 11, 233
Indigeneity, 13, 246, 247
indigenization, 13, 237
Indigenous identity, 12, 13
Indo-European languages, 34, 35, 37, 38, 80
inferiority, 117, 121, 220, 224, 240, 241, 246
Islam, 111
Italians, 32, 56, 71, 77, 132, 133

Italy, 71, 76, 78, 132, 181
ius sanguinis, 214

jazz, 219–224
Jewish people, 10, 15, 30, 32, 33, 41, 57, 58, 66, 70, 75, 78, 81, 82, 89–95, 97–105, 108, 109, 111–122, 134, 139, 146, 156, 157, 161–163, 166, 167, 194, 239, 246, 251
  Jewishness, 10, 15, 90, 98, 99, 101–104, 116–118, 121, 122
Judaism, 89, 91, 98, 99, 102–104, 108, 111, 118, 122
justice system, 129, 130, 144, 148, 150, 246

Kirchner, Ernst Ludwig, 54
Klabund (writer), 46, 54, 61
Klagges, Dietrich, 75
Kolnberger, Anton M., 31
Küas, Richard, 48, 51, 52
Kumsteller, Friedrich, 75, 78–81
Kunst und Rasse, 17, 56, 174–176, 192–197
Kunstwart debate, 90, 94, 98, 101
Kurella, Alfred, 133

Lagarde, Paul de, 81, 83, 94, 95, 97, 183
Lebensreform movement, 4, 5, 175, 177, 178, 180, 181, 183, 184, 201
liberalism, 5, 7, 11, 82, 155, 161, 170
Lissauer, Ernst, 15, 89–105
Liszt, Franz von, 133, 134
literary fromations, 14, 15, 31, 33, 45–48, 50, 52–54, 56–60, 89, 101, 102, 195, 234, 238
Lombroso, Cesare, 16, 132, 133, 140, 147
loss of the German colonies, 242
Lutheran, 15, 108, 114, 115

Mann, Heinrich, 53
masculinity, 159, 187, 216, 223, 224, 237, 248, 250
May, Karl, 12, 233, 238
Mein Kampf, 72–74

Meiser, Hans, 15, 109, 112, 114, 115, 118, 120–122
Mendel, Gregor, 59
mental mechanism, 14, 30, 41
Milieutheorie, 175, 177, 191, 192
miscegenation, 14, 44–60, 70–72, 74, 77, 80, 82, 109, 110, 113, 167, 239, 253
　hybridity, concepts of, 45, 48, 51, 59
　interraciality, 14, 46, 47, 53, 54, 234, 235, 244
missionaries, 114, 121, 231
mixed race, 45, 46, 48–50, 52–54, 59, 60, 79, 109–111, 113, 116, 117, 120, 121, 143, 214
modernism, 5–7, 12, 18, 47, 52, 57, 81, 93, 156, 158, 161, 174, 191, 222–224, 226, 235
monogenism, 9, 233, 238
motivation, 29, 40, 41, 141
Müller, Robert, 46

narratives of origin, 27, 28, 34, 38, 39
nation, 4–7, 14, 16, 17, 27, 29, 32, 33, 36–38, 44, 45, 47–50, 52–54, 57–59, 70, 74, 79, 80, 82, 83, 89–95, 97, 99–102, 118, 121, 130, 134, 139, 140, 144, 154, 155, 157–159, 161, 164, 169, 180, 181, 184, 185, 192, 195, 198, 211, 212, 214, 220, 221, 226, 227, 247, 251, 253, 254
National Socialism, 2, 4, 7, 16–18, 31, 65, 66, 71, 72, 74, 81, 82, 89, 90, 114, 119, 122, 157, 160, 169, 174, 175, 185, 190, 191, 193, 194, 196, 197, 222, 230, 247, 251, 253, 254
　Nazi, 16, 30, 31, 46, 47, 53, 55, 56, 58, 65, 66, 71, 74, 75, 81–83, 90, 95, 100, 101, 115, 119, 157, 158, 190, 230, 239
nationalism, 4, 5, 10, 13, 19, 28, 81, 93, 94, 96, 145, 159, 160, 169, 193, 237, 238
nationality, 17, 32, 93, 94, 131, 137, 139, 141, 143, 144, 147, 168
nationalization, 1, 109

nationhood, concepts of, 81, 91, 94, 95, 101, 104
Negrophilia, 220, 222
Niceforo, Alfredo, 133
Nietzsche, Friedrich, 53, 60, 68, 72, 82, 183
Nordic, 31, 57, 65, 68, 70–73, 77–80, 176, 183, 188, 190, 193, 195, 251
normativity, 4, 6, 9, 11, 132, 178, 180, 182, 186, 198, 216, 217, 231, 232, 238, 241
novel, 14, 32, 33, 46–50, 52–54, 59, 186, 195, 221
NSDAP, 15, 122, 160, 176, 196
Nuremberg Laws, 74

Oriental, 37, 77, 78, 80, 188, 201
origin mechanism, 14
　ancestral tales, 3, 251
　origin myth, 27
　origin-story, 31–40
　origin metaphor. *See* origin mechanism
Othering, 130, 131, 146
Otto the Great, 76

Pacific (region), 232, 233, 242
Pan-German (party), 158, 160
　GDVP, 158–162, 165, 166, 168
Papuan peoples, 2
passivity (racial character), 217, 218, 241
Penka, Karl, 14, 34–36, 39
Persia, 65, 72, 73, 77, 80
philosemitism, 10, 11, 239
phylogentic origin, 234, 238
physiognomy, 31, 56, 175, 183, 192, 201, 202, 235, 237, 252
Pinthus, Kurt, 211
Plato, 55, 79, 195
poems, 102, 103
poetry, 53, 90, 102
Poland, 16, 33, 129–131, 134–148, 214
political participation, 154, 164
polygenism, 9, 233, 238
Polynesians, 233, 253

popular culture, 3, 18, 155, 211, 214, 219, 221, 224, 226, 227, 231, 233
Porten, Henny, 18, 209–219, 222–227
Posen (Poznań), 132, 136, 139, 141–145, 149, 150
prehistory, 33, 37, 38, 80, 235, 253
  Stone Age, concepts of, 19, 235, 236, 242
primitivism, 9, 11, 19, 33, 36, 38, 46, 47, 52–54, 57, 58, 60, 61, 133, 220, 224, 230, 233–238, 241, 242, 245, 246, 248, 250, 253, 254
primordiality, idea of, 10, 33, 34, 55, 92, 235, 246
propaganda, 118, 157, 160, 161, 163, 197, 198, 220, 244
Protestant, 4, 89, 108, 111, 114, 115, 119, 120, 122, 160, 161
Prussia, 16, 82, 100, 109, 112, 129–132, 134, 136, 138–140, 142, 143, 145, 149, 150
purity, concepts of, 14, 45–47, 51, 54, 56–60, 68, 71, 73, 74, 110, 168, 174, 198, 217, 234

racial beauty, 1, 18, 52, 55, 177, 178, 180, 182, 184–187, 190, 209, 213, 218, 232–234, 236, 238, 241, 251, 252
racial breeding, ideas of, 46, 59, 71, 73, 155, 194. *See also* miscegenation
racial difference, 13, 18, 211, 219, 235
racial health, 110, 118, 176–178, 180, 183, 184, 186, 187, 190, 191, 193, 195, 223, 241
racial hierarchies, 2, 8, 9, 18, 44, 50–52, 55, 57, 80, 130, 131, 160, 197, 198, 217, 220, 230, 233, 235, 238, 240–244, 246, 251, 253, 254
racial inscriptions, 240, 241
racial intelligence, 49, 232, 241–243
  mental ability, 235
racial mixing, 14, 15, 45–47, 52–54, 71, 73, 74, 81, 109–111, 113, 120, 233. *See also* miscegenation

racial mixture. *See* miscegenation
racial state, 46
racial studies, 113
racial theory, 6, 17, 53, 57, 58, 60, 70, 71, 73, 83, 174, 193
racialist diachronics, 14, 31, 39, 40
racialist synchronics, 14, 39, 40
racialization, 2, 4, 6–13, 15, 17, 66, 193, 214, 227, 231, 234, 235, 237, 239–241, 246, 247, 251, 253, 254
racism, 7–10, 14, 17–19, 27–30, 33, 35, 36, 40, 44, 45, 47, 53, 55, 57, 68, 70, 94, 97, 104, 105, 119, 155, 156, 160–162, 165–168, 174, 219, 220, 222, 224, 227, 238–241, 254
  ridicule, 11, 18, 91, 102, 199, 220, 226
Ranke, Leopold von, 28, 29
Rassenkunde, 71, 194, 195, 202
rationality, idea of, 53
Rehoboth people, 59, 109
relativism, 27–30
Renaissance, 56
Renan, Ernest, 27
Rhineland, 110, 138, 141, 214, 220
Roman Empire, 16, 65, 76–79
romanticism, 4, 5, 238
Rosenberg, Alfred, 55–57, 61, 65, 69, 71, 72, 83, 175
Ross, Colin, 230, 234, 238, 239
Russia, 66, 67, 83, 134

Samoa, 59
savagery, ideas of, 11, 233, 234, 236, 238, 241–243, 246
  animalism, 11, 30, 71, 155, 217, 220, 235, 241, 252
  noble savage, 233, 238
Schemann, Ludwig, 70
schematic narrative template, 16, 66–68, 74–78
Schirmacher, Käthe, 164, 169, 170
Schleicher, August, 34–36
Schneider, Maria, 48, 78–81, 165–167, 170
Schultze-Naumburg, Paul, 17, 55, 56, 61, 174–198, 201

sensuality, idea of, 53
sexuality, 3, 14, 44, 45, 47–51, 53, 55, 57, 59, 210, 214, 216, 217, 220, 223, 227, 241
Silesia, 100, 129, 140
Slavic peoples, 16, 35, 131, 147
Social Democrats, 112, 156, 159, 160, 163, 166
society, 6, 17, 37, 90, 91, 93, 98, 100, 109–111, 113, 116, 118, 122, 130–132, 156, 157, 160, 185, 191, 198, 211, 222, 224
Socrates, 79
Sonderweg, 4, 7
Sparta, 65, 72, 79, 82, 84
Spencer, Baldwin, 235–238
Spengler, Oswald, 55, 65, 69, 72
stereotypes, 2, 16, 18, 19, 46, 97, 115, 129–131, 139, 141, 146–148, 194, 209, 211, 212, 220
Stratz, Carl Heinrich, 18, 187
Streicher-group, 119
superiority, 13, 18, 28, 32, 33, 40, 73, 139, 214, 219, 226, 230, 231, 238, 240, 245, 253, 254

Tacitus, 37, 38
taxonomy, 9
textbooks, 66–68, 74–76, 78, 83, 84
Third Reich, 4, 5, 16, 65, 66, 68, 72, 75, 82, 197
    Thousand-Year Reich, 197
Thirty Years' War, 77, 80, 188, 190
tolerance, 10, 11, 222, 239, 244
tradition, concepts of, 4, 5, 12, 27, 29, 30, 36, 53, 67, 68, 93, 134, 147, 174, 181, 186, 199, 220, 234–236, 248, 252
transnationalism, 1, 2, 12, 13, 17, 19, 122, 127, 147, 219, 231, 234–236, 245, 253
Trutzgau Weimar, 17, 174

Urgeschichte, 33, 34, 140
Ursprache, 32, 34, 36
Urvolk, 34, 36–39
Urzeit, 33–34

utopia, 46, 47, 53, 57, 58, 115–117, 165, 196, 197

valorization, 112, 121, 242
veritism, 29
Vernegerung, ideas of, 49, 60
    negroing, 219
Verkafferung, ideas of, 49, 50, 60
violence, 45, 137, 141, 143–146, 162, 192, 196, 220, 239, 244, 245, 247, 250
    physical assault, 137, 138, 141, 143–145
Voegelin, Eric, 55
Vogel, Paul, 75, 76
Volk, 7, 36, 38, 48, 55, 56, 60, 73, 75, 81, 93, 102, 106, 165–167, 169, 195
völkisch nationalism, 5, 35, 56, 71, 76, 83, 89, 93–95, 97, 105, 154, 157, 158, 160–165, 167, 174, 183, 193, 195, 199, 237, 238, 251, 253, 254
Volksgemeinschaft, 17, 154–159, 161–170, 175, 198
    community of the people, 17
Volkskörper, ideas of, 18, 55, 58, 175–177, 191, 195, 197, 202, 203
Volkstum, 94, 102, 196

Wagner, Richard, 33, 35, 68–70, 81, 83
Wehrmacht, 31
Weimar period, 5, 17, 18, 46, 47, 55, 58, 99, 160, 165, 174–176, 185, 188, 190, 193, 196, 197, 209, 211, 212, 214, 220, 221, 223, 224, 226, 227
Wertsch, James, 16, 66, 67, 83
white hegemony, 18, 214, 226, 231, 232, 240
whiteness, 12, 44, 211–214, 216–219, 223–227, 231, 232, 234, 241, 245
    white peoples, 53, 245
    white race, 216, 217, 240, 253
Wilhelmine period, 2, 6, 7, 17–19, 89, 90, 174–178, 196, 198, 219, 220
    Kaiserreich, 14, 44, 45, 47, 134, 145, 146, 148

Wilhelminian age, 210, 218
women, 17, 31, 49, 50, 52, 57, 60, 78, 144, 154, 155, 157–159, 162–169, 175, 177, 178, 180, 183, 187–191, 209, 210, 213, 214, 216–218, 223, 230, 236, 238, 244, 252
women's suffrage, 17, 158, 166
women's movements, 17
world history, interpretation of, 16, 65, 103

World War I, 2, 15, 28, 47, 54, 55, 90, 91, 93–95, 98, 105, 156, 158, 163, 167, 192, 195, 210, 211, 214, 216, 218, 219, 227, 254
  Great War, 113
World War II, 28

"Zigeuner". *See* "Gypsies"
Zionism, 15, 90, 91, 93, 95, 98, 99, 101–103, 105, 116, 117

www.ingramcontent.com/pod-product-compliance
Lightning Source LLC
Chambersburg PA
CBHW071336080526
44587CB00017B/2860